TAKING SIDES

Clashing Views on Controversial

Psychological Issues

ELEVENTH EDITION

TAKING SIDES

Clashing Views on Controversial

Psychological Issues

ELEVENTH EDITION

Selected, Edited, and with Introductions by

Brent Slife
Brigham Young University

Dushkin/McGraw-Hill
A Division of The McGraw-Hill Companies

To my three garrulous sons, Conor, Nathan, and Jacob

Photo Acknowledgment
Cover image: © 2000 by PhotoDisc, Inc.

Cover Art Acknowledgment
Charles Vitelli

Manufactured in the United States of America

Eleventh Edition

1234567890BABA1

Library of Congress Cataloging-in-Publication Data
Main entry under title:
Taking sides: clashing views on controversial psychological issues/selected, edited, and with introductions by Brent Slife.—11th ed.
Includes bibliographical references and index.
1. Psychology. 2. Human behavior. I. Slife, Brent, *comp.*
150

0-07-237142-0
ISSN: 1098-5409

Printed on Recycled Paper

Preface

Critical thinking skills are a significant component of a meaningful education, and this book is specifically designed to stimulate critical thinking and initiate lively and informed dialogue on psychological issues. In this book I present 36 selections, arranged in pro and con pairs, that address a total of 18 different controversial issues in psychology. The opposing views demonstrate that even experts can derive conflicting conclusions and opinions from the same body of information.

A dialogue approach to learning is certainly not new. The ancient Greek philosopher Socrates engaged in it with his students some 2,400 years ago. His point-counterpoint procedure was termed a *dialectic*. Although Socrates and his companions hoped eventually to know the "truth" by this method, they did not see the dialectic as having a predetermined end. There were no right answers to know or facts to memorize. The emphasis in this learning method is on how to evaluate information—on developing reasoning skills.

It is in this dialectical spirit that *Taking Sides: Clashing Views on Controversial Psychological Issues* was originally compiled, and it has guided me through this 11th edition as well. To encourage and stimulate discussion and to focus the debates in this volume, each issue is expressed in terms of a single question and answered with two points of view. But certainly the reader should not feel confined to adopt only one or the other of the positions presented. There are positions that fall between the views expressed, or totally outside them, and I encourage you to fashion your own conclusions.

Some of the questions raised in this volume go to the very heart of what psychology as a discipline is all about and the methods and manner in which psychologists work. Others address newly emerging concerns. In choosing readings I was guided by the following criteria: the readings had to be understandable to newcomers to psychology; they had to have academic substance; and they had to express markedly different points of view.

Plan of the book Each issue in this volume has an issue *introduction*, which defines each author's position and sets the stage for debate. Also provided is a set of point-counterpoint statements that pertain to the issue and that should help to get the dialogue off the ground. Each issue concludes with *challenge questions* to provoke further examination of the issue. The introduction and challenge questions are designed to assist the reader in achieving a critical and informed view on important psychological issues. Also, at the beginning of each part is a list of Internet site addresses (URLs) that should prove useful as starting points for further research. At the back of the book is a listing of all the *contributors to this volume*, which gives information on the psychologists, psychiatrists, philosophers, professors, and social critics whose views are debated here.

i

In the interest of space, the reference lists of many of the original articles have been omitted or severely curtailed. Although I welcome further scholarly investigations on these issues, I assume that readers who engage in such investigation will want to look up the original articles (with the original reference lists) anyway. Furthermore, many of the articles have been heavily edited.

Changes to this edition   This edition represents a considerable revision. There are 8 completely new issues: *Does Genetic Testing Have Negative Psychological Effects?* (Issue 4); *Is Love a Mechanism of Evolution?* (Issue 5); *Does Spanking Children Lead Them to Become More Violent?* (Issue 6); *Should the Theory of Multiple Intelligences Be Abandoned?* (Issue 8); *Do Adults Repress Childhood Sexual Abuse?* (Issue 9); *Is Brief Therapy as Effective as Long-Term Therapy?* (Issue 13); *Does the Internet Have Psychological Benefits?* (Issue 16); and *Does Pornography Cause Men to Be Violent Toward Women?* (Issue 18). In all, there are 16 new selections. The issues that were dropped from the previous edition were done so on the recommendation of professors who let me know what worked and what could be improved.

A word to the instructor   An *Instructor's Manual With Test Questions* (multiple-choice and essay) is available through the publisher for the instructor using *Taking Sides* in the classroom. A general guidebook, *Using Taking Sides in the Classroom*, which discusses methods and techniques for integrating the pro-con approach into any classroom setting, is also available. An online version of *Using Taking Sides in the Classroom* and a correspondence service for *Taking Sides* adopters can be found at http://www.dushkin.com/usingts/.

   Taking Sides: Clashing Views on Controversial Psychological Issues is only one title in the Taking Sides series. If you are interested in seeing the table of contents for any of the other titles, please visit the Taking Sides Web site at http://www.dushkin.com/takingsides/.

Acknowledgments   In working on this revision I received useful suggestions from many of the users of the previous edition, and I was able to incorporate many of their recommendations for new issues and new readings. I particularly wish to thank the following professors:

Cyrus Azimi
Columbia College

Robert Jensen
California State University-Sacramento

Edward Crothers
University of Colorado-Boulder

James J. Kotleba
Elgin Community College

Steven Haggbloom
Arkansas State University

Linda Lockwood
Metropolitan State College of Denver

Harold Herzog
Western Carolina University

Lyla Maynard
Des Moines Area Community College

Jack Hesson
Metropolitan State College of Denver

Rona J. McCall
Regis University

Gary Nickell
Moorhead State University

Richard Spong
High Point University

David A. Probst
Clarkson College

Inger Thompson
Glendale Community College

Marc Riess
Middlebury College

Frank J. Vattano
Colorado State University

James Siemen
Washington College

John P. Wilson
Cleveland State University

In addition, special thanks go to Theodore Knight, list manager for the Taking Sides series at Dushkin/McGraw-Hill, for his support and perspective.

Brent Slife
Brigham Young University

Contents In Brief

Contents

Psychologist Diana Baumrind argues that Stanley Milgram's study of obedience did not meet ethical standards for research, because participants were subjected to a research design that caused undue psychological stress that was not resolved after the study. Social psychologist Stanley Milgram, in responding to Baumrind's accusations, asserts that the study was well designed, the stress caused to participants could not have been anticipated, and the participants' anguish dissipated after a thorough debriefing.

Elizabeth Baldwin, a research ethics officer for the American Psychological Association's Science Directorate, maintains that the benefits of behavioral research with animals are substantial and that the animals are being treated humanely. Professor of educational psychology Alan D. Bowd and Kenneth J. Shapiro, executive director of Psychologists for the Ethical Treatment of Animals, argue that the harm done to animals in this research is not widely known and that the "benefits" are not sufficient to balance this cruelty.

Psychotherapy researcher Martin E. P. Seligman defends the conclusion of *Consumer Reports* that psychotherapy is effective by pointing to the importance of client satisfaction in the actual settings in which the clients are treated. Psychotherapy researchers Neil S. Jacobson and Andrew Christensen contend that the *Consumer Reports* study is essentially the same as 40-year-old studies that have long been rejected as inadequate.

PART 2   BIOLOGICAL ISSUES   53

Katharine A. Rimes and Paul M. Salkovskis, both researchers in genetics and bioethics, argue that although genetic testing may have benefits, the negative psychological consequences of such testing may actually increase the risk of developing a disorder or exacerbating a problem. Carol Lynn Trippitelli and her colleagues, researchers of the effects of genetic testing, maintain that although there may be ethical and psychosocial issues involved in genetic testing, their study showed that patients and their spouses feel that the advantages of genetic testing outweigh the risks.

Anthropologist Helen Fisher contends that love is a chemical mechanism through which natural selection initiates and sustains human pair-bonds. Further, she maintains that serial monogamy has adaptive advantages and is visible in worldwide patterns of divorce. Freelance writers Jeffrey S. Reber and Marissa S. Beyers contend that love is not merely biological but also fundamentally relational, social, and psychological. Additionally, they argue that Fisher's commitment to an evolutionary perspective leads to a biased interpretation of the evidence.

PART 3   HUMAN DEVELOPMENT   93

Professor of sociology Murray A. Straus, citing several studies that show a link between childhood spanking and aggressive behavior in later life, argues that spanking teaches a child violence and that there are always nonaggressive alternatives to spanking. John K. Rosemond, a family psychologist, maintains that the research on spanking is politically skewed. Because the research makes no distinction between spanking and beating, he argues, it misrepresents loving parents who appropriately discipline their children.

Issue 7.   Does Viewing Television Increase a Child's Aggression?   116

Brandon S. Centerwall, an epidemiologist, argues that children act out the violence they see on television and carry the violent behaviors into adulthood. Brian Siano, a writer and researcher, contends that children with nonnurturing parents, regardless of the children's television viewing habits, tend to be more aggressive than children who closely identify with either parent.

PART 4   COGNITIVE PROCESSES   139

Issue 8.   Should the Theory of Multiple Intelligences Be Abandoned?   140

Perry D. Klein, who is on the University of Western Ontario's Faculty of Education, contends that Howard Gardner's theory of multiple intelligences can be boiled down to a collection of trivial statements or a circular argument. He argues that the theory says little about intelligence. Professor of human development Howard Gardner counters that Klein has misunderstood his theory and that his theory offers the educational system hope of reaching more students.

Issue 9.   Do Adults Repress Childhood Sexual Abuse?   154

May Benatar, a clinical social worker and lecturer, asserts that recent publicity on memories of sexual abuse has focused more on the "hype" of sexual abuse rather than on the actual prevailing act of sexual abuse. She maintains that repressed memories are a common response of child sexual abuse and that they can be recovered in adulthood. Susan P. Robbins, an associate professor of graduate social work, contends that there is little support for the idea of repressed or dissociated memories of child sexual abuse in scientific studies. She also argues that outside sources can trigger or influence many inaccurate memories of child abuse.

Issue 10.   Is There a Racial Difference in Intelligence?   178

Professor of psychology J. Philippe Rushton argues that there is irrefutable scientific evidence of racial differences in intelligence that are attributable to genetic differences. Teacher and psychologist Zack Z. Cernovsky argues that Rushton's data is based not on contemporary scientific research standards but on racial prejudice that is reflective of Nazi dogma.

PART 5 MENTAL HEALTH   191

Issue 11.   Is Schizophrenia a Biological Disorder?   192

Clinical psychiatrist Nancy C. Andreasen asserts that a variety of modern technologies, including neuroimaging and animal modeling, show that although schizophrenia is a disease that manifests itself in the mind, it arises from the brain. Clinical psychologist Victor D. Sanua contends that the assumption that schizophrenia is a biological disorder is not supported by research but is, instead, maintained by many scientists who have a misguided faith in an elusive future technology that will supposedly show the connection between mind and brain.

Issue 12.   Have Antidepressant Drugs Proven to Be Effective?   204

Psychiatrist Peter D. Kramer argues that antidepressant drugs such as Prozac can transform depressed patients into happy people with almost no side effects. Professors of psychology Seymour Fisher and Roger P. Greenberg assert that the studies that demonstrate the effectiveness of antidepressants are seriously flawed.

PART 6   PSYCHOLOGICAL TREATMENT   227

Issue 13.   Is Brief Therapy as Effective as Long-Term Therapy? 228

Researcher Brett N. Steenbarger argues that although psychologists may underestimate the long-lasting effects of brief therapy, studies show that the most dramatic changes in patient behavior take place after only eight therapy sessions. Therapist and researcher Charles J. Gelso contends that although initial behavior change may be rapid, long-term therapy is needed in order for a client to maintain lasting and deep personality changes.

Issue 14.   Should Psychologists Be Allowed to Prescribe Drugs? 242

Psychologist and lawyer Patrick H. DeLeon and Jack G. Wiggins, Jr., former president of the American Psychological Association, argue that giving prescription privileges to psychologists will allow them to address society's pressing needs. Psychologists Steven C. Hayes and Elaine Heiby maintain that prescription privileges will cost the discipline of psychology its unique professional identity and compromise public safety.

Issue 15.   Classic Dialogue: Do Diagnostic Labels Hinder Treatment?   256

Psychologist D. L. Rosenhan describes an experiment that he contends demonstrates that once a patient is labeled "schizophrenic," his behavior is seen as such by mental health workers regardless of the true state of the patient's mental health. Psychiatrist Robert L. Spitzer argues that diagnostic labels are necessary and valuable and that Rosenhan's experiment has many flaws.

PART 7   SOCIAL PSYCHOLOGY   291

Research scientist James E. Katz and Philip Aspden, executive director of the Center for Research on the Information Society, contend that the Internet has positive effects on the lives of its users. They also maintain that the Internet creates more opportunities for people to foster relationships with people, regardless of their location. Robert Kraut, a professor of social psychology and human computer interaction, and his colleagues at Carnegie Mellon University question how beneficial Internet use really is. They argue that Internet use reduces the number and quality of interpersonal relationships that one has.

David B. Larson, president of the National Institute for Healthcare, maintains that religious commitment improves mental health and that spirituality can be a medical treatment. Albert Ellis, president of the Institute for Rational-Emotive Therapy, challenges Larson's studies and questions particularly whether a religious commitment of "fanatic" proportions is truly mentally healthy.

Author Elizabeth Cramer and her colleagues maintain that pornography often depicts women in violent and degrading ways, thus desensitizing the viewer of such pornography and making violence acceptable. Professor of sociology Kimberly A. Davies argues that pornography is a scapegoat for many societal problems, including violence and abuse toward women.

Introduction

Unresolved Issues in Psychology

Brent Slife

Stephen C. Yanchar

Eminent psychologist Edward Bradford Titchener (1867–1927) once stated that although psychology has a short history, it has a long past. He meant that even though the science of psychology is of relatively recent origin, the subject matter of psychology extends back to ancient history. Unfortunately, this dual history—the short and the long—is rarely treated in psychology texts; most texts focus almost exclusively on the shorter history. This shorter history is thought to be guided by the scientific method, so texts are generally filled with the scientific facts of the discipline. However, we cannot fully understand psychology without also understanding its longer intellectual history, a history of age-old questions that have recently been addressed by science but rarely been completely answered. Some history texts portray this longer intellectual history, but they do not deal with its contemporary implications. *Taking Sides: Clashing Views on Controversial Psychological Issues* is dedicated to the unresolved issues that still plague psychologists from this longer history.

Why Are There Unresolved Issues?

The subject matter of psychology is somewhat different from the subject matter of the natural sciences. In fact, psychology has been termed a "soft" science because it deals with neither the "hard" world of observable entities and physical elements—like zoology, biology, physiology, and chemistry—nor the rigorous computational analyses of mathematics, physics, and astronomy. These hard sciences are disciplines in which the crucial questions can usually be answered through scientific observation and experimentation.

Psychologists, on the other hand, deal with the warm, "soft" world of human beings—the thoughts, attitudes, emotions, and behaviors of people interacting with other people. Psychologists are therefore concerned with many of the philosophical questions that seem so central and unique to humanity. These questions have no quick and simple answers. Indeed, these questions have occupied thinkers—scientists and philosophers alike—since at least the time of the ancient Greeks.

For example, psychologists regularly deal with the topic of mind and matter, or what is sometimes referred to as the mind-body problem. The mind-body problem essentially asks, Does the mind (which is often viewed as *not* being entirely composed of matter) control the body (which *is* entirely composed of matter), or does the brain control the mind? Yet the essence of what we mean by the mind-body problem has been a topic of debate since at least the time of the Greek philosopher Aristotle (Robinson, 1989). Aristotle (384–322 B.C.) believed that the human mind had to be distinct from the crude matter of the human body. While the human body would eventually die and decay, the human mind (or soul) was imperishable. Aristotle accounted for much of human psychology on biological grounds (i.e., in terms of matter), but he still considered the higher rational activities of a human to be aspects of a mind that are independent of the body (Robinson, 1986). However, what is left out of his and other accounts is a precise explanation of how mind and body are connected. That is, if we assume that the mind is *not* composed of matter and is thus intangible, then how can it connect or interact with something material and tangible like the body? If, on the other hand, we decide that the mind *is* tangible and material, then we inherit a host of other problems associated with reductionism (see Slife & Williams, 1995, for details).

The point is that these and other such questions may not be resolved merely through scientific observation and experimentation. Scientific method is helpful for answering certain empirical questions, but its benefits are limited for many philosophical questions. And, for better or worse, psychology is infused with philosophical questions as well as empirical questions. There are basically two reasons for this infusion: the complexity of psychology's subject matter and the methods that psychologists use to study their subject matter.

Human beings—the primary subject matter of psychology—appear to operate with wills of their own within a hopelessly complex network of situations and relationships. This, it would seem, hinders the ability of scientists to attain the kind of certainty with people that they can attain with inanimate objects. Perhaps more important, it is difficult to know *why* people act in a particular manner because we cannot directly observe their intentions, thoughts, and desires. Thus, there are some aspects of human beings that elude the traditional methods of natural science.

The scientific method itself provides no irrefutable verification of an explanation. This is because data alone do not provide answers. Scientists sometimes talk as if the data from their experiments "tell" them what to believe or "give" them results, but this is somewhat misleading. Data are meaningless until they have been interpreted by the scientist (Slife & Williams, 1995). That is, scientists have a lot to do with their findings. Because there are a number of possible interpreters, there are, in principle, a number of possible interpretations. As some of the issues in this volume show, results that seem to supply indubitable proof for one interpreter might appear quite dubious to another. The reason for this is that the scientific method is set up in a manner that requires interpretation. As many who have studied this method have noted (e.g., Popper, 1959; Rychlak, 1988), the scientific method basically takes the form of a logical if-then statement: *If* my theory is correct, *then* my data will come out as I predict. However, problems can occur when we use this logic inappropriately. What if we know, for example, that we have the "then" portion of our statement, that the data did come out as I predicted? Do we then know that my theory is correct? Of course we cannot know this, because there can be an alternative theory (or many alternatives) that could explain the same data.

Unfortunately, however, this is the way in which science is conducted. We do not know the "if" portion of our logical statement—that my theory is correct; we can only know the "then" portion—that my data came out as I predicted. And our knowledge of our data cannot tell us that our theory is correct. All we can ever do is *interpret* what our data mean because our data can always mean something else.[1]

So, as a little logic has shown, data from human subjects can always be interpreted in different ways. In fact, because of these possible interpretations, there can never be a final and definitive experiment to determine what is really true about human beings (Slife & Williams, 1995). This is what scientists mean when they say that they cannot *prove* a theory but can only *support* it. Unfortunately, this simple distinction leaves many important questions unresolved, such as the mind-body problem. Still, this lack of resolution does not mean that scientists can ignore these issues. Just because certain issues are not amenable to scientific methods does not mean they go away. The issue of whether or not the mind controls matter, for example, is vital to cancer patients who wonder whether or not positive mental attitudes will alter the course of their disease. Such issues require exploration and debate regardless of the state of scientific knowledge. Whatever scientific information is available is important, and the lack of a complete scientific answer cannot prevent us from debating what information we do have, particularly when we may never get a complete scientific answer.

A Dialectical Approach

This volume introduces some of the most important contemporary debates in psychology as well as some classical issues that remain unresolved. As mentioned, this volume is different from texts that focus exclusively on what is known scientifically. Most texts with an exclusive scientific focus adopt a "banking conception" of education.

The banking conception of education assumes that students are essentially "banks" in which scientific facts are "deposited." Because psychology is considered a science, there are presumably many scientific psychological facts, derived from experiments, that need to be deposited in students' minds. The banking conception makes teachers and textbooks fact distributors or information transmitters. Lectures are monologues through which the facts of experiments or the findings of method are distributed and transmitted into the mental "banks" of students. At test time, then, teachers make information "withdrawals" to discern how well students have maintained the deposits of educational currency referred to as knowledge.

Since the time of the Greek philosopher Socrates (470–399 B.C.), the banking conception of education has not been considered effective for learning about unresolved conceptual issues. One reason for this is that nestled within the banking conception lies the assumption that knowledge is above reasonable criticism and that the facts of a scholarly discipline are approximations of truth—distilled and ready for distribution to students. This is the notion of education that considers knowledge to be strictly objective. Students are thought to acquire a clear and objective picture of reality—the way things really are. As we have observed, however, it is questionable whether teachers of the "soft" sciences have access to clear and objective facts only. In many cases, the "facts" are not so clear and objective but rather puzzling and debatable. Indeed, interpretations of data are always debatable, in principle.

An alternative to the banking tradition of education is the *dialectical* tradition of education. In this tradition, there can be no meaning (and thus no knowledge) without opposition. For example, there is no way to understand what "beauty" or "upness" means without implicitly understanding what "ugliness" or "downness" is, respectively. To judge the beauty of a work of art, one must have some notion of the contrast to beauty. In other words, opposing notions only make sense when considered at the same time, one complementing the other and together forming a complete concept. In this Greek conception of the dialectic, there are no quick and easy answers to difficult questions, and there are few incontestable facts to present. Instead, there are at least two sides to every issue.

Socrates taught his students that we may begin in error or falsity, but we will eventually arrive at truth if we continue our dialectical conversation. This is because truth, for Socrates, involves uncovering what is already there. Because all conceptions—true or false—supposedly have their dialectical complements implicit within them, truth is itself already implicit and waiting to be revealed. Truth, then, according to Socrates, is uncovered by a rational analysis of the relevant (and perhaps even false) ideas and arguments already under discussion.

The discipline of psychology is often considered to be dialectical, at least in part. Any student who has studied the many different theories of human behavior (e.g., humanism, behaviorism, psychoanalysis) can attest to this. Psychology frequently consists of two or more voices on the same psychological issue. Consequently, many of the ideas of psychology develop through conversation that takes place among psychologists or among the students of psychology. Although this is understandable when we consider the complexity of psychology's subject matter, it can create problems for the banking approach to education. What can be deposited in a mental bank when two or more voices are possible and the conversation among the voices is ongoing? Some information distribution is certainly important. However, information distribution alone cannot capture this type of knowledge in the discipline, because that knowledge is dialectical in nature.

Benefits of a Dialectical Approach

The dialectical approach is the focus of this volume: Psychological issues are presented in true dialectical fashion, with two distinct sides. Students are asked to familiarize themselves with both sides of an issue, look at the supporting evidence on both sides, and engage in constructive conversation about possible resolutions. This approach to education requires students to take an active role in making sense of the issues. In so doing, students benefit in several ways.

First, students come to a richer understanding of the subject matter of psychologists. It is important to understand that there is a dialectical, or humanities, side of psychology as well as an informational, or scientific, side of psychology. As necessary as data may be, there will always be a human interpreter of the data that will never permit psychology to dispense with humanities entirely.

Second, students develop a healthy respect for both sides of a debate. There is a natural tendency to underestimate reasonable arguments on one side or the other of a debate. Often, of course, the side one favors is the "most reasonable." Without exception, the issues in this book have reasonable people and reasonable arguments *on both sides*. That is, these issues are issues in psychology precisely because they have reasonable arguments and evidence on either side. This is not to say that both sides are correct (although this too is possible). It is to say, rather, that a proper appreciation of both sides is necessary to understanding what is at issue and thus to begin to find a resolution.

A third benefit of this dialectical approach is that students better understand the nature of psychological knowledge in general. Although contemporary psychologists have taken up the scientific challenge of exploring behavior and mind, many questions are still far from being answered. Psychology's parent, like all sciences, is philosophy. Hence, philosophical (or theoretical) issues always lurk behind the activities of psychologists. Issues such as mind versus body, free will versus determinism, nature versus nurture, and the philosophy of science are both philosophical and psychological questions. Students will necessarily have to entertain and explicate these types of issues as they learn about and advance the discipline.

Fourth, students become more aware of alternative views on controversial psychological issues. People often do not even realize that there is another point of view to an issue or evidence to the contrary. This realization, however, can help students to be more cautious in their knowledge. As the dialectician Socrates once noted, this caution is sometimes the first step toward true wisdom —knowing what it is that you don't know.

Finally, the dialectical approach promotes critical thinking skills. As authorities on critical thinking have noted (e.g., Brookfield, 1987), thinking skills require an awareness of what one *does* believe and a knowledge of alternatives regarding what one *could* believe. *Taking Sides: Clashing Views on Controversial Psychological Issues* provides both elements. Finely honed critical skills give students a better position from which to examine the psychological literature critically and to select or develop their own positions on important psychological issues.

Note

1. Unfortunately, falsifying the consequent—the "then" portion of our logical statement—does not prevent us from needing to interpret either, as Slife and Williams (1995) have shown.

References

Brookfield, S. (1987). *Developing critical thinkers: Challenging adults to explore alternative ways of thinking.* San Francisco: Jossey-Bass.

Popper, K. (1959). *The logic of scientific discovery.* New York: Basic Books.

Robinson, D. (1986). *An intellectual history of psychology.* Madison, WI: University of Wisconsin Press.

Robinson, D. (1989). *Aristotle's psychology.* New York: Columbia University Press.

Rychlak, J. F. (1988). *The psychology of rigorous humanism* (2d ed.). New York: New York University Press.

Slife, B. D., & Williams, R. N. (1995). *What's behind the research: Discovering hidden assumptions in the behavioral sciences.* Thousand Oaks, CA: Sage Publications.

On the Internet ...

Abraham A. Brill Library

The Abraham A. Brill Library, perhaps the largest psychoanalytic library in the world, contains data on over 40,000 books, periodicals, and reprints in psychoanalysis and related fields. Its holdings span the literature of psychoanalysis from its beginning to the present day.

http://plaza.interport.net/nypsan/

Psychnet

Information on psychology may be obtained at this Web site through the site map or by using the search engine. You can access the American Psychological Association's newspaper, the *APA Monitor,* APA books on a wide range of topics, PsychINFO—an electronic database of abstracts on over 1,350 scholarly journals—and the Help Center for information on dealing with modern life problems.

http://www.apa.org/psychnet/

I-A-P: Inventory for the Assessment of Psychology

This site, created and maintained by Ira Rietz and Svenja Wahl at the University of Hamburg, is an ongoing survey on attitudes toward psychology among psychologists and members of the general public.

http://www.unibw-hamburg.de/PWEB/psypae/eng.html

Psychology Research on the Net

Psychologically related experiments on the Internet can be found at this site. Biological psychology/neuropsychology, clinical psychology, cognition, developmental psychology, emotions, health psychology, personality, sensation/perception, and social psychology are just some of the areas addressed.

http://psych.hanover.edu/APS/exponnet.html

PART 1

Research Issues

*R*esearch *methods allow psychologists to investigate their ideas and subject matter. How psychologists perform their research is often a subject of controversy. For example, sometimes animals are used to test experimental procedures before they are applied to humans. Is this right? Should animals be experimented upon—and sometimes sacrificed—in the service of humans? Similarly, what limits, if any, should be set on psychological research that is conducted on humans? Are there some experiments that are so potentially psychologically harmful to people that they should not be performed?*

- Classic Dialogue: Was Stanley Milgram's Study of Obedience Unethical?

- Should Animals Be Used in Psychological Research?

- Is the *Consumer Reports* Conclusion That "Psychotherapy Helps" Valid?

ISSUE 1

Classic Dialogue: Was Stanley Milgram's Study of Obedience Unethical?

YES: Diana Baumrind, from "Some Thoughts on Ethics of Research: After Reading Milgram's 'Behavioral Study of Obedience,'" *American Psychologist* (vol. 19, 1964)

NO: Stanley Milgram, from "Issues in the Study of Obedience: A Reply to Baumrind," *American Psychologist* (vol. 19, 1964)

ISSUE SUMMARY

YES: Psychologist Diana Baumrind argues that Stanley Milgram's study of obedience did not meet ethical standards for research, because participants were subjected to a research design that caused undue psychological stress that was not resolved after the study.

NO: Social psychologist Stanley Milgram, in responding to Baumrind's accusations, asserts that the study was well designed, the stress caused to participants could not have been anticipated, and the participants' anguish dissipated after a thorough debriefing.

Are there psychological experiments that should not be conducted? Is the psychological distress that participants experience in some studies too extreme to justify the experimental outcomes and knowledge gained? Or is it sometimes necessary to allow participants to experience some anguish so that a researcher can better understand important psychological phenomena? These questions lie at the heart of ethical considerations in psychological research. They have traditionally been answered by the researcher, who attempts to weigh the costs and benefits of conducting a given study.

The problem is that a researcher's ability to accurately anticipate the costs and benefits of a study is severely limited. Researchers are likely to have an investment in their studies, which may lead them to overestimate the benefits and underestimate the costs. For these and other reasons, in 1974 the United States Department of Health, Education, and Welfare established regulations for the protection of human subjects. These regulations include the creation of institutional review boards, which are responsible for reviewing research proposals and ensuring that researchers adequately protect research participants.

The establishment of these regulations can be traced to past ethical controversies, such as the one raised in the following selection by Diana Baumrind regarding Stanley Milgram's famous 1963 study of obedience. Baumrind's primary concern is that the psychological welfare of the study's participants was compromised not only through the course of the study but also through the course of their lives. She contends that participants were prone to obey the experimenter because of the atmosphere of the study and the participants' trust in the experimenter. As a result, participants behaved in ways that disturbed them considerably. Baumrind maintains that these disturbances could not be resolved through an after-study debriefing but rather remained with the participants.

In response to these accusations, Milgram argues that the atmosphere of a laboratory generalizes to other contexts in which obedience is prevalent and is thus appropriate to a study of obedience. Furthermore, he and a number of other professionals never anticipated the results of the study; they were genuinely surprised by its outcome. Milgram also asserts that the psychological distress experienced by some participants was temporary, not dangerous, and that it dissipated after the true nature of the study was revealed.

POINT

- Milgram's indifference toward distressed participants reveals his lack of concern for their well-being.
- A study of obedience should not be conducted in the laboratory because subjects are particularly prone to behave obediently and to put trust in the researcher.
- The psychological distress experienced by participants exceeded appropriate limits.
- Participants experienced long-term, negative psychological consequences as a result of their participation in Milgram's experiment.
- In planning and designing the study, Milgram ignored issues regarding the extreme psychological distress that was experienced by some participants.

COUNTERPOINT

- Milgram made special efforts to assure participants that their behavior was normal.
- The laboratory setting is well suited to a study of obedience because it is similar to other contexts in which obedience is prevalent.
- The psychological distress was brief and not injurious.
- Participants spoke positively about the experiment, indicating that it was psychologically beneficial.
- The extreme psychological tension experienced by some participants was unanticipated by Milgram and many other professionals.

Diana Baumrind

Some Thoughts on Ethics of Research

Certain problems in psychological research require the experimenter to balance his career and scientific interests against the interests of his prospective subjects. When such occasions arise the experimenter's stated objective frequently is to do the best possible job with the least possible harm to his subjects. The experimenter seldom perceives in more positive terms an indebtedness to the subject for his services, perhaps because the detachment which his functions require prevents appreciation of the subject as an individual.

Yet a debt does exist, even when the subject's reason for volunteering includes course credit or monetary gain. Often a subject participates unwillingly in order to satisfy a course requirement. These requirements are of questionable merit ethically, and do not alter the experimenter's responsibility to the subject.

Most experimental conditions do not cause the subjects pain or indignity, and are sufficiently interesting or challenging to present no problem of an ethical nature to the experimenter. But where the experimental conditions expose the subject to loss of dignity, or offer him nothing of value, then the experimenter is obliged to consider the reasons why the subject volunteered and to reward him accordingly.

The subject's public motives for volunteering include having an enjoyable or stimulating experience, acquiring knowledge, doing the experimenter a favor which may some day be reciprocated, and making a contribution to science. These motives can be taken into account rather easily by the experimenter who is willing to spend a few minutes with the subject afterwards to thank him for his participation, answer his questions, reassure him that he did well, and chat with him a bit. Most volunteers also have less manifest, but equally legitimate, motives. A subject may be seeking an opportunity to have contact with, be noticed by, and perhaps confide in a person with psychological training. The dependent attitude of most subjects toward the experimenter is an artifact of the experimental situation as well as an expression of some subjects' personal need systems at the time they volunteer.

The dependent, obedient attitude assumed by most subjects in the experimental setting is appropriate to that situation. The "game" is defined by the experimenter and he makes the rules. By volunteering, the subject agrees

From Diana Baumrind, "Some Thoughts on Ethics of Research: After Reading Milgram's 'Behavioral Study of Obedience,'" *American Psychologist,* vol. 19 (1964). Copyright © 1964 by The American Psychological Association. Reprinted by permission.

implicitly to assume a posture of trust and obedience. While the experimental conditions leave him exposed, the subject has the right to assume that his security and self-esteem will be protected.

There are other professional situations in which one member—the patient or client—expects help and protection from the other— the physician or psychologist. But the interpersonal relationship between experimenter and subject additionally has unique features which are likely to provoke initial anxiety in the subject. The laboratory is unfamiliar as a setting and the rules of behavior ambiguous compared to a clinician's office. Because of the anxiety and passivity generated by the setting, the subject is more prone to behave in an obedient, suggestible manner in the laboratory than elsewhere. Therefore, the laboratory is not the place to study degree of obedience or suggestibility, as a function of a particular experimental condition, since the base line for these phenomena as found in the laboratory is probably much higher than in most other settings. Thus experiments in which the relationship to the experimenter as an authority is used as an independent condition are imperfectly designed for the same reason that they are prone to injure the subjects involved. They disregard the special quality of trust and obedience with which the subject appropriately regards the experimenter.

Other phenomena which present ethical decisions, unlike those mentioned above, *can* be reproduced successfully in the laboratory. Failure experience, conformity to peer judgment, and isolation are among such phenomena. In these cases we can expect the experimenter to take whatever measures are necessary to prevent the subject from leaving the laboratory more humiliated, insecure, alienated, or hostile than when he arrived. To guarantee that an especially sensitive subject leaves a stressful experimental experience in the proper state sometimes requires special clinical training. But usually an attitude of compassion, respect, gratitude, and common sense will suffice, and no amount of clinical training will substitute. The subject has the right to expect that the psychologist with whom he is interacting has some concern for his welfare, and the personal attributes and professional skill to express his good will effectively.

Unfortunately, the subject is not always treated with the respect he deserves. It has become more commonplace in sociopsychological laboratory studies to manipulate, embarrass, and discomfort subjects. At times the insult to the subject's sensibilities extends to the journal reader when the results are reported. Milgram's (1963) study is a case in point. The following is Milgram's abstract of his experiment:

> This article describes a procedure for the study of destructive obedience in the laboratory. It consists of ordering a naive S to administer increasingly more severe punishment to a victim in the context of a learning experiment. Punishment is administered by means of a shock generator with 30 graded switches ranging from Slight Shock to Danger: Severe Shock. The victim is a confederate of E. The primary dependent variable is the maximum shock the S is willing to administer before he refuses to continue further. 26 Ss obeyed the experimental commands fully, and administered the highest shock on the generator. 14 Ss broke off the experiment at some point after the victim protested and refused to provide further answers. The procedure created ex-

treme levels of nervous tension in some Ss. Profuse sweating, trembling, and stuttering were typical expressions of this emotional disturbance. One unexpected sign of tension—yet to be explained—was the regular occurrence of nervous laughter, which in some Ss developed into uncontrollable seizures. The variety of interesting behavioral dynamics observed in the experiment, the reality of the situation for the S, and the possibility of parametric variation within the framework of the procedure, point to the fruitfulness of further study [p. 371].

The detached, objective manner in which Milgram reports the emotional disturbance suffered by his subject contrasts sharply with his graphic account of that disturbance. Following are two other quotes describing the effects on his subjects of the experimental conditions:

I observed a mature and initially poised businessman enter the laboratory smiling and confident. Within 20 minutes he was reduced to a twitching, stuttering wreck, who was rapidly approaching a point of nervous collapse. He constantly pulled on his earlobe, and twisted his hands. At one point he pushed his fist into his forehead and muttered: "Oh, God, let's stop it." And yet he continued to respond to every word of the experimenter, and obeyed to the end [p. 377].

In a large number of cases the degree of tension reached extremes that are rarely seen in sociopsychological laboratory studies. Subjects were observed to sweat, tremble, stutter, bite their lips, groan, and dig their fingernails into their flesh. These were characteristic rather than exceptional responses to the experiment.

One sign of tension was the regular occurrence of nervous laughing fits. Fourteen of the 40 subjects showed definite signs of nervous laughter and smiling. The laughter seemed entirely out of place, even bizarre. Full-blown, uncontrollable seizures were observed for 3 subjects. On one occasion we observed a seizure so violently convulsive that it was necessary to call a halt to the experiment ... [p. 375].

Milgram does state that,

After the interview, procedures were undertaken to assure that the subject would leave the laboratory in a state of well being. A friendly reconciliation was arranged between the subject and the victim, and an effort was made to reduce any tensions that arose as a result of the experiment [p. 374].

It would be interesting to know what sort of procedures could dissipate the type of emotional disturbance just described. In view of the effects on subjects, traumatic to a degree which Milgram himself considers nearly unprecedented in sociopsychological experiments, his casual assurance that these tensions were dissipated before the subject left the laboratory is unconvincing.

What could be the rational basis for such a posture of indifference? Perhaps Milgram supplies the answer himself when he partially explains the subject's destructive obedience as follows, "Thus they assume that the discomfort caused the victim is momentary, while the scientific gains resulting from the experiment are enduring [p. 378]." Indeed such a rationale might suffice to justify the means used to achieve his end if that end were of inestimable value to humanity or were not itself transformed by the means by which it was attained.

The behavioral psychologist is not in as good a position to objectify his faith in the significance of his work as medical colleagues at points of break-through. His experimental situations are not sufficiently accurate models of real-life experience; his sampling techniques are seldom of a scope which would justify the meaning with which he would like to endow his results; and these results are hard to reproduce by colleagues with opposing theoretical views.... [T]he concrete benefit to humanity of his particular piece of work, no mat-ter how competently handled, cannot justify the risk that real harm will be done to the subject. I am not speaking of physical discomfort, inconvenience, or experimental deception per se, but of permanent harm, however slight. I do regard the emotional disturbance described by Milgram as potentially harmful because it could easily effect an alteration in the subject's self-image or ability to trust adult authorities in the future. It is potentially harmful to a subject to commit, in the course of an experiment, acts which he himself considers unwor-thy, particularly when he has been entrapped into committing such acts by an individual he has reason to trust. The subject's personal responsibility for his ac-tions is not erased because the experimenter reveals to him the means which he used to stimulate these actions. The subject realizes that he would have hurt the victim if the current were on. The realization that he also made a fool of him-self by accepting the experimental set results in additional loss of self-esteem. Moreover, the subject finds it difficult to express his anger outwardly after the experimenter in a self-acceptant but friendly manner reveals the hoax.

A fairly intense corrective interpersonal experience is indicated wherein the subject admits and accepts his responsibility for his own actions, and at the same time gives vent to his hurt and anger at being fooled. Perhaps an ex-perience as distressing as the one described by Milgram can be integrated by the subject, provided that careful thought is given to the matter. The propriety of such experimentation is still in question even if such a reparational expe-rience were forthcoming. Without it I would expect a naive, sensitive subject to remain deeply hurt and anxious for some time, and a sophisticated, cynical subject to become even more alienated and distrustful.

In addition the experimental procedure used by Milgram does not ap-pear suited to the objectives of the study because it does not take into account the special quality of the set which the subject has in the experimental situa-tion. Milgram is concerned with a very important problem, namely, the social consequences of destructive obedience. He says,

> Gas chambers were built, death camps were guarded, daily quotas of corpses were produced with the same efficiency as a manufacture of appliances. These inhumane policies may have originated in the mind of a single person, but they could only be carried out on a massive scale if a very large number of persons obeyed orders [p. 371].

But the parallel between authority-subordinate relationships in Hitler's Germany and in Milgram's laboratory is unclear. In the former situation the SS man or member of the German Officer Corps, when obeying orders to slaughter, had no reason to think of his superior officer as benignly disposed towards himself or their victims. The victims were perceived as subhuman and not worthy of consideration. The subordinate officer was an agent in a great cause. He did not need to feel guilt or conflict because within his frame of reference he was acting rightly.

It is obvious from Milgram's own descriptions that most of his subjects were concerned about their victims and did trust the experimenter, and that their stressful conflict was generated in part by the consequences of these two disparate but appropriate attitudes. Their distress may have resulted from shock at what the experimenter was doing to them as well as from what they thought they were doing to their victims. In any case there is not a convincing parallel between the phenomena studied by Milgram and destructive obedience as that concept would apply to the subordinate-authority relationship demonstrated in Hitler Germany. If the experiments were conducted "outside of New Haven [Connecticut] and without any visible ties to [Yale University]," I would still question their validity on similar although not identical grounds. In addition, I would question the representativeness of a sample of subjects who would voluntarily participate within a noninstitutional setting.

In summary, the experimental objectives of the psychologist are seldom incompatible with the subject's ongoing state of well being, provided that the experimenter is willing to take the subject's motives and interests into consideration when planning his methods and correctives. Section 4b in *Ethical Standards of Psychologists* (APA, undated) reads in part:

> Only when a problem is significant and can be investigated in no other way, is the psychologist justified in exposing human subjects to emotional stress or other possible harm. In conducting such research, the psychologist must seriously consider the possibility of harmful aftereffects, and should be prepared to remove them as soon as permitted by the design of the experiment. Where the danger of serious aftereffects exists, research should be conducted only when the subjects or their responsible agents are fully informed of this possibility and volunteer nevertheless [p. 12].

From the subject's point of view procedures which involve loss of dignity, self-esteem, and trust in rational authority are probably most harmful in the long run and require the most thoughtfully planned reparations, if engaged in at all. The public image of psychology as a profession is highly related to our own actions, and some of these actions are changeworthy. It is important that as research psychologists we protect our ethical sensibilities rather than adapt our personal standards to include as appropriate the kind of indignities to which Milgram's subjects were exposed. I would not like to see experiments such as Milgram's proceed unless the subjects were fully informed of the dangers of serious aftereffects and his correctives were clearly shown to be effective in restoring their state of well being.

References

AMERICAN PSYCHOLOGICAL ASSOCIATION. Ethical Standards of Psychologists: A summary of ethical principles. Washington, D.C.: APA, undated.

MILGRAM, S. Behavioral study of obedience. *J. abnorm. soc. Psychol.*, 1963, 67, 371–378.

NO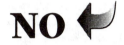

Stanley Milgram

Issues in the Study of Obedience: A Reply to Baumrind

Obedience serves numerous productive functions in society. It may be ennobling and educative and entail acts of charity and kindness. Yet the problem of destructive obedience, because it is the most disturbing expression of obedience in our time, and because it is the most perplexing, merits intensive study.

In its most general terms, the problem of destructive obedience may be defined thus: If X tells Y to hurt Z, under what conditions will Y carry out the command of X, and under what conditions will he refuse? In the concrete setting of a laboratory, the question may assume this form: If an experimenter tells a subject to act against another person, under what conditions will the subject go along with the instruction, and under what conditions will he refuse to obey?

A simple procedure was devised for studying obedience (Milgram, 1963). A person comes to the laboratory, and in the context of a learning experiment, he is told to give increasingly severe electric shocks to another person. (The other person is an actor, who does not really receive any shocks.) The experimenter tells the subject to continue stepping up the shock level, even to the point of reaching the level marked "Danger: Severe Shock." The purpose of the experiment is to see how far the naive subject will proceed before he refuses to comply with the experimenter's instructions. Behavior prior to this rupture is considered "obedience" in that the subject does what the experimenter tells him to do. The point of rupture is the act of disobedience. Once the basic procedure is established, it becomes possible to vary conditions of the experiment, to learn under what circumstances obedience to authority is most probable, and under what conditions defiance is brought to the fore (Milgram, in press).

The results of the experiment (Milgram, 1963) showed, first, that it is more difficult for many people to defy the experimenter's authority than was generally supposed. A substantial number of subjects go through to the end of the shock board. The second finding is that the situation often places a person in considerable conflict. In the course of the experiment, subjects fidget, sweat,

From Stanley Milgram, "Issues in the Study of Obedience: A Reply to Baumrind," *American Psychologist*, vol. 19 (1964). Copyright © 1964 by Stanley Milgram. Reprinted by permission of Alexandra Milgram.

and sometimes break out into nervous fits of laughter. On the one hand, subjects want to aid the experimenter; and on the other hand, they do not want to shock the learner. The conflict is expressed in nervous reactions.

In a recent issue of *American Psychologist,* Diana Baumrind (1964) raised a number of questions concerning the obedience report. Baumrind expressed concern for the welfare of subjects who served in the experiment, and wondered whether adequate measures were taken to protect the participants. She also questioned the adequacy of the experimental design.

Patently, "Behavioral Study of Obedience" did not contain all the information needed for an assessment of the experiment. But . . . this was only one of a series of reports on the experimental program, and Baumrind's article was deficient in information that could have been obtained easily. . . .

At the outset, Baumrind confuses the unanticipated outcome of an experiment with its basic procedure. She writes, for example, as if the production of stress in our subjects was an intended and deliberate effect of the experimental manipulation. There are many laboratory procedures specifically designed to create stress (Lazarus, 1964), but the obedience paradigm was not one of them. The extreme tension induced in some subjects was unexpected. Before conducting the experiment, the procedures were discussed with many colleagues, and none anticipated the reactions that subsequently took place. Foreknowledge of results can never be the invariable accompaniment of an experimental probe. Understanding grows because we examine situations in which the end is unknown. An investigator unwilling to accept this degree of risk must give up the idea of scientific inquiry.

Moreover, there was every reason to expect, prior to actual experimentation, that subjects would refuse to follow the experimenter's instructions beyond the point where the victim protested; many colleagues and psychiatrists were questioned on this point, and they virtually all felt this would be the case. Indeed, to initiate an experiment in which the critical measure hangs on disobedience, one must start with a belief in certain spontaneous resources in men that enable them to overcome pressure from authority.

It is true that after a reasonable number of subjects had been exposed to the procedures, it became evident that some would go to the end of the shock board, and some would experience stress. That point, it seems to me, is the first legitimate juncture at which one could even start to wonder whether or not to abandon the study. But momentary excitement is not the same as harm. As the experiment progressed there was no indication of injurious effects in the subjects; and as the subjects themselves strongly endorsed the experiment, the judgment I made was to continue the investigation.

Is not Baumrind's criticism based as much on the unanticipated findings as on the method? The findings were that some subjects performed in what appeared to be a shockingly immoral way. If, instead, every one of the subjects had broken off at "slight shock," or at the first sign of the learner's discomfort, the results would have been pleasant, and reassuring, and who would protest?

Table 1

Excerpt from Questionnaire Used in a Follow-up Study of the Obedience Research

Now that I have read the report and all things considered . . .	Defiant	Obedient	All
1. I am very glad to have been in the experiment	40.0%	47.8%	43.5%
2. I am glad to have been in the experiment	43.8%	35.7%	40.2%
3. I am neither sorry nor glad to have been in the experiment	15.3%	14.8%	15.1%
4. I am sorry to have been in the experiment	0.8%	0.7%	0.8%
5. I am very sorry to have been in the experiment	0.0%	1.0%	0.5%

Note—Ninety-two percent of the subjects returned the questionnaire. The characteristics of the nonrespondents were checked against the respondents. They differed from the respondents only with regard to age; younger people were overrepresented in the nonresponding group.

Procedures and Benefits

A most important aspect of the procedure occurred at the end of the experimental session. A careful post-experimental treatment was administered to all subjects. The exact content of the dehoax varied from condition to condition and with increasing experience on our part. At the very least all subjects were told that the victim had not received dangerous electric shocks. Each subject had a friendly reconciliation with the unharmed victim, and an extended discussion with the experimenter. The experiment was explained to the defiant subjects in a way that supported their decision to disobey the experimenter. Obedient subjects were assured of the fact that their behavior was entirely normal and that their feelings of conflict or tension were shared by other participants. Subjects were told that they would receive a comprehensive report at the conclusion of the experimental series. In some instances, additional detailed and lengthy discussions of the experiments were also carried out with individual subjects.

When the experimental series was complete, subjects received a written report which presented details of the experimental procedure and results. Again their own part in the experiments was treated in a dignified way and their behavior in the experiment respected. All subjects received a follow-up questionnaire regarding their participation in the research, which again allowed expression of thoughts and feelings about their behavior.

The replies to the questionnaire confirmed my impression that participants felt positively toward the experiment. In its quantitative aspect (see Table 1), 84% of the subjects stated they were glad to have been in the experiment; 15% indicated neutral feelings, and 1.3% indicated negative feelings. To be sure, such findings are to be interpreted cautiously, but they cannot be disregarded.

Further, four-fifths of the subjects felt that more experiments of this sort should be carried out, and 74% indicated that they had learned something of personal importance as a result of being in the study. . . .

The debriefing and assessment procedures were carried out as a matter of course, and were not stimulated by any observation of special risk in the experimental procedure. In my judgment, at no point were subjects exposed to danger and at no point did they run the risk of injurious effects resulting from participation. If it had been otherwise, the experiment would have been terminated at once.

Baumrind states that, after he has performed in the experiment, the subject cannot justify his behavior and must bear the full brunt of his actions. By and large it does not work this way. The same mechanisms that allow the subject to perform the act, to obey rather than to defy the experimenter, transcend the moment of performance and continue to justify his behavior for him. The same viewpoint the subject takes while performing the actions is the viewpoint from which he later sees his behavior, that is, the perspective of "carrying out the task assigned by the person in authority."

Because the idea of shocking the victim is repugnant, there is a tendency among those who hear of the design to say "people will not do it." When the results are made known, this attitude is expressed as "if they do it they will not be able to live with themselves afterward." These two forms of denying the experimental findings are equally inappropriate misreadings of the facts of human social behavior. Many subjects do, indeed, obey to the end, and there is no indication of injurious effects.

The absence of injury is a minimal condition of experimentation; there can be, however, an important positive side to participation. Baumrind suggests that subjects derived no benefit from being in the obedience study, but this is false. By their statements and actions, subjects indicated that they had learned a good deal, and many felt gratified to have taken part in scientific research they considered to be of significance. A year after his participation one subject wrote:

> This experiment has strengthened my belief that man should avoid harm to his fellow man even at the risk of violating authority.

Another stated:

> To me, the experiment pointed up ... the extent to which each individual should have or discover firm ground on which to base his decisions, no matter how trivial they appear to be. I think people should think more deeply about themselves and their relation to their world and to other people. If this experiment serves to jar people out of complacency, it will have served its end.

These statements are illustrative of a broad array of appreciative and insightful comments by those who participated.

The 5-page report sent to each subject on the completion of the experimental series was specifically designed to enhance the value of his experience. It laid out the broad conception of the experimental program as well as the logic of its design. It described the results of a dozen of the experiments, discussed the causes of tension, and attempted to indicate the possible significance of the experiment. Subjects responded enthusiastically; many indicated a desire to be in further experimental research. This report was sent to all subjects several years ago. The care with which it was prepared does not support Baumrind's assertion that the experimenter was indifferent to the value subjects derived from their participation.

Baumrind's fear is that participants will be alienated from psychological experiments because of the intensity of experience associated with laboratory procedures. My own observation is that subjects more commonly respond with distaste to the "empty" laboratory hour, in which cardboard procedures are employed, and the only possible feeling upon emerging from the laboratory is that one has wasted time in a patently trivial and useless exercise.

The subjects in the obedience experiment, on the whole, felt quite differently about their participation. They viewed the experience as an opportunity to learn something of importance about themselves, and more generally, about the conditions of human action.

A year after the experimental program was completed, I initiated an additional follow-up study. In this connection an impartial medical examiner, experienced in outpatient treatment, interviewed 40 experimental subjects. The examining psychiatrist focused on those subjects he felt would be most likely to have suffered consequences from participation. His aim was to identify possible injurious effects resulting from the experiment. He concluded that, although extreme stress had been experienced by several subjects,

> none was found by this interviewer to show signs of having been harmed by his experience.... Each subject seemed to handle his task [in the experiment] in a manner consistent with well established patterns of behavior. No evidence was found of any traumatic reactions.

Such evidence ought to be weighed before judging the experiment.

Other Issues

Baumrind's discussion is not limited to the treatment of subjects, but diffuses to a generalized rejection of the work.

Baumrind feels that obedience cannot be meaningfully studied in a laboratory setting: The reason she offers is that "The dependent, obedient attitude assumed by most subjects in the experimental setting is appropriate to that situation [p. 421]." Here, Baumrind has cited the very best reason for examining obedience in this setting, namely that it possesses "ecological validity." Here is one social context in which compliance occurs regularly. Military and job situations are also particularly meaningful settings for the study of obedience precisely because obedience is natural and appropriate to these contexts. I reject Baumrind's argument that the observed obedience does not count because it occurred where it is appropriate. That is precisely why it *does* count. A soldier's obedience is no less meaningful because it occurs in a pertinent military context. A subject's obedience is no less problematical because it occurs within a social institution called the psychological experiment.

Baumrind writes: "The game is defined by the experimenter and he makes the rules [p. 421]." It is true that for disobedience to occur the framework of the experiment must be shattered. That, indeed, is the point of the design. That is why obedience and disobedience are genuine issues for the subject. *He must really assert himself as a person against a legitimate authority.*

Further, Baumrind wants us to believe that outside the laboratory we could not find a comparably high expression of obedience. Yet, the fact that ordinary citizens are recruited to military service and, on command, perform far harsher acts against people is beyond dispute. Few of them know or are concerned with the complex policy issues underlying martial action; fewer still become conscientious objectors. Good soldiers do as they are told, and on both sides of the battle line. However, a debate on whether a higher level of obedience is represented by *(a)* killing men in the service of one's country, or *(b)* merely shocking them in the service of Yale science, is largely unprofitable. The real question is: What are the forces underlying obedient action?

Another question raised by Baumrind concerns the degree of parallel between obedience in the laboratory and in Nazi Germany. Obviously, there are enormous differences: Consider the disparity in time scale. The laboratory experiment takes an hour; the Nazi calamity unfolded in the space of a decade. There is a great deal that needs to be said on this issue, and only a few points can be touched on here.

1. In arguing this matter, Baumrind mistakes the background metaphor for the precise subject matter of investigation. The German event was cited to point up a serious problem in the human situation: the potentially destructive effect of obedience. But the best way to tackle the problem of obedience, from a scientific standpoint, is in no way restricted by "what happened exactly" in Germany. What happened exactly can *never* be duplicated in the laboratory or anywhere else. The real task is to learn more about the general problem of destructive obedience using a workable approach. Hopefully, such inquiry will stimulate insights and yield general propositions that can be applied to a wide variety of situations.

2. One may ask in a general way: How does a man behave when he is told by a legitimate authority to act against a third individual? In trying to find an answer to this question, the laboratory situation is one useful starting point —and for the very reason stated by Baumrind—namely, the experimenter does constitute a genuine authority for the subject. The fact that trust and dependence on the experimenter are maintained, despite the extraordinary harshness he displays toward the victim, is itself a remarkable phenomenon.

3. In the laboratory, through a set of rather simple manipulations, ordinary persons no longer perceived themselves as a responsible part of the causal chain leading to action against a person. The means through which responsibility is cast off, and individuals become thoughtless agents of action, is of general import. Other processes were revealed that indicate that the experiments will help us to understand why men obey. That understanding will come, of course, by examining the full account of experimental work and not alone the brief report in which the procedure and demonstrational results were exposed.

At root, Baumrind senses that it is not proper to test obedience in this situation, because she construes it as one in which there is no reasonable alternative to obedience. In adopting this view, she has lost sight of this fact: A substantial proportion of subjects do disobey. By their example, disobedience is shown to be a genuine possibility, one that is in no sense ruled out by the general structure of the experimental situation.

Baumrind is uncomfortable with the high level of obedience obtained in the first experiment. In the condition she focused on, 65% of the subjects obeyed to the end. However, her sentiment does not take into account that within the general framework of the psychological experiment obedience varied enormously from one condition to the next. In some variations, 90% of the subjects *diso*beyed. It seems to be *not* only the fact of an experiment, but the particular structure of elements within the experimental situation that accounts for rates of obedience and disobedience. And these elements were varied systematically in the program of research.

A concern with human dignity is based on a respect for a man's potential to act morally. Baumrind feels that the experimenter *made* the subject shock the victim. This conception is alien to my view. The experimenter tells the subject to do something. But between the command and the outcome there is a paramount force, the acting person who may obey or disobey. I started with the belief that every person who came to the laboratory was free to accept or to reject the dictates of authority. This view sustains a conception of human dignity insofar as it sees in each man a capacity for *choosing* his own behavior. And as it turned out, many subjects did, indeed, choose to reject the experimenter's commands, providing a powerful affirmation of human ideals.

Baumrind also criticizes the experiment on the grounds that "it could easily effect an alteration in the subject's... ability to trust adult authorities in the future [p. 422]." But I do not think she can have it both ways. On the one hand, she argues the experimental situation is so special that it has no generality; on the other hand, she states it has such generalizing potential that it will cause subjects to distrust all authority. But the experimenter is not just any authority: He is an authority who tells the subject to act harshly and inhumanely against another man. I would consider it of the highest value if participation in the experiment could, indeed, inculcate a skepticism of this kind of authority. Here, perhaps, a difference in philosophy emerges most clearly. Baumrind sees the subject as a passive creature, completely controlled by the experimenter. I started from a different viewpoint. A person who comes to the laboratory is an active, choosing adult, capable of accepting or rejecting the prescriptions for action addressed to him. Baumrind sees the effect of the experiment as undermining the subject's trust of authority. I see it as a potentially valuable experience insofar as it makes people aware of the problem of indiscriminate submission to authority.

Conclusion

My feeling is that viewed in the total context of values served by the experiment, approximately the right course was followed. In review, the facts are these: *(a)* At the outset, there was the problem of studying obedience by means of a simple experimental procedure. The results could not be foreseen before the experiment was carried out. *(b)* Although the experiment generated momentary stress in some subjects, this stress dissipated quickly and was not injurious. *(c)* Dehoax and follow-up procedures were carried out to insure the subjects' well-being. *(d)* These procedures were assessed through questionnaire and psychiatric studies and were found to be effective. *(e)* Additional steps were taken to enhance the value of the laboratory experience for participants, for example, submitting to each subject a careful report on the experimental program. *(f)* The subjects themselves strongly endorse the experiment, and indicate satisfaction at having participated.

If there is a moral to be learned from the obedience study, it is that every man must be responsible for his own actions. This author accepts full responsibility for the design and execution of the study. Some people may feel it should not have been done. I disagree and accept the burden of their judgment.

Baumrind's judgment, someone has said, not only represents a personal conviction, but also reflects a cleavage in American psychology between those whose primary concern is with *helping* people and those who are interested mainly in *learning* about people. I see little value in perpetuating divisive forces in psychology when there is so much to learn from every side. A schism may exist, but it does not correspond to the true ideals of the discipline. The psychologist intent on healing knows that his power to help rests on knowledge; he is aware that a scientific grasp of all aspects of life is essential for his work, and is in itself a worthy human aspiration. At the same time, the laboratory psychologist senses his work will lead to human betterment, not only because enlightenment is more dignified than ignorance, but because new knowledge is pregnant with humane consequences.

References

BAUMRIND, D. Some thoughts on ethics of research: After reading Milgram's "Behavioral study of obedience." *Amer. Psychologist,* 1964, **19**, 421–423.

LAZARUS, R. A laboratory approach to the dynamics of psychological stress. *Amer. Psychologist,* 1964, **19**, 400–411.

MILGRAM, S. Behavioral study of obedience. *J. abnorm. soc. Psychol.,* 1963, **67**, 371–378.

MILGRAM, S. Some conditions of obedience and disobedience to authority. *Hum. Relat.,* in press.

CHALLENGE QUESTIONS

Classic Dialogue: Was Stanley Milgram's Study of Obedience Unethical?

1. Investigate the role that your college's institutional review board (see the introduction to this issue) plays in protecting subjects from undue harm.
2. Sometimes people make the wrong decisions and end up hurting other people. Apart from utilizing institutional review boards, what can researchers do to avoid making wrong decisions regarding potentially harmful studies?
3. Imagine that you have just participated in Milgram's study. How would you feel about the deception that occurred? Is it ever appropriate to deceive participants in research studies? If so, when? If not, why not?
4. Both Baumrind and Milgram might agree that there are cases in which some low-level tension for research participants is allowable. Under what conditions might it be acceptable to allow participants to experience some distress? Under what conditions is it inappropriate to subject participants to any distress?
5. Baumrind raises the issue of trust. Do you think the participants in the Milgram study lost trust in psychological researchers or authority figures in general? Why, or why not?
6. If you were on an ethics review board and the Milgram study was brought before you, would you allow Milgram to run the study? Support your answer.

ISSUE 2

Should Animals Be Used in Psychological Research?

YES: Elizabeth Baldwin, from "The Case for Animal Research in Psychology," *Journal of Social Issues* (vol. 49, no. 1, 1993)

NO: Alan D. Bowd and Kenneth J. Shapiro, from "The Case Against Laboratory Animal Research in Psychology," *Journal of Social Issues* (vol. 49, no. 1, 1993)

ISSUE SUMMARY

YES: Elizabeth Baldwin, a research ethics officer for the American Psychological Association's Science Directorate, maintains that the benefits of behavioral research with animals are substantial and that the animals are being treated humanely.

NO: Professor of educational psychology Alan D. Bowd and Kenneth J. Shapiro, executive director of Psychologists for the Ethical Treatment of Animals, argue that the harm done to animals in this research is not widely known and that the "benefits" are not sufficient to balance this cruelty.

Until relatively recently, humans were thought to be distinctly different from lower animals. Only humans were considered to have self-consciousness, rationality, and language. Today, however, these distinctions appear to have been blurred by modern research. Many scientists, for example, believe that chimpanzees use language symbols and that many animals have some type of consciousness.

This apparent lack of hard and fast distinctions between humans and other animals has many implications. One of these concerns the use of animals in experimental research. For hundreds of years animals have been considered tools of research. In fact, research ethics has demanded that most experimental treatments be tested on animals before they are tested on humans. Another view, however, has come to the fore. Because there is no clear distinction between lower and higher animals, this view asserts that the lower animals should be accorded the same basic rights as humans. Animal experimentation, from this perspective, cannot be taken for granted; it must be justified on the same moral and ethical grounds as research on humans. This perspective has recently gained considerable momentum as supporters have become politically organized.

Elizabeth Baldwin disagrees with this perspective. In the following selection, she argues that animals should be used in psychological research and that although people should be held responsible for the humane treatment of animals, animals do not have the same rights as humans. Baldwin describes the important role that animals have played in improving the human condition through research and how animal research benefits the health and welfare of other animals. Baldwin argues that many people are not aware of the many federal regulations and laws that protect animals from inhumane treatment. Ultimately, she contends, humans and animals cannot be viewed as essentially the same, with the same ethics and rights.

In the second selection, Alan D. Bowd and Kenneth J. Shapiro do not concur with this view. Their case against the use of animals for psychological research hinges on the idea that these animals are denied basic rights. Bowd and Shapiro have developed what they call a "scale of invasiveness," which is an index of the suffering and harm done to animals before, during, or after an experimental procedure. Unlike Baldwin, they argue that federal laws and regulations are not sufficient because they do not consider the animals. Bowd and Shapiro also maintain that the research revealing the harm done to animals is not being published and, in turn, is not being sufficiently recognized. Consequently, they suggest that alternatives to the use of animals in laboratory research be found.

POINT

- Animals do not have the same rights as humans, but people have a responsibility to ensure the humane treatment of animals.

- There are elaborate federal regulations protecting animals in research, as well as state laws and professional guidelines on the care of animals.

- Society has made a collective judgment that the benefits derived from animal research far outweigh the costs.

- Animals have played a pivotal role in improving the human condition and, in return, society should strive to treat them well.

COUNTERPOINT

- Those who accord rights to human beings and deny them to other species must show a morally relevant difference between these species.

- Many species are not covered by the Animal Welfare Act and are therefore not reported as part of federally mandated inspections.

- In contrast to the uncertain benefits of laboratory animal research, the cost to animals is clear and real.

- The benefits of animal research are indeterminate because they depend on unknowns, such as human welfare.

Elizabeth Baldwin  **YES**

The Case for Animal Research
in Psychology

Animal liberationists do not separate out the human animal. A rat is a pig is a dog is a boy.

— Ingrid Newkirk, Director, People for the
Ethical Treatment of Animals.

The shock value of this quote has made it a favorite of those defending the use of animals in research. It succinctly states the core belief of many animal rights activists who oppose the use of animals in research. Although some activists work for improved laboratory conditions for research animals, recent surveys suggest that most activists would like to eliminate animal research entirely (Plous, 1991). These activists believe animals have rights equal to humans and therefore should not be used as subjects in laboratory research.

The debate over animal research can be confusing unless one understands the very different goals of animal welfare organizations and animal rights groups. People concerned with animal welfare seek to improve laboratory conditions for research animals and to reduce the number of animals needed. These mainstream goals encompass traditional concerns for the humane treatment of animals, and most researchers share these goals. In contrast, the views of animal rights activists are *not* mainstream, since there are few people who would agree with the above quote from Ingrid Newkirk. Indeed, in a national poll conducted by the National Science Foundation, half the respondents answered the following question affirmatively: "Should scientists be allowed to do research that causes pain and injury to animals like dogs and chimpanzees if it produces new information about human health problems?" (National Science Board, 1991). These findings are particularly impressive given the explicit mention of "pain and injury" to popular animals such as dogs and chimpanzees. My own position is that animals do not have rights in the same sense that humans do, but that people have a responsibility to ensure the humane treatment of animals under their care. Animals have played a pivotal role in improving the human condition, and in return, society should strive to treat them well.

From Elizabeth Baldwin, "The Case for Animal Research in Psychology," *Journal of Social Issues*, vol. 49, no. 1 (1993), pp. 121–129. Copyright © 1993 by The Society for the Psychological Study of Social Issues. Reprinted by permission of Blackwell Publishers. References omitted.

Background

The modern animal rights movement is intellectual and spiritual heir to the Victorian antivivisection movement in Britain (Sperling, 1988). This 19th-century movement was a powerful force in Britain and arose in part from accelerating changes brought about by science and technology (and the resulting challenges to the prevailing view of humanity's relationship to nature).

The British movement peaked in 1876 with the passage of the Cruelty to Animals Act. This compromise legislation required licenses for conducting animal research, but recognized the societal value of continuing to use animals in research. It was about this time that the scientific community began to organize a defense of animal research. Several challenges to animal research were made in the ensuing 20 years, but in the end, the medical and scientific community were able to successfully protect their interests. The Victorian antivivisection movement, however, did bring about the regulation of research and helped prevent outright abuse (Sperling, 1988).

The beginning of the modern animal rights movement is generally dated to the 1975 publication of *Animal Liberation* by philosopher Peter Singer. Although Singer himself is not an advocate of animal "rights," he provided the groundwork for later arguments that animals have rights—including the right not to be used in research. Most animal rights activists believe animals have a right not to be used for research, food, entertainment, and a variety of other purposes. An inordinate amount of attention is devoted to animal research, however, even though far fewer animals are used for research than for other purposes (Nicoll & Russell, 1990).

There has been a phenomenal growth in the animal rights movement since the publication of Singer's book. People for the Ethical Treatment of Animals (PETA), the leading animal rights organization in the United States, has grown from 18 members in 1981 to more than 250,000 members in 1990. (McCabe, 1990). By any standard, the animal rights movement is a force to be reckoned with.

Philosophical Issues

There are two basic philosophies that support the animal rights movement, although activists are often unable to articulate them (Sperling, 1988). These two positions are summarized by Herzog (1990) as the *utilitarian* argument and the *rights* argument.

The utilitarian position is that the greatest good is achieved by maximizing pleasure and happiness, and by minimizing suffering and pain. Although traditionally applied only to humans, Singer argues that animals should be included when considering the greatest good. He states, "No matter what the nature of the being, the principle of equality requires that its suffering be counted equally with the like suffering—insofar as rough comparisons can be made—of any other being" (Singer, 1990, p. 8). Utilitarians would thus argue that animals have an interest equal to that of humans in avoiding pain and suffering, and should therefore not be used in experiments that could cause them harm. Two problems with this philosophy are that (1) it is hard to draw a line between creatures that suffer and creatures that do not, and (2) the argument does not address *qualitative* differences in pain and pleasure across species (Herzog, 1990).

The rights position states that animals possess certain rights based on their inherent value. This philosophy, first developed by Tom Regan (1983), argues that animals have a right not to be used by humans in research (and for many other purposes). Major problems with this position arise in deciding just what rights are and in determining who is entitled to hold them (Herzog, 1990).

While the above positions have been developed relatively recently, the alternative view of animals as qualitatively different from humans has a long history in Judeo-Christian thought. Traditionally, humans were believed to have been created in the image of God and to have dominion over animals. Robb (1988) uses this perspective in arguing that humans are unique by virtue of their capacity for moral choice. Because of this capacity, humans can be held responsible for their choices, and can therefore enter into contractual agreements with binding rights and responsibilities for *both* parties. Robb acknowledges that some animals have human capacities in certain areas, but he argues that this does not make them morally equal to humans or give them rights that take precedence over human needs.

The most persuasive argument for using animals in behavioral research, however, is the untold benefit that accrues to both humans and animals. The benefits of behavioral research with animals have been enumerated by such authors as Miller (1985) and King and Yarbrough (1985), and for most people, these benefits are the reason that they support the continued use of animals in research. This argument—which is basically utilitarian—is the one most often cited by the research community in defense of animal research. In contrast to Singer's utilitarianism, however, animals are not given the same degree of consideration as people.

In conclusion, both sides in the animal rights debate have philosophical underpinnings to support their position, but what often emerges in the rhetoric is not reasoned debate but emotion-laden charges and personal attacks. This is not surprising, given the strong passions aroused in the discussion.

Framing the Debate

In the 1980s, activists targeted certain researchers or areas of research that they viewed as vulnerable to attack, and researchers were forced to assume a defensive posture. Unfortunately, activists were right about the vulnerability of individual scientists; little or no institutional defense was mounted against these early attacks. The prevailing attitude was to ignore the activists in hopes that they would go away, and thus attract less attention from the public and the press. This passivity left the early targets of animal rights activists in the position of a man asked, "Why do you beat your wife?" No matter how researchers responded, they sounded defensive and self-serving. It took several years for the research community to realize that animal rights activists were not going away, and that the activists' charges needed to be answered in a systematic and serious manner.

This early failure on the part of the research community to communicate its position effectively left the public with little information beyond what was provided by the animal rights activists. Framing the debate is half the battle, and the research community was left playing catch-up and answering the question, "Why do you abuse your research animals?"

The research community also faced the daunting task of explaining the use of animals in research to a public whose understanding of the scientific method was almost nil. The most difficult misconception to correct was the belief that every research project with animals should produce "useful" results (Orem, 1990). Social scientists who have received Senator William Proxmire's "Golden Fleece Award" are well aware of this line of thinking—a line of thinking that displays a complete misunderstanding of how science works, and ignores the vast amount of basic research that typically precedes each "useful" discovery.

It is difficult for scientific rationales to compete with shocking posters, catchy slogans, and soundbites from the animal rights movement. The most effective response from the scientific community has been to point out innumerable health advances made possible by the use of animals as research models. This approach is something that most people can relate to, since everyone has benefited from these advances.

The early defensive posture of scientists also failed to allay public concerns about the ability of researchers to self-regulate their care and use of research animals. Unlike the participation of humans in research (who are usually able to speak in their own defense and give consent), there seemed to be no one in the system able to "speak" for the animals. Or so people were encouraged to believe by animal rights activists. As discussed below, there are elaborate federal regulations on the use of animals in research, as well as state laws and professional guidelines on the care and use of animals in research.

Restoring Trust

Scientists, research institutions, and federal research agencies finally came to realize that the charges being leveled by animal rights activists needed to be publicly—and forcefully—rebutted. Dr. Frederick Goodwin, former Administrator of the Alcohol, Drug Abuse, and Mental Health Administration (ADAMHA), was one of the first federal officials to defend animal research publicly, and point out the difference between animal welfare and animal rights (Booth, 1989). Recently, many more federal officials and respected researchers have publicly spoken on the importance of animal research (Mervis, 1990).

Countering Misinformation

Animal rights literature often uses misleading images to depict animal research —images such as animals grimacing as they are shocked with electricity. These descriptions lead readers to believe animals are routinely subjected to high volt-age shocks capable of producing convulsions (e.g., Singer, 1990, pp. 42–45). Such propaganda is far from the truth. In most cases, electric shock (when used at all) is relatively mild—similar to what one might feel from the discharge of static electricity on a cold, dry day. Even this relatively mild use of shock is care-fully reviewed by Institutional Animal Care and Use Committees before being approved, and researchers must demonstrate that alternate techniques are not feasible. Stronger shock *is* used in animal research, but it is used to study med-ical problems such as epilepsy (a convulsive disorder). It is also used to test the effectiveness and side effects of drugs developed to control such disorders. It is not within the scope of this article to refute the myriad charges issued against animal research in general, specific projects, and individual researchers. Suffice it to say that such allegations have been persuasively refuted (Coile & Miller, 1984; Feeney, 1987; Johnson, 1990; McCabe, 1986).

Benefits to Animals

Animal rights activists often fail to appreciate the many benefits to animals that have resulted from animal research. Behavioral research has contributed to improvements in the environments of captive animals, including those used in research (Novak & Petto, 1991). The list of benefits also includes a host of veterinary procedures and the development of vaccines for deadly diseases such as rabies, Lyme disease, and feline leukemia. Research in reproductive biology and captive breeding programs are also the only hope for some animals on the brink of extinction (King et al., 1988).

Regulations and Guidelines

It is clear that many people concerned about the use of animals in research are not aware of the elaborate structure that exists to regulate the care and use of animals in research. This system includes federal regulations under the Animal Welfare Act (U.S. Department of Agriculture, 1989, 1990, 1991), Public Health Service (PHS) policy (Office for Protection from Research Risks, 1986), and state laws that govern the availability of pound animals for research.

The Animal Welfare Act, most recently amended in 1985, is enforced by the USDA's Animal and Plant Health Inspection Service (APHIS). The regula-tions connected with this law include 127 pages of guidelines governing the use of animals in research. It also includes unannounced inspections of animal research facilities by APHIS inspectors who do nothing but inspect research facilities. Their inspections are conducted to ensure compliance with regula-tions that include everything from cage size, feeding schedules, and lighting to exercise requirements for dogs and the promotion of psychological well-being among nonhuman primates.

In addition to APHIS inspectors who make unannounced inspections of animal research facilities, there are local Institutional Animal Care and Use Committees (IACUCs) that review each proposed research project using ani-mals. Research proposals must include a justification for the species used and the number of animals required, an assurance that a thorough literature review has been conducted (to prevent unnecessary replication of research), and a consideration of alternatives if available. IACUCs are also responsible for inspecting local animal research facilities to check for continued compliance with state protocols.

Each grant proposal received by a PHS agency (National Institutes of Health, and the Centers for Disease Control) that proposes using animals must contain an assurance that it has been reviewed by an IACUC and been approved. IACUCs must have no less than five members and contain at least one veterinarian, one practicing scientist experienced in research involving animals, one member who is primarily concerned in nonscientific matters (e.g., a lawyer or ethicist), and one member who is not affiliated with the institution in any way and is not an immediate family member of anyone affiliated with the institution (Office for Protection from Research Risks, 1986; USDA, 1989).

Beyond federal animal welfare regulations, PHS policy, and the PHS Guidelines (National Research Council, 1985), there are professional guidelines for the care and use of research animals. Examples include the American Psychological Association's (APA) *Ethical Principles of Psychologists* (1990) and *Guidelines for Ethical Conduct in the Care and Use of Animals* (1993), and the Society for Neuroscience's Handbook (Society for Neuroscience, 1991).

The APA also has a Committee on Animal Research and Ethics (CARE) whose charge includes the responsibility to "review the ethics of animal experimentation and recommend guidelines for the ethical conduct of research, and appropriate care of animals in research." CARE wrote the APA's *Guidelines for Ethical Conduct in the Care and Use of Animals,* and periodically reviews it and makes revisions. These guidelines are widely used by psychologists and other scientists, and have been used in teaching research ethics at the undergraduate and graduate level. The APA's Science Directorate provided support for a conference on psychological well-being of nonhuman primates used in research, and published a volume of proceedings from that conference (Novak & Petto, 1991). The APA also helps promote research on animal welfare by membership in and support for such organizations as the American Association for the Accreditation of Laboratory Animal Care (AAALAC).

AAALAC is the only accrediting body recognized by the PHS, and sets the "gold standard" for animal research facilities. To receive AAALAC accreditation, an institution must go beyond what is required by federal animal welfare regulations and PHS policy. AAALAC accreditation is highly regarded, and those institutions that receive it serve as models for the rest of the research community.

Even with all these safeguards in place, some critics question the ability of the research community to self-regulate its use of animals in research. The system can only be considered self-regulating, however, if one assumes that researchers, institutional officials, members of IACUCs (which must include a member not affiliated with the institution), USDA inspectors, animal care and lab technicians, and veterinarians have identical interests. These are the individuals with the most direct access to the animals used in research, and these are the specialists most knowledgeable about the conditions under which animals are used in research.

In several states, animal rights activists have succeeded in gaining access to IACUC meetings where animal research proposals are discussed. On the whole, however, research institutions have fought—and are still fighting —to keep these meetings closed to the general public. There is a very real fear among researchers that information gleaned from such meetings will be used to harass and target individual researchers. Given the escalating nature of illegal break-ins by such organizations as the Animal Liberation Front, this is a legitimate concern. Indeed, on some campuses "reward posters" offer money to individuals who report the abuse of research animals.

Even though IACUC meetings are generally closed to the public, the elaborate system regulating animal research is by no means a closed one. The most recent animal welfare regulations were finalized after five years of proposals recorded in the *Federal Register;* comments from the public, research institutions, professional associations, animal welfare groups, and animal rights groups; the incorporation of these comments; republication of the revised rules; and so forth. Neither researchers nor animal rights groups were entirely pleased with the final document, but everyone had their say. Although certain elements of the regulatory system rely on researchers, it is hard to imagine a workable system that would fail to use their expertise. The unspoken assumption that researchers cannot be trusted to care for their research animals is not supported by the records of APHIS inspections. Good science demands good laboratory animal care, and it is in a researcher's best interest to ensure that laboratory animals are well cared for.

The Benefits of Behavioral Research With Animals

The use of animals in psychological and behavioral research was an early target of animal rights activists. This research was perceived as a more vulnerable target than biomedical research, which had more direct and easily explained links to specific human health benefits. Psychological and behavioral research also lacked the powerful backing of the medical establishment (Archer, 1986).

There is, of course, a long list of benefits derived from psychological research with animals. These include rehabilitation of persons suffering from stroke, head injury, spinal cord injury, and Alzheimer's disease; improved communication with severely retarded children; methods for the early detection of eye disorders in children (allowing preventive treatment to avoid permanent impairment); control of chronic anxiety without the use of drugs; and improved treatments for alcoholism, obesity, substance abuse, hypertension, chronic migraine headaches, lower back pain, and insomnia (Miller, 1985). Behavioral research with nonhuman primates also permits the investigation of complex behaviors such as social organization, aggression, learning and memory, communication, and growth and development (King et al., 1988).

The nature of psychological and behavioral research makes the development and use of alternatives difficult. It is the behavior of the whole organism, and the interaction among various body systems, that is examined. Computer models may be used, but "research with animals will still be needed to provide basic data for writing computer software, as well as to prove the validity and reliability of computer alternatives" (U.S. Congress, Office of Technology Assessment, 1986). The alternative of using nonliving systems may be possible with epidemiologic data bases for some behavioral research, but chemical and physical systems are not useful for modeling complex behaviors. Likewise, in vitro cultures of organs, tissues, and cells do not display the characteristics studied by psychologists.

Conclusion

Research psychologists have been asked to eschew emotionalism, and bring logic and reason to the debate over animal research (Bowd, 1990). This is certainly the style most researchers are comfortable with—yet they have also been advised to quit trying to "apply logic and reason in their responses [to animal rights activists]" (Culliton, 1991). Culliton warns that while "animal rights people go for the heart, the biologists go for the head" and are losing the public in the process.

Which path is best? A reasoned approach draws high marks for civility, but will it help scientists in their trench warfare with animal rights activists?

Do animals have rights that preclude their use in laboratory research? I, and the psychologists I help represent, would say no. But researchers do have responsibilities to the animals they use in their research. These responsibilities include ensuring the humane care of their research animals, using the minimum number of animals necessary, and seeing to it that all laboratory assistants are adequately trained and supervised. As stated in the APA's *Ethical Principles,* "Laws and regulations notwithstanding, an animal's immediate protection depends upon the scientist's own conscience" (APA, 1990).

Researchers and others concerned with animal welfare can engage in a useful dialogue as standards of care and use evolve. This dialogue has proven fruitless with animal rights activists, though, since they seem unwilling to compromise or consider other viewpoints. What is the middle ground for a discussion with someone whose goal is the elimination of all research on animals?

The collective decision society has made is that the benefits derived from animal research far outweigh the costs. As public opinion polls indicate, most people are willing to accept these costs but want assurances that animals are humanely cared for. Yes, I'm "speciesist" in the eyes of Ingrid Newkirk—I will never believe my son is a dog is a pig is a rat.

Alan D. Bowd and Kenneth J. Shapiro  **NO**

The Case Against Laboratory Animal Research in Psychology

In this article, we will (1) present empirical evidence documenting several serious problems with the use of animals in psychology, (2) consider philosophical objections to the use of animals in invasive research, (3) give an overview of how the research community has responded to these concerns, and (4) suggest directions for change.

The Problem

The number of nonhuman animals used in psychological research in the United States is difficult to estimate. Many species are not covered by the Animal Welfare Act and are therefore not reported as part of federally mandated inspections (Rowan & Andrutis, 1990). The Animal Legal Defense Fund (a nonprofit animal protection group) is currently challenging this loophole, but at present, rats, mice, and birds—which comprise roughly 90% of all nonhuman research subjects—are not considered "animals" under the Animal Welfare Act. Attempts to arrive at estimates from departmental surveys, analyses of *Psychological Abstracts,* and extrapolations from countries where better records are kept all have their limitations, but integrating these sources of information, we estimate that roughly 1–2 million animals are used in psychological research each year.

Although some laboratory animals are obtained from shelters—a practice that is illegal in 14 states and is abhorred by a majority of the public—most laboratory animals are "purpose bred" for research. This method of procuring subjects is not without problems, however. For example, the legal office of the United States Department of Agriculture is currently investigating a major producer of animals for alleged abuse (Holden, 1990). Other problems with producing animals for laboratory research arise from selective breeding and genetic engineering. Producing animals that are susceptible to audiogenic seizures or cancerous tumors, or that adapt well to confinement, raises significant ethical questions (President's Commission, 1982).

From Alan D. Bowd and Kenneth J. Shapiro, "The Case Against Laboratory Animal Research in Psychology," *Journal of Social Issues,* vol. 49, no. 1 (1993), pp. 133–142. Copyright © 1993 by The Society for the Psychological Study of Social Issues. Reprinted by permission of Blackwell Publishers. References omitted.

Invasiveness in Research

In reviewing laboratory practices, it is important to distinguish between the experimental procedure itself and pre- or postexperimental care (i.e., "husbandry"). It is also critical to separate individual cases of abuse from customary practices. The case of the Silver Spring monkeys, for example, is an instance of individual abuse that became a cause célèbre of the animal rights movement. Charges against psychologist Edward Taub centered on abusive husbandry practices—inadequate veterinary care, food, ventilation, and cage space. However, much of the public outcry reflected objections to the experimental procedure (deafferentation) itself (Shapiro, 1989).

An example of a routine experimental procedure under scrutiny is the use of chair restraints. Primates that are chair restrained as part of a study spend a mean time of 5.7 hours confined in the chair each day (Bayne, 1991). An example of a customary husbandry practice under scrutiny is the housing of primates in individual cages. In one survey, 84% of the investigators housed their adult primates singly (Bayne, 1991), despite the importance of social interaction to these animals. Thus, quite apart from any trauma induced by experimental procedures, the animals suffered from routine husbandry practices.

Contrary to what defenders of animal research often say, a good deal of psychological research is highly invasive. Many studies involve stress, pain, punishment, social and environmental deprivation, and induced emotional and intellectual deficits. In their "scale of invasiveness," Field and Shapiro (1988) operationalized the term to encompass suffering and harm before, during, or after an experimental procedure. By this definition, most investigators targeted by the animal rights movement have conducted highly invasive research (e.g., maternal deprivation and drug addiction in macaques, physiology of taste in rats, visual deprivation in kittens). Beyond their invasiveness, these studies have been criticized for their nongeneralizability, redundancy, purely theoretical focus, parametric tinkering, and diversion of funds from treatment programs.

Areas of highly invasive research have shifted over time. In 1947, electroconvulsive shock and audiogenic seizures were prevalent, while in 1967 punishment, brain lesioning, and the administration of curare were more common (Field, 1988). The most frequently cited invasive studies in popular college introductory psychology textbooks (1984–1988 editions) are infant maternal deprivation, perceptual restriction in newborns, brain studies of the eating/satiety center, and learned helplessness (Field, 1990).

As a popular college major, psychology influences thousands of students each year. Typically, psychology coursework includes direct exposure to animal research in laboratories and/or indirect exposure through texts and audiovisual materials that feature animal research. Yet descriptions of invasive research in popular psychology textbooks are often sanitized (Field, 1989). For example, most discussions of Harlow's work on maternal deprivation—the most frequently cited invasive experiment—minimize the suffering involved, present pictures of "cute" animals, and omit reference to the subjective experience of the animals.

Ethical Issues

The animal rights movement began to have an impact on psychology shortly after the publication of Singer's *Animal Liberation* and Ryder's *Victims of Science* (both in 1975). Both books targeted behavioral research in particular for its painful and unnecessary experiments. The ethical foundation of the animal rights movement has since been broadened to include several other discourses: Regan (1983) provided a theory of rights to complement Singer's utilitarianism, Adams (1990) developed a feminist discourse that linked the subjugation of animals with patriarchy, and several authors provided theological perspectives on the use of animals (Linzey, 1987; McDaniel, 1989; Regenstein, 1991).

Experimental psychologists have been forced to defend their ethical positions with rational arguments. Many psychologists consider ethics a matter of personal preference, a view that exempts individuals from public scrutiny and justifies individual self-regulation. Others have attempted to reduce ethics to science, arguing that ethics is a naturally evolved phenomenon and that regulation from outside the field is inappropriate (e.g., Gallup & Suarez, 1980). However, the burgeoning field of moral philosophy suggests that ethical positions—like any other human beliefs—are subject to logical examination, and may be found to be ambiguous or contradictory.

Following Ryder (1989) and Rollin (1981), here we propose an ethic that draws upon the work of both Singer and Regan. To wit:

Interests and rights are not the sole preserve of the human species, and should be evaluated consistently and with due consideration to an animal's capacity to suffer. Our ethical obligations extend to individuals who are intellectually unable to reciprocate them, within and beyond our own species. Those who would accord rights to human beings but deny them to all other species must make the case that there is a morally relevant difference separating *Homo sapiens* from other creatures. We do not believe such a difference exists.

All creatures capable of experiencing pain and other forms of suffering have an interest in being spared it, and the rights that flow from this interest vary from individual to individual and species to species. Although this point may seem obvious, animal protectionists are often ridiculed for believing all animals are identical or for advocating that farm animals be given the right to vote. Such caricatures (usually based on quotations taken out of context) make easy targets and avoid serious discussion.

Many proponents of invasive research argue that the work is justified by morally relevant differences that exist between the human species and all others. However, by focusing on attributes such as intelligence, empathy, and a sense of moral responsibility (e.g., Fox, 1986; King, 1986), they exclude young children and developmentally delayed adults from moral consideration. Because humans and nonhumans overlap on some of these dimensions (e.g., intelligence, self-awareness), and because young or impaired humans wholly lack other characteristics (e.g., empathy, sense of moral responsibility), there is simply no morally relevant attribute that separates humans from nonhumans. To base ethical decisions on species membership alone in the absence of such an attribute is as arbitrary as relying on skin color or gender in hiring decisions.

The most morally relevant factor in a decision to cause suffering to others is their ability to experience it. Cognitive competence and related abilities are relevant to certain human rights (such as the right to vote), but not to other rights (such as the freedom to move one's limbs or to interact with others). Research justified by consequent human benefit abridges these rights. We feel methods involving inescapable pain, deprivation, or fear are unacceptable because each sentient being, regardless of its other capabilities, has an interest in being spared suffering. Modern-day society rejects the notion of performing painful experiments on humans who are incapable of granting consent, regardless of the benefits which might accrue to others. In the absence of morally relevant distinctions between ourselves and other animals, painful research on sentient nonhumans should be rejected for the same reasons.

The Response from Psychologists

Social constructionists and others have recently noted the Western, ethnocentric, and male-dominated agenda of traditional psychological research (Gergen, 1985; Hare-Mustin & Marecek, 1990; Irvine & Berry, 1988). The broad cultural changes represented by the women's movement, environmentalism, and the animal rights movement have been instrumental in fomenting the current debate within psychology regarding animal research, and many analysts now view the practice of invasive laboratory-based research as symptomatic of anthropocentrism in psychology.

Within the psychological community, a growing number of individuals have expressed reservations about animal research on both scientific and ethical grounds (Bowd, 1980, 1990; Fox, 1982; Giannelli, 1985; Segal, 1982; Shapiro, 1991; Ulrich, 1991). Nonetheless, many psychologists have defended current practices. We will first examine organizational responses and then discuss responses within the professional literature. The focus will be on developments in the United States, though it should be noted that similar debates are taking place among psychologists in Canada, Great Britain, Australia, and other countries.

Organizational Responses

In 1981, the American Psychological Association (APA) amended its Ethics Code to include the treatment of animals (American Psychological Association [APA], 1981). However, the APA Ethics Committee considered only one animal welfare case from 1982 to 1990 (APA, 1991)—a period during which the animal rights movement charged several laboratories with specific animal welfare violations. The Ethics Committee considered the case of Edward Taub, a psychologist who studied deafferentation (the severing of sensory nerves) in macaque monkeys at the Institute for Behavioral Research in Maryland. This case came to light after Alex Pacheco, cofounder of People for the Ethical Treatment of Animals, documented several explicit violations of animal welfare regulations.

According to Principle 10 of the current Ethics Code, researchers must ensure that "The acquisition, care, use and disposal of all animals are in compliance of current Federal, state or provincial, and local laws and regulations" (APA, 1981). After reviewing Pacheco's evidence, the National Institutes of Health (NIH) suspended Taub's grant because of violations in NIH guidelines, and Taub was convicted of cruelty to animals under Maryland law (a verdict that he later appealed). Nevertheless, even though the suspension of funding and the conviction of animal cruelty were known by members of the APA Ethics Committee, the panel cleared Taub of any wrongdoing on a split vote.

A second APA body charged with overseeing animal welfare, the Committee on Animal Research and Ethics (CARE), was established in 1925 "to combat attempts to prevent or restrict [animal experimentation]" (Young, 1928). In fact, the two events that led to the formation of CARE were both legislative efforts, outside APA, to curtail animal research (Young, 1928; Young, 1930). For the first 50 years of its existence, CARE's stated purpose was to defend and protect animal *research*, not *animals*. It was not until the early 1980s that the task of protecting animals was added (CARE, 1980), and even then the meetings continued to focus on the protection of animal research and animal researchers (Bernstein, personal communication, 1990). Furthermore, Field, Shapiro, and Carr (1990) found that the animal research conducted by recent CARE chairs was more invasive than comparable research published in leading journals. Thus, the APA responded to ethical challenges by forming advocacy groups rather than impartial or balanced review panels.

Responses Within the Professional Literature

APA publications have discussed animal welfare with increasing frequency in recent years (Phillips & Sechzer, 1989). However, in its scientific and news publications, the APA often takes a one-sided position (Bowd, 1990). We examined issues of the *APA Monitor* from 1980 to 1986, and found 30 articles and 43 letters dealing with the ethics of animal research. By our estimate, roughly 60% supported animal research and only 10% opposed it explicitly. Similarly, the *American Psychologist* published 17 relevant articles or commentaries during the same period, 10 advocating animal research and 7 opposing it. Of the 5 full-length articles that appeared during this interval, 4 explicitly supported animal research.

A recent article in the *APA Monitor* typifies this slant in coverage. Moses (1991) described how psychology students were upset by a laboratory break-in, but failed to mention a much more widespread source of student concern about animal research—the refusal of faculty to provide alternatives to the laboratory study of animals. In a recent survey of 300 psychology departments, one of the authors (KJS) found that 50% of the departments used animals in education, and of these, only 40% had a policy to accommodate students who objected.

Indeed, not only do APA publications neglect to mention such problems —the APA actively discourages their discussion. For example, the APA refused to sell exhibit space at its 1991 convention to Psychologists for the Ethical Treatment of Animals for the purpose of displaying publications, although other organizations were provided with space to display animal research publications and catalogues of laboratory equipment (Shapiro, 1990).

Turning to the scientific literature, most accounts defend animal research with some version of the following arguments: (1) animal research leads to applications that improve human welfare; (2) the costs to animals are relatively small; (3) whatever harm the animals incur is necessary, because there are no viable alternatives to animal research (Gallup & Suarez, 1985; King, 1984; Miller, 1985).

The tenor of these articles tends to be indignant, adversarial, and defensive. In fact, in their survey of the scientific literature, Phillips and Sechzer (1989) found a marked increase in defensiveness between the 1960s and the 1980s. Gluck and Kubacki (1991) have also described a "strategic defensive posture" assumed by researchers, part of which is to trivialize the issue of animal protection. For example, some researchers trivialize the issue by pointing out that laboratory rats fare better than their uncaged city conspecifics (e.g., Gallup & Suarez, 1987). Typically, there is little empirical evidence offered to support such assertions, and in many cases, the arguments are specious (Shapiro, 1988). For example, Gallup and Suarez (1987) failed to provide evidence about the relative welfare of laboratory and feral rats, although data are available regarding invasiveness of procedures undergone by the former, and Hendrickson (1983) found that rats in urban nonlaboratory settings often proliferate and live quite well. Furthermore, the suffering of laboratory rats is additional; its cost must be added to whatever suffering other rats endure. The argument advanced by Gallup and Suarez (1987) is particularly ironic given their portrayal of scientists as rational and animal activists as illogical and emotional.

Assessment of Costs and Benefits

Miller (1985) and other authors have claimed that animal research generates applications that improve human welfare. However, Kelly (1986) found that in the 1984 volume of the *Journal of Consulting and Clinical Psychology* (a journal devoted to studies of the treatments Miller explicitly linked to animal research), only 0.3% of more than 3,000 citations were of laboratory animal studies. In addition, Giannelli (1985) found that only seven of the 118 citations selected by Miller to demonstrate the value of animal research were listed in the 1985 Association for Advanced Training in the Behavioral Sciences, a well-known and comprehensive course for national licensure in psychology. Even more problematically, the potential benefits of any animal research are indeterminate, for they depend on several unknowns: the applicability of the results to human welfare, the question of whether the study will get published (rejection rates for mainstream psychology journals are over 50%), and more subtly, the *missed benefits of studies not undertaken.* Any research program implies paths not taken.

In contrast to the uncertain benefits from laboratory animal research, the cost to animals is clear and real. Reliable measures of the cost to animals do exist (Field & Shapiro, 1988), yet virtually no published study—or study proposal —presents detailed analyses of the costs of husbandry conditions, experimental procedures, and disposition of the animals. In any case, any analysis of costs to animals presumes they are willing participants. In truth, in the current research enterprise they are commodities produced, confined, and harmed in a system in which they are only incidental beneficiaries. Yet in our Western tradition, individuals have rights that safeguard against their welfare being compromised for the benefit of others. Because of these operational and ethical problems, cost–benefit analyses are an unsatisfactory tool in the assessment of the use of animals in research.

Suggested Directions

As an interim strategy, we favor the following: (1) the development of alternatives to laboratory animal research; (2) the specification and prohibition of experimental procedures that are deemed "intrinsically objectionable" (Heim, 1978)—that is, procedures generally agreed to be so invasive that they are objectionable regardless of possible benefits; and (3) a reduced reliance on the search for animal models of complex, culturally generated human phenomena. These practices should replace the hollow, justificatory language of cost–benefit analyses. In the longer term, we favor a shift from laboratory-based invasive research to minimally manipulative research conducted in naturalistic and seminaturalistic settings.

We urge psychologists, individually and through professional societies such as the APA, to (1) establish advocacy committees charged solely with the protection of animals used in psychology-related settings, (2) develop alternatives for students who object to the use of laboratory animals, and (3) include balanced coverage of animal welfare issues and a discussion of ethical issues in professional and textbook publications. Such policies will not only contribute to animal welfare—they will contribute to *human* welfare by broadening the education of tomorrow's psychologists.

CHALLENGE QUESTIONS

Should Animals Be Used in Psychological Research?

1. How and where would you draw the line on the use of animals in research? Even if the use of animals is justified in research that saves human lives, is the use of animals justified in cosmetic or plastic surgery research? Why, or why not?
2. Assuming you were against all instances of animal research, would you turn down medical procedures for yourself or your children because they were developed at the expense of animals? Would there be exceptions, such as vaccinations for your children or a cure for a life-threatening illness?
3. Baldwin makes the case that experimentation with animals has produced many important medical and psychological findings. Are there other types of research that use animals? Is this other research justified? Why, or why not?
4. Baldwin argues that the use of animals in research has been beneficial to animals as well as to humans. Does this assertion change the debate?
5. Locate the federal and state regulations on the use and care of animals in psychological research, and evaluate both authors' arguments regarding the sufficiency of those regulations.

ISSUE 3

Is the *Consumer Reports* Conclusion That "Psychotherapy Helps" Valid?

YES: Martin E. P. Seligman, from "The Effectiveness of Psychotherapy: The *Consumer Reports* Study," *American Psychologist* (December 1995)

NO: Neil S. Jacobson and Andrew Christensen, from "Studying the Effectiveness of Psychotherapy: How Well Can Clinical Trials Do the Job?" *American Psychologist* (October 1996)

ISSUE SUMMARY

YES: Psychotherapy researcher Martin E. P. Seligman defends the conclusion of *Consumer Reports* that psychotherapy is effective by pointing to the importance of client satisfaction in the actual settings in which the clients are treated.

NO: Psychotherapy researchers Neil S. Jacobson and Andrew Christensen contend that the *Consumer Reports* study is essentially the same as 40-year-old studies that have long been rejected as inadequate.

In 1994 *Consumer Reports* (*CR*), the well-known evaluator of appliances and automobiles (among other things), decided to evaluate something it had never evaluated before—the effectiveness of psychotherapy. True to its own philosophy, *CR* surveyed the consumers of psychotherapy to determine how these consumers felt about their treatment. Twenty-six questions about people's experiences with mental health professionals were asked, including questions about presenting problems, therapist competence, type of therapy, and satisfaction with treatment.

In the November 1995 issue *CR* published its controversial but seemingly clear-cut findings. Perhaps the most noteworthy finding was that over 90 percent of the people who responded to the survey found psychotherapy to be beneficial. Although this specific percentage can be disputed, other research has supported the overall conclusion that psychotherapy is generally helpful. (See, for example, Allen E. Bergin and Sol L. Garfield, eds., *Handbook of Psychotherapy and Behavior Change*, John Wiley, 1994). This general conclusion is not the root of the controversy. The root of the controversy is the methods that *CR* used to reach its conclusion. Most mainstream psychotherapy researchers favor experimental methods—with control groups and manipulated variables—to evaluate psychotherapy's effectiveness. *CR*'s conclusions were reached without such methods. Were *CR*'s methods valid? If they were not, then the conclusion that "psychotherapy helps" would itself be in question.

In the following selection, Martin E. P. Seligman defends *CR*'s methods by making a distinction between efficacy research and effectiveness research. Efficacy research pertains to the experimental type of design that most researchers favor. Although Seligman believes that these designs have some advantages, he contends that they also have many disadvantages, which he feels the *CR* type of study (effectiveness research) can complement. The types of studies that *CR* conducts have their own problems, Seligman admits, but they can reveal whether or not people feel that psychotherapy is effective. In this case, the answer is yes.

In the second selection, Neil S. Jacobson and Andrew Christensen, on the other hand, compare the *CR* survey to outmoded studies that therapy researchers rejected long ago. Jacobson and Christensen point to "two fundamental problems" with retrospective surveys, or surveys based on participants' recollections of previous experiences. They admit that "consumer satisfaction is far from trivial." However, such ratings of satisfaction are "uncorrelated with... general [client] functioning." These authors contend that psychotherapy researchers were initially correct in rejecting these types of studies long ago.

POINT	COUNTERPOINT
• There are two types of therapy research—efficacy and effectiveness—that complement one another.	• The "effectiveness" type of research was found to be inadequate many years ago.
• *CR*'s survey type of study has many advantages, such as greater realism and comprehensiveness.	• Surveys have two fundamental problems that disallow their use as serious studies of effectiveness.
• *CR*'s study is large in scale and cost-effective.	• If such a study is not valid, its scale and minimal cost mean little.
• The *CR* study has several clear-cut results.	• Some of the results of the *CR* study are strikingly different from the results of more highly controlled studies.
• *CR* has pioneered a whole new type of therapy outcome study.	• The *CR* study is essentially the same as studies that were performed and subsequently rejected many years ago.

Martin E. P. Seligman  **YES**

The Effectiveness of Psychotherapy: The *Consumer Reports* Study

How do we find out whether psychotherapy works? To answer this, two methods have arisen: the *efficacy study* and the *effectiveness study*. An efficacy study is the more popular method. It contrasts some kind of therapy to a comparison group under well-controlled conditions....

The high praise "empirically validated" is now virtually synonymous with positive results in efficacy studies, and many investigators have come to think that an efficacy study is the "gold standard" for measuring whether a treatment works....

But my belief has changed about what counts as a "gold standard." And it was a study by *Consumer Reports* (1995, November) that singlehandedly shook my belief. I came to see that deciding whether one treatment, under highly controlled conditions, works better than another treatment or a control group is a different question from deciding what works in the field (Muñoz, Hollon, McGrath, Rehm, & VandenBos, 1994). I no longer believe that efficacy studies are the only, or even the best, way of finding out what treatments actually work in the field. I have come to believe that the "effectiveness" study of how patients fare under the actual conditions of treatment in the field, can yield useful and credible "empirical validation" of psychotherapy and medication. This is the method that *Consumer Reports* pioneered....

Consumer Reports Survey

Consumer Reports (CR) included a supplementary survey about psychotherapy and drugs in one version of its 1994 annual questionnaire, along with its customary inquiries about appliances and services. *CR*'s 180,000 readers received this version, which included approximately 100 questions about automobiles and about mental health. *CR* asked readers to fill out the mental health section "if at any time over the past three years you experienced stress or other emotional problems for which you sought help from any of the following: friends, relatives, or a member of the clergy; a mental health professional like a psychologist or a psychiatrist; your family doctor; or a support group." Twenty-two thousand readers responded. Of these, approximately 7,000 subscribers responded to the mental health questions. Of these 7,000 about 3,000 had just talked to friends, relatives, or clergy, and 4,100 went to some combination of mental health professionals, family doctors, and support groups. Of these 4,100, 2,900 saw a mental health professional: Psychologists (37%) were the most frequently seen mental health professional, followed by psychiatrists (22%), social workers (14%), and marriage counselors (9%). Other mental health professionals made up 18%. In addition, 1,300 joined self-help groups, and about 1,000 saw family physicians. The respondents as a whole were highly educated, predominantly middle class; about half were women, and the median age was 46. . . .

There were a number of clear-cut results, among them:

- Treatment by a mental health professional usually worked. Most respondents got a lot better. Averaged over all mental health professionals, of the 426 people who were feeling *very poor* when they began therapy, 87% were feeling *very good, good,* or at least *so-so* by the time of the survey. Of the 786 people who were feeling *fairly poor* at the outset, 92% were feeling *very good, good,* or at least *so-so* by the time of the survey. These findings converge with meta-analyses of efficacy (Lipsey & Wilson, 1993; Shapiro & Shapiro, 1982; Smith, Miller, & Glass, 1980).
- Long-term therapy produced more improvement than short-term therapy. This result was very robust, and held up over all statistical models. . . .
- There was no difference between psychotherapy alone and psychotherapy plus medication for any disorder (very few respondents reported that they had medication with no psychotherapy at all).
- While all mental health professionals appeared to help their patients, psychologists, psychiatrists, and social workers did equally well and better than marriage counselors. Their patients' overall improvement scores (0–300 scale) were 220, 226, 225 (not significantly different from each other), and 208 (significantly worse than the first three), respectively.
- Family doctors did just as well as mental health professionals in the short term, but worse in the long term. Some patients saw both family doctors and mental health professionals, and those who saw both had more severe problems. For patients who relied solely on family doctors, their overall improvement scores when treated for up to six months was 213, and it remained at that level (212) for those treated longer than six months. In contrast, the overall improvement scores for patients of mental health professionals was 211 up to six months, but climbed to 232 when treatment went on for more than six months. The advantages of long-term treatment by a mental health professional held not only for the specific problems that led to treatment, but for a variety of general functioning scores as well: ability to relate to others,

coping with everyday stress, enjoying life more, personal growth and understanding, self-esteem and confidence.

- Alcoholics Anonymous (AA) did especially well, with an average improvement score of 251, significantly bettering mental health professionals. People who went to non-AA groups had less severe problems and did not do as well as those who went to AA (average score = 215).

- Active shoppers and active clients did better in treatment than passive recipients (determined by responses to "Was it mostly your idea to seek therapy? When choosing this therapist, did you discuss qualifications, therapist's experience, discuss frequency, duration, and cost, speak to someone who was treated by this therapist, check out other therapists? During therapy, did you try to be as open as possible, ask for explanation of diagnosis and unclear terms, do homework, not cancel sessions often, discuss negative feelings toward therapist?").

- No specific modality of psychotherapy did any better than any other for any problem. These results confirm the "dodo bird" hypothesis, that all forms of psychotherapies do about equally well (Luborsky, Singer, & Luborsky, 1975). They come as a rude shock to efficacy researchers, since the main theme of efficacy studies has been the demonstration of the usefulness of specific techniques for specific disorders.

- Respondents whose choice of therapist or duration of care was limited by their insurance coverage did worse, ... (determined by responses to "Did limitations on your insurance coverage affect any of the following choices you made? Type of therapist I chose; How often I met with my therapist; How long I stayed in therapy").

These findings are obviously important, and some of them could not be included in the original *CR* article because of space limitations. Some of these findings were quite contrary to what I expected, but it is not my intention to discuss their substance here. Rather, I want to explore the methodological adequacy of this survey. My underlying questions are "Should we believe the findings?" and "Can the method be improved to give more authoritative answers?"

Consumer Reports Survey: Methodological Virtues

Sampling   This survey is, as far as I have been able to determine, the most extensive study of psychotherapy effectiveness on record. The sample is not representative of the United States as a whole, but my guess is that it is roughly representative of the middle class and educated population who make up the bulk of psychotherapy patients. It is important that the sample represents people who choose to go to treatment for their problems, not people who do not "believe in" psychotherapy or drugs. The *CR* sample, moreover, is probably weighted toward "problem solvers," people who actively try to do something about what troubles them.

Treatment duration   *CR* sampled all treatment durations from one month or less through two years or more. Because the study was naturalistic, treatment, it can be supposed, continued until the patient (a) was better, (b) gave up unimproved, or (c) had his or her coverage run out. This, by definition, mirrors what actually happens in the field. In contrast to all efficacy studies, which are of fixed treatment duration regardless of how the patient is progressing, the *CR* study informs us about treatment effectiveness under the duration constraints of actual therapy.

Self-correction   Because the *CR* study was naturalistic, it informs us of how treatment works as it is actually performed—without manuals and with self-correction when a technique falters. This also contrasts favorably to efficacy studies, which are manualized and not self-correcting when a given technique or modality fails.

Multiple problems   The large majority of respondents in the *CR* study had more than one problem. We can also assume that a good-sized fraction were "subclinical" in their problems and would not meet *DSM-IV* [Diagnostic and Statistical Manual of Mental Disorders, 4th Ed.] criteria for any disorder. No patients were discarded because they failed exclusion criteria or because they fell one symptom short of a full-blown "disorder." Thus the sample more closely reflected people who actually seek treatment than the filtered and single-disordered patients of efficacy studies.

General functioning   The *CR* study measured self-reported changes in productivity at work, interpersonal relations, well-being, insight, and growth, in addition to improvement on the presenting problem. . . . Importantly, more improvement on the presenting problem occurred for treatments which lasted longer than six months. In addition, more improvement occurred in work, interpersonal relations, enjoyment of life, and personal growth domains in treatments which lasted longer than six months. Since improvements in general functioning, as well as symptom relief, is almost always a goal of actual treatment but rarely of efficacy studies, the *CR* study adds to our knowledge of how treatment does beyond the mere elimination of symptoms.

Clinical significance   There has been much debate about how to measure the "clinical significance" of a treatment. Efficacy studies are designed to detect statistically significant differences between a treatment and control groups, and an "effect size" can be computed. But what degree of statistical significance is clinical significance? How large an effect size is meaningful? The *CR* study leaves little doubt about the human significance of its findings, since respondents answered directly about how much therapy helped the problem that led them to treatment—from *made things a lot better* to *made things a lot worse*. Of those who started out feeling *very poor*, 54% answered treatment *made things a lot better*, and another one third answered it made things *somewhat better*.

Unbiased Finally, it cannot be ignored that *CR* is about as unbiased a scrutinizer of goods and services as exists in the public domain. They have no axe to grind for or against medications, psychotherapy, managed care, insurance companies, family doctors, AA, or long-term treatment. They do not care if psychologists do better or worse than psychiatrists, marriage and family counselors, or social workers. They are not pursuing government grants or drug company favors. They do not accept advertisements. They have a track record of loyalty only to consumers. So this study comes with higher credibility than studies that issue from drug houses, from either APA [American Psychiatric Association], from consensus conferences of the National Institute of Mental Health, or even from the halls of academe....

The Ideal Study

The *CR* study, then, is to be taken seriously—not only for its results and its credible source, but for its method. It is large-scale; it samples treatment as it is actually delivered in the field; it samples without obvious bias those who seek out treatment; it measures multiple outcomes including specific improvement and more global gains such as growth, insight, productivity, mood, enjoyment of life, and interpersonal relations; it is statistically stringent and finds clinically meaningful results. Furthermore, it is highly cost-effective.

Its major advantage over the efficacy method for studying the effectiveness of psychotherapy and medications is that it captures how and to whom treatment is actually delivered and toward what end. At the very least, the *CR* study and its underlying survey method provides a powerful addition to what we know about the effectiveness of psychotherapy and a pioneering way of finding out more.

The study is not without flaws, the chief one being the limited meaning of its answer to the question "Can psychotherapy help?" This question has three possible kinds of answers. The first is that psychotherapy does better than something else, such as talking to friends, going to church, or doing nothing at all. Because it lacks comparison groups, the *CR* study only answers this question indirectly. The second possible answer is that psychotherapy returns people to normality or more liberally to within, say, two standard deviations of the average. The *CR* study, lacking an untroubled group and lacking measures of how people were before they became troubled, does not answer this question. The third answer is "Do people have fewer symptoms and a better life after therapy than they did before?" This is the question that the *CR* study answers with a clear "yes."

NO

**Neil S. Jacobson and
Andrew Christensen**

Studying the Effectiveness
of Psychotherapy

[T]here is considerable debate about the merits of a recent *Consumer Reports (CR)* survey (1995).... This survey has received a great deal of attention within psychology and has been publicized in the popular press. Seligman (1995) suggested that this is the best study ever conducted on the effectiveness of psychotherapy.

Much like Freud's case studies, the report by *CR* (1995) is very persuasive and will probably have a great deal of influence on the public perception of psychotherapy. However, the purpose of this article is to show that most of what the *CR* study says has already been proven to the satisfaction of both practitioners and psychotherapy researchers. Moreover, those findings from the *CR* study that have not been previously established are highly questionable because of the study's methodological shortcomings. Finally, controlled experiments that avoid the methodological pitfalls of the *CR* study can answer virtually all of the questions considered by Seligman (1995) to be beyond the scope of clinical trials. In fact, it would be unfortunate if the field of psychotherapy research abandoned the controlled experiment when attempting to answer questions regarding the effectiveness of psychotherapy. Although clinical trials have their limitations and may need to be supplemented by other types of methodologies, they are far superior to the type of design reflected in the *CR* study, a design that has already been debated and rejected by both practitioners and researchers....

A Critique of the New Findings
from the *Consumer Reports* Survey

The methodological shortcomings of the *CR* (1995) survey greatly limit their evidentiary value. Seligman (1995) mentioned some of these shortcomings but not others; the ones he did mention tended to be minimized. Here are a sample of these shortcomings.

A Retrospective Survey Is Not an Ideal
Prototype for Effectiveness Research

Seligman (1995) suggested that the CR (1995) study is a well-done effectiveness study and was careful to distinguish this study from an efficacy study—a randomized clinical trial. However, in fact, the CR survey is not necessarily a good model for an effectiveness study as that term is typically used. The main virtue of the CR survey, according to Seligman, is its "realism"; that is, it is a report about real therapy, conducted by real therapists, with real clients, in the real world. The retrospective biases that are impossible to rule out are not seen as fatal flaws but simply as aspects of the design that need to be refined.

There are two fundamental problems with retrospective surveys. The first is that, because they are retrospective, there is no opportunity to corroborate respondents' reports. When participants are reporting on their own previous experiences, whether in therapy or otherwise, there is no way of assessing their accuracy. Various biases may contaminate their responses, ranging from demand characteristics to memory distortion. With a prospective study, some of these biases can be minimized, whereas others can be evaluated, using corroborative measures coming from different modalities. For example, self-report data can be supplemented with observational data. With retrospective surveys, such validation is impossible, and thus the responses are hard to interpret.

The second problem with retrospective surveys is the possibility that an unrepresentative subsample of those surveyed returned their questionnaires. Although it cannot be proven that those who benefited from psychotherapy were more likely to complete the survey than were those who did not, neither can that possibility be disproven. With a prospective study, one doesn't have to guess. This additional problem makes the improvement rates reported in the CR (1995) survey hard to interpret.

The most striking example of this selectivity problem is in the findings pertaining to Alcoholics Anonymous (AA), which had the highest mean improvement rate of any treatment category reported by Seligman (1995). In fact, as a treatment, AA significantly outperformed other mental health professionals. This finding can be contrasted with the lack of evidence supporting the efficacy of AA in prospective studies (McCrady & Delaney, 1995). Seligman acknowledged the strong possibility of sampling bias in AA and offered some speculations on why one might expect AA to be particularly susceptible to such biases. However, he then inexplicably minimized the likelihood of similarly extensive biases operating in the sample as a whole, suggesting that

> a similar kind of sampling bias, *to a lesser degree,* [italics added] cannot be overlooked for other kinds of treatment failures. At any rate, it is quite possible that there was a *large* [italics added] oversampling of successful AA cases and a *smaller* [italics added] oversampling of successful treatment for problems other than alcoholism.(p. 971)

Is it not possible that the oversampling of successful cases was as large for other problems as it was for AA? Is there any evidence to the contrary?

In addition to contaminating the overall estimates of treatment gains, sampling bias could easily explain the apparent superiority of long-term therapy reported by the respondents in the CR (1995) study. Unlike Howard et al. (1986), who found a negatively accelerated dose–response relationship, the CR survey found a linear relationship: the more therapy, the better the outcome. This would indeed be an important finding if it were interpretable; unfortunately, it is not interpretable. Seligman (1995) argued against the possibility of sampling bias by focusing on one potential source. He suggested that, if early dropouts are treatment failures and those who remain in treatment are beneficiaries, then earlier dropouts should have lower rates of "problem resolution" than later dropouts. In fact, the rates are uniform: About two thirds of dropouts quit because the problem is resolved, whether they quit therapy one month or two years after they started.

The problem with Seligman's (1995) refutation is that it fails to rule out the primary source of interpretive ambiguity—spontaneous remission. The longer people stay in therapy, the greater the opportunity for factors other than therapy to produce improvement. There is no way of knowing whether the superiority of long-term therapy is due to the treatment itself or simply to increased opportunities for other factors to produce improvements.

Seligman (1995) argued that the main virtue of the CR (1995) study is its realism. If one thinks of realism using the metaphor of a snapshot, the implication is that the CR survey provides a snapshot of what psychotherapy is really like. But, because the study is retrospective, the snapshot may be out of focus. With a prospective study, one can take a snapshot of psychotherapy whose focus is indisputable. But, with a retrospective survey, the negatives are gone forever.

The Absence of Control Groups of Any Kind Constitutes an Additional Fatal Flaw

Seligman (1995) fully acknowledged the problems introduced by the uncontrolled nature of the study but suggested that there are "internal controls" that can be used as surrogates. Unfortunately, none of Seligman's internal controls can be considered adequate substitutes for control groups.

First, he suggested that the inferior performance of marriage counselors allowed them to serve as a reference group because they controlled for various nonspecific factors such as the presence of an attentive listener. However, because marriage counselors may have differed systematically from other professionals in the client population with whom they worked, their performance cannot be compared with that of other mental health professionals who may have treated more mental health problems that were not primarily related to marital distress. In other words, there may have been a systematic confounding between type of problem treated and profession, which rendered marriage counselors useless as an internal control.

Second, Seligman (1995) noted that long-term treatment worked better than short-term treatment, thus allowing the use of the first point in the dose–response curve as a control group. As we have already suggested, this internal control is useless because of the confound with greater opportunity for spontaneous remission in long-term therapy.

Third, according to Seligman (1995), because it is known that drugs outperform placebos, and because psychotherapy did as well as psychotherapy plus drugs in the CR (1995) study, one can infer that psychotherapy would have outperformed an adequate placebo if one had been included in the CR study. This argument is specious for a number of reasons: It is not known what drugs were used for which problems in the CR study; it is not known whether the pharmacotherapy performed was adequate (compliance, dosage, etc.); and most importantly, it is not known whether the sample of patients in the CR study was similar to those in which drugs typically outperform placebos.

Fourth, family doctors did not perform as well as mental health professionals when treatment continued beyond six months, thus suggesting family doctors as an internal control. However, family doctors saw clients for a fewer number of sessions than did mental health professionals, creating a confound that Seligman (1995) himself acknowledged.

Seligman (1995) concluded that spontaneous remission is an unlikely explanation for the high improvement rates reported by respondents in the CR (1995) study. We come to a different conclusion, because none of the proposed internal controls are adequate. We conclude that factors other than psychotherapy might very well have accounted for the improvement rates reported by the respondents. We come to this conclusion for several reasons. First, there is no adequate control to rule it out, thus no compelling reason to reject the null hypothesis. Second, because the 4,000 respondents in the CR study were, to use Seligman's (1995) terminology, "middle class and educated" (p. 969) and "a good-sized fraction were 'subclinical'... and would not meet *DSM-IV [Diagnostic and Statistical Manual of Mental Disorders*, 4th Edition; American Psychiatric Association, 1994] criteria for any disorder" (p. 970), we have the kind of sample that is most likely to spontaneously remit, or to benefit from any treatment, specific or nonspecific (Jacobson & Hollon, 1996). As Seligman noted, in most clinical trials, the single largest basis for exclusion is that the client is not sufficiently distressed or dysfunctional to be included.

For example, in research on depression, by far the most common basis for exclusion is that not enough symptoms are present for the patient to meet criteria for major depressive disorder; even if *DSM-IV* criteria are met, participants are often excluded because the major depressive disorder is not severe enough (Jacobson et al., 1996). In efficacy studies, there is a good reason to exclude these participants: They seem to get better no matter what they receive. Even the less severe patients who make it into these trials tend to respond as well to placebos as they do to active treatments (cf. Jacobson & Hollon, 1996). Thus, it is a fair assumption that many of the respondents to the CR (1995) survey who improved would have improved without therapy.

The Measures in the *Consumer Reports* Survey Were Not Only Unreliable but Unrevealing

The *CR* (1995) survey measured little more than consumer satisfaction. Consumer satisfaction is far from trivial. However, consumer satisfaction ratings are uncorrelated with symptomatic outcome and general functioning. In the *CR* survey, three questions were asked in the assessment of improvement, one pertaining to "satisfaction with therapist," a second pertaining to "improvement in the presenting problem," and a third pertaining to "improvement in overall functioning." The latter measure was a change score, derived by subtracting posttest scores from pretest scores (both obtained retrospectively); the other two measures were simply posttest scores. Seligman (1995) seized on these three questions to argue that three different constructs are being measured: consumer satisfaction, symptom relief, and general functioning. However, since all three questions are global and retrospective and have method variance in common, they cannot be considered independent assessments of functioning or to be measuring different constructs. Furthermore, the three questions were combined into a multivariate composite for the calculation of improvement rates, thus making it impossible to separate out consumer satisfaction from the other items.

The Specificity Question Revisited: The *Consumer Reports* Survey Did Not Assess Which Therapies Led to Improvement in Which Problems

Researchers are long past the stage of referring to psychotherapy as if it were uniform, without specifying the nature of the problem being treated or the treatment used. Yet, the *CR* (1995) study failed to inform the public about any particular treatment for any particular problem and thus provides little information that advances knowledge about psychotherapy. The data may be available to answer more specific questions. But even if they were available, and were released, they would be based on respondent reports: Respondents would be reporting what their presenting problem was and the kind of treatment they received (we have already seen some data on this latter question), and they would be defining both the profession and the theoretical orientation of the therapist. How reliable are survey respondents at describing the theoretical orientation of their therapist or at fitting their presenting problem into one of a series of choices on a survey, especially in retrospect? Both of us have small private practices, and a large proportion of our clients are couples. We have heard ourselves referred to as marriage counselors, psychologists, and even, on occasion, psychiatrists. We doubt whether the number of our clients who could correctly identify our theoretical orientation would much exceed chance.

Even Assuming Methodological Adequacy, the Results as Reported by *Consumer Reports* and by Seligman Are Misleading

Although the sound bite coming out of both the *CR* (1995) report and Seligman's (1995) article says that 90% of the respondents found psychotherapy beneficial, it is worth noting that this figure comes from combining those who were helped "a great deal," "a lot," and "somewhat." Only 54% reported that they were helped "a great deal." This is not a very impressive figure from the standpoint of clinical significance, especially when one takes into account the number of subclinical respondents in the sample and the possibility that the respondents may be overrepresented by those who found treatment to be helpful.

The Eysenck Evaluation Revisited

The *CR* (1995) survey bears remarkable resemblance to the controversial evaluation of psychotherapy reported by Eysenck (1952). In this report, Eysenck summarized the results of 24 reports of psychoanalytic and eclectic psychotherapy with more than 7,000 neurotic patients treated in naturalistic settings. Using therapist ratings of improvement, Eysenck reported a 44% improvement rate for psychoanalytic therapy and a 64% improvement rate for eclectic psychotherapy. Unlike the *CR* survey, however, these reports were prospective in that the therapist evaluations occurred at the time of termination. Also unlike the *CR* survey, Eysenck used control groups: One consisted of all improved patients who had been discharged from hospitals in New York between 1917 and 1934 for "neurotic" conditions, receiving nothing but custodial care; the other consisted of 500 disability claimants who were periodically evaluated by general practitioners without receiving psychotherapy, so it could be determined whether they were improved enough to go back to work. Improvement for this latter control group was defined as their ability to return to work, which was decided by the general practitioner. Eysenck reported, on the basis of these two control groups, that the spontaneous remission rate for these minimally treated patients was 72% and that psychotherapy was therefore ineffective.

The merits of these findings and the methodology supporting them were debated vigorously for 20 years. Initially, Luborsky (1954) criticized the study on the grounds that the measures of improvement were flawed, the control groups were inadequate, and the treatments were lacking on both uniformity and representativeness. Similar critiques were registered by Rosenzweig (1954) and De Charrus, Levy, and Wertheimer (1954). These and more recent critiques (e.g., Bergin, 1971) argued, with considerable merit, that Eysenck (1952) had underestimated the success of therapy and overestimated the spontaneous remission rate. As recently as the mid-1970s, Eysenck's study was subject to refutation by more optimistic appraisals and interpretations of psychotherapy's impact (Luborsky et al., 1975; Meltzoff & Kornreich, 1970). Now, the controversy has largely subsided, and Eysenck's study has been rejected by clinical scientists. In fact, in the most recent edition of Bergin and Garfield's (1994) *Handbook of Psychotherapy and Behavioral Change* the study is not even cited.

When it is referenced nowadays, it is primarily for its historical impact and its heuristic value.

What is interesting about examining Eysenck's (1952) study in light of the *CR* (1995) survey is that virtually all of the criticisms leveled at Eysenck's evaluation also apply to the *CR* survey, even though Eysenck's evaluation was more sophisticated from a methodological perspective. Eysenck had a sample that was almost twice as large as the sample reported in the *CR* survey; he did at least include control groups, however inadequate they might have been; the measures of improvement were concurrent rather than retrospective; and the measures were obtained from trained therapists rather than from the clients themselves. Given Seligman's (1995) assumptions that therapists are able to self-correct their therapeutic work and cannily select which clients need drugs and psychotherapy, therapists should also be better judges of when clients have made genuine improvement versus transitory symptom change. However, the field was correct in rejecting Eysenck's evaluation: The control groups and the measures of outcome were inadequate. We don't see any reason to revert to a methodology that was rejected for its methodological inadequacies 20 years ago.

CHALLENGE QUESTIONS

Is the *Consumer Reports* Conclusion That "Psychotherapy Helps" Valid?

1. You have probably learned about the difference between correlation and causation in research and methods. How does this difference pertain to the controversy over the *Consumer Reports* study?
2. Do you think that psychotherapy is effective? Assert your own conclusion and support it with scientific research.
3. Jacobson and Christensen discuss the parallels between Hans Eysenck's 1952 study of psychotherapy and *CR*'s study. Look up Eysenck's original study and describe how it is also different from the *CR* study.
4. Why are "experimental" designs favored by not only therapy researchers but also psychological researchers in general?
5. How important do you feel "consumer satisfaction" should be in the evaluation of psychotherapy? Support your answer.

On the Internet ...

Ask NOAH About: Mental Health

This enormous resource contains information about child and adolescent family problems, mental conditions and disorders, suicide prevention, and much more, all organized in a "clickable" outline form.

```
http://www.noah.cuny.edu/illness/mentalhealth/
mental.html
```

Biological Changes in Adolescence

This site offers a discussion of puberty, sexuality and biological changes, cross-cultural differences, and nutrition for adolescents, including obesity and its effects on adolescent development.

```
http://www.personal.psu.edu/faculty/n/x/nxd10/
biologic2.htm
```

Serendip

Organized into five subject areas (brain and behavior, complex systems, genes and behavior, science and culture, and science education), Serendip contains interactive exhibits, articles, links to other resources, and a forum area for comments and discussion.

```
http://serendip.brynmawr.edu/serendip/
```

SHPM.com: Various Views Related to Genetic Testing

This section of the *Self-Help and Psychology Magazine* Web site offers articles on the psychological impact of genetic testing.

```
http://www.shpm.com/articles/health/hsgentest.html
```

PART 2

Biological Issues

*N*o behavioral or mental activity can take place without biology. Biological processes are fundamental to all mental functions, including emotion, perception, and mental health. Does this mean that differences in behavior are essentially the result of biological differences? Are differences between males and females or between thin people and fat people primarily biological?

- Does Genetic Testing Have Negative Psychological Effects?

- Is Love a Mechanism of Evolution?

ISSUE 4

Does Genetic Testing Have Negative Psychological Effects?

YES: Katharine A. Rimes and Paul M. Salkovskis, from "Psychological Effects of Genetic Testing for Psychological Disorders," *Behavioural and Cognitive Psychotherapy* (vol. 26, 1998)

NO: Carol Lynn Trippitelli et al., from "Pilot Study on Patients' and Spouses' Attitudes Toward Potential Genetic Testing for Bipolar Disorder," *American Journal of Psychiatry* (July 1998)

ISSUE SUMMARY

YES: Katharine A. Rimes and Paul M. Salkovskis, both researchers in genetics and bioethics, argue that although genetic testing may have benefits, the negative psychological consequences of such testing may actually increase the risk of developing a disorder or exacerbating a problem.

NO: Carol Lynn Trippitelli and her colleagues, researchers of the effects of genetic testing, maintain that although there may be ethical and psychosocial issues involved in genetic testing, their study showed that patients and their spouses feel that the advantages of genetic testing outweigh the risks.

Sarah is a 28-year-old college graduate with a stable job and a loving husband. She has had a relatively healthy adult life and an equally healthy childhood. But she has recently learned that a close family member is schizophrenic. Ever since, she has worried that she, too, might be susceptible to schizophrenia. Sarah is considering having herself tested for genetic defects such as schizophrenia, but she is not sure that she wants to.

On one hand, Sarah is a healthy individual who has no prior reason to question her health. And the testing itself would cause her some anxiety and discomfort. However, on the other hand, knowing her genetic tendencies might give her an early edge on treatment, if necessary. Would knowing that she had a gene associated with schizophrenia make her feel schizophrenic? Would it be more beneficial or more harmful for her to know?

Recently, many studies have been conducted to weigh the costs and benefits of predictive genetic testing for psychological disorders. In some instances, genetic testing may prove beneficial in that it can increase awareness and allow individuals to obtain preventive treatment earlier. But are psychological disorders caused only by genetics? Many psychologists assert that genetic testing may not be as beneficial as it seems. The knowledge that one carries a supposed "gene of disorder" could induce psychological dysfunction that might not otherwise surface. That is, a self-fulfilling prophecy might induce the disorder.

In the following selection, Katharine A. Rimes and Paul M. Salkovskis argue that genetic testing will do more harm than good. Advances in such testing, they say, introduce a number of negative psychological effects, including worry, stress, and even suicidal tendencies. These effects may seem ludicrous, given the seemingly inconsequential nature of such testing. But many people are tremendously fearful of their genes. Also, Rimes and Salkovskis propose that genetic testing may cause psychological and behavioral reactions that actually maintain existing problems.

In the second selection, Carol Lynn Trippitelli and her colleagues describe a pilot study in which attitudes toward genetic testing for bipolar disorder were measured. For this study the researchers gathered information on patients' and spouses' attitudes toward genetic testing and found that an overwhelming majority of people favor knowing that they may be genetically susceptible to bipolar disorder over not knowing. The authors use this evidence to refute the contention that the psychological effects of genetic testing are negative. They contend that, in actuality, the vast majority of people are in favor of genetic testing and that ignorance is not bliss. Knowing that one is genetically predisposed to a psychological disorder could enable one to better control it.

It is important to note that Trippitelli et al. admit that it is not yet clear whether or not it is possible to construct an accurate genetic test for bipolar disorder. They also agree that if a sufficiently accurate genetic test could be constructed, pretest and posttest counseling should be done for all individuals involved and that such counseling should be available as well for the family members of those who are considering testing or participating in testing.

POINT

- Genetic testing may increase a person's risk of mental illness.
- Genetic testing may cause stress, worry, and even suicidal preoccupation.

- Because psychological disorders are not based primarily in genetics, genetic testing for psychological disorders is not as sure as genetic testing for physical disorders.
- Once genetic testing is done, the knowledge can never be undone.

COUNTERPOINT

- Genetic testing may result in earlier preventive treatment.
- Patients with bipolar disorder and their spouses agree that the benefits of knowing about one's genes outweigh the risks.
- Patients and spouses seem to realize that psychological disorders are not 100 percent heritable.

- It is better to know than to not know.

Katharine A. Rimes and
Paul M. Salkovskis

 **YES**

Psychological Effects of Genetic Testing for Psychological Disorders

Introduction

It is likely that genetic factors contribute to some extent to psychological disorders and it has been suggested that in the near future many relevant genes may be identified (see Farmer and Owen, 1996, Rutter and Plomin, 1997 and Gelernter and Crowe, 1997 for discussions of current findings). Such developments may have important implications for our understanding and treatment of psychological disorders. However, there are also reasons for caution. The emphasis on identification of genetic factors could lead to other aetiological and maintaining factors being relatively ignored, even though these may be more amenable to intervention. Furthermore, advances in genetics will introduce the possibility of genetic testing for vulnerability to psychological disorders, raising a number of ethical and psychosocial issues. Some of these issues concern the possible effects of testing on the individual and their family. The question of whether or not genetic testing should be widely available (and whether a particular individual should undergo testing) should take into account the anticipated costs and benefits to the person tested. Examination of these issues regarding testing should begin now, at a relatively early stage, because it is possible that once relevant genes are identified there will be demands for testing to be quickly introduced. Consideration of the psychological effects of genetic testing also raises issues relevant to current practice, since some mental health professionals already provide clients with estimates (or general judgements) of the importance of the genetic component of their current problem. This paper is intended to highlight and discuss some of the possible effects of providing genetic information about psychological disorders....

There are many ethical and social issues raised by the prospect of genetic testing for psychological disorders, but here we will focus on the possible psychological and behavioural effects of testing. Previous research findings concerning testing for Huntington's Disease [a neurodegenerative disorder] will be described, as this is the only disease with psychological symptoms for which there is a body of research about the effects of genetic testing....

Edited from Katharine A. Rimes and Paul M. Salkovskis, "Psychological Effects of Genetic Testing for Psychological Disorders," *Behavioural and Cognitive Psychotherapy*, vol. 26 (1998). Copyright © 1998 by The British Association for Behavioural and Cognitive Psychotherapies. Reprinted by permission of the authors and Cambridge University Press. Acknowledgments and references omitted. Paul Salkovskis is a Wellcome Trust Senior Research Fellow.

Psychological Reactions to an *Increased*-Risk Result from Genetic Testing

After genetic testing for Huntington's Disease (HD), psychological reactions include shock, anger, pessimism about the future, depression, increased preoccupation with HD, guilt about possibly passing on the gene to their children, finding the result an emotional burden, continued feelings of uncertainty and even suicide attempts (e.g. Tyler, Morris, et al., 1992; Codori & Brandt, 1994; Tibben, Roos, & Niermeijer, 1997). All of these reactions can be expected after genetic testing for other psychological disorders. However, the reactions of those receiving a high-risk result from genetic testing in HD have generally been less severe than expected. It is tempting to conclude that the same will be true for other types of genetic testing, but there are several reasons why this may not be so. Firstly, HD is a dominantly inherited disorder with 100% penetrance, so that someone with a parent with HD has a 50% chance of having the gene, and people with the gene will all develop the disorder, if they reach the age of onset. This means that genetic testing allows the individual who has a family history of HD to move from uncertainty to relative certainty (whether good or bad news), which may help to reduce distress. This will not be the case for genetic testing involving multifactorial disorders, in which there are both genetic and non-genetic causal factors—here uncertainty may actually be increased after testing. For example, a positive genetic test result for a multifactorial disease may increase the estimate of a person's risk from 1% (population risk) to 30%. If they are found to have the relevant gene, the odds are still in favour of them *not* developing the disease, but the uncertainty is now greater. Another reason why it should not be assumed that genetic testing for other disorders will have similar effects to those reported after HD testing is that people who have undergone testing for HD in research settings have received extensive pre- and post-test counselling. It is not known what the psychological consequences would be if it was not possible to give this amount of counselling (as will be the case in most clinical settings). Furthermore, people who have current psychological problems or signs of vulnerability to them are generally excluded from genetic testing, so little is known about the likely effects of testing these patients (e.g. Tyler, Ball, et al., 1992; Tibben, Timman, Bannink, & Duivenvoorden, 1997). People who accept testing for HD also seem to be a self-selected group; they are less likely to anticipate negative emotional reactions than those who refuse testing (Codori, Hanson, & Brandt, 1994) and have high levels of resourcefulness (Bloch et al., 1989). Finally, it should be noted that Tyler, Morris, et al. (1992), Wiggins et al. (1992) and others report that some people refused to take part in follow-ups because they were too distressed (e.g. 17% of Tyler, Morris, et al.'s increased risk group), which indicates that the degree of psychological distress in those who receive a high risk result from HD testing may be higher than is generally reported.

There is a need for research into how people who are known to be at increased risk react if they become symptomatic. It has been reported that some HD carriers who initially coped well after testing have become severely depressed and suicidal when they develop symptoms of HD (Tibben et al., 1997).

There is also a need for data concerning the psychological consequences of reaching the expected time of onset for people who know that they are at increased risk. Many of those tested for HD are not at the expected age of onset at the time of the test result and the follow-up data are not yet available. It is important to note that HD has a later mean onset than psychological disorders such as anxiety disorders, mood disorders, eating disorders and so on. Many of the people tested for these psychological disorders will already be at or near the typical age of onset, which could result in more severe psychological reactions. This is partly because of the meaning of the result (i.e. they are facing an immediate rather than delayed threat of illness) and partly because these people's response to testing may already be *directly* influenced by their genetic vulnerability. It has been well documented that adverse life events are associated with an increased risk for many psychological disorders, particularly if the individual has a pre-existing psychological vulnerability (e.g. Brown & Harris, 1989), and receiving a high risk test result will be an adverse event for many people. The stress of the genetic test result could prove to be an aetiological factor in the person's first episode of the illness in question.

People who are at high genetic risk for psychological disorders are also likely to be at increased environmental risk. At times, a parent with a psychological disorder may not be able to give their child the level of care that they would otherwise have been capable of, and in some cases the child may as a result develop maladaptive coping strategies or negative beliefs about themselves. This means that some people whose parents have psychological problems may already be more at risk for psychological disorder than their genetic risk would indicate and may react particularly badly to news about their genetic risk.

An increased-risk result is likely to have effects on interpersonal relationships. In HD testing it has been found that partners of a gene carrier report increased psychological distress after risk notification which is still apparent three years later (Tibben et al., 1997) and couples in which one partner has received a high-risk result report lower marital satisfaction than couples who received a low-risk result (Quaid & Wesson, 1995). Byrne and Bamforth (1994) report a case where a woman with a high-risk result became depressed and reported suicidal preoccupation after her fiancé called off the marriage because she had the HD gene. It is likely that in some cases the person with a high-risk result will feel guilty about being a current or future burden to their family or about possibly passing on the gene in question to their children, which may cause relationship difficulties. They may also feel anger towards the parent who passed on the gene in question. There may be problems outside of the family too: the person may face discrimination from others, since there is much prejudice about psychological problems in Western societies.

It is important to remember that even a high risk result can have benefits; Codori and Brandt (1994) found that patients who have received a high risk result from HD testing reported at least one positive effect of testing. However, many of these effects (e.g. relief of uncertainty and ability to plan for the future) may only apply to conditions such as HD where there was great uncertainty before testing, which is reduced by the test result. Some people who have already suffered psychological problems (or who go on to experience difficulties in the future) may feel that simply understanding more about the possible causes of their problems is beneficial. An increased-risk result for a multifactorial disease could have long-term positive psychological effects if the patient receives earlier diagnosis or treatment as a result or if they receive help to prevent episodes of psychological problems.

Psychological Implications of *Decreased*-Risk Test Results

... An important feature of genetic and non-genetic health testing is that a negative or low-risk result is not always completely reassuring (e.g. Tibben et al., 1992; Rimes, 1996). For example, Tibben et al. (1992) found that 56% of non-carriers in their group remained preoccupied with the threat of HD and 44% sometimes questioned the reliability of the test. For multifactorial disorders, a decreased-risk result is even less reassuring, because someone who does not have a particular gene may still be at a considerable risk for the condition. Thus one of the often-cited advantages of health testing—reassurance—may be very limited after tests for multifactorial psychological disorders.

In genetic testing for multifactorial psychological disorders there are further possible negative psychological consequences. For example, if a person is found to be a low genetic risk but has suffered from the problem anyway or goes on to suffer it in the future, they are likely to consider why this has happened. If they cannot blame their genes, they may blame their environment, for example, poor parenting. This may cause more problems in their relationships with their parents than a genetic causal attribution would have done, because genes are likely to be perceived as less under the parents' control than their style of parenting. Alternatively, the person may consider that there is something intrinsically wrong with them as a person; for example, that they are somehow weak or defective. Since poor self-image is risk factor for psychological problems, this type of attribution will increase their risk of persistent psychological distress (Abramson, Seligman, & Teasdale, 1978).

Testing People With a Current Psychological Disorder

Genetic testing of people with a current psychological illness poses particular problems. It is likely that these people will have fewer resources with which to cope with the testing process and may respond to testing in ways that increase their distress. For example, there is evidence that people who tend to be anxious selectively attend to threatening information and are more likely to interpret ambiguous situations in particularly negative ways (e.g., Mathews & MacLeod, 1986; Clark et al., 1988; McNally & Foa, 1987), so it is likely that they will be more distressed by genetic testing than people without anxiety problems. Similarly, people suffering from depression may tend to view bad news from a genetic test as further evidence that the future is hopeless. Such hopelessness may prolong the depression and increase the risk of suicide. In the case of addictive behaviours, news of increased risk may result in beliefs such as "there's no use trying to fight it [the urge to use the substance], it's in my genes"—which could facilitate further abuse of the substance in question. Someone with an addiction may also use the substance to help them cope with the distress caused. Many people with psychological problems have low self-esteem and they may conclude that the results of a genetic test confirm their low opinion of themselves; this will probably have the effect of maintaining or worsening their problems. For all psychological problems, an increased risk result may cause fatalistic attitudes towards their current problems and decrease their motivation to try to resolve their difficulties. Research is needed to examine the extent to which these kinds of responses occur after genetic testing.

In previous genetic testing research, attempts have been made to avoid these kinds of problems by excluding people with current psychological problems from the testing process. At the present time it does not appear that there are clear treatment benefits in testing patients who are currently suffering from psychological problems, although this situation may change. If such patients are to receive testing, effective ways of providing psychological support need to be developed and evaluated. Testing could then be offered in combination with psychological support at every stage from trained professionals. Each patient should receive pre-test assessment from a professional who should identify the type of reactions that the patient is likely to experience, determine whether the patient is likely to be able to cope with the testing process, help the patient to decide whether they definitely want to be tested, and help prepare the patient to deal with the test results. If testing of people with current psychological problems does occur, this should initially take place in research settings so that the impact of testing and the effectiveness of psychological support can be evaluated.

Individual Differences in Reactions to Medical Tests

There is a need for theoretical models of psychological reactions to genetic testing. Such models would allow the generation of hypotheses regarding factors that determine how different people react to genetic testing. An understanding of such factors would inform the development of methods for preventing and reducing distress associated with testing. Furthermore, if genetic testing for psychological disorders becomes widespread there will be insufficient resources to offer everyone intensive pre- and post-test counselling. If factors that determine individual differences in reactions to testing were better understood, it may be possible to use pre-test assessments to identify people who are at relatively higher risk of suffering adverse psychological effects, and target counselling resources at these people. We have proposed that a cognitive-behavioural (CB) model of health anxiety can be usefully applied to the assessment and prediction of different responses to predictive testing for physical illness (Salkovskis & Rimes, 1997). One reason why this model seems particularly promising is that it has given rise to an intervention for health anxiety that has been shown to be effective in controlled trials (e.g. Warwick, Clark, Cobb, & Salkovskis, 1996). [See Salkovskis & Rimes, 1998 for a fuller discussion of this approach.] ...

Ways of Coping With the Test Result

Research is needed into the ways in which people cope with the result from their genetic test. For example, there is evidence suggesting that one way in which some people may cope with a high-risk result from a health test is to "minimize" the risk itself or the seriousness of having the risk factor (Rimes, Salkovskis, & Shipman, submitted; Codori & Brandt, 1994; Croyle & Ditto, 1990). We found that women who were told they have low bone density rated low bone density as less serious than women who had high bone density, and showed significantly lower seriousness ratings after their result than before-hand. This minimization was *not* associated with fewer preventative behaviours. Codori and Brandt (1994) found that at 6 months after the test, gene carriers estimated their risk as much lower (60%) than was initially revealed at disclosure (>95%). Minimization may also occur in predictive genetic testing for other psychological disorders. The mechanisms behind minimization are not known, although it is possible, for example, that relatively optimistic seriousness beliefs are sometimes the result of selective comparison, e.g. the person telling themselves that their high risk result is not as serious as being at risk for certain other psychological disorders or as being at risk for certain *physical* disorders. In genetic testing for multifactorial conditions, the person who finds that they are at relatively high genetic risk may also be able to conclude that *overall* they are not at high risk because they are at low risk in terms of non-genetic factors. It is important to make the distinction between minimization, which may be an adaptive response, and complete denial, which may sometimes be associated with poor coping (Davey, 1993). The mechanisms of these and other reactions to genetic testing need to be investigated so that successful coping strategies can be encouraged and help can be given to people who use potentially maladaptive coping strategies.

Further Issues: Problems of Reliability and Validity of Diagnosis and the Provision of Genetic Information in Current Practice

Evaluation of the contribution of genetic factors to particular psychological disorders, both for the disorder in general and for particular individuals, requires the reliable and valid identification of those suffering from the problem in question. However, the criteria for diagnosing "psychological disorders" vary enormously in their reliability and validity, from the "Axis II" disorders ("Personality disorders") which tend to have poor reliability and validity (Perry, 1992; Steiner, Tebes, Sledge, & Walker, 1995) through to the relatively more robust criteria for manic-depressive disorders. An alternative to the use of diagnostic interviewing would be the use of biological markers (e.g. the use of neurochemical challenge tests). However, Philibert, Egeland, Paul and Ginns

(1997) point out that even in bipolar affective disorder, where the contribution of biological factors is relatively well established, biological markers of the disorder have not been identified. This means that researchers and clinicians rely exclusively on relatively unreliable categorical diagnoses based on clinical interview data. A further complication is that differential diagnosis often takes family history into account (DSM-IV; American Psychiatric Association, 1994, p. 355), which could lead to an overestimation of the contribution of genetic factors.

The identification of genetic influences on behaviour does not necessarily mean that psychological problems are best viewed as inherited diseases with a specific pathophysiology. Opinions vary on whether disease models are appropriate as a way of conceptualizing psychological problems. It is possible that mental health professionals may lose sight of the impact on their patients of their adoption of particular views concerning the nature of psychological problems. Some professionals and patients may regard the identification of genetic factors as indicating that the person's problem is purely biologically determined. Clinical experience suggests that, given a choice, patients generally prefer treatments that they believe deal with what they perceive to be causal factors rather than "symptomatic" approaches. The patient who firmly believes their anxiety is caused by genetic factors is likely to prefer an intervention that they believe will correct the "cause" of their problem rather than one which will change the way in which they react psychologically to potentially stressful situations. This belief could prevent some patients from accepting or engaging fully in well validated psychological treatments.

The present paper has considered the effects of genetic information in the context of genetic testing, with a view to considering how best to manage the likely consequences of such testing if it was to become technically feasible. However, many of these issues are also relevant to current practice, in terms of the way that clinicians describe the importance of genetic contributions to their psychological problem. This may be done in a general way by specifying that a particular disease is known to have a genetic basis, or genetic information may be elicited in the form of family pedigrees and then explained to the patient as indicating that their problem has a genetic basis. Those making such pronouncements clearly need to consider the likely impact of such suggestions on the patient's psychological well-being. There is an urgent need within mental health settings for research into the impact of providing patients with particular explanations for the aetiology of psychological problems.

Conclusions

There are many reasons to be concerned about the psychological and behavioral effects of genetic testing for psychological disorders. Such testing should initially be carried out in research settings so that the range of psychological responses to different types of testing can be monitored, both in the person tested and their family. This will inform the debate over the possibility of such testing being widely available. If it is shown that adverse psychological reactions are common or long-lasting, it may be decided that the costs of this testing out-weigh the benefits. The intention to offer psychological help as part of genetic counselling should not be used to justify the availability of tests that can create much distress, unless it can be demonstrated that psychological interventions given to those tested do in fact help to reduce their distress and help them to cope with the result. Genetic counselling should also be evaluated with regard to its effect on patient understanding and decision-making.

In the consideration of the advisability and possible implementation of genetic testing for psychological disorders, there is a need for a theoretical ba-sis for understanding the psychological issues involved in such testing. This could then be used to generate hypotheses for research concerning the type of variables that predict the range of psychological and behavioural responses to testing. Once factors determining different responses to testing have been identified, this will aid the development of interventions to prevent or reduce strong and persistent adverse reactions. It should also make it possible to iden-tify people who are likely to react in particularly negative ways; these people should be given extra psychological help focused on their individual needs. If genetic testing for psychological problems does becomes available, everyone who receives a high-risk result should be offered psychological interventions that not only help them to cope with the distress caused by the test result but also educate them about the disorder in question, such as how to recognize the symptoms and when to seek help. Preventative interventions should be devel-oped for those with a high-risk result in order to minimize their chances of developing the disorder or experiencing a worsening of an existing problem. It is important that a high-risk result does not become a self-fulfilling prophecy.

Pilot Study on Patients' and Spouses' Attitudes Toward Potential Genetic Testing for Bipolar Disorder

There is compelling evidence from twin, family, and adoption studies to suggest that bipolar disorder is genetically transmitted. Data from genetic linkage studies indicate the probability that familial bipolar disorder results from multiple genetic loci acting independently or in concert. Although results of genetic linkage studies of bipolar disorder have not been consistently replicated, positive evidence for linkage with chromosome 18 markers in bipolar families has been reported by three independent research groups. Furthermore, three groups have independently reported linkage of bipolar disorder to loci on human chromosome 21q....

The purpose of our study was to gain information about the attitudes of individuals with bipolar disorder and of their spouses toward some of the issues that are arising from advancing genetic research on bipolar disorder. There have been no previous studies comparing the knowledge and attitudes of bipolar patients and spouses with respect to genetic information....

Method

A 46-item questionnaire was distributed to 90 patients with bipolar disorder and to their spouses (a total of 180 questionnaires) between June and September 1993. Subjects with bipolar disorder were drawn from participants in the Johns Hopkins University bipolar disorder genetic linkage study, members of the Depression and Related Affective Disorders Association, and inpatients and outpatients of the affective disorders division of the John Hopkins University Hospital. An introductory letter describing the purpose and nature of the study was sent to 84 linkage study participants; this letter was followed, in turn, by a phone call from a researcher asking permission to send a questionnaire. Questionnaires were sent to 32 of the 84 linkage study participants and their spouses. Support group leaders of the Depression and Related Affective Disorders Association in Maryland, Pennsylvania, and Washington, D.C., were contacted to

Edited from Carol Lynn Trippitelli, Kay R. Jamison, Marshal F. Folstein, John J. Bartko, and J. Raymond DePaulo, "Pilot Study on Patients' and Spouses' Attitudes Toward Potential Genetic Testing for Bipolar Disorder," *American Journal of Psychiatry*, vol. 155, no. 7 (July 1998). Copyright © 1998 by The American Psychiatric Association. Reprinted by permission of The American Psychiatric Association and the authors. References omitted.

request permission to distribute questionnaires to their group members. Questionnaires were given to 52 of the members and their spouses. Some individuals completed the questionnaires at their group meeting, and others completed them at home and mailed them back. Questionnaires were also given to three outpatients and their spouses, only one member of a married couple could have a diagnosis of bipolar disorder. All of the outpatients couples mailed the questionnaires back to us, while all of the inpatient couples completed them in the hospital.

After complete description of the study to all subjects, written informed consent was obtained. Patients and spouses were asked to complete the questionnaires independently. In most instances, a researcher was present to answer any questions that the subjects had. In instances where no researcher was present, the phone number of a researcher was given to the subjects so that they could call if they had any questions....

Results

Of the 180 questionnaires distributed, 90 were returned to us. Thirty-four of the questionnaires received were completed by bipolar type I patients and their spouses, 42 were completed by bipolar type II patients and their spouses, and 14 were completed by couples for whom we were unable to ascertain the specific type of bipolar disorder in the affected individual. Of the 45 couples who responded, the patients in 16 were participants in the genetic linkage study, the patients in 23 were members of the Depression and Related Affective Disorders Association, and there were three outpatients and three inpatients of the affective disorders unit of the Johns Hopkins University Hospital. The majority of the questionnaires were fully completed; however, some questions were left blank by certain subjects....

Knowledge of Probability of Inheritance

Both patients and their spouses were asked to give their estimate of the probability that a child will inherit a gene for bipolar disorder if one partner but not the other has bipolar disorder. The mean estimate was 46.7% for the patients and 41.4% for the spouses.

Attitudes Toward Genetic Testing for Bipolar Disorder and Disclosure of Genetic Information to Third Parties

The great majority of the subjects with bipolar disorder indicated that they would definitely or probably take a blood test to determine whether they are carrying a gene for bipolar disorder, and the majority of their spouses said that they too would want to know the results of such a test. Of the individuals with bipolar disorder, 85.4% (N = 35 of 41) indicated that they would definitely take a blood test to determine whether they are carrying a gene for bipolar disorder, and 14.6% (N = 6 of 41) said that they would probably take the test; however, of the spouses, only 46.3% (N = 19 of 41) said that they would definitely take the test themselves, and 34.1% (N = 14 of 41) said that they would probably take the test, a significant difference ($\chi^2 = 18.8$, df $= 1$, p < 0.001). Those spouses who were less certain about whether they would take advantage of genetic testing for bipolar disorder themselves may believe that their risk of carrying a gene is minimal in the absence of any clinical signs or symptoms of bipolar disorder. Furthermore, most of the spouses (85.4%, N $= 35$ of 41) said that they would definitely or probably want to know the results of their affected partner's genetic test. Of note, when gender was looked at separately, there were no statistically significant differences between the responses of male patients and female patients on this issue. There were also no statistically significant differences between male and female spouses.

When the subjects with bipolar disorder and their spouses were asked whether minors (children under age 18) should be tested for a gene for bipolar disorder, the majority of the bipolar patients and the majority of the spouses said that minors should definitely or probably be tested. Among the bipolar individuals (N $= 40$ for this question), 77.5% (N $= 31$) said that minors should definitely or probably be tested, 12.5% (N $= 5$) were uncertain, and 10.0% (N $= 4$) said that they should definitely not or probably not be tested.

There was more of a gradation in respondents' views about testing a fetus. While 43.9% (N $= 18$) of 41 patients and of their spouses said that they would definitely or probably test a fetus, 39.0% (N $= 16$) of the patients and 41.5% (N $= 17$) of the spouses felt that they would definitely not or probably not test a fetus. Respondents also expressed more uncertainty about testing a fetus than about testing minors: 17.1% (N $= 7$) of 41 patients and 14.6% (N $= 6$) of 41 spouses were uncertain about testing a fetus.

When asked about the disclosure of genetic information to third parties, the large majority of patients and spouses indicated that they would want their genetic information to be given to their doctor but not to their insurance company. Of the individuals with bipolar disorder, 75.0% (N $= 30$ of 40) said that they would definitely or probably want researchers to give their genetic information to their doctor, and the majority of their spouses (65.0%, N $= 26$) expressed the same view. When asked whether they would want researchers to give their genetic information to their insurance company, the majority of individuals with bipolar disorder (76.9%, N $= 30$ of 39) and the majority of their spouses (84.6%, N $= 33$), said that they would definitely not or probably not want this to be done.

Overall, patients and spouses were in agreement about their attitudes toward genetic testing and the disclosure of genetic information to third parties.

Benefits and Risks of Having Bipolar Disorder Genetic Information

The bipolar patients and spouses were asked to choose from a variety of reasons for undergoing genetic testing those that they believed were potential benefits of knowing whether they or their spouse carries a gene for bipolar disorder. Of the benefits that they acknowledged, they were asked to mark those that they felt were most important. The majority (67.5%, N $= 27$ of 40) of both patients and spouses indicated that the most important benefit was "to obtain treatment to prevent attacks." The second most important benefit selected was "I think that I (or my spouse) have the gene, and I want to be more certain of that." This was ranked most important by 12.5% (N = 5) of the patients and by 5.0% (N = 2) of their spouses. Both of these potential benefits were ranked more important than "to decide whether or not to have children," "to decide whether or not to get married," and "to make financial plans."

The bipolar patients and their spouses were next asked to choose from a variety of reasons for genetic testing those that they felt were potential risks of knowing whether they or their spouse carries a gene for bipolar disorder. They were also given the option of indicating that there are no real risks of knowing. In addition, of the reasons they acknowledged, they were asked to mark those that they felt were most important. There was less agreement between patients and spouses about the risks of knowing their bipolar disorder genetic information than there was about the benefits of knowing.... Twenty-five percent (N = 10 of 40) of the patients felt most strongly that there were no real risks of knowing their bipolar disorder genetic information. This response was ranked most important by the patients more frequently than any of the risks that were proposed. Among the patients, the prospect of their insurance company finding out was most frequently selected as the most important risk. Among the spouses, two risks were most frequently selected as most important: the prospect of their insurance company finding out and the prospect that a positive test might upset them because of worries about their children. When gender was looked at separately, there were no statistically significant differences between the responses of male patients and female patients or between those of male and female spouses on any of the questions that addressed potential risks. In addition, there were no significant differences between the attitudes of patients and spouses regarding the relative importance of various benefits and risks of knowing whether one carries a gene for bipolar disorder.

The vast majority of the bipolar patients and their spouses indicated that the benefits of knowing whether they or their spouses carry a gene for bipolar disorder outweigh the risks. None of the respondents said that the risks outweighed the benefits of genetic knowledge. Only 22.0% (N = 9 of 41) of the patients and 14.6% (N = 6) of their spouses were uncertain. Moreover, there were no statistically significant differences in responses to this question between male patients and female patients or between male and female spouses.

Attitudes Toward Abortion

Figure 1 shows patients' and spouses' attitudes toward aborting a fetus that carries a gene for bipolar disorder. When asked about this, the majority of the patients with bipolar disorder, 55.0% (N = 22 of 40) and their spouses, 65.0% (N = 26) said that they would definitely not abort the fetus.

Patients and spouses were also asked about their attitudes toward abortion under other genetic risk circumstances (e.g., increased genetic risk of a serious, painful or debilitating, incurable neurologic disorder or extreme untreatable obesity). The majority of both the patients and their spouses expressed the opinion that abortion was definitely not or probably not justified in any of

Figure 1

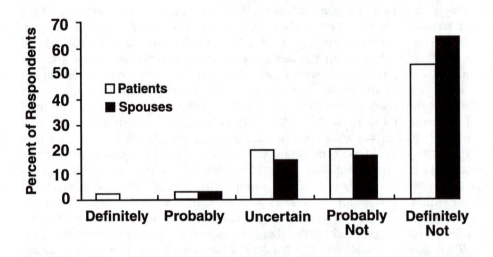

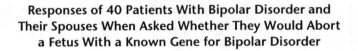

Responses of 40 Patients With Bipolar Disorder and
Their Spouses When Asked Whether They Would Abort
a Fetus With a Known Gene for Bipolar Disorder

these cases. They were most inclined to justify abortion in the case of a serious, painful, and incurable neurologic disorder beginning at age 40, with 22.0% (N = 9 of 41) of the patients and 24.4% (N = 10) of their spouses indicating that they would definitely or probably choose to abort a fetus that would develop such a condition.

In addition, there were no significant differences in responses to any of the questions regarding abortion between male and female patients or between male and female spouses.

Attitudes Toward Marriage and Childbearing

Most respondents—92.1% (N = 35 of 38) of the patients and 78.9% (N = 30) of their spouses—said that they would have definitely or probably gotten married even if a blood test had detected a gene for bipolar disorder. In addition, the majority of respondents—55.0% (N = 22 of 40) of the patients and 57.5% (N = 23) of their spouses—said that knowing that they or their spouse had a gene for bipolar disorder would definitely not or probably not have deterred them from having children.

There were no statistically significant differences between patients' and spouses' predicted attitudes toward marriage and childbearing given this genetic information. However, there was more uncertainty about childbearing than about marriage among both patients and spouses; 17.5% (N = 7 of 40) of the patients and 25.0% (N = 10) of their spouses were uncertain whether they would have children if they knew that they had a gene for bipolar disorder, compared to 7.9% (N = 3 of 38) of the patients and 21.1% (N = 8) of their spouses who indicated that they were uncertain whether they should still have gotten married if they knew that they had a gene for bipolar disorder.

When responses to questions about marriage and childbearing were analyzed separately by gender, there were no statistically significant differences between male and female patients or male and female spouses.

Discussion

Our data indicate that attitudes toward presymptomatic and prenatal testing for bipolar disorder were quite positive. The majority of the bipolar patients and their spouses stated that they would want to take advantage of presymptomatic and prenatal genetic tests for bipolar disorder if they became available. Furthermore, the majority of both patients and spouses were in favor of testing minors for the gene. The greatest degree of uncertainty for both patients and spouses involved the testing of a fetus.

Importantly, the vast majority of patients and spouses believed that the benefits of knowing whether they or their spouse carries a gene for bipolar disorder outweigh the risks. The benefit ranked most important by both patients and spouses was to obtain treatment to prevent episodes of illness. Only a small group of patients (10.0%) and spouses (15.0%) felt that knowing that one carried a gene for bipolar disorder would make it harder for that person to reach his or her goals in life.

The overwhelming majority of the bipolar patients and spouses indicated that they would not choose to abort a fetus with a gene for bipolar disorder. Overall, respondents were less likely to justify abortion for carrying a gene for bipolar disorder than they were for carrying a gene for any of the other hypothetical conditions presented. This is in agreement with a study by Smith et al. which showed that members of bipolar disorder support groups, psychiatric residents, and medical students would all be more inclined to abort a fetus for another life-threatening or severely debilitating disorder than they would for bipolar disorder. However, compared to our patient and spouse groups, a greater percentage of their respondents indicated that they would end a pregnancy if the fetus were to definitely develop an unspecified course of bipolar disorder. This may be because our question left open the possibility that an individual may in fact have a gene for bipolar disorder but not develop any clinical symptoms. (When asked to estimate the likelihood that one could have a gene for bipolar disorder but not show any signs of the disorder at all, our patients gave a mean estimate of 31.7%, and the spouses gave a mean estimate of 30.5%.) Smith et al. also found that the intention to abort a fetus would be influenced by the projected severity of the illness and the likelihood of developing bipolar disorder. However, given the multifactorial nature of bipolar disorder, it is possible that a positive result of a genetic test for the disorder would still leave uncertainty about whether one will in fact develop the disorder. In addition, a positive genetic test result might not provide information about the severity of the illness.

It is interesting to note that there were no significant differences between the attitudes of patients and those of their spouses toward most of the issues addressed.

The relatively high rate of uncertain responses regarding childbearing, prenatal testing, and abortion indicate areas in which patients and spouses perceive a need for more information.

This was a pilot study, and several limitations may have influenced our results. First, we had a 50% response rate to our questionnaire, which is comparable to the general response rate for medical questionnaires. Another limitation of the study was the small size of the study group. Trends that did not reach statistical significance in our study might well have reached significance with a larger group. In addition, it is apparent that our subject group was in some respects quite skewed; ascertainment was not systematic, and most respondents were well-educated and in their first marriage. The patients in their first marriage may represent those whose illness has caused less marital disruption. Most of the patient respondents were members of support groups or participants in a genetic study and would be expected to be better-educated and more willing to disclose personal information about the genetics of their disease.

Our study did not explore the length of time that affected individuals had been treated for bipolar disorder or how efficacious their treatment had been. These factors would be expected to affect attitudes toward marriage, childbearing, and disclosure of genetic information. In addition, we had no method of ensuring that patients were euthymic at the time that they completed the questionnaire. Finally, we had no normal (nonclinical) control group.

Despite the limitations of the study, the results are of considerable interest and value in terms of providing a basis for further research. The trends we observed suggest a strong likelihood that individuals will make use of genetic tests for bipolar disorder once they become available. In addition, they convey attitudes that may shed light on some of the concerns that have been raised regarding the possible misuse of genetic information. However, we must be careful about extrapolating from hypothetical intentions to actual requests for genetic testing. In the case of Huntington's disease—an incurable, genetic (autosomal dominant) neuropsychiatric degenerative disease for which genetic testing is now available—the current demands for testing are substantially below the rate predicted by early surveys (18, 19). A study by Quaid and Morris (20) surveyed 66 people at risk for Huntington's disease who chose not to undergo testing for the disorder. The five most important reasons that they cited for declining testing were lack of a treatment, increased risk to their children, the prospect of losing health insurance, financial costs of testing, and "the inability to undo the knowledge."

The discovery of a genetic test for bipolar disorder will inevitably raise some similar concerns, but bipolar disorder differs in many respects from Huntington's disease. The availability of treatment, high rates of response to treatment, and aspects of the illness that might confer advantages to the individual, to interpersonal relationships, and to society may outweigh the potential disadvantages at the time of actual testing.

Additional studies with larger study groups and broader sampling of the population would be useful. It would be informative to address the issue of how the degree of accuracy of a genetic test for bipolar disorder would influence people's attitudes toward testing. It is not clear how much genetic information will be required to justify making a genetic test for bipolar disorder available. Careful consideration must be given to the issue of testing minors. The question of whether parents' desire to know that their child has a gene for bipolar disorder outweighs the child's right to privacy—particularly if such knowledge could lead to earlier treatment and avoiding potential harm to the child—remains to be answered. Related issues, such as circumstances under which it might be permissible to deny testing to individuals and whether there might ever be circumstances that warrant mandatory testing, have already become real issues in the genetic testing for Huntington's disease and will undoubtedly have to be addressed in future testing for bipolar disorder. Data from continuing research on the issues identified here will be essential in facilitating the development of appropriate guidelines for the eventual genetic testing for bipolar disorder.

Acknowledgment

Research funded by the Drs. Kienle Center for Humanistic Medicine at the Pennsylvania State University College of Medicine and the Dana Corsortium for the Genetic Basis of Manic-Depressive Illness.

CHALLENGE QUESTIONS

Does Genetic Testing Have Negative Psychological Effects?

1. As a healthy, happy adult, would you seek genetic testing if a family member was diagnosed with schizophrenia? Explain.
2. Analyze the issues of genetic testing in the movie *Gattaca* in terms of the readings. Which side of the controversy would the movie's screenwriter be on, and why?
3. Review the research literature on self-fulfilling prophecies, and discuss their implications for the genetic testing issue.
4. How would you conduct a follow-up study to the investigation conducted by Trippitelli et al.? Include a discussion of your objective, methods, and possible results.

ISSUE 5

Is Love a Mechanism of Evolution?

YES: Helen Fisher, from "The Nature of Romantic Love," *The Journal of NIH Research* (April 1994)

NO: Jeffrey S. Reber and Marissa S. Beyers, from "Love Is Not an Evolutionarily Derived Mechanism," An Original Essay Written for This Volume (January 2000)

ISSUE SUMMARY

YES: Anthropologist Helen Fisher contends that love is a chemical mechanism through which natural selection initiates and sustains human pair-bonds. Further, she maintains that serial monogamy has adaptive advantages and is visible in worldwide patterns of divorce.

NO: Freelance writers Jeffrey S. Reber and Marissa S. Beyers contend that love is not merely biological but also fundamentally relational, social, and psychological. Additionally, they argue that Fisher's commitment to an evolutionary perspective leads to a biased interpretation of the evidence.

Many people would argue that of all the human emotions, love seems to be the most universal and important. It is an emotion shared by almost every culture, present and past, and it is the subject of countless tales, poems, and songs. Given its pervasiveness and significance to human beings, love is a vital area of psychological investigation. Indeed, psychologists have been concerned with providing a full understanding of this emotion, both as it originates and as it is experienced.

Evolutionary psychologists argue that the powerful emotion of love can be understood in terms of selective pressures. According to the renowned naturalist Charles Darwin, who formalized and popularized the theory of evolution during the nineteenth century, natural selection has directed the progression and development of all living organisms. Therefore, love is like any other attribute of living organisms. It has evolved because it ensures the progression of the species; thus, feelings of love are adaptive.

Consistent with this evolutionary perspective, Helen Fisher proposes in the following selection that all aspects of love—from attachment to detachment

—can be explained in terms of evolutionarily driven, biochemical determinants. She cites patterns of divorce and other statistics to bolster her case. Her evolutionary understanding of love is best exemplified through the sexual strategy of serial monogamy, wherein intimate relationships exist to produce viable offspring. Love is the mechanism through which these relationships are formed, and it exists at least until the successful production of viable offspring is accomplished.

In the second selection, Jeffrey S. Reber and Marissa S. Beyers take issue with Fisher's assertion that love can be adequately understood in terms of evolutionarily driven, biochemical determinants. They argue that the notion of chemically derived emotions negates the possibility of other defining features that are necessary to fully understand love. Furthermore, Reber and Beyers assert that divorce statistics are not evidence that serial monogamy is a human sexual strategy. They contend that Fisher's work is guided more by her commitment to evolutionary theory than by a commitment to a full account of how humans truly experience love.

POINT

- Love can be explained in terms of biochemical components.

- Serial monogamy is the primary sexual strategy of human beings as evidenced by divorce statistics and shared evolutionary origins.

- Cultural forces and free will may influence human pair-bonding.

- Attachment patterns support love's role in evolution.

COUNTERPOINT

- Love is not merely biological but also fundamentally social, relational, and psychological.

- Serial monogamy is not the primary sexual strategy of human beings; Fisher misinterprets divorce statistics and relies on badly fitted animal analogues to support the contention that it is.

- Fisher's perspective reduces cultural forces and free will to mere functions of natural selection; their roles in feelings of love are actually much more profound.

- Divorce and remarriage rates do not support an evolutionary account of love.

Helen Fisher  **YES**

The Nature of Romantic Love

Oh eyes be strong, you cherish people and then they're gone." Safia, a middle-aged Bedouin woman of Egypt's Western Desert, recited this short poem about lost love. She is not the only human being who has felt the angst or ecstasy of romance. In 1992, anthropologists William Jankowiak and Edward Fischer surveyed 166 societies and found evidence of romantic love in 88.5 percent of them. In some cultures, people sang love songs. Some eloped. Some informants recounted their anguish to the anthropologists, who lived among them. And the mythology of many societies portrayed romantic entanglements. So Jankowiak and Fischer concluded that romantic love, which they equate with "passionate love," constitutes a human universal. They attributed the absence of evidence for romantic love in the balance of these cultures to "ethnographic oversight," or lack of access to the folklore of the culture.

What is this thing called love? From the responses to a series of questionnaires administered at and around the University of Bridgeport, Conn., psychologist Dorothy Tennov identified a constellation of psychological characteristics common to the condition of "limerence," her term for being in love. Limerence, she notes, begins the moment another individual takes on "special meaning"; the other person could be a stranger or an old friend seen in a new perspective. But as one informant put it, "My whole world had been transformed. It had a new center, and that center was Marilyn."

... Why is it that scientists have failed to study such a profound and universal emotional state? Affiliative behavior plays a crucial role in the mating process of all birds and mammals—and mating is the single most important act of any individual of any sexually reproducing species. Yet in the 1970s, Sen. William Proxmire gave the Golden Fleece Award (for wasting public funds) to a group of psychologists studying romantic behavior.

Perhaps we think love is too private, too intangible, or too frivolous for scientific investigation. First, humankind studied the stars, plants, and animals; only in the past two centuries have the fields of psychology, sociology, and anthropology developed to examine human behavior systematically. Even now, as scientists explore the biochemistry of the basic emotions, investigations focus on the physiology of aggression, dominance, depression, and anxiety. Studies are just beginning on the biochemistry of affiliation.

The Chemistry of Attraction and Attachment

In seminal research done in the 1980s, psychiatrist Michael Liebowitz divided human romantic love into two basic stages, attraction and attachment, and he proposed that specific physiological events in the brain were involved in each. After analyzing the effects of antidepressant drugs that inhibit monoamine oxidase (MAO) that were administered to lovesick patients, Liebowitz concluded that the exhiliration of attraction is associated with phenylethylamine (PEA), which is chemically related to the amphetamines, and/or with the action of the monoamine neurotransmitters norepinephrine, dopamine, and serotonin in the limbic system and associated areas of the brain.

Liebowitz attributed the second stage of romantic love, attachment, and its concomitant feelings of tranquility and peace to heightened production of the endorphins, peptide neurotransmitters that are chemically related to morphine. Newer data suggest that oxytocin and vasopressin, peptide neurotransmitters that play central roles in male-female bonding, group bonding, and mother-infant bonding in other mammalian species, may also be involved in human attachment.

Moreover, human attraction and attachment have analogues in birds and other mammals—suggesting that these emotions evolved. Birds and mammals distinguish among potential mates, judge which would make better breeding partners, and exhibit interest in some individuals more than others. Much like humans, chimpanzees, gorillas, baboons, elephants, wolves, and many other social mammals express attraction with an array of pats, rubs, taps, gazes, licks, and nibbles, as well as with close body contact, play gestures and tolerance of one another. And while courting, many mammals are energized....

Does a male elephant feel attraction as he strokes a female's back with his trunk just before he mounts her? Does a male wolf feel attachment as he nudges a chunk of meat toward his hungry mate while she is nursing in their den? Questions about the animal correlates of the human emotions remain. But the... data suggest that attraction and attachment are emotions as primitive and universal as fear, anger, and surprise, which are (at least in part) psychopharmacological events arising from arousal circuits located primarily in the limbic system and surrounding regions of avian and mammalian brains.

I think these emotions evolved in birds and mammals to initiate mating and sustain male-female associations long enough to ensure reproduction and survival of the young. (Because each species has a distinctive breeding system, the brain anatomy and physiology for these emotions undoubtedly vary to correspond with each species-specific mating cycle.) Then, with the evolution of the cerebral cortex among the first hominids, our ancestors began to build on this core of primitive emotions associated with reproduction, eventually developing complex romantic feelings and elaborate traditions to celebrate and curb what European cultures would come to call romantic love.

How Love Progresses

"When two people are first together, their hearts are on fire and their passion is very great. After a while, the fire cools and that's how it stays. They continue to love each other, but it's in a different way—warm and dependable." So said Nisa, a !Kung San woman of the Kalahari Desert of southern Africa to anthropologist Marjorie Shostak in her 1981 book, *Nisa: The Life and Words of a !Kung Woman.* At some point, that magic wanes. Tennov measured the duration of limerence from the moment infatuation hit to the moment a "feeling of neutrality" for one's love object began. She concluded that the most frequent duration of "being in love," as well as the average, was between approximately 18 months and three years. Sexologist John Money agrees, proposing that once you begin to see your sweetheart regularly, the elation typically lasts two to three years.

Liebowitz has hypothesized that the transition from attraction to the second stage of romantic love, attachment, is also grounded in brain physiology; either neurons in the limbic system become habituated to the brain's natural stimulants or concentrations of PEA and/or other endogenous amphetamine-like substances begin to drop. Then, the endorphin system begins to take over, giving partners feelings of safety, stability, tranquility, and peace. Perhaps as feelings of attachment grow, the production of oxytocin and/or vasopressin or the sensitivity of the receptor sites for these peptides increases as well.

No one has examined how long human attachment lasts, but clearly many mateships end. So, for some men and women, there is a third stage of romantic love, detachment. To my knowledge, the physiology of detachment has not been explored. But in trying to explain why birds abandon their nests at the end of the breeding season to join a flock and why many creatures leave the safety of their natal home after infancy, ethologist Norbert Bischof has theorized that an animal gets an "excess of security," to which it responds by withdrawing from the object of attachment. The same phenomenon may occur in humans. At some point in some long relationships, the brain's receptor sites for the endorphins, oxytocin, vasopressin, and/or other neurochemicals may become desensitized. Thus attachment wanes and sets up the mind for separation.

None of the above is meant to suggest that men and women are biologically *compelled* to fall in love, to attach or detach from one another. Cultural forces play a powerful role in directing behavior, as does one's idiosyncratic perspective—what philosophers have long called "free will." But marriage is a cultural universal and divorce is common in societies around the world. Moreover, worldwide data on marriage and the timing of divorce suggest that, like attraction and attachment, the physiology of detachment evolved to direct the ebb and flow of our ancestral hominid mating system (discussed below).

Human Reproductive Strategies

Records going back to the mid-1800s indicate that over 90 percent of American men and women in every birth cohort marry. The 1982 *Demographic Yearbook of the United Nations* lists the number of men and women who have married by age 49 in 97 industrial and agricultural countries: Between 1972 and

1981, an average of 93.1 percent of women and 91.8 percent of men married in these 97 countries. These figures have not changed significantly since then. Although no worldwide tabulations have been made on the percentage of men and women who marry in horticultural and hunter-gatherer cultures, the ethnographic literature confirms that marriage is a pancultural custom; in nonindustrial communities, men and women who have never married are rare.

Moreover, most men and women are monogamous; they wed only one individual at a time. What is permissible to each gender varies,however. In 99.5 percent of 853 cultures for which anthropologists have data, women are permitted to marry only one man at a time, monandry. Each woman forms a social and economic relationship that entails sexual rights and privileges with only that one man.

... [D]ata on monogamy does not suggest that human beings are sexually faithful to their spouses, however. Extra-pair copulations are commonly seen in monogamous species of birds and mammals; adultery is clearly a secondary *opportunistic* reproductive strategy in humans. However, this article addresses only the primary human reproductive strategy: monogamy, specifically *serial* monogamy, because human pairing displays several patterns of decay that are relevant to understanding the evolution and nature of human romantic love.

Human Divorce Patterns

With a few exceptions, peoples from Amazonia to Siberia divorce. Several patterns of divorce have purely cultural explanations, but four of these patterns do not correlate with the divorce rate. These four patterns, I think, evolved in humans and resulted in the characteristic ebb and flow of human romantic love.

The first pattern is reflected in the duration of marriage that ends in divorce. Data from the demographic yearbooks of the United Nations on 62 available industrial and agricultural societies for all obtainable years between 1947 and 1989 (188 graphs, or cases, each showing the divorce profile for a specific country, area, or ethnic group in a specific year) indicate that divorces exhibit a skewed distribution, characterized by the occurrence of the mode (or divorce peak) during and around the fourth year, followed by a gradual, long-tailed decline in divorce counts. Divorces peak during and around four years after marriage.

The second common aspect of human divorce patterns evident in the demographic yearbooks of the United Nations is the age at which divorce occurs. Age at highest divorce risk was tabulated for 24 available societies in selected years (80 cases each showing the divorce profile for a specific country in a specific year) between 1966 and 1989. Divorce risk was highest among men in the age category 25 to 29; divorce risk for women was equally highest in age categories 20 to 24 and 25 to 29. Across the 62 sampled societies (188 cases), the mean percent of divorces that involved women under age 45 was 81 percent; the mean percent of divorces that involved men under age 45 was 74 percent. Thus, in the above cross-cultural sample, divorce risk was greatest at the height of reproductive and parenting years.

The third pattern is seen in the number of children per couple who divorce. In the 59 societies recorded between 1950 and 1989, 39 percent of divorces occurred among couples with no dependent children, 26 percent occurred among those with one dependent child, 19 percent occurred among couples with two dependent children, 7 percent occurred among those with three children, 3 percent occurred among couples with four young, and couples with five or more dependent young rarely split. Hence, divorce counts were highest among couples with no children and one dependent child, and they decreased with increasing numbers of dependent young. (The demographic yearbooks of the United Nations do not provide comparative cross-cultural data sufficient to establish divorce risk by number of dependent young.)

The fourth pattern of human pair-bonding concerns remarriage. The U.S. Census Bureau reports that approximately 75 percent of American women and 80 percent of American men who divorce remarry, and one-half of the American remarriages take place within three years of a divorce. Moreover, most remarriages occur during reproductive years: 76.3 percent of American women who divorce during their 20s remarry; 56.2 percent of those who divorce in their 30s remarry; and 32.4 percent of those who divorce in their 40s remarry. In 1979, the modal age at remarriage for American men was 30 to 34 years, and the modal age at remarriage for American women was 25 to 29 years.

Cross-culturally, remarriage by divorced individuals also peaks among men and women of reproductive age. Among the 98 peoples surveyed by the United Nations between 1971 and 1982, the modal age at remarriage among men was 30 to 34 years; women who remarried after a divorce were modal age of 25 to 29 years. The United Nations Statistical Office does not tabulate the percent of divorced individuals who remarry. Remarriage is frequent, however, in those places for which data are available, and remarriage rates are highest for men and women of reproductive age.

Human marriages, then, have several general patterns of decay. They tend to disband during and around the fourth year of existence. Man and women around the world tend to divorce while in their twenties—the height of reproductive and parenting years. Men and women regularly abandon a partnership that has produced no children or one dependent child. Most divorced individuals of reproductive age remarry. And the longer a mateship lasts, the older the spouses get, and/or the more children they bear, the more likely a couple is to remain together.

Why Love Ends—and Begins Again

Why do human beings pair up, establish a home base, build networks of business associates, family, and friends, and bear and nurture children—only to leave each other and pair anew? From a Darwinian perspective, it is remarkable that we pair at all. Monogamy is rare in mammals; only 3 percent pair up, and they do so only under specific circumstances. Many of these circumstances may have contributed to the evolution of monogamy in hominids. But a factor proposed by [D. G.] Kleiman is particularly relevant. She writes that monogamy is favored in evolution "whenever more than a single individual (the female) is needed to rear the young."

Canid species are good examples. The female red fox bears as many as five altricial kits that need to be fed almost continuously, so she must stay in the den to attend to them; she needs a mate to bring her food. For the male fox, polygyny is impractical because resources are usually spread out; he cannot acquire enough food to feed a harem. So, a male and female fox form a pair-bond in midwinter and raise their young together during the spring and early summer. But the pair-bond lasts only through the breeding season; as the kits become independent, mates part company. Serial monogamy in conjunction with a breeding season is also a common reproductive strategy among birds. In at least 50 percent of the 9,000 or so avian species, individuals pair at the beginning of the mating season, rear their chicks together until the young are fledged, and then part to join a flock. Some pair together at the beginning of the next breeding season, while others choose new mates.

Homo sapiens shares traits with seasonally parenting foxes and birds. The modal duration of marriage that ends in divorce, four years, conforms to the traditional period between human successive births, four years. So, I propose that the human tendency to pair up and remain together for a modal duration of about four years reflects an ancestral hominid reproductive strategy to pair and remain together throughout the infancy of a single highly dependent child. Once a child living in a hunter-gatherer society could join a multi-age play group at about age 4, however, and be raised by other members of the band, a pair-bond broke up—enabling both partners to choose new mates and bear more varied young. And I think the physiologically based emotions associated with romantic love—specifically attraction, attachment, and restlessness during long relationships—evolved to stimulate this ancestral *cyclic* breeding system, serial monogamy....

Despite the social disruption that detachment entails in humans (and many other species), serial monogamy may have had several genetic benefits in our prehistoric past. Variety in one's lineage has been mentioned. Furthermore, males who dissolved one partnership for another acquired the opportunity to select a younger mate more likely to produce more viable offspring. Ancestral females who dissolved an unsatisfactory relationship, on the other hand, acquired the opportunity to choose a mate who provided better protection, food, and nurturance for her, her children, and her forthcoming infants. So, regardless of the social complexities inherent in changing partners, serial monogamy *during reproductive years* became an adaptive reproductive strategy, leaving this legacy not only in contemporary worldwide patterns of divorce and remarriage but in our universal struggle with primitive, powerful, and often transitory reproductive emotions that many associate with romantic love.

Nature, Culture, and Romantic Love

Someone once asked Margaret Mead why all of her marriages failed. Mead reportedly replied, "I beg your pardon, I had three marriages and none of them was a failure." Most Americans do not view marriage so pragmatically. Even fewer are willing to consider the possibility of genetic components to divorce—largely because this perspective threatens their concept of free will. Many scientists resist exploring the biological bases of attraction, attachment, and divorce for an historical reason. Soon after Darwin proposed the concept of natural selection by survival of the fittest, these ideas were marshaled by conservatives to vindicate the social hierarchy of Victorian England. Women, poor people, immigrants, colonized peoples, and the outcasts of society were dismissed as "less fit." This credo led to a bitter reaction by the 1920s and ushered in several decades of "cultural determinism." Today, many lay people and scientists still hold that love is a purely cultural phenomenon, outside the realm of scientific inquiry.

But romantic love is a elegant example of the complex mixture of environment and heredity. Culture, for example, plays an essential role in one's *choice* of partner and the *timing* and *process* of courting. As children, for example, we develop specific likes and dislikes in response to family, friends, and experiences. So, by the teenage years, each individual carries within him or her an unconscious mental template, or "love map," a group of physical, psychological, and behavioral traits that he or she finds attractive in a mate. People fall in love when they are ready. Barriers (such as geographic or social constraints) enhance infatuation, as does novelty and unfamiliarity. And cultural beliefs regularly tie partners together. In fact, 50 percent of Americans marry for life—an excellent example, I believe, of the triumph of culture and personal commitment over nature.

So, culture plays a crucial role in *whom* you find attractive, *when* you court, *where* you woo, *how* you pursue a potential partner, *how* you resolve your problems, and (depending on economic factors) *how many* people stay together. But beliefs, traditions, family, friends, books, songs, and other cultural phenomena do not teach one *what to feel* as one falls in love, becomes attached to a mate, or becomes restless in a long relationship. Instead, these emotions are generated by brain-body physiology. They evolved long ago to direct the ebb and flow of our primary reproductive strategy, serial monogamy, and they came across the eons to invigorate and complicate our lives.

Love Is Not an Evolutionarily Derived Mechanism

Many Greek tragedies, Shakespeare's sonnets, and countless other pieces of literature, art, music, and poetry are all based on love. This overflow of artistic expression is a testament to the profound meaning that all of us associate with love and intimate relationships. Yet, in Helen Fisher's article, "The Nature of Romantic Love," she seems content to explain love in such a way that its profound meaning is irrelevant and impossible. Granted, this irrelevancy and impossibility are not immediately apparent in her article. In fact, Fisher begins with the feelings and emotions involved in the meaningful experience of love. However, because she attributes this experience to an evolutionarily adaptive strategy, she ultimately renders love meaningless.

The problem is that Fisher's evolutionary perspective assumes that all human behaviors are the product of natural selection and biology. Fisher speaks about the importance of culture and free will but she does not consider them primary in her explanation of love. They are instead the byproducts of natural selection and biology. Fisher argues that these conclusions are forced on her by scientific evidence. However, we will show how the research findings she reports do not necessitate an evolutionary/biological explanation. Indeed, the correlations she cites between biochemical substances in the brain and feelings of love, or between animals and humans, can be accounted for by a number of alternative, equally viable, explanations. For this reason, we contend that Fisher's evolutionary perspective fails to prove that love is the product of natural selection and biology. We also argue that her evolutionary/biological account negates the rich and profound meaning of love as well as the primary role of culture and free will in that meaning.

Can we account for love in a way that preserves its meaning? Herein we offer an alternative account that gives sufficient weight to free will and culture. According to this alternative, human beings are not merely biological; they are also fundamentally relational, social, and psychological. Although we hold that biology is very much a part of human experience and thus, the experience of love, this biology does not constitute or cause love. On the contrary, we propose that love, culture, free will, and the meaning we attach to intimate relationships *give rise to* the biological experience of love. Because love is rooted in the meaningful experience of intimate relationships, rather than in our biology or any universalized sexual strategy, natural laws and forces cannot and do not determine love. The relationships and meanings themselves determine love.

Love Is Not Merely Biological

Fisher's assertion that feelings of love arise out of brain chemicals, structures, and processes cannot offer a sufficient account of love. We agree that love has its physiological correlates. Anyone who has experienced love can attest to the butterflies in the stomach, the dry mouth, and racing heart that accompany it. But to say that biological activity is associated with love is not the same thing as Fisher's assertion that feelings of love originate in our biology. It is our contention that Fisher's assertion that feelings associated with love and intimacy arise from neurological brain patterns is mistaken. We will argue that a full accounting of love cannot be possible using *solely* biological correlates. The focus of this section, then, is twofold: 1) we will illustrate how an understanding of the biological activity associated with love fails to provide a sufficient explanation for the rich and full meaning of love as experienced in intimate relationships; and 2) we will argue that biology doesn't produce love, but that the special meaning we attach to a person and a relationship actually gives rise to biological activity.

For Fisher, the psychological experience of love is *really just* biological activity. She contends that our "complex romantic feelings and elaborate traditions" stem from a core of primitive emotions that arise from arousal circuits located in the brain. In other words, the rich meaning of love that is expressed in literature, music, and especially between lovers ultimately reduces to primitive brain structures and neurotransmitters such as vasopressin and oxytocin. Any particular accounting of love, such as the one Fisher refers to: "My whole world had been transformed. It had a new center, that center was Marilyn," is explainable in terms of "particular brain chemistry for attachment." This perspective replaces an experience of love that is rich with psychological, social, relational, and biological components with one made up of *solely* biological components. As a result, the psychological, social, and relational components of love become merely by-products or secondary manifestations of what is *really* going on. For Fisher, all of the rich meaning and emotion shared in loving relationships, the cultural traditions and rituals of marriage, and the sense of satisfaction and fulfillment that accompanies child-rearing exist *only* as the byproducts of neuronal activity.

At this point it is important to ask whether there is anything wrong with a completely biological account of love and intimate relationships. We are, after all, biologically embodied. Isn't it therefore reasonable to assume that love arises from our bodies? It is our contention that although such an assumption may seem reasonable, it is, in fact, impossible. That is, a completely biological account of love fails because it reduces love to neurotransmitters and peptides that in and of themselves are meaningless and can tell us nothing of the rich variety of thoughts and feelings that are central to loving relationships. Vasopressin has no inherent meaning; nor can oxytocin love anything at all! Chemical components cannot create a poem or a love song. Neurotransmitters do not love other neurotransmitters. Rather, we contend that they are part of a greater psychological process wherein biological components receive their meaning from people in particular contexts or relationships. A racing heart, for example, means very different things in the context of a mugging, where it is associated with fear, or in a fight, where it is understood in terms of anger, or in an embrace, wherein it is assigned the meaning of love. In short, the biological activity described by Fisher can tell us very little about ourselves without being connected to the meaningful context of our experience.

Biological activity, then, must be understood within a greater context. We contend that biology depends on the human experience of love for its meaning. That is, it isn't until we assign meaning and importance to a person that the biological activities are relevant or even begin. We don't get butterflies in the stomach, a racing heart, and increased endorphin production for just anyone or anything. We reserve such responses for that one person who is important to us, that particular person who "takes on special meaning." Hence, love originates not in our biology, but in a relationship between two people that is sufficiently meaningful to engage the whole person—mind and body. That is, the meaning we assign to a person not only affects our thoughts and feelings, but also our very physiology. The person with whom we are in love means so much to us that even the chemicals in the deepest recesses of our brain respond. So yes, we agree that love has its biological components, but those components are not solely responsible for love—they do not give rise to love.

The evolutionary perspective Fisher advocates identifies all aspects of life as arising from biology and consequently, Fisher misinterprets the causal nature of the biological activity associated with love. In so doing, she has blinded herself to the possibility—indeed, we would claim, the very reality—that love gives rise to biology; not in the sense that love creates the biology, but in the sense that without love the biology would be meaningless and its activity dormant. There would be no racing heart or increased endorphins were it not for the special meaning that is assigned to a particular person and one's relationship to that person. Because Fisher's account fails to acknowledge this centrality of meaning, we find her biological explanation of love to be neither sufficient nor compelling.

Love Has No Meaning If It Is Determined by Evolutionary Forces

Fisher's endorsement of evolutionary theory negates a meaningful account of love. We propose that this meaninglessness occurs because, according to the evolutionary philosophy undergirding Fisher's account, persons are not directing their behavior, natural forces are. Consequently, feelings of love for another or behaving lovingly can be about as meaningful as a rock rolling down a hill. A rock rolling down a hill merely reacts to forces acting upon it (i.e., gravity). The rock does not decide to roll down the hill, nor can it choose to stop; its rolling and the direction that rolling takes are completely determined by the natural forces acting upon it. Hence, there can be no meaning attached to the rock's "behavior" because the rock has no ability to intervene or behave differently.

In a similar fashion, natural forces are thought to determine human behavior. Specifically, Fisher's account rests on the assumption that loving behavior is determined by natural selection. That is, because the evolutionary perspective views human beings as natural organisms that are essentially the same as other natural organisms (e.g., mammals, birds, insects, etc.), and because natural laws determine the actions of natural organisms, human beings are determined by natural laws. Accordingly, because natural selection is a natural law, human beings are determined by natural selection. As a result our behavior is not really our behavior. Rather, for Fisher, we, like the rock, are objects that can be moved and shaped according to natural pressures and forces that exist to progress the species. Hence, we love because love leads to mating, we mate because mating leads to offspring—the spread of our genetic material—and we care for our offspring to ensure the survival of our genes. This is the agenda of natural selection, and, as a natural law, natural selection *is* the ultimate cause of love and intimate relationships.

If, as Fisher's argument demands, we are *not* the arbiters of our own behaviors, then it becomes all too clear that our own behaviors are devoid of meaning. Sure, we may assign meaning to our relationships and loved ones. We may call them special or our reason for living. We may share rich cultural traditions with them, like marriage, where we express publicly our undying love. But through it all, it is natural selection, not our own will, which causes us to do those things. A groom may think he chooses his bride because he feels a meaningful connection to her, but according to this perspective, she is *really just* a satisfactory target for reproduction. That is, she is sufficiently young, healthy, and hardy to produce viable offspring and raise them to survive. The meaning in this marriage exists *only* as a function of the ever-present agenda of natural selection that governs behavior just as gravity governs the behavior of a rock rolling down a hill.

In light of this determinism, Fisher's claims regarding the influence of culture and free will sound hollow. Cultural forces and free will cannot "play a powerful role in directing behavior" in any genuine sense. They cannot ultimately "triumph over nature" because they too are the products of nature and are governed by natural law. That is, culture exists only because it facilitates specific human mating rituals that ensure genetic fitness and viable offspring. Similarly, free will is not free, as it too must fall under the reign of natural selection. Like the experience of love, culture and any feelings of free will are byproducts or manifestations of selection. Neither has causal power in and of itself, but like biological mechanisms, each ultimately serves as a tool to bring about evolutionary ends.

Because Fisher's argument denies culture, free will, and love any real status or influence and because her account renders irrelevant any meaning that we might attach to other people and our loving relationships, we cannot accept her explanation of love. We do agree that there are natural aspects to human beings and that humans share some biological commonality with other natural organisms, but we cannot agree that we are *merely* natural organisms. In the previous section we showed how the meaning we attach to our relationships actually gives rise to our biology, proving that, although love may have its biological components, it is more fundamentally relational. As a result, we contend that love is not under the governance of natural selection. If it were, why would we ever love people with whom we do not mate? Why would we care for children that share no biological make-up with us whatsoever?

From an evolutionary perspective, wherein we are merely natural organisms determined by natural selection, these questions are not easily answered. However, when we recognize that we are not merely natural organisms, but that also and more fundamentally, we are relational beings, the answers to these questions become clear. It is the meaning that we assign to a person and our willingness to commit ourselves to them that causes us to love our partner and care for our children, regardless of any evolutionary agenda. So, just as gravity may affect our bodies, but cannot affect our minds or our feelings, natural selection cannot affect the non-natural, non-biological activity of relational beings. When it comes to human relationships and love, natural selection simply is not relevant.

Human Beings Are Not Serially Monogamous

Fisher does not show serial monogamy to be the primary sexual strategy of human beings. Serial monogamy requires the detachment phase and, as we will show, the evidence she provides does not support her assertion regarding this phase of love. According to Fisher, monogamous relationships are inconsistent with evolutionary theory, as they do not allow for the widest spread of genetic material and progression of the species. Serial monogamy, however, allows for the increased genetic fitness and progression required by natural selection. To stay consistent with her evolutionary perspective then, Fisher asserts that serial monogamy is the primary sexual strategy for human beings. In order for serial monogamy to be *primary* however, detachment, as a necessary stage of serial monogamy, must be universal to the majority of human beings across relationships and cultures. If detachment is not universal, then serial monogamy cannot be primary, because it would mean that most couples do not transition out of the attachment stage.

Current marriage and divorce statistics do not reflect a universal detachment phase in the majority of intimate relationships. Consequently, there is no compelling reason to conclude that serial monogamy is the primary sexual strategy of human beings. It is our contention then, that Fisher's assertion is more an expression of her evolutionary bias (wherein serial monogamy is adaptive and monogamy is not) than an objective report of the evidence. Fisher's assertions regarding detachment, though consistent with the assumptions of evolutionary theory, simply are not supported by the evidence she provides.

Consider as an example her discussion regarding divorce. According to the most recent report of the United Nations, which investigated divorce rates in a sample of 36 countries, more couples stay together than divorce. Yet Fisher bases her discussion only on those individuals who do divorce. Conveniently, she skips right to this population, never indicating to the reader that this population itself is a very small subset of the population to which she refers. Remember, her claims of the universality of love (and its three stages) are thought by her to apply to *all* people in *all* cultures. However, the divorce rates in most countries are low, varying between .15 to 3.36 per 1,000 people. Even in the United States where divorce rates are among the highest in the world (4.95 per 1,000), the incidence of divorce is no higher than 40%. Mathematically speaking, her explanations and proposals regarding both the incidence of detachment and serial monogamy are only applicable to 40% of the people in this country and considerably fewer people in the rest of the world.

On this point alone, Fisher's explanatory justification loses much of its power. She seems less interested in understanding love and intimate relationships and more interested in supporting her evolutionary account. Unfortunately, this misdirected focus leads her to misrepresent the data on marriage and divorce. Consequently, she runs the risk of misleading the reader into believing that serial monogamy is the primary sexual strategy of human beings, when it clearly is not. Although we agree that detachment and serial monogamy occur, they are not universal experiences. They don't even capture the majority of human beings. A true account of love would be based on what most people do, which is marry and stay married.

Love as Meaningful Experience

At this point we must conclude that Fisher fails to illuminate the nature of romantic love. Her claim that love exists and is universal because it is the product of some universal force or law (i.e., natural selection) reduces love to meaningless biological activity that is always in the service of evolutionary ends. According to her account, vasopressin and endorphins replace intimacy and passion. She demeans our experience by equating it with the behavior of red foxes, elephants, and birds. She denies culture and free will any genuine status or influence. Last but not least, her account turns children and partners into tools of genetic proliferation, in whom we are invested only to secure the progress of the species.

Fisher's explanatory strategies and their consequences remove love from its context (i.e., the human realm) wherein it is experienced and is meaningful. Once removed from the human realm love no longer connects to human experience. In this transition, love loses the characteristics and qualities that comprise its very nature. Consequently, Fisher has to rely on badly fitted animal analogues (e.g., red foxes), flimsy correlational evidence, and even irrelevant statistics (e.g., divorce rates) to uphold an explanation that has become more important than what she is trying to explain. Fisher moves directly to an evolutionary/biological accounting of love, not because the evidence demands it, but because of her evolutionary assumptions about human life. In so doing, she disregards a number of other, equally feasible explanations that would adequately explain the data *and* preserve the rich meaning and culture of love and intimate relationships.

Paradoxically, in all her efforts to explain love, Fisher has essentially explained it away. However, the meaningful experience of love cannot be explained away. Love cannot be transformed into a principle or force in any meaningful way, and as we have argued, any effort to do so, changes it so fundamentally that it no longer connects to human experience. Hence, love must be understood in terms of love, an experience that is universal to being human. But it is not just the universality of love that makes it worthy of investigation. As discussed initially, love and intimate relationships are fundamental to human life. Love is universal because it defines us, because it is so important to us. If it were universally present, but unimportant, few if any would be concerned with it. But it is perhaps the most meaningful aspect of our lives. Given its centrality and the necessity of understanding it as it is experienced in the human realm, the meaningful experience of love must be fundamental.

Once the meaningful experience of love is understood as fundamental, the focus of investigation changes completely. The relationship and the feelings of the people involved become central to an understanding of love. Love remains full of possibility and cannot be captured by any singular account or explanation. Literature, art, music, and other expressions of love play an important role in understanding the full and rich meaning of this experience. For example, the phrase, "My whole world had been transformed. It had a new center and that center was Marilyn," is taken as the reality and is studied in terms of the meaning it expresses. In this quote, the man clearly feels changed by Marilyn so completely that she now has become the most important thing in his life. She seems to have created in him feelings of love so penetrating that he can do nothing but think of her. He does not conceive of Marilyn as a target for mating. She cannot be relegated to the status of an object to be used and then discarded after she fulfills her role in this evolutionary scheme. On the contrary, she is central to this man's world. She is more important to him than anything else. She is part of a relationship that is filled with passion, intimacy, and commitment, not because it satisfies some evolutionary goal, but because she, together with the man, created it and because they both care about it and each other.

CHALLENGE QUESTIONS

Is Love a Mechanism of Evolution?

1. Describe how evolutionary explanations have become so popular in psychological theory, both historically and logically. Why do you suppose this is an attractive thesis?
2. Why is it difficult for Fisher to account for culture as a separate influence if she endorses an evolutionary explanation of love? What effects follow from the assumption that human emotions and behavior are caused by our genes?
3. How do Reber and Beyers account for biological correlates without assuming a causal relationship? How might you explain other emotions, such as anger and depression, with the same thesis?
4. Research other aspects of evolutionary psychology. What strengths and weaknesses do you find in this research?

On the Internet ...

Mental Health Risk Factors for Adolescents

This collection of Web resources is part of the Adolescence Directory On-Line (ADOL), an electronic guide to information on adolescent issues provided by the Center for Adolescent Studies at Indiana University. It covers a great deal of topics, including abuse, conduct disorders, stress, and support.

`http://education.indiana.edu/cas/adol/mental.html`

American Psychological Association's Division 20, Adult Development and Aging

At this site Division 20, which is dedicated to studying the psychology of adult development and aging, provides links to research guides, laboratories, instructional resources, and other related areas.

`http://www.iog.wayne.edu/APADIV20/lowdiv20.htm`

Behavior Analysis Resources

Those who are interested in the behaviorist approach to human development should check out the links at this site.

`http://www.coedu.usf.edu/behavior/bares.htm`

The Jean Piaget Society: Society for the Study of Knowledge and Development

This is the home page of the Jean Piaget Society: Society for the Study of Knowledge and Development. From here you can link to information on the society, symposia, conferences, and publications, as well as links to related sites.

`http://www.sunnyhill.bc.ca/Lalonde/JPS/`

PART 3

Human Development

*T*he goal of developmental psychologists is to document the course of our physical, social, and intellectual changes over a life span. Considerable attention has been paid to the childhood part of that life span because this period of development seems to set the stage for later periods. Two potential influences on childhood are debated here: spanking and television.

- Does Spanking Children Lead Them to Become More Violent?

- Does Viewing Television Increase a Child's Aggression?

ISSUE 6

Does Spanking Children Lead Them to Become More Violent?

YES: Murray A. Straus, from *Beating the Devil Out of Them: Corporal Punishment in American Families and Its Effects on Children* (Lexington Books, 1994)

NO: John K. Rosemond, from *To Spank or Not to Spank: A Parent's Handbook* (Andrews & McMeel, 1994)

ISSUE SUMMARY

YES: Professor of sociology Murray A. Straus, citing several studies that show a link between childhood spanking and aggressive behavior in later life, argues that spanking teaches a child violence and that there are always nonaggressive alternatives to spanking.

NO: John K. Rosemond, a family psychologist, maintains that the research on spanking is politically skewed. Because the research makes no distinction between spanking and beating, he argues, it misrepresents loving parents who appropriately discipline their children.

In developmental psychology, there has always been a lot of discussion about the impact of early childhood events. Sigmund Freud would say that the lessons that you learn in the first few years set the pattern for the rest of your life. If that is true, then a heavy burden is placed upon the young and inexperienced parent. Even seasoned parents may feel the burden of shaping their children's futures. Make the wrong choices, say the wrong words, or use the wrong disciplinary technique, and parents fear that they may permanently damage the psychological well-being of their children.

Discipline is a special concern to most parents in this regard. Were you spanked as a child? Did you turn out okay? Will you spank your own children? Everyone seems to have an opinion about how people should discipline their children, from the family pediatrician to the children's grandparents. One concern is that spanking emotionally confuses children and teaches them that anger allows one to hit others, even loved ones. According to Murray A. Straus, the author of the first of the following selections, this is the conclusion that many children draw when their loving parents hit them in anger. If you were spanked as a child, do you remember being confused or believing that it was okay to hit others because your parents hit you? John K. Rosemond, the author of the second selection, is willing to bet that you do not.

In the following selection, Straus presents and then attempts to refute several myths about spanking that he believes allows parents to convince themselves that spanking is an acceptable form of punishment. He argues that spanking is not effective, that it results in violent teenage and adult behavior, and that it leads to child abuse. He asserts that spanking should never, under any circumstances, be permitted.

Rosemond, on the other hand, contends that the evidence against spanking is vastly overrated. He maintains that studies on spanking do not distinguish between spanking and beating and, thus, overestimate the harmful effects of spanking. By taking spanking out of context, he says, researchers like Straus mislead the public into thinking that spanking makes children grow up to be violent toward their spouses and aggressive toward their peers. Rosemond argues that such information has led to a dangerous and intrusive campaign to make spanking illegal.

POINT

- Research studies show that spanking children leads to violent behavior later in life.

- Spanking weakens the bond between parent and child, causing a decreased sense of personal initiative over self-monitoring behavior.

- Spanking, like verbal abuse, should never be considered an acceptable form of punishment.

- Because the myths about spanking are so strongly held in American culture, laws protecting children from this abuse will never be passed.

COUNTERPOINT

- Methodological flaws, such as failing to distinguish spanking from beating and studying populations that are already at risk, hurts the validity of spanking research.

- Overall parenting style, rather than the use of spanking, determines an individual child's initiative.

- Spanking coupled with nurturing and other disciplinary techniques improves children's behavior.

- Legislation aimed at prohibiting spanking is intrusive and politically motivated. It has not been shown to be in the best interest of children.

Murray A. Straus  **YES**

Ten Myths That Perpetuate
Corporal Punishment

[H]itting children is legal in every state of the United States and 84 percent of a survey of Americans agreed that it is sometimes necessary to give a child a good hard spanking.... [A]lmost all parents of toddlers act on these beliefs. Study after study shows that almost 100 percent of parents with toddlers hit their children. There are many reasons for the strong support of spanking. Most of them are myths.

Myth 1: Spanking Works Better

There has been a huge amount of research on the effectiveness of corporal punishment of animals, but remarkably little on the effectiveness of spanking children. That may be because almost no one, including psychologists, feels a need to study it because it is assumed that spanking is effective. In fact, what little research there is on the effectiveness of corporal punishment of children agrees with the research on animals. Studies of both animals and children show that punishment is *not* more effective than other methods of teaching and controlling behavior. Some studies show it is less effective.

Ellen Cohn and I asked 270 students at two New England colleges to tell us about the year they experienced the most corporal punishment. Their average age that year was eight, and they recalled having been hit an average of six times that year. We also asked them about the percent of the time they thought that the corporal punishment was effective. It averaged a little more than half of the times (53 percent). Of course, 53 percent also means that corporal punishment was *not* perceived as effective about half the time it was used.

LaVoie (1974) compared the use of a loud noise (in place of corporal punishment) with withdrawal of affection and verbal explanation in a study of first- and second-grade children. He wanted to find out which was more effective in getting the children to stop touching certain prohibited toys. Although the loud noise was more effective initially, there was no difference over a longer period of time. Just explaining was as effective as the other methods.

A problem with LaVoie's study is that it used a loud noise rather than actual corporal punishment. That problem does not apply to an experiment by Day and Roberts (1983). They studied three-year-old children who had been given "time out" (sitting in a corner). Half of the mothers were assigned to use spanking as the mode of correction if their child did not comply and left the corner. The other half put their non-complying child behind a low plywood barrier and physically enforced the child staying there. Keeping the child behind the barrier was just as effective as the spanking in correcting the misbehavior that led to the time out.

A study by Larzelere (in press) also found that a combination of *non-*corporal punishment and reasoning was as effective as corporal punishment and reasoning in correcting disobedience.

Crozier and Katz (1979), Patterson (1982), and Webster-Stratton et al. (1988, 1990) all studied children with serious conduct problems. Part of the treatment used in all three experiments was to get parents to stop spanking. In all three, the behavior of the children improved after spanking ended. Of course, many other things in addition to no spanking were part of the intervention. But, as you will see, parents who on their own accord do not spank also do many other things to manage their children's behavior. It is these other things, such as setting clear standards for what is expected, providing lots of love and affection, explaining things to the child, and recognizing and rewarding good behavior, that account for why children of non-spanking parents tend to be easy to manage and well-behaved. What about parents who do these things and also spank? Their children also tend to be well-behaved, but it is illogical to attribute that to spanking since the same or better results are achieved without spanking, and also without adverse side effects.

Such experiments are extremely important, but more experiments are needed to really understand what is going on when parents spank. Still, what Day and Roberts found can be observed in almost any household. Let's look at two examples.

In a typical American family there are many instances when a parent might say, "Mary! You did that again! I'm going to have to send you to your room again." This is just one example of a non-spanking method that did *not* work.

The second example is similar: A parent might say, "Mary! You did that again! I'm going to have to spank you again." This is an example of spanking that did *not* work.

The difference between these two examples is that when spanking does not work, parents tend to forget the incident because it contradicts the almost-universal American belief that spanking is something that works when all else fails. On the other hand, they tend to remember when a *non*-spanking method did not work. The reality is that nothing works all the time with a toddler. Parents think that spanking is a magic charm that will cure the child's misbehavior. It is not. There is no magic charm. It takes many interactions and many repetitions to bring up children. Some things work better with some children than with others.

Parents who favor spanking can turn this around and ask, If spanking doesn't work any better, isn't that the same as saying that it works just as well? So what's wrong with a quick slap on the wrist or bottom? There are at least three things that are wrong:

- Spanking becomes less and less effective over time and when children get bigger, it becomes difficult or impossible.
- For some children, the lessons learned through spanking include the idea that they only need to be good if Mommy or Daddy is watching or will know about it.
- ... [T]here are a number of very harmful side effects, such as a greater chance that the child will grow up to be depressed or violent. Parents don't perceive these side effects because they usually show up only in the long run.

Myth 2: Spanking Is Needed as a Last Resort

Even parents and social scientists who are opposed to spanking tend to think that it may be needed when all else fails. There is no scientific evidence supporting this belief, however. It is a myth that grows out of our cultural and psychological commitment to corporal punishment. You can prove this to yourself by a simple exercise with two other people. Each of the three should, in turn, think of the most extreme situation where spanking is necessary. The other two should try to think of alternatives. Experience has shown that it is very difficult to come up with a situation for which the alternatives are not as good as spanking. In fact, they are usually better.

Take the example of a child running out into the street. Almost everyone thinks that spanking is appropriate then because of the extreme danger. Although spanking in that situation may help *parents* relieve their own tension and anxiety, it is not necessary or appropriate for teaching the child. It is not necessary because spanking does not work better than other methods, and it is not appropriate because of the harmful side effects of spanking. The only physical force needed is to pick up the child and get him or her out of danger, and, while hugging the child, explain the danger.

Ironically, if spanking is to be done at all, the "last resort" may be the worst. The problem is that parents are usually very angry by that time and act impulsively. Because of their anger, if the child rebels and calls the parent a name or kicks the parent, the episode can escalate into physical abuse. Indeed, most episodes of physical abuse started as physical punishment and got out of hand (see Kadushin and Martin, 1981). Of course, the reverse is not true, that is, most instances of spanking do not escalate into abuse. Still, the danger of abuse is there, and so is the risk of psychological harm.

The second problem with spanking as a last resort is that, in addition to teaching that hitting is the way to correct wrongs, hitting a child impulsively teaches another incorrect lesson—that being extremely angry justifies hitting.

Myth 3: Spanking Is Harmless

When someone says, I was spanked and I'm OK, he or she is arguing that spanking does no harm. This is contrary to almost all the available research. One reason the harmful effects are ignored is because many of us (including those of us who are social scientists) are reluctant to admit that their own parents did something wrong and even more reluctant to admit that we have been doing something wrong with our own children. But the most important reason may be that it is difficult to see the harm. Most of the harmful effects do not become visible right away, often not for years. In addition, only a relatively small percentage of spanked children experience obviously harmful effects....

Another argument in defense of spanking is that it is not harmful if the parents are loving and explain why they are spanking. The research does show that the harmful effects of spanking are reduced if it is done by loving parents who explain their actions. However, ... a study by Larzelere (1986) shows that although the harmful effects are reduced, they are not eliminated. The ... harmful side effects include an increased risk of delinquency as a child and crime as an adult, wife beating, depression, masochistic sex, and lowered earnings.

In addition to having harmful psychological effects on children, hitting children also makes life more difficult for parents. Hitting a child to stop misbehavior may be the easy way in the short run, but in the slightly longer run, it makes the job of being a parent more difficult. This is because spanking reduces the ability of parents to influence their children, especially in adolescence when they are too big to control by physical force. Children are more likely to do what the parents want if there is a strong bond of affection with the parent. In short, being able to influence a child depends in considerable part on the bond between parent and child (Hirschi, 1969). An experiment by Redd, Morris, and Martin (1975) shows that children tend to avoid caretaking adults who use punishment. In the natural setting, of course, there are many things that tie children to their parents. I suggest that each spanking chips away at the bond between parent and child....

Contrary to the "spoiled child" myth, children of non-spanking parents are likely to be easier to manage and better behaved than the children of parents who spank. This is partly because they tend to control their own behavior on the basis of what their own conscience tells them is right and wrong rather than to avoid being hit. This is ironic because almost everyone thinks that spanking "when necessary" makes for better behavior.

Myth 4: One or Two Times Won't Cause Any Damage

The evidence in this book indicates that the greatest risk of harmful effects occurs when spanking is very frequent. However, that does not necessarily mean that spanking just once or twice is harmless. Unfortunately, the connection between spanking once or twice and psychological damage has not been addressed by most of the available research. This is because the studies seem to be based on this myth. They generally cluster children into "low" and "high" groups in terms of the frequency they were hit. This prevents the "once or twice is harmless" myth from being tested scientifically because the low group may include parents who spank once a year or as often as once a month. The few studies that did classify children according to the number of times they were hit by their parents ... show that even one or two instances of corporal punishment are associated with a slightly higher probability of later physically abusing your own child, slightly more depressive symptoms, and a greater probability of violence and other crime later in life. The increase in these harmful side effects when parents use only moderate corporal punishment (hit only occasionally) may be small, but why run even that small risk when the evidence shows that corporal punishment is no more effective than other forms of discipline in the short run, and less effective in the long run.

Myth 5: Parents Can't Stop Without Training

Although everyone can use additional skills in child management, there is no evidence that it takes some extraordinary training to be able to stop spanking. The most basic step in eliminating corporal punishment is for parent educators, psychologists, and pediatricians to make a simple and unambiguous statement that hitting a child is wrong and that a child *never*, ever, under any circumstances except literal physical self-defense, should be hit.

That idea has been rejected almost without exception everytime I suggest it to parent educators or social scientists. They believe it would turn off parents and it could even be harmful because parents don't know what else to do. I think that belief is an unconscious defense of corporal punishment. I say that because I have never heard a parent educator say that before we can tell parents to never *verbally* attack a child, parents need training in alternatives. Some do need training, but everyone agrees that parents who use *psychological* pain as a method of discipline, such as insulting or demeaning, the child, should stop immediately. But when it comes to causing *physical* pain by spanking, all but a small minority of parent educators say that before parents are told to stop spanking, they need to learn alternative modes of discipline. I believe they should come right out, as they do for verbal attacks, and say without qualification that a child should *never* be hit....

This can be illustrated by looking at one situation that almost everyone thinks calls for spanking: when a toddler who runs out into the street. A typical parent will scream in terror, rush out and grab the child, and run to safety, telling the child, No! No! and explaining the danger—all of this accompanied by one or more slaps to the legs or behind.

The same sequence is as effective or more effective *without the spanking*. The spanking is not needed because even tiny children can sense the terror in the parent and understand, No! No! Newborn infants can tell the difference between when a mother is relaxed and when she is tense (Stern, 1977). Nevertheless, the fact that a child understands that something is wrong does not guarantee never again running into the street; just as spanking does not guarantee the child will not run into the street again....

Of course, when the child misbehaves again, most spanking parents do more than just repeat the spanking or spank harder. They usually also do things such as explain the danger to the child before letting the child go out again or warn the child that if it happens again, he or she will have to stay in the house for the afternoon, and so on. The irony is that when the child finally does learn, the parent attributes the success to the spanking, not the explanation.

Myth 6: If You Don't Spank, Your Children Will Be Spoiled or Run Wild

It is true that some non-spanked children run wild. But when that happens it is not because the parent didn't spank. It is because some parents think the alternative to spanking is to ignore a child's misbehavior or to replace spanking with verbal attacks such as, Only a dummy like you can't learn to keep your toys where I won't trip over them. The best alternative is to take firm action to correct the misbehavior without hitting. Firmly condemning what the child has done and explaining why it is wrong are usually enough. When they are not, there are a host of other things to do, such as requiring a time out or depriving the child of a privilege, neither of which involves hitting the child.

Suppose the child hits another child. Parents need to express outrage at this or the child may think it is acceptable behavior. The expression of outrage and a clear statement explaining why the child should never hit another person, except in self-defense, will do the trick in most cases. That does not mean one such warning will do the trick, any more than a single spanking will do the trick. It takes most children a while to learn such things, whatever methods the parents use.

The importance of how parents go about teaching children is clear from a classic study of American parenting—*Patterns of Child Rearing* by Sears, Maccoby, and Levin (1957). This study found two actions by parents that are linked to a high level of aggression by the child: permissiveness of the child's aggression, namely ignoring it when the child hits them or another child, and spanking to correct misbehavior. The most aggressive children... are children of parents who permitted aggression by the child and who also hit them for a variety of misbehavior. The least aggressive children are... children of parents who clearly condemned acts of aggression and who, by not spanking, acted in a way that demonstrated the principle that hitting is wrong.

There are other reasons why, on the average, the children of parents who do not spank are better behaved than children of parents who spank:

- Non-spanking parents pay more attention to their children's behavior, both good and bad, than parents who spank. Consequently, they are more likely to reward good behavior and less likely to ignore misbehavior.

- Their children have fewer opportunities to get into trouble because they are more likely to child-proof the home. For older children, they have clear rules about where they can go and who they can be with.
- Non-spanking parents tend to do more explaining and reasoning. This teaches the child how to use these essential tools to monitor his or her own behavior, whereas children who are spanked get less training in thinking things through.
- Non-spanking parents treat the child in ways that tend to bond the child to them and avoid acts that weaken the bond. They tend to use more rewards for good behavior, greater warmth and affection, and fewer verbal assaults on the child (see Myth 9). By not spanking, they avoid anger and resentment over spanking. When there is a strong bond, children identify with the parent and want to avoid doing things the parent says are wrong. The child develops a conscience and lets that direct his or her behavior. That is exactly what Sears et al. found.

Myth 7: Parents Spank Rarely or Only for Serious Problems

Contrary to this myth, parents who spank tend to use this method of discipline for almost any misbehavior. Many do not even give the child a warning. They spank before trying other things. Some advocates of spanking even recommend this. At any supermarket or other public place, you can see examples of a child doing something wrong, such as taking a can of food off the shelf. The parent then slaps the child's hand and puts back the can, sometimes without saying a word to the child. John Rosemond, the author of *Parent Power* (1981), says, "For me, spanking is a first resort. I seldom spank, but when I decide . . . I do it, and that's the end of it."

The high frequency of spanking also shows up among the parents [studied]. The typical parent of a toddler told us of about 15 instances in which he or she had hit the child during the previous 12 months. That is surely a minimum estimate because spanking a child is generally such a routine and unremarkable event that most instances are forgotten. Other studies, such as Newson and Newson (1963), report much more chronic hitting of children. My tabulations for mothers of three- to five-year-old children in the National Longitudinal Study of Youth found that almost two-thirds hit their children during the week of the interview, and they did it more then three times in just that one week. As high as that figure may seem, I think that daily spanking is not at all uncommon. It has not been documented because the parents who do it usually don't realize how often they are hitting their children.

Myth 8: By the Time a Child Is a Teenager, Parents Have Stopped

As we have seen, parents of children in their early teens are also heavy users of corporal punishment, although at that age it is more likely to be a slap on the face than on the behind.... [M]ore than half of the parents of 13- to 14-year-old children in our two national surveys hit their children in the previous 12 months. The percentage drops each year as children get older, but even at age 17, one out of five parents is still hitting. To make matters worse, these are minimum estimates.

Of the parents of teenagers who told us about using corporal punishment, 84 percent did it more than once in the previous 12 months. For boys, the average was seven times and for girls, five times. These are minimum figures because we interviewed the mother in half the families and the father in the other half. The number of times would be greater if we had information on what the parent who was not interviewed did.

Myth 9: If Parents Don't Spank, They Will Verbally Abuse Their Child

The scientific evidence is exactly the opposite. Among the nationally representative samples of parents [surveyed], those who did the least spanking also engaged in the least verbal aggression.

It must be pointed out that non-spanking parents are an exceptional minority. They are defying the cultural prescription that says a good parent should spank if necessary. The depth of their involvement with their children probably results from the same underlying characteristics that led them to reject spanking. There is a danger that if more ordinary parents are told to never spank, they might replace spanking by ignoring misbehavior or by verbal attacks. Consequently, a campaign to end spanking must also stress the importance of avoiding verbal attacks as well as physical attacks, and also the importance of paying attention to misbehavior.

Myth 10: It Is Unrealistic to Expect Parents to Never Spank

It is no more unrealistic to expect parents to never hit a child than to expect that husbands should never hit their wives, or that no one should go through a stop sign, or that a supervisor should never hit an employee. Despite the legal prohibition, some husbands hit their wives, just as some drivers go through stop signs, and a supervisor occasionally may hit an employee.

If we were to prohibit spanking, as is the law in Sweden (see Deley, 1988; and Haeuser, 1990), there still would be parents who would continue to spank. But that is not a reason to avoid passing such a law here. Some people kill even though murder has been a crime since the dawn of history. Some husbands continue to hit their wives even though it has been more than a century since the courts stopped recognizing the common law right of a husband to "physically chastise an errant wife" (Calvert, 1974).

A law prohibiting spanking is unrealistic only because spanking is such an accepted part of American culture. That also was true of smoking. Yet in less than a generation we have made tremendous progress toward eliminating smoking. We can make similar progress toward eliminating spanking by showing parents that spanking is dangerous, that their children will be easier to bring up if they do not spank, and by clearly saying that a child should *never,* under any circumstances, be spanked.

John K. Rosemond

To Spare or Not to Spare

In the spring of 1993, in a hotel room somewhere in America and desperate for the sound of a human voice, I turned on the television. Up popped Oprah, who was orchestrating a politically correct hoot 'n' holler over spanking. I know how these things work because I've been on several such free-for-alls (never again, I assure you). The producer, acting on behalf of the host, assembles a panel of people who are expected, perhaps even coached, to express a certain opinion. The illusion of "balance" is quickly dispelled as one realizes the host has an agenda. In this case, Ms. Winfrey's clearly was to promote to public acceptance the idea that the act of spanking is, without exception, child abuse and should be made illegal. That's right, as in *against the law!*

At one point in this ersatz discussion, Oprah approached a man in the audience whom I immediately pegged as a "plant." This very professional-looking gentleman, in response to a rogue's gallery of parents who had all confessed to spanking their children (and their intention to continue doing so), reeled off something to the effect that spankings instill a violent bent into the psyches of children and, furthermore, amount to a mixed message. The fact that parents can hit a child, yet the child cannot hit them back, he said, is horribly confusing and destructive to self-esteem. The audience roared on cue, Oprah smiled knowingly, and all was well in Talk Show Land.

With this scene fresh in mind, I subsequently asked the 250 members of an audience in Pueblo, Colorado, "Please raise a hand if you were spanked as a child." Close to 250 hands went up. "Now," I continued, "keep your hand up if you remember that as a child you were confused over or resented the fact that although your parents felt free to spank you, you were not allowed to hit them." Immediately, all hands went down.

I replicated this demonstration with several other audiences that same spring. The results were always the same. I occasionally tacked on the request that those who were spanked as kids raise their hands again if they ever recall feeling that the fact their parents spanked them meant that hitting someone in anything other than self-defense was okay. Never once did anyone raise a hand. Either the people who attend my presentations are atypical, or the politically correct rhetoric concerning the effects of spanking on children is dead wrong.

I've seen the research on spanking. In fact, this being a relatively fascinating topic, I dare say I've kept closely abreast of the research. Some of it paints an ominous picture: A person who was spanked as a child is more likely to commit violent crimes as an adult, be physically abusive toward his or her spouse and children, suffer from low self-esteem... in short, become a misfit in every possible sense.

One of the most outspoken, oft-quoted critics of spanking is sociologist Murray Straus of the University of New Hampshire Family Research Laboratory. Straus's opinions have significantly informed and shaped the rhetoric of the antispanking movement. In fact, it can legitimately be said that he is its "guru."

In a 1994 article (which appears in *Debating Children's Lives,* Mason and Gambrill, eds., Sage Publications), Dr. Straus asserts that "research showing the harmful effects of spanking is one of the best-kept secrets of American child psychology" because it implies that "almost all American parents are guilty of child abuse, *including those who write books of advice for parents* [emphasis mine, and yes, I stand accused]."

Citing a study which found that nearly all parents of toddlers spank, more than half of parents of teens spank, and 41 percent of parents feel a spanking is appropriate in the case of a child hitting another child, Straus says these parents send their children a double message: Hitting another person is bad, but it is not bad to hit someone who's done something bad. His conclusion: "Corporal punishment therefore teaches the morality of hitting."

Another aspect of spanking's "hidden curriculum," as Straus calls the supposedly irrevocable lessons he sees embedded in the act of swatting a child's rear end, is the message "those who love you, hit you." Spankings also teach, says Straus, that it is "morally acceptable to hit those you love when they 'do wrong.'" This aspect of the "hidden curriculum" is "almost a recipe for violence between spouses later in life."

After citing the results of surveys which supposedly demonstrate that spankings place children at greater risk for eventual criminal behavior, alcoholism, suicide, drug use, and lower occupational achievement, Straus comes to his point, which is a call for laws prohibiting the spanking of children *under any circumstances.* Straus firmly believes that antispanking laws will result in a "healthier, less violent, wealthier" society. He points to the fact that spanking has been against the law in Sweden since 1979. (For quite some time, Sweden has been plagued with alarmingly high rates of alcoholism, divorce, and illegitimacy. These longstanding crises, which are a direct result of Sweden's socialist politics, have contributed greatly to unusually high levels of stress in Swedish families—many of which are single-parent. As a result, Sweden's child abuse rate was—and continues to be—relatively high, prompting passage of an antispanking law which has not been shown to have reduced child abuse one iota.)

Straus proposes, however, that parents who violate these proposed laws should *not* be punished. Rather, as is the case in Sweden, the fact that they spank their children should be taken as a sign they need help, and the help should be provided. In fact, the "help" Straus refers to amounts to forced intervention into the family on the part of the state. In the case of parents who refuse this "help," the state will then be free to take clearly punitive measures, all under the guise of protecting the children, including removing them from the home, possibly permanently.

Straus's research and conclusions are full of gaping holes:

• First, his studies fail to demonstrate that spankings per se cause any problems—psychological, behavioral, or otherwise. His conclusions are based in large part on data collected from adults who report having been spanked *as teenagers.* Straus claims to have discovered that the more frequently a person was spanked as a teen, the more likely it is that as an adult that person will assault his wife, abuse his or her children, use alcohol to problematic excess, and think about committing suicide. But the mere fact that parents are spanking a teenager, and frequently at that, suggests that the teen's behavior may already be antisocial. At the very least, it speaks of serious family problems. In other words, rather than proving a link between spanking and later antisocial behavior, Straus simply demonstrates what common sense will tell us: that spankings at this age are a red flag indicating that serious problems already exist in the teen's life—in other words, that he or she is "at risk." To extend this line of thinking: We might also discover that in addition to being frequently spanked as teens, lots of criminals, wife beaters, etc., cannot remember ever being hugged or kissed or told they were loved by their parents. In that case, what "caused" their later antisocial behavior? Being spanked as children? Being starved of affection? We'll never know. All we know is that these individuals didn't have happy childhoods and that an unhappy childhood is predictive of later problems. Common sense.

• A second major problem with Straus's conclusions is that he fails—as is the case with all of the research I've ever seen that reaches blanket antispanking conclusions—to distinguish between a *beating* and a *spanking.* In effect, Straus and other antispankers feel that such a distinction does not exist. In their view, the moment a parent strikes a child—regardless of where on the child's body the strike lands, regardless of the force behind the strike, regardless of whether the parent uses a hand or some other implement, such as a belt—the parent has committed child abuse. Period. As a result of Straus's unwillingness to distinguish between a beating and a spanking . . . , his results are skewed to the negative by the life histories of people who, as children, suffered unspeakable abuse. No doubt about it, if you're beaten on as a child, you're more likely, as an adult, to pass it on. This, too, is common sense.

• Straus's spanking-leads-to-wife-beating hypothesis is contradicted by the fact that whereas the overwhelming majority of males in my generation were spanked as children, the number who beat their wives is extremely small, albeit problematic. This is yet another example of Straus's overall tendency to oversimplify extremely complex social situations, a trait that is hardly conducive to conducting worthwhile sociological study.

• Straus cannot even come close to proving his claim that spanking's "hidden curriculum" teaches children that "those who love you, hit you" and that violence is a just response to a maddening social situation. This is rhetoric, pure and simple. It is, however, emotionally seductive (which is, after all, the point of rhetoric), but in the final analysis it is nothing more than undiluted psychobabble—a construction of language, not of fact.

• Straus and other antispankers frequently argue that parents always have options other than to spank. That goes without saying, but again, the existence of other options doesn't prove that spanking is abusive or even ineffective. The question is whether any of the options, in any given situation, would be as effective as a spanking or in combination *with* a spanking. Psychologist Robert Larzelere, director of research at a residential treatment facility for children and youth and an adjunct faculty member of the University of Iowa, has found that the effectiveness of two frequently mentioned disciplinary options—verbal reprimand and time-out—actually *improves* in combination with a mild spanking, especially with children between the ages of two and six. This suggests, says Larzelere, that parents who enhance their discipline with occasional *mild* spankings during their children's earlier years may have better-behaved teens. That is certainly consistent with my own observations.

• Straus also makes the mistake of taking spanking out of context of a parent's total disciplinary style. A very well-known study which sought to determine the outcomes of various parenting styles found that children of *authoritative* parents—characterized by firm control and high nurturance—were more socially responsible and exercised greater individual initiative than children of either permissive (low control, high nurturance) or authoritarian (excessive control, low nurturance) parents. *Authoritative* parents, furthermore, were generally willing to occasionally spank. The conclusion reached was that spanking per se was not harmful, but rather that the *total pattern* of parental behavior was of utmost importance in determining the effectiveness of any disciplinary method, including spanking.

Having been trained in the scientific method, Straus is well aware that his research proves nothing. The fact that he pretends it does reveals the lack of objectivity he brings to this issue. In further fact, it suggests that Straus (and this is a problem common to antispanking "research") isn't doing research at all. He's attempting to promote a point of view. In effect, Straus is cloaking a propaganda effort in the trappings of "science."

In an interview with the *Philadelphia Inquirer* (November 1993), Straus identifies several "myths" concerning spanking, including: *I was spanked and I'm okay.* After pointing out that a *small* percentage of spanked children experience harmful effects, he asks, "Why chance it?" Again, Straus is wrong. It is *not* a myth that the overwhelming majority of people who were spanked as kids are okay as adults. In fact, he disproves his own contention by admitting that the number who do not turn out okay is small. (Keep in mind that Straus does not distinguish between a beating and a spanking. Therefore, it's probably correct to assume that the small percentage of children he refers to as being harmed come primarily from the ranks of those who were beaten.) To cite my personal example, I was spanked as a kid. I'm comfortable with myself, enjoy positive relations with my wife, children, and friends, and am satisfyingly productive. (Straus might say, however, that the fact I spanked my children proves I'm not okay at all.) In fact, I was often spanked with a belt. So was my wife: We're both okay. We spanked both of our children (albeit never with anything other than our hands), and the evidence is overwhelmingly in favor of concluding that both of our kids, as young adults, are very okay. The same can be said for the vast majority of people who were spanked as children. Straus asks, "Why chance it?" I ask, if the risk is—by his own admission—small, and the connection between being spanked and developing later problems is tenuous, and we already have laws concerning the blatant abuse of children, why do we need a law against spanking? Straus's argument here is akin to proposing that since a small number of people die during heart transplants, heart transplants should be made illegal.

Most people would, no doubt, agree that certain instances of parents striking children are, indeed, abusive. Likewise, verbal reprimands can be abusive. According to the "logic" of the antispanking argument, in the interest of not "chancing it," we should ban the use of all "negative language" when addressing children. Or, since confining a child to his room may put the child at greater risk for claustrophobia, parents should be prohibited, by law, from exercising this "more risky" form of discipline. To some degree—at least at present—these scenarios are nothing more than absurd parodies of the antispanking mentality. I for one, however, am becoming increasingly convinced that we're talking about people who, if given an inch in the social policy realm, will want a mile. These are, I fear, social engineers of the worst kind, itching to impose their influence upon the American family.

According to Straus and his cohorts in the antispanking movement, slapping a child's rear end is abuse. Only the enlightened few see through the wall of denial American parents—with the assistance of many child-rearing authorities—have erected to shield themselves from this national disgrace. Since the rest of us are unwilling to admit the error of our ways (or our advice!), the only option is to pass laws which will turn the average parent into a criminal. Not to worry, however, because offending parents won't be punished. They will be given "help." And who, pray tell, will provide this help? Why "helping professionals," of course. I think it's safe to assume that these individuals, despite their altruistic mission, will expect to be compensated for their services.

The possibility of such legislation raises a host of very conceivable possibilities, none of which is consistent with democratic principles or the privacy and stability of families. I can envision, for example, "family living education" classes in schools which would have the intended effect of encouraging children to report instances of having been "mis-parented," including having been spanked. At present, there is hardly an elementary school counselor in America who has not had a child complain that a mild spanking from his or her parents was, in the child's immature mind, abusive. Imagine the number of children who will line up outside the offices of school counselors around the country if the day comes that even a mild a spanking is, by legal definition, abuse.

Along these lines, the National Committee to Prevent Child Abuse recently published (with funds from Kmart Corporation) a Spider-Man comic book in which Spider-Man helps a father see that one reason his son is getting into fights at school is because the boy is receiving spankings at home. On page 5, Spider-Man tells the youngster that any time he is "hit" he should tell a grown-up, and keep on telling grown-ups until he finds someone who will listen and do something about it. On page 6, a spanking from a parent is equated with hitting.

In a letter to me, Richard Wexler, author of *Wounded Innocents* (Prometheus Books, 1990), had this to say about Spider-Man's message:

> Now imagine this scenario: A child gets a spanking and, following Spider-Man's advice, tells his teacher he's been "hit" by his parent. The teacher is required to report any suspicion of "child abuse." She makes such a report and a caseworker is sent to the home to investigate.... At a minimum, the child is in for a traumatic interrogation and, quite possibly, a strip-search as the worker looks for bruises. At worst, the worker will remove the child [from the home] on the spot.

By the time the book you hold in your hands is published, NCPCA's Spider-Man comic will have been distributed to thousands of children in public schools across America and discussed in many a classroom.

Amazingly enough, NCPCA denies that one of the intents of the comic is to equate spanking with abuse. During an April 1994 phone conversation and in a subsequent letter, Ann Cohn Donnelly, NCPCA's executive director, assured me they have no official position favoring anti-spanking legislation and do not feel that spankings per se are abusive. When I pointed out that their Spider-Man comic not only equates being spanked by parents with being "hit" by peers or teachers and suggests that children who are spanked should report their parents to authorities, Donnelly replied that "some people might interpret it that way" but denied that the comic was meant to imply that any and all spankings administered by parents are inappropriate. Donnelly was being evasive. The comic's introduction, written by her and addressed to children, reads:

> The stories you are about to read are about hitting and why we believe that people are not for hitting—and children are people, too. The stories are about children who are being hit by adults they know or by other children. They tell you what to do if someone is hitting you. Perhaps you or someone you know has been the object of someone else's violence....

Nowhere does the comic differentiate between being slapped in the face by, say, a teacher and being spanked on the buttocks by a parent. Quite the contrary, they are both examples of "hitting." In either case, says NCPCA, the child in question should tell adults until one listens. Regardless of Donnelly's disclaimer, the message to children reading the comic is clear: If your parents spank you, you should report them to other adult authority figures.

According to Richard Wexler, NCPCA has consistently refused to distinguish between physical abuse and corporal punishment and has gone on record as opposing any effort to do so. According to NCPCA, any statement that might be construed as condoning spanking "doesn't belong in a child abuse prevention presentation."

In 1990, NCPCA published a brochure entitled "How to Teach Your Children Discipline." It states that spanking is not a useful approach to discipline because it "is used to directly control children's behavior," teaches children "to solve problems by hitting others," and teaches children "to be afraid of the adult in charge." The brochure also implies that spankings are violent acts of "lashing out" by parents who are out of control.

Strictly speaking, Ann Cohn Donnelly is correct. NCPCA has never *explicitly* stated that spankings and child abuse are one and the same, but it is equally true that they have never taken any pains to distinguish between spankings and behaviors which are clearly abusive, such as slapping, punching, kicking, etc. Furthermore, as Richard Wexler points out, they refuse to do so, citing as rationale the sort of "data" generated by Murray Straus and like-minded ideologues. NCPCA's position statement on physical punishment, adopted May 1989, reads:

> Although physical punishment of children is prevalent in the United States, numerous studies have demonstrated that hitting, spanking, slapping, and other forms of physical punishment are harmful methods of changing children's behavior....

Ignoring for the moment the fact that this statement is not true, the tone and content of NCPCA's propaganda clearly leads to the conclusion that spanking a child on the buttocks is in the final analysis no different from slapping the child in the face.

Donnelly also told me that she didn't think antispanking legislation would ever fly in the United States because it would be regarded as too intrusive. That's true, but again, she's being disingenuous. At the present time, NCPCA knows that it would be political suicide for any legislator, state or national, to sponsor a law *specifically prohibiting parental spanking*. The prohibition, should it ever come, will more likely be the result of a judicial ruling rather than a legislative act. A group calling itself The National Task Force for Children's Constitutional Rights (NTFCCR), whose advisory board consists of a number of prominent individuals from the fields of law, psychology, medicine, and family social work, believes that the best way to protect children from mistreatment within their own families is through an amendment to the Constitution of the United States. The proposed wording of this amendment would open a judicial Pandora's box that could well lead to antispanking rulings in the courts:

> Section 1
> All citizens of the United States who are fifteen years of age or younger shall enjoy the right to live in a home that is safe and healthy... and the right to the care of a loving family or a substitute thereof....

One of NTFCCR's cofounders, Connecticut Superior Court Judge Charles D. Gill, gives approximately fifty speeches a year in which he issues the clarion call for a children's rights movement to be modeled on the women's movement. In a 1991 article for the *Ohio Northern University Law Review*, Gill equates a Children's Rights Amendment with the Equal Rights Amendment. Conceding that ERA was defeated, he notes that "nearly half of our states have enacted an Equal Rights Amendment" and "nearly all state legislatures have passed legislation that alters the status of women."

In other words, Gill is saying that while a Children's Rights Amendment to the Constitution might not fly at present, it might be possible to galvanize enough public support behind such a concept to implement its equivalent on a state-by-state basis. If such legislation is eventually enacted, it would only be a matter of time before an attorney acting on behalf of a child would file a suit asserting that a parent who spanks is failing to provide a "safe, healthy, and loving" environment, thus violating the child's protected rights. If a judge concurred, a de facto law prohibiting parental spanking would be on the books.

Support for a Children's Rights Amendment is growing. In 1991, the National Committee for the Rights of the Child (NCRC) was formed in Washington, D.C. According to Judge Gill, dozens of national groups, representing millions of Americans, met to initiate "The Next Great Movement in America."

The United Nations is even in on the act. In 1989, the UN Convention on the Rights of the Child was unanimously adopted. Article 19 of its charter states: "Parties shall take all appropriate legislative, administrative, social and educational measures to protect the child from all forms of physical or mental violence, injury or abuse ... while in the care of parents, legal guardians or any other person who has the care of the child." While this does not specifically define spanking as "physical violence," the intent of the framers is to include parental spanking in that rather broad category (Radda Barnen—Sweden's Save the Children—was intimately involved in drafting and implementing the Swedish law banning parental spanking as well as in drafting the wording of Article 19 of the UN Convention on the Rights of the Child.) The convention went into force as international law on September 2, 1990, when it was ratified by the twentieth nation. Close to one hundred nations have now ratified, thus affirming that they are legally bound by its standards. One notable holdout: the United States of America.

But an international organization calling itself End Physical Punishment of Children (EPOCH) is working diligently to enlighten American diplomats and lawmakers as to the rights of children. EPOCH's worldwide aim is that of "ending all physical punishment of children by education and legal reform." In their literature, they state that "hitting children is a violation of their fundamental rights as people and a constant confirmation of their low status," and they make it perfectly clear that spanking is hitting. As of 1992, EPOCH was able to boast that largely as a result of their efforts, physical punishment of children by parents had been legally proscribed in Sweden, Finland, Denmark, Norway, and Austria. In addition, similar bills are up for consideration in Germany, the United Kingdom, Canada, and Bolivia.

Completing the circle, the cofounder of the American chapter of EPOCH, Adrienne Hauser, is on National Staff at the National Committee to Prevent Child Abuse. (During the writing of this book, I left several messages asking Ms. Hauser to call me, but she never responded.) So although NCPCA may publicly disavow support for antispanking legislation, strong connections exist between themselves and organizations like EPOCH, the National Committee for the Rights of Children, and the National Task Force for Children's Constitutional Rights, which are working toward that end.

As reflected in much of NCPCA's literature, the distinct possibility exists that antispanking legal rulings would be just one stage in the ever-broadening legal definition of child abuse. Once spankings are defined as abusive, it's quite conceivable that raising one's voice to a child (yelling) would be next on the list of parenting behaviors to be deemed abusive (in a letter which appeared in "Dear Abby" in April of 1994, Joy Byers, an NCPCA spokesperson, writes: "Never raise your voice, or your hand, in anger") followed by banishing a child to his or her room. (If you think the latter prospect is absurd, think again. A considerable number of helping professionals are presently of the opinion that restricting a child to his room causes the development of "negative feelings" concerning what should be a "positive environment," thus increasing the risk of onset of separation anxieties, phobias, sleep disturbances, and the like, not to mention lowered self-esteem.)

Where does this end? The answer: It doesn't, for it is the inherent nature of institutional bureaucracies not only to perpetuate themselves but to expand their influence—their "mandate"—within society. As child abuse laws are liberalized, it is inevitable that the numbers of children removed from their homes and placed in the care of the state would increase, as would the number of terminations of parental rights. As one concerned reader of my syndicated newspaper column recently wrote: "I am genuinely frightened concerning the attempts of well-intentioned social engineers to effect the 'redistribution' of children to 'better' parents. The ultimate outcome is the destruction of the family as we know it." Paranoia? Keep in mind that just forty years ago, the average citizen would have regarded someone who warned of the coming of antispanking laws as nothing less than hysterical, in both senses of the term.

Murray Straus says that, under his proposed legislation, parents who spanked would not be punished, only helped. That's if, and only if, they admitted they needed help. What if, as a matter of principle, a parent refused to make such a confession? At present, if a parent clearly abuses a child and refuses to admit that his or her actions toward the child are wrong, the child is almost always immediately removed from the home until the parent's discipline has undergone successful rehabilitation. The very real possibility that this policy would be extended to parents who administer mild spankings yet refuse to confess the error of their ways is downright scary.

Straus tells us that antispanking laws will transform us into a "healthier, less violent, and wealthier society." This grand vision serves to distract from the more insidious aspects of such laws, including that for many otherwise law-abiding American parents, receiving professional "help" would no longer be a matter of choice. In short, the specter raised is one of a totalitarian family policy, one that puts the autonomy of the American family at tremendous risk.

There is evidence, furthermore, that an antispanking law might be profoundly counterproductive. It is significant to note that the outlawing of spanking in Sweden may have actually *increased* the incidence of child abuse. One study—done a year after Sweden enacted antispanking laws—found that the Swedish rate of beating a child or threatening to use or using a weapon of some sort against a child was *two to four times that of the rate in the United States.* This is especially telling of the ultimate effect of anti-spanking laws, since Sweden is by other measures a far less violent society than the United States. Their murder rate, for example, is less than half that of our own. To explain this paradox, psychologist Larzelere posits that occasional mild spankings may serve as a safety valve of sorts, preventing escalations of misbehavior and parental frustration of the sort that lead to physical explosions. He further suggests—and I second his emotion—that providing parents who intend to spank with guidelines for spanking appropriately and effectively may do more to reduce child abuse than laws which prohibit spanking altogether.

When all is said and done, this argument isn't about spanking; it's about people, zealous professionals, politics, and political correctness. It's about people who feel morally superior and therefore justified in their desire to impose their ideology on everyone, by hook or crook. The more frustrated they become, the more outrageous and dangerous they become. That's the problem with moral superiority in any form. Frustrated, it inclines toward totalitarianism.

The problem with spanking is not spanking per se. Again, it's people— people who use corporal punishment inappropriately. It's a people problem that will *not* be solved through legislation. It will, in all likelihood, never be completely solved, only mitigated. It can be mitigated through education. So let's begin the education, keeping in mind that the best, most effective educators, the ones that cause people to truly want to listen, inquire, and learn, don't promote extremist points of view.

CHALLENGE QUESTIONS

Does Spanking Children Lead Them to Become More Violent?

1. How might research on spanking draw a distinction between spanking and beating? How might this distinction affect the research?
2. What disciplinary techniques that your parents used did you think were effective? How would you discipline your children? Why?
3. Do you find Straus or Rosemond more persuasive? Why?
4. Should spanking be made illegal? Why, or why not? How might such a law be enforced?
5. How might research on spanking help to explain the current wave of youth violence evidenced in the news? Is there too much discipline or not enough?

ISSUE 7

Does Viewing Television Increase a Child's Aggression?

YES: Brandon S. Centerwall, from "Television and Violent Crime," *The Public Interest* (Spring 1993)

NO: Brian Siano, from "Frankenstein Must Be Destroyed: Chasing the Monster of TV Violence," *The Humanist* (January/February 1994)

ISSUE SUMMARY

YES: Brandon S. Centerwall, an epidemiologist, argues that children act out the violence they see on television and carry the violent behaviors into adulthood.

NO: Brian Siano, a writer and researcher, contends that children with nonnurturing parents, regardless of the children's television viewing habits, tend to be more aggressive than children who closely identify with either parent.

Survey after survey shows that one of the primary concerns of contemporary society is violence. The popular perception is that violence is on the rise. Indeed, some people believe that violence is like some contagious disease that has spread to epidemic proportions. What is the reason for this seeming "epidemic"? Why does the current generation appear to be more prone to violence than previous generations? How is today different from the "good old days"?

Many people would sum up that difference in one word—television. Television now occupies a place (or two or three) in almost every home in the United States, regardless of the inhabitants' race or level of income. And television has been cited time and again by the U.S. surgeon general, by members of the U.S. Congress, and by psychological researchers as a medium filled with many kinds of violence. It seems only natural for parents to wonder about television's impact on small children, who average over 20 hours of television viewing per week. Indeed, some have suggested that a child witnesses over 100,000 acts of violence on television before graduating from elementary school. How do these acts of violence affect a child's development?

In the following selection, Brandon S. Centerwall asserts that televised violence leads to an increase in a child's aggression, referring to numerous published studies to support this assertion. He theorizes that children have an instinctive desire to imitate behavior. Unfortunately, however, children are not born with an instinct for evaluating the appropriateness of certain actions. This means that children naturally model what they see on television and do not typically think about whether or not they *should* model what they see. Consequently, even when clearly antisocial behaviors are depicted on television, children are still likely to learn and imitate them. Centerwall believes that the danger to a child's development is so great that he advocates making television violence a part of the public health agenda.

In the second selection, Brian Siano contends that factors other than television are more influential on a child's tendency for violent actions. He points to research that contradicts Centerwall's views. For example, one study found that boys who watch nonviolent shows tend to be more aggressive than boys who watch violent television. Siano argues that style of parenting is a better indicator of the development of violent behavior. Children of nonnurturing parents and children who do not identify with their parents are the ones who are most likely to exhibit violence. Although Siano is an advocate of quality programming, he is reluctant to indiscriminately censor all violence from television, particularly when effective parenting can counter any possible ill effects.

POINT

- Research indicates that parents who watched more television as children punished their own children more severely.
- Children are incapable of discriminating between what they should and should not imitate.
- Limiting all children's exposure to television violence should become part of the public health agenda.
- Many studies demonstrate a positive relationship between television exposure and physical aggression.
- For children to be safe, television violence must be eliminated.

COUNTERPOINT

- Boys who watch nonviolent shows tend to be more aggressive than boys who watch violent shows.
- Good parents teach children how to discriminate among their behaviors.
- Violence can be used in television shows for pro-social reasons.
- Parental identification can change the way children interpret physical punishment on television.
- Indiscriminate censorship of all violence is too high a price to pay for the minimal influence of television.

Brandon S. Centerwall  **YES**

Television and Violent Crime

Children are born ready to imitate adult behavior. That they can, and do, imitate an array of adult facial expressions has been demonstrated in newborns as young as a few hours old, before they are even old enough to know that they have facial features. It is a most useful instinct, for the developing child must learn and master a vast repertoire of behavior in short order.

But while children have an instinctive desire to imitate, they do not possess an instinct for determining whether a behavior ought to be imitated. They will imitate anything, including behavior that most adults regard as destructive and antisocial. It may give pause for thought, then, to learn that infants as young as fourteen months demonstrably observe and incorporate behavior seen on television.

The average American preschooler watches more than twenty-seven hours of television per week. This might not be bad if these young children understood what they were watching. But they don't. Up through ages three and four, most children are unable to distinguish fact from fantasy on TV, and remain unable to do so despite adult coaching. In the minds of young children, television is a source of entirely factual information regarding how the world works. There are no limits to their credulity. To cite one example, an Indiana school board had to issue an advisory to young children that, no, there is no such thing as Teenage Mutant Ninja Turtles. Children had been crawling down storm drains looking for them.

Naturally, as children get older, they come to know better, but their earliest and deepest impressions are laid down at an age when they still see television as a factual source of information about the outside world. In that world, it seems, violence is common and the commission of violence is generally powerful, exciting, charismatic, and effective. In later life, serious violence is most likely to erupt at moments of severe stress—and it is precisely at such moments that adolescents and adults are most likely to revert to their earliest, most visceral sense of the role of violence in society and in personal behavior. Much of this sense will have come from television.

The Seeds of Aggression

In 1973, a remote rural community in Canada acquired television for the first time. The acquisition of television at such a late date was due to problems with signal reception rather than any hostility toward TV. As reported in *The Impact of Television* (1986), Tannis Williams and her associates at the University of British Columbia investigated the effect of television on the children of this community (which they called "Notel"), taking for comparison two similar towns that already had television.

The researchers observed forty-five first- and second-graders in the three towns for rates of inappropriate physical aggression before television was introduced into Notel. Two years later, the same forty-five children were observed again. To prevent bias in the data, the research assistants who collected the data were kept uninformed as to why the children's rates of aggression were of interest. Furthermore, a new group of research assistants was employed the second time around, so that the data gatherers would not be biased by recollections of the children's behavior two years earlier.

Rates of aggression did not change in the two control communities. By contrast, the rate of aggression among Notel children increased 160 percent. The increase was observed in both boys and girls, in those who were aggressive to begin with and in those who were not. Television's enhancement of noxious aggression was entirely general and not limited to a few "bad apples."

In another Canadian study, Gary Granzberg and his associates at the University of Winnipeg investigated the impact of television upon Indian communities in northern Manitoba. As described in *Television and the Canadian Indian* (1980), forty-nine third-, fourth-, and fifth-grade boys living in two communities were observed from 1973, when one town acquired television, until 1977, when the second town did as well. The aggressiveness of boys in the first community increased after the introduction of television. The aggressiveness of boys in the second community, which did not receive television then, remained the same. When television was later introduced in the second community, observed levels of aggressiveness increased there as well.

In another study conducted from 1960 to 1981, Leonard Eron and L. Rowell Huesmann (then of the University of Illinois at Chicago) followed 875 children living in a semirural U.S. county. Eron and Huesmann found that for both boys and girls, the amount of television watched at age eight predicted the seriousness of criminal acts for which they were convicted by age thirty. This remained true even after controlling for the children's baseline aggressiveness, intelligence, and socioeconomic status. Eron and Huesmann also observed second-generation effects. Children who watched much television at age eight later, as parents, punished their own children more severely than did parents who had watched less television as children. Second- and now third-generation effects are accumulating at a time of unprecedented youth violence.

All seven of the U.S. and Canadian studies of prolonged childhood exposure to television demonstrate a positive relationship between exposure and physical aggression. The critical period is preadolescent childhood. Later exposure does not appear to produce any additional effect. However, the aggression-enhancing effect of exposure in pre-adolescence extends into adolescence and adulthood. This suggests that any interventions should be designed for children and their caregivers rather than for the general adult population.

These studies confirmed the beliefs of most Americans. According to a Harris poll at the time of the studies, 43 percent of American adults believe that television violence "plays a part in making America a violent society." An additional 37 percent think it might. But how important is television violence? What is the effect of exposure upon entire populations? To address this question, I took advantage of an historical accident—the absence of television in South Africa prior to 1975.

The South African Experience

White South Africans have lived in a prosperous, industrialized society for decades, but they did not get television until 1975 because of tension between the Afrikaner- and English-speaking communities. The country's Afrikaner leaders knew that a South African television industry would have to rely on British and American shows to fill out its programming schedule, and they felt that this would provide an unacceptable cultural advantage to English-speaking South Africans. So, rather than negotiate a complicated compromise, the government simply forbade television broadcasting. The entire population of two million whites—rich and poor, urban and rural, educated and uneducated—was thus excluded from exposure to television for a quarter century after the medium was introduced in the United States.

In order to determine whether exposure to television is a cause of violence, I compared homicide rates in South Africa, Canada, and the United States. Since blacks in South Africa live under quite different conditions than blacks in the United States, I limited the comparison to white homicide rates in South Africa and the United States, and the total homicide rate in Canada (which was 97 percent white in 1951).[1] I chose the homicide rate as a measure of violence because homicide statistics are exceptionally accurate.

From 1945 to 1974, the white homicide rate in the United States increased 93 percent. In Canada, the homicide rate increased 92 percent. In South Africa, where television was banned, the white homicide rate declined by 7 percent.

Controlling for Other Factors

Could there be some explanation other than television for the fact that violence increased dramatically in the U.S. and Canada while dropping in South Africa? I examined an array of alternative explanations. None is satisfactory:

- **Economic growth.** Between 1946 and 1974, all three countries experienced substantial economic growth. Per capita income increased by 75 percent in the United States, 124 percent in Canada, and 86 percent in South Africa. Thus differences in economic growth cannot account for the different homicide trends in the three countries.

- **Civil unrest.** One might suspect that anti-war or civil-rights activity was responsible for the doubling of the homicide rate in the United States during this period. But the experience of Canada shows that this was not the case, since Canadians suffered a doubling of the homicide rate without similar civil unrest.

Other possible explanations include changes in age distribution, urbanization, alcohol consumption, capital punishment, and the availability of firearms. As discussed in *Public Communication and Behavior* (1989), none provides a viable explanation for the observed homicide trends.

In the United States and Canada, there was a lag of ten to fifteen years between the introduction of television and a doubling of the homicide rate. In South Africa, there was a similar lag. Since television exerts its behavior-modifying effects primarily on children, while homicide is primarily an adult activity, this lag represents the time needed for the "television generation" to come of age.

The relationship between television and the homicide rate holds *within* the United States as well. Different regions of the U.S., for example, acquired television at different times. As we would expect, while all regions saw increases in their homicide rates, the regions that acquired television first were also the first to see higher homicide rates.

Similarly, urban areas acquired television before rural areas. As we would expect, urban areas saw increased homicide rates several years before the occurrence of a parallel increase in rural areas.

The introduction of television also helps explain the different rates of homicide growth for whites and minorities. White households in the U.S. began acquiring television sets in large numbers approximately five years before minority households. Significantly, the white homicide rate began increasing in 1958, four years before a parallel increase in the minority homicide rate.

Of course, there are many factors other than television that influence the amount of violent crime. Every violent act is the result of a variety of forces coming together—poverty, crime, alcohol and drug abuse, stress—of which childhood TV exposure is just one. Nevertheless, the evidence indicates that if, hypothetically, television technology had never been developed, there would today be 10,000 fewer homicides each year in the United States, 70,000 fewer rapes, and 700,000 fewer injurious assaults. Violent crime would be half what it is.

The Television Industry Takes a Look

The first congressional hearings on television and violence were held in 1952, when not even a quarter of U.S. households owned television sets. In the years since, there have been scores of research reports on the issue, as well as several major government investigations. The findings of the National Commission on the Causes and Prevention of Violence, published in 1969, were particularly significant. This report established what is now the broad scientific consensus: Exposure to television increases rates of physical aggression.

Television industry executives were genuinely surprised by the National Commission's report. What the industry produced was at times unedifying, but physically harmful? In response, network executives began research programs that collectively would cost nearly a million dollars.

CBS commissioned William Belson to undertake what would be the largest and most sophisticated study yet, an investigation involving 1,565 teenage boys. In *Television Violence and the Adolescent Boy* (1978), Belson controlled for one hundred variables, and found that teenage boys who had watched above-average quantities of television violence before adolescence were committing acts of serious violence (e.g., assault, rape, major vandalism, and abuse of animals) at a rate 49 percent higher than teenage boys who had watched below-average quantities of television violence. Despite the large sum of money they had invested, CBS executives were notably unenthusiastic about the report.

ABC commissioned Melvin Heller and Samuel Polsky of Temple University to study young male felons imprisoned for violent crimes (e.g, homicide, rape, and assault). In two surveys, 22 and 34 percent of the young felons reported having consciously imitated crime techniques learned from television programs, usually successfully. The more violent of these felons were the most likely to report having learned techniques from television. Overall, the felons reported that as children they had watched an average of six hours of television per day—approximately twice as much as children in the general population at that time.

Unlike CBS, ABC maintained control over publication. The final report, *Studies in Violence and Television* (1976), was published in a private, limited edition that was not released to the general public or the scientific community.

NBC relied on a team of four researchers, three of whom were employees of NBC. Indeed, the principal investigator, J. Ronald Milavsky, was an NBC vice president. The team observed some 2,400 schoolchildren for up to three years to see if watching television violence increased their levels of physical aggressiveness. In *Television and Aggression* (1982), Milavsky and his associates reported that television violence had no effect upon the children's behavior. However, every independent investigator who has examined their data has concluded that, to the contrary, their data show that television violence did cause a modest increase of about 5 percent in average levels of physical aggressiveness. When pressed on the point, Milavsky and his associates conceded that their findings were consistent with the conclusion that television violence increased physical aggressiveness "to a small extent." They did not concede that television violence actually caused an increase, but only that their findings were consistent with such a conclusion.

The NBC study results raise an important objection to my conclusions. While studies have repeatedly demonstrated that childhood exposure to television increases physical aggressiveness, the increase is almost always quite minor. A number of investigators have argued that such a small effect is too weak to account for major increases in rates of violence. These investigators, however, overlook a key factor.

Homicide is an extreme form of aggression—so extreme that only one person in 20,000 committed murder each year in the United States in the mid-1950s. If we were to rank everyone's degree of physical aggressiveness from the least aggressive (Mother Theresa) to the most aggressive (Jack the Ripper), the large majority of us would be somewhere in the middle and murderers would be virtually off the chart. It is an intrinsic property of such "bell curve" distributions that small changes in the average imply major changes at the extremes. Thus, if exposure to television causes 8 percent of the population to shift from below-average aggression to above-average aggression, it follows that the homicide rate will double. The findings of the NBC study and the doubling of the homicide rate are two sides of the same coin.

After the results of these studies became clear, television industry executives lost their enthusiasm for scientific research. No further investigations were funded. Instead, the industry turned to political management of the issue.

The Television Industry and Social Responsibility

The television industry routinely portrays individuals who seek to influence programming as un-American haters of free speech. In a 1991 letter sent to 7,000 executives of consumer product companies and advertising agencies, the president of the Network Television Association explained:

> Freedom of expression is an inalienable right of all Americans vigorously supported by ABC, CBS, and NBC. However, boycotts and so-called advertiser "hit lists" are attempts to manipulate our free society and democratic process.

The letter went on to strongly advise the companies to ignore all efforts by anyone to influence what programs they choose to sponsor. By implication, the networks themselves should ignore all efforts by anyone to influence what programs they choose to produce.

But this is absurd. All forms of public discourse are attempts to "manipulate" our free society and democratic process. What else could they be? Consumer boycotts are no more un-American than are strikes by labor unions. The Network Television Association is attempting to systematically shut down all discourse between viewers and advertisers, and between viewers and the television industry. Wrapping itself in patriotism, the television industry's response to uppity viewers is to put them in their place. If the industry and advertisers were to actually succeed in closing the circle between them, the only course they would leave for concerned viewers would be to seek legislative action.

In the war against tobacco, we do not expect help from the tobacco industry. If someone were to call upon the tobacco industry to cut back production as a matter of social conscience and concern for public health, we would regard that person as simple-minded, if not frankly deranged. Oddly enough, however, people have persistently assumed that the television industry is somehow different—that it is useful to appeal to its social conscience. This was true in 1969 when the National Commission on the Causes and Prevention of Violence published its recommendations for the television industry. It was equally true in 1989 when the U.S. Congress passed an anti-violence bill that granted television industry executives the authority to hold discussions on the issue of television violence without violating antitrust laws. Even before the law was passed, the four networks stated that there would be no substantive changes in their programming. They have been as good as their word.

For the television industry, issues of "quality" and "social responsibility" are peripheral to the issue of maximizing audience size—and there is no formula more tried and true than violence for generating large audiences. To television executives, this is crucial. For if advertising revenue were to decrease by just 1 percent, the television industry would stand to lose $250 million in revenue annually. Thus, changes in audience size that appear trivial to most of us are regarded as catastrophic by the industry. For this reason, industry spokespersons have made innumerable protestations of good intent, but nothing has happened. In the more than twenty years that levels of television violence have been monitored, there has been no downward movement. There are no recommendations to make to the television industry. To make any would not only be futile but could create the false impression that the industry might actually do something constructive.

On December 11, 1992, the networks finally announced a list of voluntary guidelines on television violence. Curiously, reporters were unable to locate any network producers who felt the new guidelines would require changes in their programs. That raises a question: Who is going to bell the cat? Who is going to place his or her career in jeopardy in order to decrease the amount of violence on television? It is hard to say, but it may be revealing that when Senator Paul Simon held the press conference announcing the new inter-network agreement, no industry executives were present to answer questions.

Meeting the Challenge

Television violence is everybody's problem. You may feel assured that your child will never become violent despite a steady diet of television mayhem, but you cannot be assured that your child won't be murdered or maimed by someone else's child raised on a similar diet.

The American Academy of Pediatrics recommends that parents limit their children's television viewing to one to two hours per day. But why wait for a pediatrician to say it? Limiting children's exposure to television violence should become part of the public health agenda, along with safety seats, bicycle helmets, immunizations, and good nutrition. Part of the public health approach should be to promote child-care alternatives to the electronic babysitter, especially among the poor.

Parents should also guide what their children watch and how much. This is an old recommendation that can be given new teeth with the help of modern technology. It is now feasible to fit a television set with an electronic lock that permits parents to preset the channels and times for which the set will be available; if a particular program or time of day is locked, the set will not operate then. Time-channel locks are not merely feasible; they have already been designed and are coming off the assembly line.

The model for making them widely available comes from closed-captioning circuitry, which permits deaf and hard-of-hearing persons access to television. Market forces alone would not have made closed-captioning available to more than a fraction of the deaf and hard-of-hearing. To remedy this problem, Congress passed the Television Decoder Circuitry Act in 1990, which requires that virtually all new television sets be manufactured with built-in closed-captioning circuitry. A similar law should require that all new television sets be manufactured with built-in time-channel lock circuitry—and for a similar reason. Market forces alone will not make this technology available to more than a fraction of households with children and will exclude most poor families, the ones who suffer the most from violence. If we can make television technology available to benefit twenty-four million deaf and hard-of-hearing Americans, surely we can do no less for the benefit of fifty million American children.

A final recommendation: Television programs should be accompanied by a violence rating so that parents can judge how violent a program is without having to watch it. Such a rating system should be quantitative, leaving aesthetic and social judgments to the viewers. This approach would enjoy broad popular support. In a *Los Angeles Times* poll, 71 percent of adult Americans favored the establishment of a TV violence rating system. Such a system would not impinge on artistic freedom since producers would remain free to produce programs with high violence ratings. They could even use high violence ratings in the advertisements for their shows.

None of these recommendations would limit freedom of speech. That is as it should be. We do not address the problem of motor vehicle fatalities by calling for a ban on cars. Instead, we emphasize safety seats, good traffic signs, and driver education. Similarly, to address the problem of television-inspired violence, we need to promote time-channel locks, program rating systems, and viewer education about the hazards of violent programming. In this way we can protect our children and our society.

Note

1. The "white homicide rate" refers to the rate at which whites are the victims of homicide. Since most homicide is intra-racial, this closely parallels the rate at which whites commit homicide.

References

William A. Belson, *Television Violence and the Adolescent Boy.* Westmead, England: Saxon House (1978).

Brandon S. Centerwall, "Exposure to Television as a Cause of Violence," *Public Communication and Behavior,* Vol. 2. Orlando, Florida: Academic Press (1989), pp. 1–58.

Leonard D. Eron and L. Rowell Huesmann, "The Control of Aggressive Behavior by Changes in Attitudes, Values, and the Conditions of Learning," *Advances in the Study of Aggression*. Orlando, Florida: Academic Press (1984), pp. 139–171.

Gary Granzberg and Jack Steinbring (eds.), *Television and the Canadian Indian*. Winnipeg, Manitoba: University of Winnipeg (1980).

L. Rowell Huesmann and Leonard D. Eron, *Television and the Aggressive Child*. Hillsdale, New Jersey: Lawrence Erlbaum Associates (1986), pp. 45–80.

Candace Kruttschnitt, et al., "Family Violence, Television Viewing Habits, and Other Adolescent Experiences Related to Violent Criminal Behavior," *Criminology*, Vol. 24 (1986), pp. 235–267.

Andrew N. Meltzoff, "Memory in Infancy," *Encyclopedia of Learning and Memory*. New York: Macmillan (1992), pp. 271–275.

J. Ronald Milavsky, et al., *Television and Aggression*. Orlando, Florida: Academic Press (1982).

Jerome L. Singer, et al., "Family Patterns and Television Viewing as Predictors of Children's Beliefs and Aggression," *Journal of Communication*, Vol. 34, No. 2 (1984), pp. 73–89.

Tannis M. Williams (ed.), *The Impact of Television*. Orlando, Florida: Academic Press (1986).

NO

Brian Siano

Frankenstein Must Be Destroyed: Chasing the Monster of TV Violence

Here's the scene: Bugs Bunny, Daffy Duck, and a well-armed Elmer Fudd are having a stand-off in the forest. Daffy the rat-fink has just exposed Bugs' latest disguise, so Bugs takes off the costume and says, "That's right, Doc, I'm a wabbit. Would you like to shoot me now or wait until we get home?"

"Shoot him now! Shoot him now!" Daffy screams.

"You keep out of this," Bugs says. "He does not have to shoot you now."

"He does *so* have to shoot me now!" says Daffy. Full of wrath, he storms up to Elmer Fudd and shrieks, "And I *demand* that you shoot me now!"

Now, if you *aren't* smiling to yourself over the prospect of Daffy's beak whirling around his head like a roulette wheel, stop reading right now. This one's for a very select group: those evil degenerates (like me) who want to corrupt the unsullied youth of America by showing them violence on television.

Wolves' heads being conked with mallets in Tex Avery's *Swing Shift Cinderella*. Dozens of dead bodies falling from a closet in *Who Killed Who?* A sweet little kitten seemingly baked into cookies in Chuck Jones' *Feed the Kitty*. And best of all, Wile E. Coyote's unending odyssey of pain in *Fast and Furious* and *Hook, Line, and Stinker*. God, I love it. The more explosions, crashes, gunshots, and defective ACME catapults there are, the better it is for the little tykes.

Shocked? Hey, I haven't even gotten to "The Three Stooges" yet.

The villagers are out hunting another monster—the Frankenstein of TV violence. Senator Paul Simon's hearings in early August 1993 provoked a fresh round of arguments in a debate that's been going on ever since the first round of violent kids' shows—"Sky King," "Captain Midnight," and "Hopalong Cassidy"—were on the air. More recently, Attorney General Janet Reno has taken a hard line on TV violence. "We're fed up with excuses," she told the Senate, arguing that "the regulation of violence is constitutionally permissible" and that, if the networks don't do it, "government should respond." ...

From Brian Siano, "Frankenstein Must Be Destroyed: Chasing the Monster of TV Violence," *The Humanist*, vol. 54, no. 1 (January/February 1994). Copyright © 1994 by Brian Siano. Reprinted by permission.

Simon claims to have become concerned with this issue because, three years ago, he turned on the TV in his hotel room and was treated to the sight of a man being hacked apart with a chainsaw.... This experience prompted him to sponsor a three-year antitrust exemption for the networks, which was his way of encouraging them to voluntarily "clean house." But at the end of that period, the rates of TV violence hadn't changed enough to satisfy him, so Simon convened open hearings on the subject in 1993.

If Simon was truly concerned with the content of television programming, the first question that comes to mind is why he gave the networks an antitrust exemption in the first place. Thanks to Reagan-era deregulation, ownership of the mass media has become steadily more concentrated in the hands of fewer and fewer corporations. For example, the Federal Communications Commission used to have a "seven-and-seven" rule, whereby no company was allowed to own more than seven radio and seven television stations. In 1984, this was revised to a "12-and-12-and-12" rule: 12 FM radio stations, 12 AM radio stations, and 12 TV stations. It's a process outlined by Ben Bagdikian in his fine book *The Media Monopoly*. The net result is a loss of dissident, investigative, or regional voices; a mass media that questions less; and a forum for public debate that includes only the powerful.

This process could be impeded with judicious use of antitrust laws and stricter FCC controls—a return to the "seven-and-seven" rule, perhaps. But rather than hold hearings on this subject—a far greater threat to the nation's political well-being than watching *Aliens* on pay-per-view—Simon gave the networks a three-year *exemption* from antitrust legislation....

The debate becomes even more impassioned when we ask how children might be affected. The innocent, trusting little tykes are spending hours bathed in TV's unreal colors, and their fantasy lives are inhabited by such weirdos as Wolverine and Eek the Cat. Parents usually want their kids to grow up sharing their ideals and values, or at least to be well-behaved and obedient. Tell parents that their kids are watching "Beavis and Butt-head" in their formative years and you set off some major alarms.

There are also elitist, even snobbish, attitudes toward pop culture that help to rationalize censorship. One is that the corporate, mass-market culture of TV isn't important enough or "art" enough to deserve the same free-speech protection as James Joyce's *Ulysses* or William Burrough's *Naked Lunch*. The second is that rational, civilized human beings are supposed to be into Shakespeare and Scarlatti, not Pearl Jam and "Beavis and Butt-head." Seen in this "enlightened" way, the efforts of Paul Simon are actually for *our own good*. And so we define anything even remotely energetic as "violent," wail about how innocent freckle-faced children are being defiled by such fare as "NYPD Blue," and call for a Council of Certified Nice People who will decide what the rest of us get to see. A recent *Mother Jones* article by Carl Cannon (July/August 1993) took just this hysterical tone, citing as proof "some three thousand research studies of this issue."

Actually, there aren't 3,000 studies. In 1984, the *Psychological Bulletin* published an overview by Jonathan Freedman of research on the subject. Referring to the "2,500 studies" figure bandied about at the time (it's a safe bet that 10 years would inflate this figure to 3,000), Freedman writes:

> The reality is more modest. The large number refers to the complete bibliography on television. References to television and aggression are far fewer, perhaps around 500.... The actual literature on the relation between television violence and aggression consists of fewer than 100 independent studies, and the majority of these are laboratory experiments. Although this is still a substantial body of work, it is not vast, and there are only a small number of studies dealing specifically with the effects of television violence outside the laboratory.

The bulk of the evidence for a causal relationship between television violence and violent behavior comes from the research of Leonard Eron of the University of Illinois and Rowell Huesmann of the University of Michigan. Beginning in 1960, Eron and his associates began a large-scale appraisal of how aggression develops in children and whether or not it persists into adulthood. (The question of television violence was, originally, a side issue to the long-term study.) Unfortunately, when the popular press writes about Eron's work, it tends to present his methodology in the simplest of terms: *Mother Jones* erroneously stated that his study "followed the viewing habits of a group of children for twenty-two years." It's this sort of sloppiness, and overzealousness to prove a point, that keeps people from understanding the issues or raising substantial criticisms. Therefore, we must discuss Eron's work in some detail.

⌁⊙⌁

The first issue in Eron's study was how to measure aggressiveness in children. Eron's "peer-nominated index" followed a simple strategy: asking each child in a classroom questions about which kids were the main offenders in 10 different categories of classroom aggression (that is, "Who pushes or shoves children?"). The method is consistent with other scales of aggression, and its one-month test/retest reliability is 91 percent. The researchers also tested the roles of four behavioral dimensions in the development of aggression: *instigation* (parental rejection or lack of nurturance), *reinforcement* (punishment versus reward), *identification* (acquiring the parents' behavior and values), and *sociocultural norms.*

Eron's team selected the entire third-grade population of Columbia County, New York, testing 870 children and interviewing about 75 to 80 percent of their parents. Several trends became clear almost immediately. Children with less nurturing parents were more aggressive. Children who more closely identified with either parent were less aggressive. And children with low parental identification who were punished tended to be *more* aggressive (an observation which required revision of the behavioral model).

Ten years later, Eron and company tracked down and re-interviewed about half of the original sample. (They followed up on the subjects in 1981 as well.) Many of the subjects—now high-school seniors—demonstrated a persistence in aggression over time. Not only were the "peer-nominated" ratings roughly consistent with the third-grade ratings, but the more aggressive kids were three times as likely to have a police record by adulthood.

Eron's team also checked for the influences on aggression which they had previously noted when the subjects were eight. The persistent influences were parental identification and socioeconomic variables. Some previously important influences (lack of nurturance, punishment for aggression) didn't seem to affect the subjects' behavior as much in young adulthood. Eron writes of these factors:

> Their effect is short-lived and other variables are more important in predicting later aggression. Likewise, contingencies and environmental conditions can change drastically over 10 years, and thus the earlier contingent response becomes irrelevant.

It's at this stage that Eron mentions television as a factor:

> One of the best predictors of how aggressive a young man would be at age 19 was the violence of the television programs he preferred when he was 8 years old. Now, because we had longitudinal data, we could say with more certainty, on the basis of regression analysis, partial correlation, path analysis, and so forth, that there indeed was a cause-and-effect relation. *Continued research, however, has indicated that the causal effect is probably bidirectional: Aggressive children prefer violent television, and the violence on television causes them to be more aggressive.* [italics added]

Before we address the last comment, I should make one thing clear. Eron's research is sound. The methods he used to measure aggression are used by social scientists in many other contexts. His research does not ignore such obvious factors as the parents' socioeconomic status. And, as the above summary makes clear, Eron's own work makes a strong case for the positive or negative influence of parents in the development of their children's aggressiveness.

Now let's look at this "causal effect" business. Eron's data reveals that aggressive kids who turn into aggressive adults like aggressive television. But this is a correlation; it is not proof of a causal influence. If aggressive kids liked eating strawberry ice cream more often than the class wusses did, that too would be a predictor, and one might speculate on some anger-inducing chemical in strawberries.

Of course, the relation between representational violence and its influence on real life isn't as farfetched as that. The problem lies in determining precisely the nature of that relation, as we see when we look at the laboratory studies conducted by other researchers. Usually, the protocol of these experiments involves providing groups of individuals with entertainment calibrated for violent content, and studying some aspect of behavior after exposure—response to a behavioral test, which toys the children choose to play with, and so forth. But the results of these tests have been somewhat mixed. Sometimes the results are at variance with other studies, and many have methodological problems. For example, which "violent" entertainment is chosen? Bugs Bunny and the "Teenage Mutant Ninja Turtles" present action in very different contexts, and in one study, the Adam West "Batman" series was deemed nonviolent, despite those *Pow! Bam! Sock!* fistfights that ended every episode.

Many of the studies report that children do demonstrate higher levels of interpersonal aggression shortly after watching violent, energetic entertainment. But a 1971 study by Feshbach and Singer had boys from seven schools watch preassigned violent and nonviolent shows for six weeks. The results were not constant from school to school—and the boys watching the *nonviolent* shows tended to be more aggressive. Another protocol, carried out in Belgium as well as the United States, separated children into cottages at an institutional school and exposed certain groups to violent films. Higher aggression was noted in *all* groups after the films were viewed, but it returned to a near-baseline level after a week or so. (The children also rated the less violent films as less exciting, more boring, and sillier than the violent films—indicating that maybe kids *like* a little rush now and then.) Given the criticisms of the short-term-effects studies, and the alternate interpretations of the longitudinal studies, is this matter really settled?

Eron certainly thinks so. Testifying before Simon's committee in August, he declared that "the scientific debate is over" and called upon the Senate to reduce TV violence. His statement did not include any reference to such significant factors as parental identification—which, as his own research indicates, can change the way children interpret physical punishment. And even though Rowell Huesmann concurred with Eron in similar testimony before a House subcommittee, Huesmann's 1984 study of 1,500 youths in the United States, Finland, Poland, and Australia argued that, assuming a causal influence, television might be responsible for 5 percent of the violence in society. At *most*.

This is where I feel one has to part company with Leonard Eron. He is one of the most respected researchers in his field, and his work points to an imperative for parents in shaping and sharing their children's lives. But he has lent his considerable authority to such diversionary efforts as Paul Simon's and urged us to address, by questionable means, what only *might* be causing a tiny portion of real-life violence.

Some of Eron's suggestions for improving television are problematic as well. In his Senate testimony, Eron proposed restrictions on televised violence from 6:00 AM to 10:00 PM—which would exclude pro football, documentaries about World War II, and even concerned lawperson Janet Reno's proudest moments. Or take Eron's suggestion that, in televised drama, "perpetrators of violence should not be rewarded for violent acts." I don't know what shows Eron's been watching, but all of the cop shows I remember usually ended with the bad guys getting caught or killed. And when Eron suggests that "gratuitous violence that is not necessary to the plot should be reduced or abandoned," one has to ask just *who* decides that it's "not necessary"? Perhaps most troubling is Eron's closing statement:

> For many years now Western European countries have had monitoring of TV and films for violence by government agencies and have *not* permitted the showing of excess violence, especially during child viewing hours. And I've never heard complaints by citizens of those democratic countries that their rights have been violated. If something doesn't give, we may have to

institute some such monitoring by government agencies here in the U.S.A. If the industry does not police itself, then there is left only the prospect of official censorship, distasteful as this may be to many of us.

❧

The most often-cited measure of just how violent TV programs are is that of George Gerbner, dean of the Annenberg School of Communications at the University of Pennsylvania. Few of the news stories about TV violence explain how this index is compiled, the context in which Gerbner has conducted his studies, or even some criticisms that could be raised.

Gerbner's view of the media's role in society is far more nuanced than the publicity given the violence profile may indicate. He sees television as a kind of myth-structure/religion for modern society. Television dramas, situation comedies, news shows, and all the rest create a shared culture for viewers, which "communicates much about social norms and relationships, about goals and means, about winners and losers." One portion of Gerbner's research involves compiling "risk ratios" in an effort to discern which minority groups—including children, the aged, and women—tend to be the victims of the aggressors in drama. This provides a picture of a pecking order within society (white males on top, no surprise there) that has remained somewhat consistent over the 20-year history of the index.

In a press release accompanying the 1993 violence index, Gerbner discusses his investigations of the long-term effects of television viewing. Heavy viewers were more likely to express feelings of living in a hostile world. Gerbner adds, "Violence is a demonstration of power. It shows who can get away with what against whom."

In a previous violence index compiled for cable-television programs, violence is defined as a "clear-cut and overt episode of physical violence—hurting or killing or the threat of hurting and/or killing—in any context." An earlier definition reads: "The overt expression of physical force against self or other compelling action against one's will on pain of being hurt or killed, or actually hurting or killing." These definitions have been criticized for being too broad; they encompass episodes of physical comedy, depiction of accidents in dramas, and even violent incidents in documentaries. They also include zany cartoon violence; in fact, the indexes for Saturday-morning programming tend to be substantially higher than the indexes for prime-time programming. Gerbner argues that, since he is analyzing cultural norms and since television entertainment is a deliberately conceived expression of these norms, his definition serves the purposes of his study.

The incidents of violence (total number = R) in a given viewing period are compiled by Gerbner's staff. Some of the statistics are easy to derive, such as the percentage of programs with violence, the number of violent scenes per hour, and the actual duration of violence, in minutes per hour. The actual violence index is calculated by adding together the following stats:

%P—the *percentage* of programs in which there is violence;

2(R/P)—twice the number of violent episodes per program;

2(R/H)—twice the number of violent episodes per *hour;*

%V—percentage of *leading characters* involved in violence, either as victim or perpetrator; and

%K—percentage of leading characters involved in an actual *killing,* either as victim or perpetrator.

But if these are the factors used to compile the violence profile, it's difficult to see how they can provide a clear-cut mandate for the specific content of television drama. For example, two of the numbers used are averages; why are they arbitrarily doubled and then added to percentages? Also, because the numbers are determined by a definition which explicitly separates violence from dramatic context, the index says little about actual television content outside of a broad, overall gauge. One may imagine a television season of nothing but slapstick comedy with a very high violence profile.

This is why the violence profile is best understood within the context of Gerbner's wider analysis of media content. It does not lend itself to providing specific conclusions or guidelines of the sort urged by Senator Paul Simon. (It is important to note that, even though Simon observed little change in prime-time violence levels during his three-year antitrust exemption, the index for all three of those years was *below* the overall 20-year score.)

❦

Finally, there's the anecdotal evidence—loudly trumpeted as such by Carl Cannon in *Mother Jones*—where isolated examples of entertainment-inspired violence are cited as proof of its pernicious influence. Several such examples have turned up recently. A sequence was edited out of the film *The Good Son* in which McCaulay Culkin drops stuff onto a highway from an overhead bridge. (As we all know, nobody ever did this before the movie came out.) The film *The Program* was re-edited when some kids were killed imitating the film's characters, who "proved their courage" by lying down on a highway's dividing line. Perhaps most notoriously, in October 1993 a four-year-old Ohio boy set his family's trailer on fire, killing his younger sister; the child's mother promptly blamed MTV's "Beavis and Butt-head" for setting a bad example. But a neighbor interviewed on CNN reported that the family didn't even have cable television and that the kid had a local rep as a pyromaniac months before. This particular account was not followed up by the national media, which, if there were no enticing "Beavis and Butt-head" angle, would never have mentioned this fire at a low-income trailer park to begin with.

Numerous articles about media-inspired violence have cited similar stories—killers claiming to be Freddy Kreuger, kids imitating crimes they'd seen on a cop show a few days before, and so forth. In many of these cases, it is undeniably true that the person involved took his or her inspiration to act from a dramatic presentation in the media—the obvious example being John Hinckley's fixation on the film *Taxi Driver....* But stories of media-inspired violence are striking mainly because they're so *atypical* of the norm; the vast majority of people don't take a movie or a TV show as a license to kill. Ironically, it is the *abnormality* of these stories that ensures they'll get widespread dissemination and be remembered long after the more mundane crimes are forgotten.

Of course, there are a few crazies out there who will be unfavorably influenced by what they see on TV. But even assuming that somehow the TV show (or movie or record) shares some of the blame, how does one predict what future crazies will take for inspiration? What guidelines would ensure that people write, act, or produce something that *will not upset a psychotic*? Not only is this a ridiculous demand, it's insulting to the public as well. We would all be treated as potential murderers in order to gain a hypothetical 5 percent reduction in violence.

❧❦❧

In crusades like this—where the villagers pick up their torches and go hunting after Frankenstein—people often lose sight of what they're defending. I've read reams of statements from people who claim to know what television does to kids; but what do *kids* do with television? Almost none of what I've read gives kids any credit for thinking. None of these people seems to remember what being a kid is like.

When *Jurassic Park* was released, there was a huge debate over whether or not children should be allowed to see it. Kids like to see dinosaurs, people argued, but this movie might scare them into catatonia. . . . These objections were actually taken seriously. But kids like dinosaurs because they're big, look really weird, and scare the hell out of everything around them. Dinosaurs *kick ass.* What parent would tell his or her child that dinosaurs were *cute*? . . .

Along the same lines, what kid hasn't tried to gross out everyone at the dinner table by showing them his or her chewed-up food? Or tried using a magnifying glass on an anthill on a hot day? Or clinically inspected the first dead animal he or she ever came across? Sixty years ago, adults were terrified of *Frankenstein* and fainted at the premiere of *King Kong*. But today, *Kong* is regarded as a fantasy story, *Godzilla* can be shown without the objections of child psychologists, and there are breakfast cereals called Count Chocula and Frankenberry. Sadly, there are few adults who seem to remember how they identified more with the monsters. Who wanted to be one of those stupid villagers waving torches at Frankenstein? That's what our *parents* were like.

But it's not just an issue of kids liking violence, grossness, or comic-book adventure. About 90 percent of the cartoon shows I watched as a child were the mass-produced sludge of the Hanna-Barbera Studios—like "Wacky Races," "The Jetsons," and "Scooby Doo, Where Are You?" I can't remember a single memorable moment from any of them. But that Bugs Bunny sequence at the beginning of this article (from *Rabbit Seasoning,* 1952, directed by Chuck Jones) was done from memory, and I have no doubt that it's almost verbatim.

I know that, even at the age of eight or nine, I had some rudimentary aesthetic sense about it all. There was something hip and complex about the Warner Bros. cartoons, and some trite, insulting *sameness* to the Hanna-Barbera trash, although I couldn't quite understand it then. Bugs Bunny clearly wasn't made for kids according to some study on social-interaction development. Bugs Bunny was meant to make adults laugh as much as children. Kids can also enjoy entertainment ostensibly created for adults—in fact, that's often the most rewarding kind. I had no trouble digesting *Jaws,* James Bond, and Clint Eastwood "spaghetti westerns" in my preteen years. And I'd have no problems with showing a 10-year-old *Jurassic Park,* because I know how much he or she would love it....

I don't enjoy bad television with lots of violence, but I'd rather not lose *decent* shows that use violence for good reason. Shows like "Star Trek," "X-Men," or the spectacular "Batman: The Animated Series" can give kids a sense of adventure while teaching them about such qualities as courage, bravery, and heroism. Even better, a healthy and robust spirit of irreverence can be found in Bugs Bunny, "Ren and Stimpy," and "Tiny Toons." Some of these entertainments—like adventure stories and comic books of the past—can teach kids how to be really *alive.*

Finally, if we must have a defense against the pernicious influence of the mass media, it cannot be from the Senate's legislation or the pronouncements of social scientists. It must begin with precisely the qualities I described above —especially irreverence. One good start is Comedy Central's "Mystery Science Theater 3000," where the main characters, forced to watch horrendous movies, fight back by heckling them. Not surprisingly, children love the show, even though most of the jokes go right over their curious little heads. They recognize a kindred spirit in "MST 3000." Kids want to stick up for themselves, maybe like Batman, maybe like Bugs Bunny, or even like Beavis and Butt-head—but always against a world made by adults.

You know, *adults*—those doofuses with the torches, trying to burn up Frankenstein in the old mill.

CHALLENGE QUESTIONS

Does Viewing Television Increase a Child's Aggression?

1. Pretend that you have two young children, ages 5 and 7. After reading the selections by Centerwall and Siano, how would you handle television for your youngsters, and why?
2. Centerwall seems to imply that children have no choice but to imitate adults; imitation is instinctive. How does this explanation involve the issues of free choice and determinism? If children are truly determined by their environments and their instincts, can they be held responsible for their actions? Why, or why not?
3. Whose view does most of the research on this issue support, Centerwall's or Siano's? Review the research at your library to help you form a judgment.
4. There is considerable research on children who watch television with their parents. One set of findings indicates that parents who actively comment upon and engage their children in discussions about television programs minimize the impact of television's ill effects. How might such research affect the debate between Centerwall and Siano?

On the Internet ...

Basic Neural Processes

This is a highly interactive site tutorial on brain structures by Dr. John H. Krantz of Hanover College.

`http://psych.hanover.edu/Krantz/neurotut.html`

Cognitive Science Society, Inc.

This is the home page for the Cognitive Science Society, Inc.

`http://www.umich.edu/~cogsci/`

Max Planck Institute for Psychological Research

Several behavioral and cognitive development research projects are available at this site.

`http://www.mpipf-muenchen.mpg.de/BCD/bcd_e.htm`

Psychology Tutorials

A collection of interactive tutorials and simulations, primarily in the areas of sensation and perception, is available at this site.

`http://psych.hanover.edu/Krantz/tutor.html`

Your Mind's Eye

This site is a multimedia museum exhibit on illusions, which is a natural teaching device that will inform and delight the user about something that is most central to us: how we think and perceive.

`http://illusionworks.com/html/jump_page.html`

PART 4

Cognitive Processes

*T*he nature and limitation of our mental (or cognitive) processes pose fundamental questions for psychologists. Are mental capacities, such as intelligence, determined at birth? And if so, could there be innate differences between racial groups? Is it even valid to speak of intelligence as one entity, or are there mutiple intelligences? Also, can we trust our memories? For example, are memories of early sexual abuse always reliable? Can they be trusted enough to bring alleged abusers to trial?

- Should the Theory of Multiple Intelligences Be Abandoned?

- Do Adults Repress Childhood Sexual Abuse?

- Is There a Racial Difference in Intelligence?

ISSUE 8

Should the Theory of Multiple Intelligences Be Abandoned?

YES: Perry D. Klein, from "Multiplying the Problems of Intelligence by Eight: A Critique of Gardner's Theory," *Canadian Journal of Education* (vol. 22, no. 4, 1997)

NO: Howard Gardner, from "A Reply to Perry D. Klein's 'Multiplying the Problems of Intelligence by Eight,'" *Canadian Journal of Education* (vol. 23, no. 1, 1998)

ISSUE SUMMARY

YES: Perry D. Klein, who is on the University of Western Ontario's Faculty of Education, contends that Howard Gardner's theory of multiple intelligences can be boiled down to a collection of trivial statements or a circular argument. He argues that the theory says little about intelligence.

NO: Professor of human development Howard Gardner counters that Klein has misunderstood his theory and that his theory offers the educational system hope of reaching more students.

J ohn has never been as good as Sally at math. However, John can take apart a broken clock and fit it back together so that it runs like new, while Sally cannot. Is John nevertheless less intelligent than Sally? What about Jennifer, who can dance effortlessly, as though she were born to dance? Is her dancing proof of her intelligence? Most intelligence tests only attempt to measure one supposedly general form of intelligence—one form that presumably affects all abilities and skills. A conventional test of intelligence would not even ask about John's clock-repairing ability or Jennifer's dancing skills. Should it?

General intelligence tests are often criticized as being biased. Either they are viewed as racist because they favor the general intelligence of a particular race or they are considered too restrictive because they do not test general intelligence adequately. Psychologists have tried over the years to correct these problems.

Howard Gardner believes that it is psychology's whole idea of intelligence that is problematic. Gardner has revolutionized the field of intelligence measurement through his contention that there are multiple kinds of intelligence, not just one. He believes that educators should attempt to incorporate all of these different intelligences in their classrooms, and many educators seem to agree with him. Eventually, Gardner hopes, psychologists will catch up with educators and recognize the importance of these intelligences too.

Perry D. Klein, however, does not agree that recognizing multiple intelligences would be a step forward in psychology. In the following selection, Klein argues that Gardner's theory does little to explain intelligence. In one sense, the theory is trivial. For example, we already know that Jennifer has bodily-kinesthetic ability because she dances well. How does it help us to formalize this ability into some bodily-kinesthetic intelligence? Gardner also maintains that these intelligences are independent brain structures. But if each type of intelligence works together, as Gardner contends, and all scientific studies show the dependence of these multiple intelligences, there is little support for Gardner's independent brain structures. Klein concludes that these so-called multiple intelligences are nothing more than special abilities or cognitive styles and that calling them "intelligences" does not help educators, let alone psychologists.

Gardner, on the other hand, argues in the second selection that Klein has gotten it all wrong. Gardner sees the naming of several different fundamental intelligences as an important step toward understanding human ability because it identifies more specific categories of human capabilities. He also asserts that understanding the multiplicity of intelligence is more true to the organization of the brain and the vast research on intelligence. Thus, the theory of multiple intelligences not only provides a useful framework for understanding human abilities and skills, but it also takes seriously the idea that each human being is unique. This, in turn, encourages educators to recognize uniqueness and to avoid racism and other biases.

POINT

- The theory of multiple intelligences is not helpful, because it describes abilities that we are already aware of.

- Gardner contends that intelligences are independent, but this independence does not account for how they must interact in daily life.

- Research shows that Gardner's intelligences are so closely related that it makes little sense to distinguish them from general intelligence.

- Telling a student that he or she is low in one kind of intelligence may discourage her or him from trying activities related to that intelligence. As such, this theory may harm more than it helps.

COUNTERPOINT

- Multiple intelligences can tell us what the fundamental categories of human activity are.

- Intelligences can be distinct without having to be completely independent of one another.

- Distinguishing between different intelligences more closely represents research on brain organization and evolution.

- The theory of multiple intelligences allows students to be different and encourages educators to present ideas in many different ways.

Perry D. Klein

 **YES**

Multiplying the Problems
of Intelligence by Eight

Howard Gardner introduced the theory of multiple intelligences (MI) in his book *Frames of Mind* (1983). In place of the traditional view that there is one general intelligence, he contended that there are seven, each operating in a specific cultural domain: linguistic, logical-mathematical, spatial, bodily-kinesthetic, musical, interpersonal, and intrapersonal. Since then, Gardner (1995) has tentatively added "the intelligence of the naturalist," which includes the ability to understand living things and to use this knowledge productively, as in farming. Each intelligence has its own core set of operations and supports specific activities. Spatial intelligence, for example, mentally represents and transforms objects, and underpins navigation, mechanics, sculpture, and geometry. Because the intelligences are independent, most individuals show an uneven profile, with some intelligences greater than others (Gardner, 1983, 1993b; Gardner & Hatch, 1989).

MI has swept education in the 15 years since its inception. ERIC citations favourable to the theory run into the hundreds, including some in prestigious or widely circulating journals (e.g., Armstrong, 1994; Gardner, 1994, 1995; Gardner & Hatch, 1989; Nelson, 1995). Most authors cite MI theory as an egalitarian alternative both to the theory that there is one general intelligence, and also to the practice of teaching a curriculum that emphasizes language and mathematics....

However, few authors have systematically evaluated MI theory. D. Matthews (1988) argued in favour of it, noting that gifted students usually excel in a single domain, such as mathematics or music. Other authors have suggested friendly revisions, such as the need for a "moral" intelligence, clarification of the theory or its implications, more evidence, or recognition of other educational concerns (Boss, 1994; Eisner, 1994; Levin, 1994). Some researchers in the psychometric tradition have rejected MI theory outright, claiming that Gardner's intelligences correlate positively with I.Q. and therefore are factors of general intelligence (Brand, 1996; Sternberg, 1983). Morgan (1992) noted the same positive correlations, and added that several of Gardner's intelligences cannot be conceptually distinguished from one another. Instead, Morgan interpreted these "intelligences" as cognitive styles. In the most sustained critique of MI, Ericsson and Charness (1994) suggested that expert performances are based on highly specific skills developed largely through extended deliberate practice, rather than on broad abilities.

Conceptual Problems

If someone were to ask, "Why is Michael a good dancer?," the MI answer would be "Because he has high bodily-kinesthetic intelligence." If the questioner then asked, "What is bodily-kinesthetic intelligence?," the answer would be "[It] is the ability to use one's body in highly differentiated and skilled ways, for expressive as well as goal-directed purposes... [and] to work skillfully with objects" (Gardner, 1983, p. 206). This explanation, however, is circular: the definition of bodily-kinesthetic intelligence is virtually a definition of dance, so the explanation says, in effect, that Michael is a good dancer because he is a good dancer. In fact, the explanation is less informative than the original question, which at least identified the type of physical activity in which Michael excels. MI's reliance on this sort of explanation makes the theory tautological, and, therefore, necessarily true (Smedslund, 1979). It also makes it trivial.

On the other hand, ascribing an achievement to an "intelligence" has a series of far-from-trivial implications. It means that performances are expressions of moderately general abilities, such as bodily-kinesthetic intelligence, rather than either very general abilities, such as general intelligence, or very specific skills, such as knowing how to dance. It also implies that whereas Michael may be better at dance than at other physical activities, his high "bodily-kinesthetic intelligence" should give him an advantage in these areas as well. Conversely, he need not be good at non-physical tasks, such as writing poems or solving mathematics problems. Furthermore, ascribing some level of achievement to an ability such as an "intelligence," rather than to an acquisition, such as "knowledge," suggests that this level will be relatively stable over time, and that its origins may be innate (Gardner, 1995).

Gardner (1983) goes even further, claiming that the "intelligences" are modules (pp. 55–56, 280–285) in approximately the sense proposed by Fodor (1983) or Allport (1980). Modules are neural structures that quickly process particular kinds of content. Colour vision, speech perception, and facial recognition have all been ascribed to modules. Each module is "computationally autonomous," meaning that it carries out its operations independently, and, for the most part, does not share resources with other modules. This autonomy implies that the internal workings of one module are not available to others, although the "output" of one module can become the "input" of another. In short, the implication of modularity for MI theory is that the mind is made up of seven (or eight) innate mechanisms, each of which works largely independently to handle one kind of content.

However, this independence makes the theory insufficient to account for some familiar experiences. Most activities involve several intelligences (Gardner, 1983, p. 304). Dance is both musical and physical; conversation is both linguistic and interpersonal; and solving a physics problem is both spatial and logical-mathematical. Modularity *per se* is not the problem, because the output of one module can become the input of another. But Gardner has defined the intelligences of MI in terms of their differing content, which raises the question of how they could exchange information. The intelligences conceivably could be coordinated by a central executive, but Gardner is reluctant to endorse this option. He and Walters (1993a, pp. 42–43) concede that there could be a "dumb executive" that simply prevents conflicts among intelligences, but this concession does not explain how they can work together productively.

. . . MI theory places our ability to use language in one intelligence, and the representation of most objects that can be spoken about in other intelligences. This breach is especially problematic when Gardner assigns "semantics" to linguistic intelligence. If the concept "mammal" is in linguistic intelligence, how does "naturalist's intelligence" function without this knowledge? And if the mammal concept is in a shared code, what becomes of modularity? The same problem arises with the overlap between, on the one hand, the pragmatic aspect of linguistic intelligence, and on the other hand, interpersonal intelligence.

The "strong" claim that humans have several distinct intelligences is difficult to defend, and Gardner sometimes presents MI theory in a "weak" form. He has written that it is "less a set of hypotheses and predictions than it is an organized framework" (Gardner, 1994, p. 578). He has allowed that the components of each intelligence can dissociate or uncouple (Gardner, 1983, p. 173). He also acknowledges that pairs of intelligences may "overlap" or be correlated (Gardner & Walters, 1993a, pp. 41–42). Finally, he has suggested that "many people can evaluate their intelligences and plan to use them together in certain putatively successful ways" (p. 43), leaving some room for an executive that spans the intelligences.

These concessions risk, however, returning Gardner to the first problem of MI theory: triviality. If the intelligences extensively exchange information, cooperate in activities, or share a common executive, then there is little warrant for characterizing them as independent entities. Of course, Gardner could claim that although the intelligences are distinct, in practice they always work together. However, this concession makes the multiplicity of the intelligences a distinction without a difference, and invites the reply that the system as a whole is one single intelligence, and specific abilities, such as spatial reasoning, are mere components of this intelligence.

These two contrasting kinds of conceptual objections place Gardner on the horns of a dilemma: If he claims that the intelligences are independent, then it is difficult to account for their interaction during many human activities. If he weakens the theory by claiming that they are not independent, then it is difficult to warrant either calling them "intelligences" or claiming that they are "modules." And if Gardner equivocates by trying to claim that both the strong and the weak versions of the theory are true, then MI theory become ambiguous and contradictory.

Fortunately, Gardner is generally committed to presenting the theory in its strong version, so that it can be meaningfully evaluated:

> Controlled experiments could either confirm or disconfirm MI. Several come to mind: a test of the independence of intelligences, for example.... If there turned out to be a significant correlation among these faculties, as measured by appropriate assessments, the supposed independence of the faculties would be invalidated. (Gardner & Walters, 1993a, p. 38)

This claim invites a review of the empirical evidence for MI theory.

Empirical Problems

Exceptional Populations

Gardner views the existence of groups that he believes to be high or low in one specific intelligence as part of the evidence for MI. The first of these are the geniuses: Yehudi Menuhin illustrates exceptional musical intelligence; Babe Ruth, outstanding bodily-kinesthetic intelligence; and Barbara McClintock, outstanding logical-mathematical intelligence (Gardner, 1993b). However, the abilities of Gardner's candidates do not appear to correspond to the categories of MI theory. Many excel in more than one domain: Barbara McClintock's work spanned the logical-mathematical and natural domains (pp. 19–20), Virginia Woolf's, the linguistic and intrapersonal domains (pp. 24–25), and Albert Einstein's, the spatial and the logical-mathematical domains (Gardner, 1993a, pp. 104–105). It is to be expected that if the intelligences are independent, then some individuals will excel in two or more domains, but if Gardner fails to show that most achieve excellence in one specific domain, then his claim that the intelligences are independent is threatened. Conversely, Gardner does not show that any of the geniuses excel throughout one of the domains defined by MI theory; instead, each seems to excel on some smaller subset of activities within a domain. Unless Gardner can show that most geniuses perform relatively well throughout a domain, then the notion that the intelligences are integrated structures is threatened. Generally, the difficulty with Gardner's discussion of genius is that many psychological theories imply some way of categorizing individuals of exceptional ability; he has not yet shown that MI theory fits the data better than other theories....

Psychometric Research

Gardner also relies on statistical research. Factor analysis is a procedure that can be used to tease out themes appearing within, or across, tests. Several factors similar to Gardner's intelligences have emerged in such analyses, including linguistic (Wiebe & Watkins, 1980), spatial (Gustafsson, 1984), and social factors (Rosnow, Skleder, Jaeger, & Rind, 1994). But this kind of research provides shaky support for MI. First, the factors in these studies typically are not independent, but instead correlate positively with one another, a fact that has been used to argue both for the existence of general intelligence and against MI (Brand, 1996; Sternberg, 1983). Although Gardner has replied that this evidence comes almost entirely from tests of logical-mathematical or linguistic intelligence (Gardner & Walters, 1993a, p. 39), it is important to note that spatial tasks correlate substantially with verbal tasks even when performance measures are used (Wechsler, 1974)....

Pedagogical Problems

One response to ... criticisms could be to claim that even though MI theory is conceptually and empirically weak, it remains a useful framework for teaching. But this is far from clear. Interpretations have been so diverse that Kornhaber has noted that "one reason for the success of MI is that educators can cite it without having to do anything differently" (cited in Gardner, 1994, p. 580)....

Some educators have claimed that a benefit of the MI framework is that children learn to identify their own "areas of strength," and some schools now issue report cards based on the theory (see Hanson, 1995; Hoerr, 1994; Wallach & Callahan, 1994). However, there is good reason to predict that these practices will backfire. The converse of being "high" in some intelligences is being "mediocre" or "low" in others. Students who believe that they are low in an ability often avoid activities that call on it, even when they might learn from the effort (Covington, 1992; Palmquist & Young, 1992). Paradoxically, students' beliefs that they are high in an ability can lead to the same result in the long run. Those who attribute their achievements to such ability approach tasks with confidence. But, when they encounter a problem that they cannot solve easily, they often quit. Apparently, their theory that achievement reflects ability leads them to interpret failure as a lack of this ability. In contrast, students who attribute achievement to effort, learning, and the application of appropriate strategies are more likely to persist when "the going gets tough," and to recover after initial failure (Dweck & Leggett, 1988).

These objections invite the fundamental pedagogical question: Is MI the right *kind* of theory for education? Although Gardner stresses the differences between general intelligence and multiple intelligences, the two frameworks nevertheless share fundamental characteristics that limit their relevance to teaching. Both identify cognitive structures far too broad to be useful for interpreting any specific educational tasks. For instance, the knowledge that basketball relies on "bodily-kinesthetic intelligence" tells a coach nothing about the skills that her players need to learn. Because both general intelligence and MI are theories of ability rather than theories of knowledge or learning, they offer only a static interpretation of children's performance; knowing that a student is high in "musical intelligence" provides no clues about how to enrich his music education; knowing that he is low in musical intelligence provides no clues about how to remedy it....

Conclusion

In examining the nature of intelligence, Gardner and his colleagues have used a wider set of tools than have traditional psychometric researchers. They have contended compellingly that the arts are as much intellectual activities as are writing, mathematics, and science (Gardner, 1982). MI researchers have drawn educators' attention to an alternative to the theory of general intelligence. And Gardner (1983, p. 297) is admirably willing to consider criticisms of his own framework. However, I contend that MI theory offers a level of analysis neither empirically plausible nor pedagogically useful.

Howard Gardner  **NO**

A Reply to Perry D. Klein's "Multiplying the Problems of Intelligence by Eight"

Domains vs. Intelligence

Like many critics, Perry Klein confuses or conflates the concepts of *Intelligence* and *domain*. As I conceive it, an intelligence is a biopsychological potential. Because of evolutionary pressures, human beings have evolved over a long period of time to be sensitive to certain kinds of information in the environment or culture, and to process this content in certain ways. Specific neurological structures subserve each of the several intelligences. In the absence of proper stimulation, however, an intelligence will not develop; it is not an instinct.

Whereas the notion of "intelligences" comes initially from the biological sciences, "domain" is a cultural concept. Every culture features a large number of disciplines, crafts, activities, and so on, in which at least some members attain expertise. Activities ranging from chess to psychology to ballet to mechanics are all domains. Both the boundaries and the details of domains will change over time, depending on individual and cultural values and practices.

It is easy to see why intelligences can be confused with domains; indeed, I have done so myself. But they are different concepts. Any intelligence (like spatial intelligence) can be drawn on in many domains (ranging from chess to sailing to sculpture); and, in turn, any domain can involve one or more intelligences (for example, chess presumably draws on spatial, logical, personal, and perhaps other intelligences as well).

Starting with his very first example, Klein confuses these concepts throughout his paper. He claims that MI theory is circular because being "a good dancer" is the same as having "high bodily kinesthetic intelligence." But the domain of dancing involves several intelligences, and one can be a credible dancer even with modest bodily-kinesthetic intelligence. By the same token, possession of high bodily potential does not mean that one will become a good dancer. One has to decide to pursue this domain and then to have considerable practice, good teachers, cultural support, and the like. Inasmuch as dancing is in no sense equivalent to bodily kinesthetic intelligence, the charge of circularity evaporates.

Size of Unit and Scholarly Goals

Much of Klein's paper is an attack on the notion of intelligence as a viable psychological construct. On the one hand, he seems sympathetic to the notion of a single "general intelligence" and he expresses regret that I have broken this venerable concept down into a number of varieties. On the other hand, he is also partial to the notion that individuals have very specific kinds of abilities or skills, and he critiques my intelligences for being too broad and undifferentiated a concept.

Klein would like to have it both ways but he can't. All constructs have regions where they are appropriate and applicable, and other regions where they involve a stretch or are manifestly inappropriate. When speaking of diseases, it has traditionally been appropriate to speak at the level of tissues and organs; and in recent years, it has sometimes been possible to add explanations at the cellular or even the molecular level. In analyzing social structures, one may speak of entities ranging from the family or the local neighbourhood to the entire nation or the "global community." One level of analysis does not vitiate or invalidate the others; each has its proper scope.

... I go on at great length in *Frames of Mind* (1983/1993b) to illustrate that each intelligence is itself composed of subintelligences, which may... operate in modular fashion; and I indicate that an individual might be strong in one subintelligence (say, dealing with wide spaces, or solving human conflict) while not as strong in another associated subintelligence (dealing with circumscribed spaces, or directing others in battle).

The question, then, is not "one intelligence or several intelligences or dozens of subintelligences." Rather, the question is: Under which circumstances does it make most scientific sense to invoke concepts at these varying levels of analysis? I believe that the positing of a small number of relatively independent intelligences has several virtues: it respects neural organization; it reflects a plausible evolutionary course; it organizes a vast amount of data in a convenient way; it provides a framework that can guide (and has guided) teachers who are concerned with questions of pedagogy, curriculum, and assessment. Indeed, although this is not in itself evidence for the theory, I am quite sure that "MI" theory would have been ignored in both psychological and educational circles if, like J. P. Guilford (1967), I had asserted the existence of 120 or 150 different intelligences. George Miller's magic number 7 (Miller, 1956) has relevance that extends beyond the limits of short-term memory.

Klein questions whether the correlation among the various subintelligences is sufficiently great to legitimate their grouping under a single label. This is a reasonable question and it might well yield different answers for different candidate subintelligences. At present, we lack sufficient data to answer the question.

My own prediction is that, for two reasons, future research will confirm the utility of speaking of "linguistic" or "spatial" or "interpersonal" intelligences rather than referring only to the candidate subintelligences— for example, "foreign-language-learning intelligence" or "conflict-resolution intelligence." First of all, the neural regions involved in the subintelligences-of-one-intelligence are closer to one another and are more likely to work in consort. Second, most *tasks in a domain* call on more than one of the subintelligences. As individuals become practised at these tasks, they will necessarily strengthen the associated subintelligences, and so measures of subintelligences drawn from the same family will show higher correlations than measures of subintelligences drawn from two separate intelligences.

Having made these two general points, let me now turn to Klein's more specific comments.

Conceptual Issues

... In challenging the intelligences, Klein questions how the concept of mammal can be construed without linguistic intelligence. However, infants without language, globally aphasic patients, and individuals in cultures without a Linnaean taxonomy can all make plausible groupings of animals, which might even be equivalent to the distinction between mammal (except for dolphins!) and nonmammal. The principal intelligence at work would be naturalist intelligence—the capacity to recognize patterns in the natural world. When an individual organizes these discriminations and perceptions, she uses logical intelligence; if she codifies the classification in language, she uses linguistic intelligence.

Klein says that the intelligences cannot be both independent and interactive in many human activities. This simply does not follow. Members of a quartet are independent organisms who interact well and subtly in the performance of musical compositions. Moreover, I have never claimed that intelligences are completely independent; rather, they are relatively independent from one another, as illustrated by the fact that strength in one intelligence does not predict strength or weakness in other intelligences.

Empirical Issues

Klein notes that exceptional individuals (genius is his word, not one that I favour) are often outstanding in more than one intelligence. I not only grant this point, I insist on it and suggest that the extraordinariness is a function of strength in two or more intelligences, often ones unusual for the domain (Gardner, 1993a). But Klein misses the point here. If exceptional lawyers were all strong in linguistic and personal intelligences, my analysis would be suspect. But some lawyers stand out by virtue of their combination of linguistic and logical analysis; some by virtue of their logical and interpersonal skills; still others (say, entertainment or patent lawyers) for their musical or spatial intelligences.

I would agree that an individual may be outstanding in a domain, even if some of his associated subintelligences are less striking than others. No doubt there are great writers who are not skilled in learning foreign languages or in performing grammatical parsing. However, for the reasons stated above, I'd bet that writers are more likely to be excellent in these domains than, say, a comparison group of architects or physicists....

Pedagogy

Although I continue to work on the theory of multiple intelligences, my own work over the past 15 years has been primarily on practical applications and implications of the theory. I have written dozens of articles on this subject, authored a book (Gardner, 1993c), and drafted another (Gardner, unpublished manuscript). And my own efforts have represented but a few drops in the ocean of writings by educators of many persuasions.

I agree with Klein that many applications of MI theory, though well intentioned, have been superficial and ill advised (Gardner, 1995). I would add the point, missed by Klein, that one should never proceed directly from psychological or scientific theory to educational practices. Educational practice is a co-function of one's values, on the one hand, and one's reflections on efforts to achieve successful learning and pedagogy, on the other. Neither falls directly from scientific discovery, though both can be informed by relevant scientific work....

I've elected not to review Klein's educational comments point by point, since I have dealt with these points elsewhere (e.g., Gardner 1993c, 1995, in press-a). Far more useful, I believe, is a brief statement of the two major educational implications that I have drawn from the theory, after many years of thought and experimentation:

1. We need to take differences among individuals very seriously. Rather than teaching all students the same content in the same way, and assessing them in the same way, we now have the opportunity (especially through technology) to individualize education. The intelligences offer one initial way in which we might begin to think about individual differences in the classroom and in other educational environments.

2. Important curricular ideas can and should be presented to students in many ways. MI theory suggests a number of different entry points (how to introduce the topic); various analogies and metaphors (where unfamiliar materials are illuminated by more familiar instances); and different "model languages" or "ways of representing" the key points of a concept, theory, or idea (Gardner, in press-b, unpublished manuscript).

When the variety of intelligences is exploited in the presentation of curricula, two desirable outcomes are obtained. First, more students are reached. Second, students are exposed to expert knowledge—because experts are individuals who have multiple representations of the same content.

Concluding Comment

In my view, multiple intelligences theory is a far richer, more flexible, and more useful set of ideas than Klein's article implied. On the conceptual level, MI theory insists not on a domination by a single middle-level construct, but rather on a place for that construct in between the overarching notion of a general intelligence and an endless list of specific skills and subskills. On the empirical level, it provides a far better explanation for many groups and behaviours than does either the general or the local perspective. Finally, despite inevitable caricatures, the theory lays the groundwork for an education that can reach more students and do so in a way that deepens their understanding.

CHALLENGE QUESTIONS

Should the Theory of Multiple Intelligences Be Abandoned?

1. What do you think the goal of intelligence testing should be in psychology? In education? Does acknowledging the existence of multiple intelligences help or hinder that goal? Why?
2. How might a psychologist test Gardner's "other" intelligences? Pick one of the eight intelligences mentioned in the selections and outline what such a test would be like. What questions or activities would be involved, and how would they be scored?
3. Klein contends that scoring a child low in a particular intelligence might discourage that child from trying something new. This is the same type of criticism leveled against traditional intelligence tests—that they discourage children from trying activities the intelligence tests have told them they are not talented at. Do you think the theory of multiple intelligences helps to alleviate this problem or only makes it worse by increasing the number of problematic categories? Explain.
4. Intelligence testing has a checkered history. Briefly review some of the other criticisms of intelligence testing. Would Gardner's theory affect these criticisms positively or negatively? Explain.

ISSUE 9

Do Adults Repress Childhood Sexual Abuse?

YES: May Benatar, from "Running Away from Sexual Abuse: Denial Revisited," *Families in Society: The Journal of Contemporary Human Services* (May 1995)

NO: Susan P. Robbins, from "Wading Through the Muddy Waters of Recovered Memory," *Families in Society: The Journal of Contemporary Human Services* (October 1995)

ISSUE SUMMARY

YES: May Benatar, a clinical social worker and lecturer, asserts that recent publicity on memories of sexual abuse has focused more on the "hype" of sexual abuse rather than on the actual prevailing act of sexual abuse. She maintains that repressed memories are a common response of child sexual abuse and that they can be recovered in adulthood.

NO: Susan P. Robbins, an associate professor of graduate social work, contends that there is little support for the idea of repressed or dissociated memories of child sexual abuse in scientific studies. She also argues that outside sources can trigger or influence many inaccurate memories of child abuse.

I t is hard to imagine a more heinous crime than sexual abuse. Yet, perhaps surprisingly, it is a crime that often goes unpunished. Frequently, sexual abusers are family members and their victims are children who are too young to protest or too naive to know that they are being violated. This problem is part of the reason why memories have become so significant to the sexual abuse issue. Often it is not until the victims become adults that they realize they were abused.

Complicating the issue is that the reliability of memory itself is questionable. In the courtroom, for example, eyewitness testimony has lost much of its credibility because memories of a single occurrence can vary from witness to witness. Suggestive questions may even change the memory of a witness. More pertinently, the so-called repression or dissociation of sexual abuse memories has been called by some "false memories." Many feel that "memories" of sexual abuse are not always real; that is, memories can be changed by outside influences, such as suggestions, "trigger" questions, and hypnosis. If a therapist or another investigator is suspected of manipulating subject responses and "creating" memories of sexual abuse, then the validity of "recovered" memories becomes questionable. On the other hand, some therapists believe that there is an overemphasis on the validity of memories, sometimes referred to as "hype." Their concern is that by getting too bogged down in the "hype" of sexual memories, people are ignoring the pain of the victims.

In the following selection, May Benatar asserts that too much attention is indeed being paid to this "hype" and to the mistrust of children with memories of sexual abuse. She questions the value being placed on the welfare of children, stating, "The author asks whether we are panicking over child abuse. Is criminal prosecution tantamount to panic? And if it is, is the abuse of children not worthy of such a response?" But Benatar emphasizes that a lack of explicit memories of sexual abuse does not mean that abuse did not occur. Many times, child sexual abuse has occurred regardless of the victim's recollection of explicit details.

In the second selection, Susan P. Robbins refutes Benatar's arguments and calls for greater attention in distinguishing conjecture from fact. Robbins sides with the critics and points out that critics are skeptical of recovered memories because there is no support from reproducible scientific evidence. She states, "[The critics] contend that the growing body of research on memory has consistently shown memory to be subject to inaccuracy, distortion, and fabrication." Robbins also calls attention to the differences between child sexual abuse and the "recovered memories" of abuse, a distinction often lost on proponents of prosecuting child sexual abuse.

POINT

- Denial of child sexual abuse comes from a backlash against feminism.

- One out of every three girls and one out of every seven to ten boys is sexually abused.

- Clinicians have been trained to deny that their clients have been sexually abused because Sigmund Freud was politically pressured to abandon his theory of repressed sexual abuse.

- Traumatic memories are stored in a special part of the brain and are retrieved in response to a number of stimuli, such as suggestion.

- By focusing on cases of "false memories" of sexual abuse, society is denying the pain of its children.

COUNTERPOINT

- The real feminist issue is the victimization of clients who may have traumatic memories implanted by a therapist.

- Because statistics regarding sexual abuse are so difficult to accurately gather, they should always be viewed with caution.

- Freud never denied his clients' conscious memories of sexual abuse; he only questioned their unconscious and recovered memories.

- Memory experts agree that memory is not stored in the brain but is reconstructed meaningfully.

- Questioning the veracity of recovered or repressed memories is not the same as doubting that child sexual abuse occurs.

May Benatar  **YES**

Running Away from Sexual Abuse: Denial Revisited

After a period of increased professional and public awareness of how pervasive the sexual maltreatment of children is in our society, we appear to be in danger of vaulting away from hard-won insights into this major public health issue. Both propounding and expressing the prejudices of the culture, the press and other media have taken to indicting the veracity of traumatic memories of survivors of sexual abuse, minimizing the toxic long-term effects of the sexual maltreatment of children, and casting doubt on both the skill and good intentions of clinicians treating both child victims and adult survivors. We have seen front-page articles on the purported "false" memories of adult survivors of abuse; examples of "false" accusations of innocent parents, grandparents, or teachers; or speculations that therapists, many of whom are survivors themselves, intentionally or unintentionally suggest events to their patients that never took place.

A 1993 *Newsweek* cover photograph showed a middle-age couple convicted of molesting their grandchildren. The caption asks: "When does the fight to protect our kids go too far?" Does this strange juxtaposition of material imply that convicting child molesters is "going too far?" The article inside (Shapiro, 1993) reviews a few recent court cases and one reversal and addresses the issue of child testimony; the author asks whether we are panicking over child abuse. Is criminal prosecution tantamount to panic? And if it is, is the abuse of children not worthy of such a response?

In the *New Yorker,* Wright (1993a, 1993b) wrote a two-part article on the case of a Washington state deputy sheriff, who, after being accused of child abuse by his two daughters, confessed to sexually abusing them, prostituting them to family friends, and being part of a satanic cult. The case unraveled when it was discovered that at least some of the accusations and confessions by both parents resulted from overzealous questioning and suggestions by police interrogators on what were alleged to be highly suggestible subjects. The article clearly implies that this case represents one of many instances of modern-day witch hunts—the innocent "witches" in this case being those accused of perpetrating unthinkable crimes such as ritual sexual abuse, torture, and murder.

In *Mother Jones,* a well-regarded if somewhat off-beat publication, Watters (1993) also expressed concern about false memories and false accusations in a report of a young woman's delayed discovery of childhood abuse. The woman entered therapy following a severe depressive episode and while in therapy recovered memories of sexual abuse. Although the facts of the case neither ex-culpate the accused nor affirm the victim's accusations, the author uses this case to propose that "a substantial segment of the therapy community has charged ahead, creating a *growth* industry around the concept of recovered memories."

Even Carol Tavris (1993), a noted feminist author, cast a skeptical eye on what she termed the "incest-survivor machine," an umbrella term for therapists working with adult survivors, writers of self-help books for survivors, and the grass-roots recovery movement of adult survivors.

For clinicians working with patients to address the post-traumatic effects of childhood sexual abuse and for adult survivors struggling to take their own stories seriously and understand the difficulties of their adult lives as sequelae of and adaptation to violations that occurred during childhood, this emphasis on the "hype" of sexual abuse is deeply troubling.

Child Abuse: Past and Present Findings

The reality of child abuse is well established. Why then is it currently accept-able, even fashionable, to doubt the victims, those who prosecute for them, and those who treat their post-traumatic illnesses? This backlash against sexual-abuse survivors has social, cultural, political, and psychological roots. One reading is that this backlash is a response to the evolution in law regarding the issue of incest—an evolution that now allows some adult survivors to seek legal redress many years, even decades, after the commission of crimes. An-other reason for this backlash may be related to the cultural mysogyny that Faludi (1991) documents in her book *Backlash,* which refers to the social forces that thwart the gains that women have achieved in society. On another level of analysis, we may understand this phenomenon of denial of social realities as "cultural dissociation." As a society we are unable to accept the reality of the cruelty, sadism, neglect, and narcissism that adults inflict upon children. In a world where some people still debate the reality of Nazi death camps, it is not surprising that we have difficulties acknowledging that 1 of every 3 girls and 1 of 7 to 10 boys are "used" by an adult in a manner that brings great harm to them for the rest of their lives.

The epidemiology of child sexual abuse has been carefully documented. Kinsey found in the early 1950s that 24% of his female sample of 4,000 women reported sexual abuse in childhood (before the age of puberty) (Brownmiller, 1975). Dozens of studies have confirmed this finding. Thirty years later, Russell (1986) carefully surveyed a nonclinical population of nearly 1,000 women. She reported that 38% of the sample reported being molested before the age of 18 and 28% before puberty. In addition, she found that most abusers are known to the child as trusted individuals who occupy a position of authority over the child.

In another significant study, Herman and Schatzow (1987) discussed recall of traumatic memories from childhood often dissociated by the child in an effort to maintain secrecy and safety. Fifty-three female patients in group psychotherapy reported delayed recall of traumatic memory; 74% of the women confirmed their memories of abuse by obtaining independent corroborating evidence—physical evidence, diaries, pictures, confirmation by perpetrators and/ or corroboration by other family members who had also been victimized. This study appears to strengthen Russell's and Kinsey's data. Even those with delayed recall, when seeking confirmation of the reality of their memories many years after the fact, are able to confirm the memory. To my knowledge, no comparable study demonstrates *false* recall of childhood-abuse memories.

Interestingly, the conflict between the reality of child abuse and the voices of disbelief and disavowal is not unique to the 1990s; a century ago western psychiatry experienced a similar struggle and process. Masson (1984), in *The Assault on Truth,* presented important work done in 19th-century France regarding the criminal brutalization and sexual abuse of children. In setting the stage for his explanation of why Freud first adopted and later abandoned the "seduction theory" to explain the origins of hysterical neurosis, Masson discusses child abuse in Europe during that period. Forensic psychiatrists uncovered shocking facts about child abuse. Ambrose Tardieu, a professor and dean of forensic medicine at the University of Paris and president of the Academy of Medicine in Paris in 1860, published "A Medico-Legal Study of Cruelty and Brutal Treatment Inflicted on Children." He presented case after case of detailed medical evidence indicating severe child abuse, including the sexual abuse of children. He indicated that the phenomenon was not rare and that perpetrators were often parents and that victims were often very young and primarily girls.

Paul Brouardel, Tardieu's successor to the chair of legal medicine in Paris and also a contemporary of Freud, described perpetrators as "excellent family men" who were often the fathers of the victims. Brouardel was a collaborator of Jean-Martin Charcot, a neurologist who demonstrated the efficacy of hypnosis in the treatment of psychiatric patients, particularly female hysterics. Freud was fascinated by Charcot's work and came to Paris to study with him. Masson argues that Freud and his contemporaries were more than likely aware of the work of Tardieu, Brouardel, and other forensic psychiatrists in France through their studies with Charcot. Freud's early struggles to understand the underpinnings of neurosis suggest his awareness of the traumatic origins of psychic disturbance as well as the influence that the French pioneers had on his clinical awareness. In the late 1890s Freud (1984) wrote movingly and persuasively in *The Aetiology of Hysteria* about 18 cases of hysterical neurosis in which an early experience of sexual abuse had led to hysterical symptoms in adult life— symptoms similar to what we categorize today as post-traumatic stress disorder or dissociative disorder.

However, it was Pierre Janet, another visitor to Charcot's seminars, who developed both a complex theoretical understanding and efficacious treatment model for hysteria. Janet published many of his findings the year before Freud's *Aetiology of Hysteria* appeared, but unlike Freud he held fast to the trauma model that Freud renounced. Janet described many cases of what we have come to understand as dissociative disorders and multiple personality disorder. Janet understood his patients' symptoms, much as trained clinicians do today, as ingenious and creative adaptations to overwhelming childhood stress such as physical and/or sexual abuse. He saw hysterical symptoms, not as compromise formations of drive derivatives or expressions of drive conflicts, but rather as fossils from the past, derivatives of traumatic memory, communications of early betrayals and overwhelming affects (van der Kolk & van der Hart, 1989).

Yet for most of the 20th century, Janet was *not* studied and *not* employed in our attempts to understand mental life. Freud's development of psychoanalysis obliterated Janet's work. To read Janet today, 100 years later, is to be struck with how little modern trauma psychology and our understandings of traumatic memory can add to his understandings, how clearly he explicated what we have come to rediscover in the past decade and a half, and how brilliantly he anticipated modern findings on the psychophysiology of memory.

Herman (1992) and others have proposed that Freud and his students moved away from trauma theory or the "seduction theory," because the zeitgeist of the time and place could not support such conclusions. Earlier in the century, in Tardieu's and Charcot's France, the political atmosphere was one of reform: challenges to the monarchy and the church enabled a movement toward understanding mental illness as a rational, not magical, pursuit. They viewed mental illness as a sequela of early experience that could be understood and addressed by science. These sociopolitical forces ushered in an era of more humane treatment of the mentally ill that approached mental illness as trauma based. Freud's science grew in different soil—Viennese soil—where trauma-based theory was unable to take root.

For a brief period in the 1800s, clinicians and students of forensic psychiatry knew that many children were severely abused by their families and that such abuse led to dramatic effects in the mental health of adults. They also understood effective treatment of these symptoms involved revisiting early memory and processing these memories in the context of a solid therapeutic alliance. By the beginning of the 20th century, after Freud had published *The Aetiology of Hysteria,* the political winds had shifted, as had the politics of psychiatry. Traumatic etiology was relegated to the background and endogenous intrapsychic conflicts moved to the foreground. We stopped looking at the environmental surround—the maltreatment of children—and turned our scientific gaze inward toward fantasy formation and the intricate topography of the mind.

Where Do We Go Today?

It has taken us nearly a century to get back to where we started—the work of Janet. Two concurrent social movements helped to reawaken our awareness of childhood trauma. In the 1970s, the returning Vietnam War veterans became quite active in seeking validation for their catastrophic experiences during the war. They organized themselves to obtain services from veterans hospitals and recognition for their suffering from their communities. Their illnesses became the focus for legal activity and psychiatric attention. Psychiatrists rediscovered "war neurosis" and learned from their patients about the aftereffects of severe, intense, and acute traumatic experience. Post-traumatic stress disorder became a diagnostic entity and was entered into the *Diagnostic and Statistical Manual of Mental Disorders* in 1980.

The other major social change that contributed to the reemergence of our awareness of childhood sexual abuse was the women's movement in the 1970s. Women meeting in consciousness-raising groups, helping one another to name their fears, their frustrations, and their hopes, began telling stories of sexual manipulation, sexual violence, and early experiences of sexual violation at the hands of family members. Women Against Rape centers sprang up across the country; from these centers rape-crisis-counseling centers were developed. Today, a strong grass-roots recovery movement exists, carrying the message about child abuse and dissociative disorders to the public. Individuals help one another in 12-step-type recovery groups, generating art, newsletters, books, workshops, and conferences to help heal themselves as well as educate clinicians and lay individuals.

As a result of these two powerful movements for social change, survivors of childhood sexual abuse found a voice and clinicians began to listen. By the 1980s we began to see new journals devoted to exploring the effects and the treatment of individuals so affected. A whole new subspecialty in psychiatry, psychology, and social work emerged: working with dissociative disorders. Today, however, troubling signs indicate that public and political retrenchment from various interconnecting and interactive factors are contributing to renewed denial and disavowal of the prevalence of child sexual abuse. Moreover, social, legal, political, and psychological pressures are undermining all that we have learned about the etiology and sequelae of this devastating societal problem.

Factor One

In many ways, the mass media have focused more attention on survivors than has the mental health establishment. Oprah, Phil, and Sally Jesse have featured shows alerting the public to the painful experiences of adult survivors, which has led to a "Geraldoizing" effect. Despite the fact that Geraldo Rivera has actually done a couple of interesting shows on multiple personality disorder and has devoted more time and attention to the consequences of severe childhood trauma than have many mental health professionals, his and other popular talk shows tend to be associated with sensationalism and exploitation. As a result, real problems are trivialized in the public mind. If Geraldo thinks it is interesting, it must be hype. The overall effect is chilling. Clients wonder whether their memories and intense psychic, even physical, pain associated with their abuse histories are merely childish bids for attention. A client who kept her childhood rape secret for 40 years spoke of her dread of being perceived as having the "designer" affliction of our time.

Factor Two

The effect on memory is one sequela of childhood trauma that muddies the water for both the layperson and professional. How reliable is memory?

Police and prosecutors of violent crime understand that survivors of psychological trauma make very poor witnesses. Janet brilliantly described the differences between what he termed "narrative memory" and "traumatic memory" (van der Kolk & van der Hart, 1989). Narrative memory is what we generally mean when we speak of memory. It involves a complex process whereby new experiences are integrated into preexisting schema or mental categories, along with the slow evolution and expansion of those schema. Traumatic memory is different. Trauma is an event or series of events that lies outside the ordinary, expectable events of life. It is overwhelming in its affective impact on the individual. It does not easily fit into preexisting schema, nor does it evolve easily with other memories. Traumatic memories are "dissociated." To use a computer analogy, narrative memory is stored on drive C, the drive that is generally available to consciousness and voluntary control processes. Although drive C may have subdirectories of unconsciousness as well, that is, memories that are repressed but can be brought into consciousness through psychoanalysis, dream work, free association, and the like, drive B, or dissociated, memories arise unexpectedly when someone or something triggers them into actualization: therapy, a child reaching a developmental milestone, a movie, a book, a television show, a death. Dissociated memories are fragmentary, illusive, uncertain, even terrifying.

If the trauma is not verifiable and if it occurred early in life and was severe, these dissociated states act as containers for memories and pain and assume the coherence of alternative selves, that is, separate personality or ego states that hold particular memories together. During the therapeutic process, the therapist and patient attempt to understand the nature of these drive B materials, retrieve them, and integrate them into drive C consciousness. In so doing, traumatic memory is integrated and assimilated into narrative memory.

For example, a 36-year-old woman who has been in therapy for three years struggling with depression and periodic panic attacks glances at her four-year-old daughter playing at the beach and suddenly remembers being raped by her father when she was four years old. In the following days, she questions her sanity and is unable to understand what is happening to her. Her therapist may also wonder about this bewildering experience. She will likely try to forget or trivalize it.

The impulse to both know the secrets of early trauma, and to tell it most typically fight with the impulse to keep the secret: what emerges is often jumbled and contradictory. That is the nature of traumatic memory! This is why victims are poor witnesses. The most common scenarios for survivors is to want to discredit their dissociated memories, not particularly to elevate them to heroic status. False memories, or memories that are iatrogenically induced during therapy, are not that common. Although some types of memories can be distorted or implanted in the minds of individuals under certain circumstances, evidence does not indicate that this occurs frequently, or even occasionally, in psychotherapeutic work with survivors of trauma.

Factor Three

Faludi (1991) states that approximately every 30 years a cultural backlash arises against nascent feminism. Even modest status gains by women are quickly followed by a cultural response indicating that these changes and gains are not good for society or women.

Sexual abuse and sexual violence are cast as women's issues, despite the fact that children of both sexes are affected by abuse. Attacks on feminism focus energy on maintaining the *status quo* in power relationships. As a result, child victims and adult survivors may be discredited under the rubric of women's issues. Faludi points to the 1980s as a decade of government retrenchment on women's issues, disproportionate cuts in funding for women's programs, and decreased commitment in government funding for battered women's programs, despite increases in domestic violence. A dramatic rise in sexual violence against women, an increase that outstrips other types of violent crimes, has been met with indifference at all levels of government.

The retreat from renewed awareness of child-abuse problems in general and sexual abuse in particular reflects this backlash. Interestingly, patients' veracity in therapy was never an issue until we began discussing issues of sexual abuse.

Factor Four

The changing legal climate regarding prosecution in civil incest suits has also affected adult-survivor issues. In the early 1980s, legal scholars began to reconsider the problem of seeking legal redress for crimes involving sexual abuse years after the commission of these crimes and after the statute of limitations had expired. In the *Harvard Women's Law Review*, Salten (1984) persuasively argued, "Given the latent nature and belated detection of many incest related injuries, the parent's special duty of care to his [sic] child, the youth of the incest victim, and the likelihood of psychological disabilities which preclude timely action, a tort suit for latent incestuous injuries is perhaps the paradigmatic example of special circumstances requiring equitable preservation of a potential remedy" (p. 220). As a result of this and other legal arguments, several U.S. state and Canadian provincial legislatures are considering changes in the law that toll the statute of limitations for both criminal prosecution of incest (incest *is* a crime) and civil incest suits from age 21 and/or from the time the facts of the crime are discovered. These changes in the law would acknowledge both the powerlessness of children to bring suit or initiate prosecution and the problem of associative memory, whereby memories of child sexual abuse may not be available to the victim until many years after the victimization.

This "delayed discovery" approach to civil litigation has precedent in cases involving injuries from asbestos and other harmful substances. Perpetrators are now within reach of the law years, even decades, after the commission of their crimes. This evolution in the law, however, has invigorated attacks against delayed memory in adult survivors. The False Memory Syndrome Foundation is dedicated to disseminating information on what its spokepersons describe as the growing threat of false accusations of incest and sexual abuse.

Part of its mission is to provide financial assistance to families in need of legal services or legal counseling.

Conclusion

Freud anticipated the skepticism and criticism that would greet his views on sexual trauma as a cause of hysteria. Nevertheless, his views are as relevant today as they were 100 years ago. Freud discussed three aspects of work with traumatized patients:

- Patients reexperiencing an early life experience in a dissociative manner clearly demonstrate suffering, pain, shame, terror, and extreme helplessness. Suggested memories do not have this quality.
- Patients resist these memories both consciously and unconsciously and often disavow the memories immediately after the experience. People do not want to believe that they were betrayed by the adults whom they trusted for protection. Typically, such a belief requires a reorientation of one's frame of reference.
- Freud mentions that when he successfully suggested a scene to a patient, even the most compliant patients are unable to reproduce such scenes with the intensely appropriate affect and detail characteristic of dissociated memory. Although Freud did not speak of "dissociated memory" as such, he described it very sympathetically in *The Aetiology of Hysteria*.

Freud's critics had the final say, and Freud changed his mind about traumatic memories. The legacy of this intellectual struggle in psychiatry has affected tens of thousands of people whose early-life trauma has been ignored. For the past 15 years, we have struggled to reverse this legacy. We have made great strides in our understanding of female psychology, trauma, memory, and self-formation. Countervailing reactionary forces that are not grounded in scientific skepticism or informed by a spirit of inquiry would erase these gains. Both professionals and the lay public must meet this challenge by refusing to dishonor the struggles of those who refuse to forget.

References

Brownmiller, S. (1975). *Against our will: Men, women and rape.* New York: Simon and Schuster.

Faludi, S. (1991). *Backlash: The undeclared war against American women.* New York: Crown Publishers.

Freud, S. (1984). The aetiology of hysteria. In J. M. Masson (Ed.), *Freud: The assault on truth* (pp. 251–282). London: Faber and Faber.

Herman, J. L. (1992). *Trauma and recovery: The aftermath of violence from domestic abuse to political terror.* New York: Basic Books.

Herman, J. L., & Schatzow, E. (1987). Recovery and verification of memories of childhood sexual trauma. *Psychoanalytic Psychology, 4,* 1–14.

Masson, J. (1984). *Freud: The assault on truth.* London: Faber and Faber.

Russell, D. (1986). *The secret trauma: Incest in the lives of girls and women.* New York: Basic Books.

Salten, M. (1984). Statutes of limitations in civil incest suits: Preserving the victim's remedy. *Harvard Women's Law Journal, 7,* 189–220.

Shapiro, L. (1993, April 19). Rush to judgment. *Newsweek,* 54–60.

Tavris, C. (1993, January 3). Beware the incest-survivor machine. *New York Times,* Sect. 7, p. 1.

van der Kolk, B., & van der Hart, O. (1989). Pierre Janet and the breakdown of adaptation. *American Journal of Psychiatry, 146,* 1530–1540.

Watters, E. (1993, January–February). Doors of memory. *Mother Jones,* p. 24.

Wright, L. (1993a, May 17). Remembering Satan, part I. *New Yorker,* pp. 60–81.

Wright, L. (1993b, May 24). Remembering Satan, part II. *New Yorker,* pp. 54–76.

Susan P. Robbins

Wading Through the Muddy Waters
of Recovered Memory

In her essay "Running Away from Sexual Abuse: Denial Revisited" Benatar (1995) addresses a timely and important topic—recovered memories of childhood sexual abuse. Delayed recovery of memories of traumatic events and the nature, validity, and accuracy of these memories have been at the center of a controversial and bitter debate among mental health professionals and researchers (see Berliner & Williams, 1994; Butler, 1995; Byrd, 1994; Ewen, 1994; Gleaves, 1994; Gold, Hughes, & Hohnecker, 1994; Gutheil, 1993; Lindsay & Read 1994; Loftus & Ketcham, 1994; Peterson, 1994; Pezdek 1994; Pope & Hudson, 1995; Slovenko, 1993; Wylie, 1993; Yapko, 1994a, 1994b).

Proponents of recovered memory believe that many victims of repeated childhood sexual abuse repress or dissociate all memory of their trauma as a mechanism for coping. Although conscious memory of the trauma is not available to the victim, it nonetheless is believed to affect one's social and psychological functioning in adulthood. Seeking therapy for various problems such as substance abuse, eating disorders, depression, or marital difficulties, unhappy adults (primarily white, middle- and upper-class women in their thirties and forties) report memories of abuse that usually surface during the course of therapy. Such memories may also surface while participating in recovery groups, attending self-help conferences, reading incest-recovery books, or as the result of a specific trigger event. These memories typically appear as terrifying images or flashbacks that proponents believe are genuine, if not precise, memories of earlier abuse. Professional knowledge about recovered memory is derived primarily from clinical case reports, and most proponents accept these case studies as confirming evidence.

Critics are skeptical of recovered memories because no reproducible scientific evidence supports these claims. They contend that the growing body of research on memory has consistently shown memory to be subject to inaccuracy, distortion, and fabrication. They have also raised serious questions about the therapeutic methods used to help clients "recover" memories, and some claim that the real feminist issue is the victimization of clients by their therapists who, either knowingly or unconsciously, are suggesting, implanting, and reinforcing memories of abuse that never happened. Many critics have expressed concern that indiscriminate acceptance of recovered memories will lead to a serious backlash of disbelief in authentic cases of abuse.

In the past five years, a rapidly growing body of literature has supported both sides of this contentious debate. Although social workers are often cited as central figures in this debate, leading social work journals have not previously addressed this controversy. Benatar's essay, although timely, adds little to this debate and is a prime example of practice prescriptions based on ideology and theoretical conjecture. In addition to a woefully inadequate review of the current literature in this area, the essay suffers from a lack of conceptual clarity, unwarranted assumptions, and factual inaccuracy.

At the outset, the issue of child sexual abuse is confused with that of "recovered memories" of abuse. These are, in fact, two different issues that have recently come to be associated with each other. The former deals with a well-documented phenomenon—the sexual abuse of children by parents, relatives, other adult caretakers, friends, acquaintances, and strangers. The latter involves the debate about traumatic memory, including the repression of traumatic events and delayed recovery of these memories. According to Loftus and Ketcham (1994), this is a debate about memory and not a debate about childhood sexual abuse.

Benatar expresses disdain for the popular media's skeptical stance about delayed memory, the techniques used to uncover such memories, and the growing incest-survivor industry. Casting this skepticism as an antifeminist backlash against sexual-abuse survivors, she discounts the crucial issue of "false memories" and asserts that those who even question the veracity of traumatic memories are eroding the important gains made in our recognition of childhood abuse. Throughout, she improperly equates skepticism about recovered memories with denial of child sexual abuse.

Adding to this conceptual confusion, Benatar fails to draw distinctions among children who are current victims of abuse, adults who have always remembered traumatic incidents of childhood abuse, and those who have only recently recovered previously amnesic memories. Because this important point is neither addressed nor explored, all client reports of childhood abuse (which she refers to as "their own stories") are inferentially cast as being equally valid descriptions of historical events.

Child Abuse: Past and Present Findings

Benatar correctly notes that "the reality of child abuse is well established." Given the increasing empirical evidence substantiating the reality of child abuse, it is most unfortunate that her ensuing discussion is based on specious analogies, incomplete data, and the use of unverified historical theories.

For example, labeled as "cultural dissociation," she equates the denial of the reality of Nazi death camps to what she believes is a prevalent societal denial of child abuse. In comparing the widely discredited beliefs of a relative few to a broader cultural misogyny that disavows child abuse, she engages in fallacious and distorted logic based on improper generalization and false analogy (see Fischer, 1970).

More problematic is the narrow sample of studies Benatar cites to support her discussion on the epidemiology of child sexual abuse, a problem further compounded by the lack of any critical analysis or discussion of the methodological limitations of these studies. A more thorough review of the literature reveals a broad range in the estimated prevalence of childhood sexual abuse. Although studies on child sexual abuse date back to 1929, few systematic studies utilizing careful statistical analyses were done before the late 1970s and early 1980s (see Demause, 1991). Retrospective surveys have reported base rates ranging from 6% to 62% for women (Burnam, cited in Peters, Wyatt, & Finkelhor, 1986; Wyatt, 1985) and between 3% and 31% for men (Landis, 1956; National Committee for the Prevention of Child Abuse, cited in Goldstein & Farmer, 1994). Researchers attribute the wide disparity in prevalence rates to the varying methodologies and definitions of sexual abuse used in each study. Studies that broadly define sexual abuse to include verbal propositions, for example, yield much higher estimates than do those using narrower definitions that only include forced sexual contact. Other definitions have included exposure, peeping, masturbation, unwanted kissing, and fondling (see Baker & Duncan, 1985; Finkelhor, Hotaling, Lewis, & Smith, 1990; Lindsay & Read, 1994; Russell, 1986, 1988; Williams & Finkelhor, 1992). Further complicating this problem, some studies fail to clarify the definition of sexual abuse being used (see Wassil-Grimm, 1995).

Because the primary focus of Benatar's essay is on recovered memories of abuse, the data she cites are also shaded by her failure to distinguish between incestuous and nonincestuous abuse. This is a critical point because the pathogenic and traumagenic nature of child sexual abuse has been linked in numerous studies to incest by a biological parent in general and, more specifically, to repeated molestation by fathers involving contact abuse and the use of force specifically (see Conte & Berliner, 1988; Elliott & Briere, 1992; Herman, 1981; Russell, 1986). Significantly, recovered memories typically involve repeated incest (see Bass & Davis, 1994).

It is difficult to obtain reliable data on incest because most studies do not make sufficient distinctions in their categorization of abusers. Based on a small number of retrospective studies, estimates indicate that approximately 4% to 5% of girls have reported being abused by a father, adoptive father, or stepfather before the age of 18 (Wassil-Grimm, 1995). Data from Williams and Finkelhor (1992) and Russell (1986) indicate that between 1% to 2.8% of girls are abused by a biological father. The rates are higher, of course, when abuse by other family members is included. Further, most cases of sexual abuse involve exhibition, masturbation, and both nongenital and genital touching rather than forced penetration (Lindsay & Read, 1994; Wakefield & Underwager, 1992). Russell's (1986) data showed a marked trend toward stepfathers abusing more frequently, using verbal threats, and being more severely abusive.

Two separate reviews of retrospective studies of childhood sexual abuse (Lindsay & Read, 1994; Wassil-Grimm, 1995) concluded that the preponderance of surveys indicate that the prevalence of intrafamilial incest is lower than the rates reported in the memory-recovery literature. In contrast, Demause (1991) contended that the known rates should be increased by 50% in order to correct for factors that lead to underreporting, including repression. Although the factors he cited are valid, his figures are based on pure speculation. Likewise, Bradshaw (1992) claimed that approximately 60% of all incest is repressed. To date, no replicable scientific evidence supports these claims. In a critique of what she sees as a "cycle of misinformation, faulty statistics, and unvalidated assertions" by incest-recovery authors, Tavris (1993) noted that inaccurate and sometimes concocted statistics are "traded like baseball cards, reprinted in every book and eventually enshrined as fact."

Another issue that is rarely discussed in the recovery literature is that not all children who are sexually abused experience the abuse as traumatic or develop psychological problems as an adult (Browne & Finkelhor, 1986; Kendall-Tacket, Williams, & Finkelhor, 1993; Russell, 1986). A review of recent empirical studies by Kendall-Tacket et al. (1993) found that many women are totally asymptomatic. Contradictory evidence also surrounds the relationship of sexual abuse to high levels of dissociation and multiple personality disorder (see Beitchman, Zucker, Heed, deCosta, & Cassavia, 1992; Brier & Elliott, 1993; Hacking, 1995; Kluft, 1985; Lindsay & Read, 1994; Nash, Hulsey, Sexton, Herralson, & Lambert, 1993a, 1993b). These findings should not minimize the severe trauma and psychological distress that some abuse victims experience; rather, they should alert us to the fact that the sequelae of childhood sexual abuse is not the same for all victims. Not surprisingly, those who demonstrate higher levels of traumatization and psychopathology are more often found in clinical samples than in the population in general (Russell, 1986).

It should be clear from the above discussion that *all* statistics on child sexual abuse should be interpreted very cautiously. Because of its hidden nature, child sexual abuse is seriously underreported. However, data from clinical samples, especially those samples undergoing therapy for childhood sexual abuse, are likely to overestimate its prevalence. Conversely, underestimates are likely if the data are based on retrospective surveys of adults in the general population, because some may choose not to report their abuse and some may not remember it. Despite discrepancies in the data, it is painfully clear that sexual abuse of children is a serious and pervasive problem that occurs more often than previously believed. As Pope and Hudson (1995) have astutely pointed out, even when conservative estimates of 10% for women and 5% for men are used, this means that 14,000,000 adults in the United States are former victims.

Revisiting Freud and Janet

Benatar gives a brief description of Freud and Janet's theories of repressed or dissociated trauma, supported only by historical case studies. Although case studies are an important source of information, they should not be confused with scientific findings. Despite a widespread belief in the validity of case reports that show repression or dissociation to be a common response to sexual abuse (see Blume, 1990; Chu & Dill, 1990; Courtois, 1988, 1992; Ellenson, 1989;

Erdelyi & Goldberg, 1979; Fredrickson, 1992; Kluft, 1985; Mennen & Pearlmutter, 1993), little support for this belief can be found in empirical studies. In a review of 60 years of research, Holmes (1990) could not find any controlled studies that supported the concept of repression.

The few studies that were initially thought to provide possible evidence of repression (Briere & Conte, 1993; Herman & Schatzow, 1987; Loftus, Polonsky, & Fullilove, 1994; Williams, 1994) have yielded divergent results, with rates ranging from 18% to 59%. Methodological limitations, however, restrict the ability of any of these studies to support fully the mechanism of repression or dissociation (see Lindsay & Read, 1994; Loftus, 1993; Pope & Hudson, 1995). Despite Benatar's assertion that the Herman and Schatzow study supports the claim of delayed traumatic recall, this study has received widespread criticism because of its nonrepresentative sample, lack of specification of methodology (including criteria for confirmation of abuse), the use of composites of cases, little or no amnesia in the majority of cases, and the possibility of suggestion during therapy (see Lindsay & Read, 1994; Pope & Hudson, 1995; Wassil-Grimm, 1995). In short, Herman and Schatzow's study is far from conclusive.

Studies have shown to the contrary that people typically remember their past abuse. Loftus, Polonsky, and Fullilove (1994) found that in their sample of 105 women involved in outpatient treatment for substance abuse, the majority (54%) reported a history of childhood sexual abuse; the vast majority (81%) had always remembered their abuse. In Williams's (1994) study of 100 women with documented histories of sexual abuse, the majority (62%) acknowledged their abuse when asked by the researcher. Because no follow-up interview was conducted in either of these studies, it is impossible to know whether those failing to report their past abuse did so due to repression, ordinary forgetting, normal childhood amnesia, or the desire not to disclose a painful event. Femina, Yeager, and Lewis's (1990) longitudinal study of 69 adults with documented histories of child abuse (primarily physical) found no evidence of total amnesia. The majority (62%) readily reported their abuse to the interviewer. Those who initially denied or minimized their abuse acknowledged in a follow-up "clarification" interview that they did, in fact, remember their abuse but chose to withhold the information for various reasons.

In order for us to validate the clinical impressions gained from current and historical case histories, we need carefully designed studies to test the repression/dissociation hypothesis. Pope and Hudson (1995) suggested that the design of the Williams study is a useful starting point. Strict criteria for inclusion and the use of clarification interviews, similar to those used by Femina et al. (1990) would be a necessary addition to the study design. Pope and Hudson proposed that a series of case reports could be used to present preliminary evidence if they strictly adhered to the research criteria. They noted that given the high prevalence of repression suggested by many authors, this area "begs further carefully designed studies to resolve one of its most critical questions." In sum, both the existence and prevalence of repression have yet to be scientifically validated; the same is true for the type of dissociative amnesia hypothesized in the recovery literature.

Traumatic Memory

In her discussion of traumatic memory, Benatar exhibits a serious misunderstanding of memory, in general, and memory organization, storage, and retrieval, in particular. Based on a narrow and inaccurate reading of van der Kolk and van der Hart's (1989) article, she presents an oversimplified typology of memory and compounds it with a misleading computer analogy.

Memory researchers widely accept that memory is *constructive* and *reconstructive,* not reproductive (Loftus, 1993; Loftus & Ketcham, 1994; Rose, 1992; Squire, 1987). Neuroscientist Steven Rose (1992) cautioned against the use of a flawed brain/computer metaphor:

> Brains do not work with information in the computer sense, but with *meaning* [which] is a historically and developmentally shaped process ... because each time we remember, we in some senses do work on and transform our memories; they are not simply being called up from store.... Our memories are recreated each time we remember [emphasis added].

In their review of current research on memory processing, encoding, and state-dependent learning, van der Kolk and van der Hart (1989) reappraise Janet's early theory of psychopathological dissociation in an attempt to link it with recent findings. However, in contrast with Benatar's firm assertion that "traumatic memory is different," this is not what the authors conclude. They state that

> [Janet's notion] that traumatic memories are stored in memory in ways different from ordinary events is as challenging today as it was ... almost 100 years ago. One century later, much remains to be learned about how memories are stored and keep on affecting emotions and behavior.

Likewise, in her ensuing discussion of trauma, dissociation, and memory, Benatar confuses theory with fact, stating that "if the trauma is verifiable and if it occurred early in life and was severe, these dissociated states act as containers for memories and pain and assume the coherence of alternate selves." Numerous studies on verifiable traumas (Leopold & Dillon, 1963; Malmquist, 1986; Pynoos & Nader, 1989; Strom et al., 1962; Terr, 1979, 1983) have shown to the contrary that vivid (although not necessarily accurate) recall of traumatic events is common. No subjects in these studies repressed the event or developed dissociative amnesia. Post-traumatic symptomatology most commonly involves intrusive images, flashbacks, nightmares, and anxiety attacks, such as those seen in Vietnam veterans.

It is also well established that adults rarely have recall of any events prior to the age of two or three and only sketchy memories up until age five (Fivush & Hudson, 1990; Loftus & Ketcham, 1994; Pendergast, 1995; Usher & Neisser, 1993). This normal "infantile amnesia" is developmentally based and is not due to trauma. Traumatic amnesia in adults is a well-documented phenomenon and involves either large portions of the memory (one's name, address, and other personal information) or circumscribed traumatic events, with good recall of everything prior to and subsequent to the event. In both cases, people are *aware* of the fact that they have amnesia (see Loftus & Ketcham, 1994).

In the last decade, with the revival of Freud's seduction theory and Janet's theory of dissociation, some clinicians and researchers have begun *theorizing* that traumatic memories of *repeated* childhood sexual abuse are encoded differently from other traumas and result in a total loss of awareness of not only the events but of the amnesia itself (see Herman, 1992; Terr, 1991, 1994). The idea that these painful memories are somehow "split off" or dissociated into compartmentalized areas of the mind remains an untested hypothesis. To date, attempts to establish a link between dissociated or repressed trauma and current findings in the neurobiology of memory have been speculative at best. Despite her personal conviction that traumatic memories and ordinary memories are qualitatively different, Herman (1992) acknowledged that "the biological factors underlying ... traumatic dissociation remain an enigma." To paraphrase Klein (1977), we must avoid confusing what a theorist has merely claimed or believed with what she or he has actually proved or demonstrated. Even van der Kolk and van der Hart (1989) conceded that "we can neither confirm or [sic] contradict most of Janet's observations on memory disturbances following traumatization."

Veracity of Client Reports

Benatar is partly correct in her assertion that "veracity in therapy was never an issue until we began discussing issues of sexual abuse." However, this conclusion is based on the faulty premise that acceptance of a client's narrative truth is presumed to be an accurate historical account of events, which is not necessarily the case. In most cases, the veracity of a client's narrative report of life events is not an issue unless the therapist becomes aware of contradictions. It is important to note that allegations of sexual abuse, when made by children or adolescents, are now routinely subjected to extensive collateral verification by an independent investigator (Faller, 1988).

Although psychoanalysts since Freud have been trained to believe that memories of seduction and sexual abuse are incestuous wishes (Masson, 1990), the response on the part of most mental health professionals has been to ignore, minimize, or avoid the topic of sexual abuse (Craine, Henson, Colliver, & MacLean 1988; Jacobson, Koehler, & Jones-Brown, 1987; Post, Willett, Franks, House, & Weissberg, 1980; Rose, Peabody, & Stratigeas, 1991). Whether this is a result of disbelief is, according to Rose et al. (1991), a topic of endless debate. The fact that clinicians have routinely failed to inquire about or respond to reports of sexual abuse represents a serious omission, especially given the prevalence of abuse found in clinical populations.

Contrary to Masson's (1984) and Miller's (1984) assertions that Freud abandoned his theory about the primacy of incest in the etiology of hysteria, Demause (1991) argued that an unbiased reading of Freud shows that he continued to believe in his patients' spontaneous reports of *conscious* memories of abuse. Freud concluded that only *unconscious* memories of early infantile scenes of seduction were "phantasies which my patients had made up or which myself had perhaps forced on them" (cited in Demause, 1991). If Demause is correct, it would appear that even Freud came to question the veracity of *recovered* memories of sexual abuse but did not doubt those memories that were always remembered. In a similar vein, Hacking (1995) noted that Janet revised his early formulations and dropped the concept of dissociation in his later writings. He eventually came to believe that double (or multiple) personality was a special and rare case of bipolar disorder, which he termed "les circulaires." It is interesting that the proponents of recovered memory extensively cite his earlier work while ignoring his later ideas.

It is widely acknowledged that it is impossible to verify charges of sexual abuse in the absence of external corroboration. Because of its hidden nature and the tendency for perpetrators to deny their guilt, it is sometimes difficult to find the necessary corroboration, especially decades after the alleged abuse occurred. But we must be clear that clinical judgment alone is not a sufficient predictor of veracity. In his discussion of the child sexual abuse accommodation syndrome, Summit (1983, 1992) acknowledged that "there is no clinical method available to distinguish valid claims from those that should be treated as fantasy or deception." He further cautioned that "the capacity to listen and the willingness to believe . . . is not an admonition to interrogate or assume that every disclosure is real" (Summit, 1992). Clearly, we must be open to listening to our clients and willing to help them explore issues of past abuse. However, we must be cautious about accepting a client's narrative truth as historical fact in the absence of corroboration. This is especially true in the case of recovered memories; some memories may be fully accurate, some may be partly accurate, and some may be totally false. This does not imply that we should disbelieve our clients but rather that we maintain a neutral stance about historical accuracy. Historical accuracy becomes mandatory, however, when this debate is moved from the therapist's office into the courtroom (see Gutheil, 1993; Slovenko, 1993).

A more controversial but intricately related issue that Benatar fails to address is that of recovered memories of satanic ritual abuse, alien abductions, past lives, preverbal body memories, in *utero* trauma, and cellular memory (see Goldstein & Farmer, 1993, 1994; Mack, 1994; Mulhern, 1991; Pendergrast, 1995; Richardson, Best, & Bromley, 1991; Robbins, 1995; Smith, 1995; Victor, 1993). These memories raise interesting questions regarding both the veracity of client reports and the therapeutic methods used to retrieve or recover them: Are all such memories possible? If not, which ones are? Where do we draw the line? Based on what criteria? How can we determine their accuracy? These questions are significant because a growing number of therapists involved in memory-recovery therapy believe in the validity and accuracy of all recovered memories (Loftus, Garry, Brown, & Rader, 1994; Smith, 1995; Yapko, 1994a, 1994b). Not surprisingly, their clients come to believe in them as well.

False Memories: Fact or Fiction?

Skepticism about "false memories" is often voiced by proponents of recovered memory because it is seen as a backlash to the discovery of childhood sexual abuse and an attempt to silence the victims; as such, false memories are equated with "denial" of abuse (Bloom, 1995; Rockwell, 1995). In the past several years this has become the subject of debate in scholarly journals and professional conferences. Because these issues become tangled and confused, it is important once again to make the distinction between the debate about memory and the documented reality of abuse; the false-memory debate is not about the latter.

A growing body of research has shown that partially and wholly inaccurate memories are not an unusual phenomenon. Because memory is extremely malleable, it is influenced by various factors, and false memories can be created through exposure to misinformation (Loftus, 1993; Terr, 1994). According to Terr, a false memory can be "a strongly imagined memory, a totally distorted memory, a lie, or a misconstructed impression." Numerous studies have shown that people can be led to construct not only inaccurate and confabulated details of past events, but detailed memories of entire events that never happened (see Haugaard, Reppucci, Laurd, & Nauful, 1991; Loftus, 1993; Loftus & Ketcham, 1994; Neisser & Harsch, 1992; Pynoos & Nader, 1989; Spanos, Menary, Gabora, DuBreuil, & Dewhirst, 1991).

Evidence about erroneous memory has sparked concern that memories of abuse are being created by therapists who, through well-intentioned but misguided therapeutic methods, may directly or indirectly evoke specious memories with the use of hypnosis, guided visualization, "truth" drugs, abreactive therapy, dream and body memory interpretation, or suggestive questioning (Byrd, 1994; Gangelhoff, 1995; Gutheil, 1993; Lindsay & Read, 1994; Loftus, 1993; Ofshe & Watters, 1994; Pendergast, 1995; Yapko, 1994a). Although proponents of recovered memory therapy incorrectly believe that false or suggested memories cannot be experienced with the same emotional intensity as can recovered memories of real trauma, evidence suggests otherwise (see Loftus & Ketcham, 1994; Yapko, 1994a). As Loftus and Ketcham noted, reconstructed memories, once adopted, come to be believed in as strongly as genuine memories. Concern about false memory is bolstered by detailed accounts of coercive therapy and lawsuits filed by "retractors"—hundreds of women who have left therapy and recanted their allegations of abuse (see Goldstein & Farmer, 1993, 1994; Pendergrast, 1995).

Studies documenting distorted and confabulated memory in children and adults have been discounted by some proponents of memory recovery because they do not speak directly to the issue of false memories of childhood sexual abuse. Benatar echoes this position along with reservations similar to those noted by Berliner and Williams (1994) and Pezdek (1994) that little scientific evidence supports the claim that false memories of abuse are common or that memory-recovery therapy is widespread. Because little research has been done in this area, this is an accurate appraisal of our lack of scientific knowledge about false memories induced in therapy. However, it is noteworthy that many who accept the "truth" of recovered memories of childhood victimization are not willing to extend the same credibility to those who claim they were victimized by their therapists. Nonetheless, methodologically sound studies are necessary to validate the phenomena of false memory as well as recovered memory; we must rely on the same standard of proof for both.

Where Do We Go from Here?

Clearly, the reluctance of clinicians to address the reality of child sexual abuse poses a serious barrier to accurate and effective assessment and treatment. Rose et al. (1991) noted that "short- and long-term sequelae result not only from sexual and physical abuse, but from inappropriate treatment and nonrecognition of the abuse." Given social work's commitment to multidimensional assessment and holistic, nondichotomous thinking (see Compton & Galaway, 1989; Haynes & Holmes, 1994; Hepworth & Larsen, 1993; Morales & Sheafor, 1995), it is critical that clinical practitioners gather accurate information about their client's past and present biopsychosocial functioning, strengths and resources, developmental history, significant life events, and reactions to and feelings about these events. In this holistic context, it would be unconscionable to fail to inquire about physical and sexual abuse—past or present. We must be sensitive to the fact that clients may choose initially not to disclose their abuse until a level of trust is developed in the therapeutic relationship. Failure to disclose should not *automatically* be assumed to be due to repression or dissociation.

We must also be cautious about hastily attributing a laundry list of non-specific symptoms to prior abuse, as this defeats the purpose of a multidimensional assessment. When a previously repressed history of sexual abuse is revealed, it is especially important to consider the use of collateral sources of information because clients may themselves be confused about these memories. However, collateral sources should never be used without the client's express permission. The use of collateral sources does not imply that the social workers should take on the dual roles of investigator and therapist, because doing so represents a serious conflict of interest (Mason, 1991). Instead, collateral information should be used to help both the practitioner and the client gain a well-rounded picture of the situation. Hepworth and Larsen (1993) noted that important factors that may otherwise be overlooked can often be identified by persons close to the client. According to van der Kolk and van der Hart (1989), Janet frequently interviewed his patients' family members and acquaintances in order to get as complete a picture as possible.

Conclusion

Social workers who work with victims of childhood sexual abuse, especially those whose claim is based solely on recovered memories, should become acquainted with the full range of clinical and social scientific literature on the topic. Clinical case studies must be balanced with scientific findings; both are crucial sources of knowledge. Many clinicians receive only training or information that supports a narrow ideology and practice methodology. As I have suggested elsewhere (Robbins, 1995), social workers must be fully informed in order to "evaluate critically these disparate ideological positions and the adequacy of the research that supports them." This is especially important because a recent study by Feld (1995) found that few social workers are provided with any content about memory or memory retrieval in their academic programs.

In addition, social workers need to be fully aware of their own personal biases in order to prevent them from interfering with assessment and treatment. Preconceived beliefs about repression, dissociation, and recovered memories may lead to an ideological stance that inhibits thorough and accurate assessment. It is imperative that we recognize the serious consequences for our clients and their families when our personal biases lead us to either underdiagnose or overdiagnose childhood sexual abuse. Further, we must remember that the imposition of our personal values and beliefs is antithetical to our deeply held value of client self-determination (Hepworth & Larsen, 1993).

As a result of the lack of scientific verification and the polemical debate shaping research and practice, we must wade cautiously through the muddy waters of recovered memory. Social workers may feel caught between two conflicting sets of claims that demand allegiance to one side or the other. It is doubtful, however, that positioning ourselves at the extremes of this debate will lead to a stance that is in the best interests of our clients. Amid the black and white positions of what Loftus and Ketcham (1994) call the "true believers" and "skeptics," a middle-ground stance is often hard to find, despite the grey areas of uncertainty and ambiguity that exist. Acknowledgment of these grey areas does not mean, however, that one is in "denial" or is uncaring or negligent as a practitioner. We must be open to new findings in this area but we must also be cautious in distinguishing between conjecture and fact.

Finally, when skepticism about the ideology of the recovery movement is based on a thorough review of valid, scientific findings, it must not be cast as antifeminist backlash. As Klein (1977) aptly noted, "Scientific questions are to be settled by appeals to evidence rather than by appeals to authority—even the authority of a Freud."

CHALLENGE QUESTIONS

Do Adults Repress Childhood Sexual Abuse?

1. Find out what Sigmund Freud believed about childhood memories. Do you believe that Freud's theories on memories of child sexual abuse are relevant today? Why, or why not?
2. Referring to the selection by Robbins, how would you account for the wide disparity in prevalence rates of child sexual abuse? How might data gathering be improved to settle the disparity?
3. If you were a therapist and your client claimed to suddenly remember being sexually abused at an early age, how would you discern whether or not your client had actually been abused? What evidence would you need?
4. What does cognitive research say about the storage and retrieval of memories? What does this research imply about traumatic memories?

ISSUE 10

Is There a Racial Difference in Intelligence?

YES: J. Philippe Rushton, from "The Equalitarian Dogma Revisited," *Intelligence* (vol. 19, 1994)

NO: Zack Z. Cernovsky, from "On the Similarities of American Blacks and Whites: A Reply to J. P. Rushton," *Journal of Black Studies* (July 1995)

ISSUE SUMMARY

YES: Professor of psychology J. Philippe Rushton argues that there is irrefutable scientific evidence of racial differences in intelligence that are attributable to genetic differences.

NO: Teacher and psychologist Zack Z. Cernovsky argues that Rushton's data is based not on contemporary scientific research standards but on racial prejudice that is reflective of Nazi dogma.

One of the most heated controversies in psychology concerns the issue of race and intelligence. No psychologist wants to be considered a racist, but research findings that seem to show racial differences in intelligence continue to pop up. If we give credence to these findings, do we support racism? Traditionally, psychological researchers have resisted racism by denying the existence of innate differences between the races, such as differences in innate intelligence. This denial is sometimes referred to as *equalitarianism*—the assumption that all races are essentially equal. The problem is that equalitarian assumptions do not always seem to fit with the research findings on intelligence.

Some argue that equalitarian assumptions are themselves biasing scientific findings. In other words, scientists do not find racial differences in their research, because it is politically incorrect to do so. This is why the publication of *The Bell Curve: Intelligence and Class Structure in American Life* (Free Press, 1994) sent shock waves through the psychological community. The authors of this book, Richard J. Herrnstein and Charles Murray, claimed that genetically determined factors lead to the racial differences often seen in intelligence research. They argued that blacks consistently score lower on IQ tests than whites do. Perhaps more controversial, Herrnstein and Murray held that differences in test scores could not be attributed to cultural biases or environmental factors.

The author of the following selection, J. Philippe Rushton, essentially agrees with the authors of *The Bell Curve*. He argues that his research shows that there are undeniable racial differences in intelligence. He begins by contending that blacks, on average, have smaller skulls and brains than many other races. He then asserts that there is a link between brain size and intelligence. His conclusion from this line of reasoning is that there is a genetic and evolutionary origin for lower levels of intelligence among black populations. Rushton also contends that because his conclusion is unpopular, his research is routinely censored. He points to dire consequences for scientific and psychological scholarship if it bases validity on political agendas rather than objective results.

In the second selection, Zack Z. Cernovsky vigorously disagrees with Rushton. Cernovsky considers the research that links brain size and intelligence to be faulty, and he argues that some of Rushton's own data contradict his position. Part of Rushton's problem, according to Cernovsky, is that he is biased by a genetic model of human nature and intelligence. Cernovsky contends that this model tends to ignore the plasticity of human beings, which is itself highly supported by empirical data. In this sense, Rushton is looking at his data through a biased lens, supported only by similarly biased and flawed research. According to Cernovsky, Rushton's research has been censored not because of its political incorrectness but because of its poor scholarship.

POINT

- On average, blacks have smaller skulls and brains than whites do.

- Brain size can be shown to correlate with intelligence; therefore, blacks are genetically predetermined to have lower intelligence levels.

- Black males have greater levels of testosterone, leading to their exhibiting more sexual activity and violent behavior than white males.

- Corruption in scholarship has led to the suppression of views that are politically incorrect.

COUNTERPOINT

- The science used by Rushton rests on the same foundation that Nazi "scientists" used to show that Jews were less intelligent and thus inferior.

- The correlation between brain size and intelligence is weak and poorly conceived.

- Rushton uses nonscientific and methodologically inadequate sources to support his claims about racial differences in behavior.

- Rushton's work is unacceptable because of its poor scholarship.

J. Philippe Rushton

 **YES**

The Equalitarian Dogma Revisited

Race Differences

The historical record shows that an African cultural disadvantage has existed, relative to Europeans and Asians, ever since Europeans first made contact 2,000 years ago (Baker, 1974; Rushton, 1995). However, until recently, it was not possible to be certain about the cause of the Black–White difference. Today the evidence has increased so much that it is almost certain that only evolutionary (and thereby genetic) theories can explain it. Surveys show that a plurality of experts in psychological testing and behavioral genetics think that a portion of the Black–White difference in IQ scores is genetic in origin (Snydermann & Rothman, 1987, 1988).

The IQ debate became international in scope when research showed that Asians scored higher on tests of mental ability than did Whites, whereas Africans and Caribbeans scored lower (Lynn, 1982, 1991; Vernon, 1982). The debate was also widened by data showing the same worldwide racial ordering in activity level, personality, speed of maturation, crime, family structure, and health (Rushton, 1995). I explored these and other variables and found that East Asians consistently averaged at one end of a continuum, Africans consistently at the other, and Caucasians consistently in between. There is, of course, enormous overlap in the distributions and thus, it is highly problematic to generalize from a group average to an individual.

The central theoretical questions are: Why should Caucasoids average so consistently between Negroids and Mongoloids on so many different dimensions? And, why is there an inverse relation between brain size and gamete production across the races? . . .

Brain Size

Rushton (1995) reviewed 100 years of scientific literature and found that across a triangulation of procedures, brains of Mongoloids average about 17 cm^3 (1 in.^{3}) larger than those of Caucasoids, whose brains average about 80 cm^3 (5 in.^{3}) larger than those of Negroids. For example, using brain mass at autopsy, Ho, Roessmann, Straumfjord, and Monroe (1980) summarized data for 1,261

Americans aged 25 to 80 after excluding obviously damaged brains. They reported a significant sex-combined difference between 811 Whites with a mean of 1,323 g (SD = 146) and 450 Blacks with a mean of 1,223 g (SD = 144). Using endocranial volume, Beals, Smith, and Dodd (1984, p. 307, Table 5) analyzed 20,000 crania and found sex-combined brain cases differed by continental area. Excluding Caucasoid areas of Asia (e.g., India) and Africa (e.g., Egypt), 19 Asian populations averaged 1,415 cm^3 (SD = 51), 10 European groups averaged 1,362 cm^3 (SD = 35), and 9 African groups averaged 1,268 cm^3 (SD = 85). Using external head measurements, Rushton (1992b) found, in a stratified random sampling of 6,325 U.S. Army personnel measured in 1988 to determine head size for fitting helmets, Asian Americans, White Americans, and Black Americans averaged 1,416 cm^3, 1,380 cm^3, and 1,359 cm^3, respectively. With data on tens of thousands of men and women collated by the International Labor Office in Geneva, Asians, Europeans, and Africans averaged, respectively, 1,308 cm^3, 1,297 cm^3, and 1,241 cm^3 (Rushton, 1994)....

Intelligence

The global literature on cognitive ability was reviewed by Lynn (1991). Caucasoids in North American, Europe, and Australasia had mean IQs of around 100. Mongoloids, measured in North America and in Pacific Rim countries, had higher means, in the range of 101 to 111. Africans living south of the Sahara, African Americans, and African Caribbeans (including those living in Britain), had mean IQs from 70 to 90. However, the question remains whether test scores are valid measures of group differences in mental ability. Basically, the answer hinges on whether the tests are culture bound. Doubts about validity linger in many quarters, although considerable technical work has disposed of this problem among those with psychometric expertise (Jensen, 1980; Syndermann & Rothman, 1987, 1988; Wigdor & Garner, 1982). This is because the tests show similar patterns of internal item consistency and predictive validity for all groups, and the same differences are found on relatively culture-free tests....

The Brain Size–IQ Link

A positive correlation between mental ability and brain size has been established in studies using magnetic resonance imaging, which *in vivo*, construct three-dimensional pictures of the brain (Andreasen et al., 1993; Raz et al., 1993; Wickett, Vernon, & Lee, 1994; Willerman, Schultz, Rutledge, & Bigler, 1991). These confirm correlations, reported since the turn of the century, from measurements of head perimeter (Wickett et al., 1994). The brain size–cognitive ability correlations range from .10 to .40.

Two studies imply that brain size differences underlie the Black–White difference in mental ability. In an adolescent sample, Jensen (1994) found that the greater the difference between White and Black children on 17 tests, the higher was the tests' correlation with head size.... In a study of 14,000 4-7-year-olds, when the White and Black children were matched on IQ, they no longer differed in head size (Jensen & Johnson, 1994).

Other Variables

... [T]he Asian–White–Black racial matrix occurs on a surprisingly wide range of dimensions. For example, the racial pattern in violent crime found within the U.S. holds internationally. I averaged several years of international police statistics to find rates of murder, rape, and serious assault to be three times higher in African and Caribbean countries than in Pacific Rim countries, again with European countries intermediate (Rushton, 1990). These results make it clear that whatever the causes of violent crime turn out to be, they must lie beyond U.S. particulars.

One neurohormonal contributor to crime is testosterone. As I review in *Race, Evolution and Behavior* (Rushton, 1995), studies show 3% to 19% more testosterone in Black college students and military veterans than in their White counterparts (e.g., Ellis & Nyborg, 1991), with the Japanese showing lower amounts than Whites. Sex hormones go everywhere in the body and have been shown to activate many brain-behavior systems involving crime, personality, and reproduction. As another example, around the world, the rate of dizygotic twinning per 1,000 births, caused by a double ovulation, is less than 4 among Mongoloids, 8 among Caucasoids, and 16 or greater among Negroids (Bulmer, 1970; Imaizumi, 1991).

Worldwide surveys show more sexual activity in Negroids compared to Caucasoids and especially to Mongoloids. Differences in sexual activity translate into consequences. International fertility rates show the racial pattern; so does the pattern of AIDS. As of January 1, 1994, World Health Organization and Centers for Disease Control and Prevention statistics showed infection rates, per hundred thousand population, for (a) Asian Americans and Asians in the Pacific Rim of less than 1, (b) European Americans and Europeans in Europe, Canada, and Australasia of 86, and (c) African Americans and Africans south of the Sahara and in the Caribbean of 355....

De Facto Censorship

It is important to draw attention to what sociologist Robert Gordon refers to as "one-party science." Irrespective of religious background, or political affiliation, virtually all American intellectuals adhere to what Linda Gottfredson (1994) called the "egalitarian fiction." For example, only politically correct hypotheses centering on cultural disadvantage are postulated to explain the differential representation of minorities in science. Analyses of aptitude test scores and behavioral genetics are taboo. Moralizing is so fierce that most sensible people avoid the taboo. This encourages vicious attacks on those who are convinced that there is a genetic basis underlying individual and group differences.

The high-placed pervasiveness of the egalitarian fiction is worrying. In an annual feature in *Science* (e.g., November 13, 1991, November 12, 1993 issues), the underrepresentation of minority scientists is documented. Unflinching statistics are accompanied by muddled analysis. First, the word *minority* is too inclusive. Only Blacks, Hispanics and American Indians are underrepresented in science: Several other minorities are overrepresented. Adopting the criterion of being listed in *American Men and Women of Science*, and using

Weyl's (1989) ethnic classification of surnames, Chinese are overrepresented relative to their numbers in the population by 620%, Japanese by 351%, and Jews by 424%. These figures cast doubt on an explanation based on prejudice and, instead, suggest factors intrinsic to the various groups. The one-party line was forcefully presented in a lead editorial in *Nature* against my work (Maddox, 1992), which likened the possibility of finding significant group differences in brain size to contradicting accepted views of an ellipsoid earth, continental drift, and relativity theory.[1] . . .

Many of my colleagues tell me, privately, that they agree with my views, not just about brain size and intelligence but also about the genetic basis of race differences in crime and other variables. I have even known senior African American police administrators who have told me that they believe biological factors underlie racial differences in crime. But, of course, my informants go on to say, "Please don't quote me." . . .

In conclusion, I suggest that it is a dereliction of duty for us to continue to put up with the egalitarian dogma. It is immoral to know, or even suspect, the truth and to remain silent. Although rational people are not immune to data, they are also influenced by the judgment of their peers. If more scientists would speak openly about the views they now voice only in private, our world would become not only a safer place, but a more enlightened one as well.

Note

1. Special sections on "Women in Science" (*Science*, April 16, 1993, March 11, 1994), as well as the editorial in *Nature* by John Maddox (1992) also ignored or denigrated sex differences in aptitudes and brain size.

Zack Z. Cernovsky

 **NO**

On the Similarities of American Blacks and Whites

The history of science teaches us that many ambitious racists attempted to manufacture scientific evidence for their beliefs. Sooner or later, their charlatan style methodology (e.g., the use of skull circumference measurement by Nazi "scientists" during the World War II) and logical inconsistencies resulted in their rejection by the scientific community. A contemporary example of this trend is the work of J. Philippe Rushton. He recently wrote a large number of repetitive articles in which he revived the old-fashioned Nazi method of skull circumference measurement and claimed that Blacks are genetically less intelligent, endowed with smaller brains, oversexed, and more prone to crime and mental disease than Whites. Only some of the numerous methodological flaws in his work are discussed in the present article.

Although Rushton (1988, 1990a, 1991) implied that Blacks are consistently found to have *smaller brains* than Whites, some of the studies listed in his reviews actually show opposite trends: North American Blacks were superior to American Whites in brain weight (see Tobias, 1970, p. 6: 1355 g vs. 1301 g) or were found to have cranial capacities favorably comparable to the average for various samples of Caucasians (see Herskovits, 1930) and number of excess neurons larger than many groups of Caucasoids, for example, the English and the French (see Tobias, 1970, p. 9). In general, skulls from people in countries with poverty and infant malnutrition are smaller regardless of race. This trend is apparent even in Rushton's (1990b) tabularly summary of Herskovits's review: Caucasoids from Cairo had far smaller crania than North American Negroes (see more details in Cernovsky, 1992). In this respect, Rushton (1990a, 1990b, 1990c) also repeatedly misrepresented findings by Beals, Smith, and Dodd (1984) on cranial capacity. Rushton implied that Beals et al. presented large-scale evidence for racial inferiority of the Blacks with respect to cranial size. De facto, extensive statistical analyses by Beals et al. showed that cranial size varies primarily with climatic zones (e.g., distance from the equator), *not* race. According to Beals et al., the correlations of brain size to race are spurious: smaller crania are found in warmer climates, irrespective of race.

And, although Rushton misleadingly reported Tobias's (1970) and Herskovits's (1930) surveys of cranial data as confirming his theory, their data are

From Zack Z. Cernovsky, "On the Similarities of American Blacks and Whites: A Reply to J. P. Rushton," *Journal of Black Studies*, vol. 25, no. 6 (July 1995). Copyright © 1995 by Sage Publications, Inc. Reprinted by permission. Notes and references omitted.

more consistent with the model presented by Beals et al. As already mentioned, in their reviews, cranial size and number of excess neurons of North American Blacks compared favorably to those of Caucasoids. It is only by pooling their data with data for Negroids from countries in hot climatic zones (notorious for famine and infant malnutrition) that Rushton obtained an illusory support for his postulates.

Rushton's (1988, Table 1) use of brain and cranial size as indicators of intelligence in humans is statistically absurd: Rushton's (1990a) own data showed that brain size and intelligence, in Homo sapiens, are only weakly related (average Pearson $r = .18$) and the highest correlations reported by Rushton were only .35, implying only 12.3% of shared variance (see critique by Cernovsky, 1991). In the past decades, even some persons with extremely small cerebral cortices were found by Lorber to have IQs in the superior range (> 120) and performed well in academic settings (Lewin, 1980). Rushton's pseudoscientific writings perpetuate lay public's misconceptions and promote racism.

Rushton (1990a, 1990c, 1991) also misrepresents the evidence for racial differences in brain/body size ratio. For example, Herskovits's (1930) data suggest that there is no consistent Black/White difference with respect to stature or crania. And, with respect to Rushton's claim about the relationships of the brain/body size ratio to intelligence, this conceptual framework is suitable for some species of animals but not necessarily for the restricted range of data. The comparison of gender differences on three different brain/body indices by Ho, Roessman, Straumfjord, and Monroe (1980) led to inconsistent results. Further empirical data in this field are necessary: Authoritarian statements "about the reality of racial differences," based on conveniently selected trends in the data, do not qualify as a scientific contribution.

Contrary to Rushton's speculations on *race and crime*, skin color would be a poor predictor of crime rate due to low base rates and very large intragroup variance. His own data (summaries of Interpol statistics, Rushton, 1990c, 1995) can be reinterpreted as showing that relying on race as an indicator of crime leads to 99.8% of false positives (Cernovsky and Litman, 1993a). The average correlations between race and crime are too low and inconsistent to support genetic racial speculations and, in fact, might point to the opposite direction than Rushton postulated (see higher crime rates in Whites than in Blacks in Interpol data analyses, Cernovsky & Litman, 1993b).

To demonstrate that Blacks are *less intelligent* and, perhaps, to allege that this is genetically given, with only minor environmental modifications, Rushton (1988, 1991) refers not only to his own biased review of brain size studies but also to Jensen's work. Yet, it has been shown that the theories favoring hereditarian over environmentalist explanations tend to be based on poor methodology (see Kamin, 1980) and that Jensen's estimates of "hereditability" are based on too many assumptions, which hardly could all be met (Taylor, 1980). Some applications of the heritability estimates were shown to have absurd consequences (Flynn, 1987a). Similarly, Jensen's recent claims about racial differences in reaction time are biased and might lack in scientific integrity (Kamin & Grant-Henry, 1987). There is no solid evidence in favor of heritability over environmental influences with respect to the development of intelligence (see a review in Kamin, 1980, and Flynn, 1987a, 1987b).

In a similar vein, some of Rushton's references to scientific literature with respect to racial differences in *sexual characteristics* turned out to be references to a nonscientific semipornographic book and to an article in the *Penthouse* Forum (see a review in Weizmann, Wiener, Wiesenthal, & Ziegler, 1991). Rushton's claims that *fertility* rates are higher in Blacks disharmonize with well-known high figures for some Caucasoids such as North American Hutterites (a group of Swiss-German ancestry, see a review in Weizmann et al., 1990, 1991). Rushton's claims about racial differences with respect to brain, intelligence, crime, sexuality, and fertility (and also twinning rates; see Lynn, 1989a, 1989b; Weizmann et al., 1991) are based on an extremely biased and inadequate review of literature.

Erroneously relying on data based on hospital admission rates, Rushton (1988) concluded that mental disease is more frequent in Blacks than Whites. Members of the lower socioeconomic class are overrepresented in official hospital admission statistics because the private and more confidential treatment resources are not accessible to them. More adequate epidemiological studies by Robins et al. (1984) based on random sampling show no significant link of lifetime prevalence to race except for simple phobias. There were no significant differences with respect to major psychiatric illness or substance abuse (see a more detailed criticism of Rushton's assumptions in this area in Zuckerman & Brody, 1988).

Rushton (1988, 1991) implies that "racial differences in behavior" are genetic and relatively immutable: He ignores the plasticity of human beings as shown in secular changes and in the intragroup variance (see more detailed criticisms in Weizmann et al., 1990, 1991). The armamentarium of clinical psychologists was shown by a host of empirical investigations to induce desirable behavioral changes in various populations (see, e.g., Turner, Calhoun, & Adams, 1981): Rushton's view of human beings is obsolete.

. . . If Rushton (1988, 1990a) could heed Jerison's (1973) warning that racial differences in brain size are at most minor and "probably of no significance for intellectual differences," he would not attempt to extend Jerison's findings across species to subgroups within modern mankind. Instead, Rushton (1991) misleadingly refers to Jerison in a manner that implies an expert support from this famous comparative neuropsychologist, without mentioning their disagreement on the most central issue.

Rushton (1991) claimed that racial differences occur "on more than 50 variables," with Blacks being consistently in a less desirable direction. The present article examined the evidence with respect to the key variables only: The examination exemplifies that his claims are fallacious. Furthermore, long lists, such as Rushton's, tend to shrink when appropriate multivariate methods (e.g., the discriminant equation) are used: These techniques eliminate redundancies and remove nonsignificant variables. And, nota bene, if a scientist would search for a suitable "finding" to lower the social prestige of Blacks and examine 50 variables and suppress evidence favorable to Blacks, he or she might, by chance alone, one day, find one or more variables on which a "significant" trend in the desired direction could be located. . . .

Finally, Rushton's most recent "scientific" contribution is the claim that women are likely to be less intelligent than men because his tape measurements of men and women in military settings indicated that males have larger heads (Rushton, 1992). Indeed, the racism is often associated with sexism.

In summary, although Rushton's writings and public speeches instill the vision of Blacks as small-brained, oversexed criminals who multiply at a fast rate and are afflicted with mental disease, his views are neither based on a bona fide scientific review of literature nor on contemporary scientific methodology. His dogma of bioevolutionary inferiority of Negroids is not supported by empirical evidence. Acceptance of similar theories should not be based on *racist prejudice* but on objective standards, that is, conceptual and logical consistency and integrity, quality of methods and data, and an analysis of disconfirmatory trends. Rushton's racial theory does not meet any of these standards.

CHALLENGE QUESTIONS

Is There a Racial Difference in Intelligence?

1. Because scientific knowledge is considered by many to be the ultimate authority, the findings of science can have a large impact on public opinion. Should "dangerous" scientific findings, such as those that would hurt people or cause hatred, be suppressed? What standards should be used, and who should enforce them? Explain.
2. How does the debate over race and intelligence reflect on women's issues? Many of the arguments in this debate are applied to debates over women's intelligence and personality. If you do not believe that there are genetic differences between races, can you justify arguments supporting genetic differences between the genders?
3. Perhaps inherent differences between races could be construed in a positive light. Can you think of reasons why some races might *want* to promote genetic differences between racial groups?
4. If there are indeed racial differences in intelligence, would this finding necessarily change political opinions and government policies? If so, how? If not, why not?

On the Internet . . .

Health Information Resources

Here is a long list of toll-free numbers for organizations that provide health-related information. The numbers do not offer diagnosis or treatment, but some do offer recorded information. Others provide personalized counseling, referrals, and/or written materials.

http://nhic-nt.health.org/Scripts/Tollfree.cfm

Mental Health Infosource: Disorders

This no-nonsense page lists hotlinks to pages dealing with psychological disorders, including anxiety, panic, phobic disorders, schizophrenia, and violent/self-destructive behaviors.

http://www.mhsource.com/disorders/

Mental Health Net

This comprehensive online guide to mental health features more than 7,000 individual resources, including resources on mental disorders; professional resources in psychology, psychiatry, and social work; and journals and self-help magazines.

http://www.cmhc.com

Suicide Awareness: Voices of Education

This is the most popular suicide site on the Internet. A very thorough site, it includes information on dealing with suicide (both before and after) and material from the organization's many education sessions.

http://www.save.org

New England Mindbody Institute's Women's Health Site

The New England Mindbody Institute's Women's Health program is devoted to helping women to achieve and maintain peak levels of psychological, physical, and spiritual health and well-being. It covers topics from premenstrual syndrome and menopause to midlife psychology and marriage.

http://www.ne-mindbody.com/women.html

PART 5

Mental Health

A mental disorder is often defined as a pattern of thinking or behaving that is either disruptive to others or uncomfortable for the person with the disorder. This definition seems straightforward; however, is it universally applicable? Certain patterns of social behavior fit this definition, but does this make them "diseases" in the medical sense? If there are biological correlates for these disorders, are they better described as physical diseases rather than mental diseases, such as schizophrenia? And if biological therapies, such as antidepressants, prove effective, does this mean that such disorders are biologically based?

- Is Schizophrenia a Biological Disorder?

- Have Antidepressant Drugs Proven to Be Effective?

ISSUE 11

Is Schizophrenia a Biological Disorder?

YES: Nancy C. Andreasen, from "Linking Mind and Brain in the Study of Mental Illnesses: A Project for Scientific Psychopathology," *Science* (March 14, 1997)

NO: Victor D. Sanua, from "The Myth of the Organicity of Mental Disorders," *The Humanistic Psychologist* (Spring 1996)

ISSUE SUMMARY

YES: Clinical psychiatrist Nancy C. Andreasen asserts that a variety of modern technologies, including neuroimaging and animal modeling, show that although schizophrenia is a disease that manifests itself in the mind, it arises from the brain.

NO: Clinical psychologist Victor D. Sanua contends that the assumption that schizophrenia is a biological disorder is not supported by research but is, instead, maintained by many scientists who have a misguided faith in an elusive future technology that will supposedly show the connection between mind and brain.

For centuries philosophers have considered the issue of how the mind and the body are connected. The man viewed by many as the father of modern philosophy, René Descartes (1596–1650), suggested that the mind and the body are linked in the pineal gland of the brain. Although this notion was later discarded, philosophers and, more recently, psychologists have continued to search for a link between the mind and the body.

Today most psychologists assume that the mind and the body are connected in some way. Furthermore, many assume that what we call the mind is not only connected to the body but arises from the body in the brain. Some researchers believe that modern technology has made it possible to show this mind/brain connection. They assume that a more sophisticated future technology will prove that all mental activity results from brain activity. Other researchers, however, consider this too optimistic—a product of philosophical bias rather than scientific data.

In the following selection, Nancy C. Andreasen notes that although there are currently no biological markers for mental illness, scientific psychopathologists maintain that mental disorders are rooted in the brain and result from a brain dysfunction of some sort. This hypothesis has been tested in numerous ways by researchers from a variety of disciplines. Andreasen contends that this multidisciplinary approach has provided considerable insight into the activities of the brain that are responsible for mental disorders. She uses the example of schizophrenia to illustrate how research that stems from several different perspectives converges on one finding—that the mind and the brain are linked.

In stark contrast, Victor D. Sanua argues in the second selection that although studies looking at how the brain might cause mental disorders have been conducted for nearly a century, the results of these studies have failed to evidence a mind/brain connection. Nevertheless, he contends, researchers such as Andreasen maintain the hope that improved technology and better research methods will eventually prove the connection. Sanua finds this hope to be unfounded because the research to date has provided so few genuine results. In conclusion, Sanua suggests that researchers might be looking in the wrong places for answers about mental illness.

POINT

- Clinicians should focus on the biological aspects of the human mind to understand mental disorders.

- Recent advances in brain research support the hypothesis that mental disorders derive from the brain.

- Schizophrenia can be used as an example to show the link between the mind and the brain.

- With increased sophistication and technology, biological markers for mental disease will be discovered.

- Multiple biopsychological disciplines should continue to investigate the biological causes of mental disorders.

COUNTERPOINT

- Clinicians should focus on the social and psychological aspects of the human mind to understand mental disorders.

- Research conducted over the last 100 years has failed to produce substantial proof that mental disorders derive from the brain.

- Investigations of schizophrenia have failed to show any link between the mind and the brain.

- More sophisticated technology will not show any link between the mind and the body.

- Psychologists should explore potential origins of mental disorders besides biology.

Nancy C. Andreasen

 **YES**

Linking Mind and Brain in the Study of Mental Illnesses

Fundamental Conceptual Issues

The relationship between mind and brain. Mental illnesses have historically been distinguished from other medical illnesses because they affect the higher cognitive processes that are referred to as "mind." The relationship between mind and brain has been extensively discussed in contemporary philosophy and psychology, without any decisive resolution. One heuristic solution, therefore, is to adopt the position that the mind is the expression of the activity of the brain and that these two are separable for purposes of analysis and discussion but inseparable in actuality. That is, mental phenomena arise from the brain, but mental experience also affects the brain, as is demonstrated by the many examples of environmental influences on brain plasticity. The aberrations of mental illnesses reflect abnormalities in the brain/mind's interaction with its surrounding world; they are diseases of a psyche (or mind) that resides in that region of the soma (or body) that is the brain.

Mind and brain can be studied as if they are separate entities, however, and this is reflected in the multiple and separate disciplines that examine them. Each uses a different language and methodology to study the same quiddity. The challenge in developing a scientific psychopathology in the 1990s is to use the power of multiple disciplines. The study of mind has been the province of cognitive psychology, which has divided mind into component domains of investigation (such as memory, language, and attention), created theoretical systems to explain the workings of those domains (constructs such as memory encoding versus retrieval), and designed experimental paradigms to test the hypotheses in human beings and animals. The study of brain has been the province of several disciplines. Neuropsychology has used the lesion method to determine localization by observing absence of function after injury, whereas neuroanatomy and neurobiology have mapped neural development and connectivity and studied functionality in animal models. The boundaries between all these disciplines have become increasingly less distinct, however, creating the broad discipline of cognitive neuroscience. The term "cognitive" has definitions that range from broad to narrow; its usage here is broad and refers to all activities of mind, including emotion, perception, and regulation of behavior.

Contemporary psychiatry studies mental illnesses as diseases that manifest as mind and arise from brain. It is the discipline within cognitive neuroscience that integrates information from all these related disciplines in order to develop models that explain the cognitive dysfunctions of psychiatric patients based on knowledge of normal brain/mind function.

Using the phenomenotype to find the biotype.   There are at present no known biological diagnostic markers for any mental illnesses except dementias such as Alzheimer's disease. The to-be-discovered lesions that define the remainder of mental illnesses are likely to be occurring at complex or small-scale levels that are difficult to visualize and measure, such as the connectivity of neural circuits, neuronal signaling and signal transduction, and abnormalities in genes or gene expression. Despite their lack of a defining objective index such as glucosuria is for diabetes, however, these illnesses are very real. Not only do they produce substantial morbidity and mortality, but advances in psychiatric nosology have produced objective, criterion-based, assessment techniques that produce reliable and precise diagnoses. In the absence of a pathological marker, the current definitions of mental illnesses are syndromal and are based on a convergence of signs, symptoms, outcome, and patterns of familial aggregation.

Finding the neural mechanisms of mental illnesses must be an iterative process; syndromal clinical definitions (or the phenomenotype) are progressively tested, refined, and redefined through the measurement of neurobiological aspects (or the biotype). This process is not fundamentally different from that used to study other diseases. The diagnosis of diabetes, for example, has evolved from the observation of glucosuria to multiple subdivisions based on age of onset, severity of symptoms and complications, degree of islet cell involvement, and genetic factors. For most mental illnesses, the task is simply made more challenging by the absence of an objective criterion that can provide an initial clue to assist in finding mechanisms, as neuritic plaques have done for Alzheimer's disease....

Linking Mind and Brain: The Example... of Schizophrenia...

Advances that have been made in the study of schizophrenia... illustrate the power of developing cognitive models that derive from different perspectives and apply techniques from multiple domains.

Finding the common thread in schizophrenia.   The name "schizophrenia" ("fragmented mind") was coined by Eugen Bleuler, who wished to emphasize that it was a cognitive disorder in which the "fabric of thought and emotion" was torn or fragmented, and normal connections or associations were no longer present. Schizophrenia poses special challenges to the development of cognitive models because of the breadth and diversity of its symptoms. The symptoms include nearly all domains of function: perception (hallucinations), inferential thinking (delusions), fluency of thought and speech (alogia), clarity and organization of thought and speech ("formal thought disorder"), motor activity (catatonia), emotional expression (affective blunting), ability to initiate and complete goal-directed behavior (avolition), and ability to seek out and experience emotional gratification (anhedonia). Not all these symptoms are present in any given patient, however, and none is pathognomonic of the illness. An initial survey of the diversity of symptoms might suggest that multiple brain regions are involved, in a spotty pattern much as once occurred in neurosyphilis. In the absence of visible lesions and known pathogens, however, investigators have turned to the exploration of models that could explain the diversity of symptoms by a single cognitive mechanism. Exemplifying this strategy are four different models that illustrate the melding of cognitive neuroscience and psychiatry, beginning at four different points of departure. The convergent conclusions of these different models are striking.

Cognitive psychology.   Approaching schizophrenia from the background of cognitive psychology, C. D. Frith has divided the symptoms of schizophrenia into three broad groups or dimensions: disorders of willed action (which lead to symptoms such as alogia and avolition), disorders of self-monitoring (which lead to symptoms such as auditory hallucinations and delusions of alien control), and disorders in monitoring the intentions of others ("mentalizing") (which lead to symptoms such as "formal thought disorder" and delusions of persecution). Frith believes that all these are special cases of a more general underlying mechanism: a disorder of consciousness or self-awareness that impairs the ability to think with "metarepresentations" (higher order abstract concepts that are representations of mental states). Frith and his collaborators are currently testing this conceptual framework using positron emission tomography (PET)....

Neurobiology.   Approaching schizophrenia from a background that blends lesion studies and single-cell recordings in nonhuman primates for the study of cognition, P. Goldman-Rakic has proposed a model suggesting that the fundamental impairment in schizophrenia is an inability to guide behavior by representation, often referred to as a defect in working memory. Working memory, or the ability to hold a representation "online" and perform cognitive operations using it, permits individuals to respond in a flexible manner, to formulate and modify plans, and to base behavior on internally held ideas and thoughts rather than being driven by external stimuli. A defect in this ability can explain a variety of symptoms of schizophrenia. For example, the inability to hold a discourse plan in mind and monitor speech output leads to disorganized speech and thought disorder; the inability to maintain a plan for behavioral activities could lead to negative symptoms such as avolition or alogia; and the inability to reference a specific external or internal experience against associative memories (mediated by cortical and subcortical circuitry involving frontal/parietal/temporal regions and the thalamus) could lead to an altered consciousness of sensory experience and would be expressed as delusions or hallucinations.

The model ... is consistent with the compromised blood flow to the prefrontal cortex seen in these patients....

Psychobiology and neurophysiology. Using techniques originally derived from neurophysiology, D. L. Braff and colleagues have developed another complementary model. This model begins from the perspective of techniques used to measure brain electrical activity, particularly various types of evoked potentials, and hypothesizes that the core underlying deficit in schizophrenia involves information processing and attention. This model derives from the empirical clinical observation that patients with schizophrenia frequently complain that they are bombarded with more stimuli than they can interpret. Consequently, they misinterpret (that is, have delusions), confuse internal with external stimuli (hallucinations), or retreat to safety ("negative symptoms" such as alogia, anhedonia, or avolition). Early interpretations of this observation ... postulated that patients had problems with early stages in serial order processing that led to downstream effects such as psychotic or negative symptoms. As serial models have been supplanted by distributed models, the deficit may be better conceptualized in terms of resource allocation: Patients cannot mobilize attentional resources and allocate them to relevant tasks....

Clinical psychiatry. Our group has used the clinical presentation of schizophrenia as a point of departure, initially attempting to localize the various symptoms in brain regions through the use of structural and functional neuroimaging techniques. This strategy has led to a search for abnormalities in specific brain regions and theories about symptom-region relationships (such as negative symptoms in the frontal cortex or hallucinations in the superior temporal gyrus), which have been examined by a variety of investigators. This approach is oversimplified, however, and we are currently testing an integrated model that explains clinical symptoms as a consequence of disruptions in anatomically identified circuits that mediate a fundamental cognitive process....

The common thread. The common thread in all these observations, spun from four different starting points, is that schizophrenia reflects a disruption in a fundamental cognitive process that affects specific circuitry in the brain and that may be improved through medications that affect that circuitry. The various teams use differing terminology and somewhat different concepts— metarepresentations, representationally guided behavior, information processing/attention, cognitive dysmetria—but they convey a common theme. The cognitive dysfunction in schizophrenia is an inefficient temporal and spatial referencing of information and experience as the person attempts to determine boundaries between self and not-self and to formulate effective decisions or plans that will guide him or her through the small-scale (speaking a sentence) or large-scale (finding a job) maneuvers of daily living. This capacity is sometimes referred to as consciousness.

Using diverse technologies and techniques—PET scanning, animal models, lesion methods, single-cell recordings, evoked potentials—the investigators also converge on similar conclusions about the neuroanatomic substrates of the cognitive dysfunction. All concur that it must involve distributed circuits rather than a single specific "localization," and all suggest a key role for interrelationships among the prefrontal cortex, other interconnected cortical regions, and subcortical regions, particularly the thalamus and striatum. Animal and molecular models are being developed that are based on knowledge of this circuitry and the fundamental cognitive process, which can be applied to understanding the mechanism of drug actions and developing new medications. . . .

Summary and Conclusion

Examples of work applying diverse techniques of cognitive neuroscience to the study of . . . schizophrenia indicate that increasingly sophisticated strategies and conceptualizations are emerging as powerful new technologies are being applied. Focal regions have been replaced by circuits and static changes by plasticity and molecular mechanisms. The power of models is enhanced by efforts to design experiments that can be used in nonhuman species, in order to obtain in vivo measures that will illuminate mechanisms. The power of neuroimaging is also permitting in vivo measures of circuits and mechanisms in the human brain. These advances have created an era in which a scientific psychopathology that links mind and brain has become a reality.

NO

Victor D. Sanua

The Myth of the Organicity
of Mental Disorders

In 1994, I attended a conference on schizophrenia arranged by the Columbia University College of Physicians and Surgeons (9th Annual Schizophrenia Conference) and the Alliance for the Mentally Ill. Herbert Pardes, Chairman of the Department of Psychiatry and Dean of the Faculty of Medicine, stated in his introductory remarks that Columbia was installing the largest Magnetic Resonance Imaging (MRI) machine in the world, which would enable scientists to see the workings of the brain. His remarks were sprinkled with optimistic adjectives like, "tremendous excitement," "new hope," and so on. The rest of the day was mostly presentations by the Columbia Faculty on the various theories about the causation of schizophrenia and the research on new antipsychotic drugs. The following are some of the areas of research on causation: genetics, immunological systems, nutritional deficiencies, exposure to influenza, obstetrical complications, structural brain changes, season of birth, neurotropic factors, loss of brain tissue, virus infecting the fetal brain, and others. Basically, schizophrenia was seen as a biological disorder whose mystery would be unveiled only by laboratory work. It should be noted that during the conference, there were no formal discussions about the relationship between neurotransmitters and schizophrenia. The hypotheses of the dysfuctions of the neurotransmitters like serotonin, endorphin and dopamine, which have been quite popular in the past, do not seem to be viable at this time.

There was a general enthusiasm that there would soon be a breakthrough with the kind of scientific research being carried out in modern laboratory facilities. However, such optimism does not seem warranted. A well-known German psychiatrist, Hafner stated, "Our knowledge of the etiology of the disease called schizophrenia has not yet made much progress from [Emil] Kraepelin's days" (1987, p. 366). The fact that there are still so many areas of research awaiting investigation at the Columbia University Conference corroborates Hafner's point. In a workshop in the afternoon, devoted to genetics, evidence for the genetic causation was the much higher concordance of schizophrenia among monozygotic twins than among dizygotic twins. When I suggested to the speaker that this could also be attributed to a similar environment for the monozygotic twins, the response of the presenter was that the evidence is further provided by

From Victor D. Sanua, "The Myth of the Organicity of Mental Disorders," *The Humanistic Psychologist,* vol. 24 (Spring 1996). Copyright © 1996 by The American Psychological Association. Reprinted by permission. References omitted.

the adoption studies of Heston (1966), Kety, Rosenthal, Wender and Schulsinger, and Jacobsen, (1975). . . .

A year later, in a similar conference by Columbia University, Malespina, a biopsychiatrist, stated that it is humbling to the profession to realize that Kraepelin had predicted that it must be left to the future to see how far his theories about schizophrenia are confirmed. According to Malespina, it seems that the future is now because of the new scientific technologies.

Thus psychiatry, at the Columbia University Conference maintained the disease model in its purest form, I never heard in the course of the day any reference to poverty, social class, child abuse, family stress, rejection, ethnicity, aggression, divorce, social conflicts, social disintegration, and [so] on which are so much part of life and which could have a major effect on abnormal behavior. The individual was presented as if it were a machine with some "broken" (Andreasen, 1984) parts, mostly in the brain, which needed to be fixed.

In 1987, Van Kammen, the editor of *Biological Psychiatry,* wrote an editorial, "5 HT, a neurotransmitter for all seasons?" about the constant appearance of studies showing how serotonin has been found to be responsible for numerous aberrations. He stated:

> As clinical researchers, we may look for low CSF 5–HIAA, decreased imipramine binding, decreased alpha receptor activity and positive DST (not again!) in patients with borderline personality disorder, alcoholism, in cocaine or marijuana abusers, cigarette smokers, compulsive gamblers, sadists, flashers and nail biters, rapists, aggressive lesbians, shoplifters, and spouse beaters. (1987, p. 1)

A cover story entitled "The Genetic Revolution" in a major periodical reported on the various ailments which result from faulty genes. Since the article did not include any references on the genetic causation of mental disorders often found in the psychiatric and popular media, I wrote a letter to the editor inquiring about the fact that there is no mention of the genetic causation of mental disorders in this otherwise well-documented article on genetic diseases. His response follows:

Dear Mr. Sanua,

Thank you for writing in response to the cover story "The Genetic Revolution." We certainly appreciate your interest in learning more about genetic indicators for medical disorders. It seems logical that there would be particular genes responsible for conditions of schizophrenia, and researchers have indeed been working to identify them. Despite ongoing study, however, *most finds to date require substantial further study, and some have been retracted because of problems with methodology* [italics added]. We hope to be able to report soon on encouraging news about genetic advances for mental disorders, of course, and we are pleased that you took the time to register your thoughts on this matter . . .

In the February 21, 1994 issue of *Time,* Overbye, an essayist for the publication entitled his essay "Born to raise hell?" in which he referred to a study which attributed aggression to genetic causation. To demonstrate, in a ludicrous way, how this ideology of genetic factors is connected to a large number of aberrations, Overbye wrote:

> Some of us, it seems were born to be bad. Scientists say they are on the verge of pinning down genetic and biochemical abnormalities that predispose their bearers to violence. An article in the journal *Science* last summer carried the headline "Evidence found for a possible 'aggression gene.'" Waiting in the wings are child-testing programs, drug manufacturers, insurance companies, civil right advocates, defense attorneys, and anxious citizens for whom the violent criminal has replaced the beady-eyed communist as the bogeyman. Crime thus joins homosexuality, smoking, divorce, schizophrenia, alcoholism, shyness, political liberalism, intelligence, religiosity, cancer and blue eyes among the many aspects of human life for which it is claimed that biology is destiny. Physicists have been pilloried for years for this kind of reductionism, but in biology it makes everybody happy: the scientists and pharmaceutical companies expand their domain; politicians have "progress" to point to; the smoker, divorces and serial killers get to blame their problems on biology, and we get the satisfaction of knowing they are sick—not like us at all. (p. 76)

Weinberger (1991), a well-known investigator on the biology of schizophrenia urged his colleagues to have a more cautious attitude about the usual claims we regularly read. He wrote:

> It would be naive to conclude that current research with its neurobiologic emphasis is totally immune to the pitfalls of prior scientific research. Many of the findings that appear rock solid today will likely turn out to be epiphenomena and trivial. This has been the case throughout this century with schizophrenia, a disorder that is still researched largely at the phenomenological level. (p. 3)

However Weinberger seems rather optimistic and belies his cautiousness when he states, on the same page, that neuroanatomical, neurochemical, and neurophysiologic correlates of schizophrenia have accumulated at a seemingly *geometric rate.* [italics added] (p. 3).

A heavy dosage of headlines on the organicity of mental disorders has had some serious influence on a small but very powerful group of clinical psychologists connected with APA [American Psychological Association] who have adopted the medical model as an ideology for the purpose of espousing "prescription privileges" for the profession. I have documented (Sanua, 1993, 1994a) the pronouncement of these psychologists who have not provided in their articles the rationale and the scientific source for their inspiration. In one case, Fox (1988) supports the need for prescription privileges for psychologists (p. 503) based on an article by Adams (1986) which appeared in the *Georgia Psychologist.* Why do biopsychiatrists continue to attribute mental disorders to organic factors, while ignoring completely social factors which offer a more parsimonious explanation for the development of mental disorders? Kovacs (1987) voiced the possibility that if organic causation is deemphasized, in time biopsychiatrists will have no reason to exist. Szasz (1987) made a very pertinent observation to the effect that books on pathology do not mention anything about schizophrenia or manic-depressive psychosis. It is felt that pathologists ought to know more than anybody else about bodily pathological dysfunctions that explain mental disorders. Thus while psychiatrists have not been able to convince pathologists, they seem to be deluding themselves that mental disorders are organic and, worse, seem to be successful in convincing the general public of their pseudo-scientific findings.

The psychiatric journals are replete with presumably sophisticated articles which basically discuss structural and functional dysfunctions of the brain, genetic inheritance, and the chemistry of the urine and blood. These are being analyzed in order to discover some aberration which could be related to the mental disorders. This is being done without ever dealing with the human aspects of the patients, his feelings, his intellect, his expectations and his anxieties about his condition. Modrow (1992) provides a good example of the organic emphasis in mental disorder. If he puts forth the whimsical theory that schizophrenia is a brain disease caused by an allergy to cats, while there are schizophrenics that have never been near a cat, it can always be said that some form of schizophrenia has been caused by an allergy to cats and some forms are not, and thus the theory cannot be falsified. To me this is not a far-fetched or whimisical theory. In the course of my attendance at the Conference on Schizophrenia at Columbia University, I made the acquaintance of a psychiatrist who told me that he knew what causes schizophrenia and he would mail me an article. The two-page article revealed that schizophrenia results from mosquito bites.

... What is hoped for is that with further development of laboratory equipment, like the imaging techniques, the "truth" about the causation of schizophrenia will soon be revealed because "it is around the corner." The "truth" around the corner has been around for almost 100 years. All I can say in reading [the] extensive literature [provided by the National Institute of Mental Health] is that there has never been so much written material that has been published with such few results.

... My analysis of the tremendous efforts spent on biological research reminds me of a story which when applied to the problem of schizophrenia reflects a tragic analogy. This is the story of a drunken man who was looking for something around the lamp post in the evening. When he was asked what he was looking for, he said that he had lost his keys. When he was asked further whether he had lost them around the lamp post, he stated that he was not sure, but that this was the only place with light and, therefore, he was going to look for his keys there.

CHALLENGE QUESTIONS

Is Schizophrenia a Biological Disorder?

1. Sanua suggests that biopsychological researchers might be looking in the wrong place for the causes of mental disorders. Where else does he imply that psychologists should look to understand the causes of mental disorders? What evidence can you find for this alternative?
2. Andreasen contends that the evidence gained from a variety of methods supports the thesis that the mind and the brain are connected. What are the advantages of multidisciplinary approaches to scientific study? What are the disadvantages?
3. Sanua concludes that the search for biological causes of mental disorders has failed. If this were true, why would scientists continue to work on this project? Are there factors that are unrelated to data that could be involved in conducting this research?
4. Both Andreasen and Sanua focus their remarks on schizophrenia. Investigate another mental disorder and report on the extent to which this disorder is biologically determined.
5. Andreasen seems to express faith in the ability of future technology to uncover the specific activities of the brain that are responsible for mental disorders. To what extent is this "faith" consistent with the scientific notion that only things that have been empirically demonstrated should be accepted as true?

ISSUE 12

Have Antidepressant Drugs Proven to Be Effective?

YES: Peter D. Kramer, from *Listening to Prozac: A Psychiatrist Explores Antidepressant Drugs and the Remaking of the Self* (Viking Penguin, 1993)

NO: Seymour Fisher and Roger P. Greenberg, from "Prescriptions for Happiness?" *Psychology Today* (September/October 1995)

ISSUE SUMMARY

YES: Psychiatrist Peter D. Kramer argues that antidepressant drugs such as Prozac can transform depressed patients into happy people with almost no side effects.

NO: Professors of psychology Seymour Fisher and Roger P. Greenberg assert that the studies that demonstrate the effectiveness of antidepressants are seriously flawed.

Antidepressants are drugs that are "anti-" or "against" depression. The use of antidepressants has recently risen dramatically. However, the relatively high number of people who report serious depression (10 percent of the population) does not account for this increase. The increasing use of antidepressants is due to the fact that more and more physicians and psychiatrists are prescribing them for psychological problems other than clinical depression. Antidepressants are now prescribed for people with "the blues," stress, obsessions, compulsions, and a host of other personal and social difficulties.

A major reason for this widespread use is that antidepressant drugs, especially Prozac, seem to work well with few side effects. Popular news magazines, such as *Newsweek* and *Time*, have heralded the supposed "miracle" power of these drugs: Not only do such drugs help cure what psychologically ails you (e.g., depression), but they are also able to "transform" your personality to a new and better you! In the past, the promise of such benefits was always balanced by the potential side effects of the drugs. People who take traditional antidepressants can experience a variety of symptoms, including dry mouth, a lack of energy, and weight gain. However, with the new types of antidepressants, such as Prozac, there appear to be very few side effects. Why not take antidepressants if they will make us better, happier people without the worry of side effects?

This is the sentiment of Peter D. Kramer, who wrote his best-selling book *Listening to Prozac* after successfully prescribing antidepressant medications to his patients. In the following selection, Kramer tells of one of his patient's experiences with Prozac: the drug not only ameliorated her depressive symptoms, but it also "reshaped [her] identity." Kramer wrestles with the implications of this success. Should such medications be prescribed more widely and more often? Is it acceptable for certain people to be on Prozac for life? These issues need to be addressed, according to Kramer, by "listening" to what drugs like Prozac have to teach us.

In the second selection, Seymour Fisher and Roger P. Greenberg contend that none of the issues that Kramer struggles with are relevant if antidepressants such as Prozac are not effective to begin with. After carefully reviewing the research, Fisher and Greenberg found that fully two-thirds of all the cases did as well with placebos (inert or nonactive pills) as they did with antidepressants. The authors also maintain that studies that do show some benefits of antidepressant medications have "crucial problems" in the methods used to evaluate such drugs.

POINT

- Antidepressant medications are amazingly effective.
- The newer antidepressants, such as Prozac, are more effective than the older antidepressants.
- Some patients who take antidepressant drugs report improvement not only in their depression but in their personalities as well.
- Research and experience have overwhelmingly indicated the effectiveness and safety of antidepressants.
- Many patients do not feel as well when they are off the medication as when they are on it.

COUNTERPOINT

- The effectiveness of antidepressant medications is mixed at best.
- Many drug researchers and manufacturers are biased in favor of new drug development.
- Such testimonials are not as reliable a measure of a drug's effectiveness as controlled studies.
- Much research is tainted by procedural and researcher biases.
- Research has shown that this may actually be a placebo effect.

 **YES**

Makeover

My first experience with Prozac involved a woman I worked with only around issues of medication....

Tess was the eldest of ten children born to a passive mother and an alcoholic father in the poorest public-housing project in our city. She was abused in childhood in the concrete physical and sexual senses which everyone understands as abuse. When Tess was twelve, her father died, and her mother entered a clinical depression from which she had never recovered. Tess—one of those inexplicably resilient children who flourish without any apparent source of sustenance—took over the family. She managed to remain in school herself and in time to steer all nine siblings into stable jobs and marriages....

Meanwhile, Tess had made a business career out of her skills at driving, inspiring, and nurturing others....

That her personal life was unhappy should not have been surprising. Tess stumbled from one prolonged affair with an abusive married man to another. As these degrading relationships ended, she would suffer severe demoralization. The current episode had lasted months, and, despite a psychotherapy in which Tess willingly faced the difficult aspects of her life, she was now becoming progressively less energetic and more unhappy. It was this condition I hoped to treat, in order to spare Tess the chronic and unremitting depression that had taken hold in her mother when she was Tess's age....

What I found unusual on meeting Tess was that the scars were so well hidden. Patients who have struggled, even successfully, through neglect and abuse can have an angry edge or a tone of aggressive sweetness. They may be seductive or provocative, rigid or overly compliant. A veneer of independence may belie a swamp of neediness. Not so with Tess.

She was a pleasure to be with, even depressed. I ran down the list of signs and symptoms, and she had them all: tears and sadness, absence of hope, inability to experience pleasure, feelings of worthlessness, loss of sleep and appetite, guilty ruminations, poor memory and concentration. Were it not for her many obligations, she would have preferred to end her life. And yet I felt comfortable in her presence....

Tess had... done poorly in her personal life. She considered herself unattractive to men and perhaps not even as interesting to women as she would have liked. For the past four years, her principal social contact had been with a married man—Jim—who came and went as he pleased and finally rejected Tess in favor of his wife. Tess had stuck with Jim in part, she told me, because no other men approached her. She believed she lacked whatever spark excited men; worse, she gave off signals that kept men at a distance.

Had I been working with Tess in psychotherapy, we might have begun to explore hypotheses regarding the source of her social failure: masochism grounded in low self-worth, the compulsion of those abused early in life to seek out further abuse.... For the moment, my function was to treat my patient's depression with medication.

⋅◦⟊◦⋅

I began with imipramine, the oldest of the available antidepressants and still the standard by which others are judged. Imipramine takes about a month to work, and at the end of a month Tess said she was substantially more comfortable. She was sleeping and eating normally—in fact, she was gaining weight, probably as a side effect of the drug. "I am better," she told me. "I am myself again."

She did look less weary. And as we continued to meet, generally for fifteen minutes every month or two, all her overt symptoms remitted. Her memory and concentration improved. She regained the vital force and the willpower to go on with life. In short, Tess no longer met a doctor's criteria for depression. She even spread the good word to one of her brothers, also depressed, and the brother began taking imipramine.

But I was not satisfied.

⋅◦⟊◦⋅

It was the mother's illness that drove me forward. Tess had struggled too long for me to allow her, through any laxness of my own, to slide into the chronic depression that had engulfed her mother.

Depression is a relapsing and recurring illness. The key to treatment is thoroughness. If a patient can put together a substantial period of doing perfectly well—five months, some experts say; six or even twelve, say others—the odds are good for sustained remission. But to limp along just somewhat improved, "better but not well," is dangerous. The partly recovered patient will likely relapse as soon as you stop the therapy, as soon as you taper the drug. And the longer someone remains depressed, the more likely it is that depression will continue or return.

Tess said she was well, and she was free of the signs and symptoms of depression. But doctors are trained to doubt the report of the too-stoical patient, the patient so willing to bear pain she may unwittingly conceal illness. And, beyond signs and symptoms, the recognized abnormalities associated with a given syndrome, doctors occasionally consider what the neurologists call "soft signs," normal findings that, in the right context, make the clinical nose twitch.

I thought Tess might have a soft sign or two of depression.

She had begun to experience trouble at work—not major trouble, but something to pay attention to. The conglomerate she worked for had asked Tess to take over a company beset with labor problems. Tess always had some difficulty in situations that required meeting firmness with firmness, but she reported being more upset by negotiations with this union than by any in the past. She felt the union leaders were unreasonable, and she had begun to take their attacks on her personally. She understood conflict was inevitable; past mistakes had left labor-management relations too strained for either side to trust the other, and the coaxing and cajoling that characterized Tess's management style would need some time to work their magic. But, despite her understanding, Tess was rattled.

As a psychotherapist, I might have wondered whether Tess's difficulties had a symbolic meaning. Perhaps the hectoring union chief and his foot-dragging members resembled parents—the aggressive father, the passive mother —too much for Tess to be effective with them. In simpler terms, a new job, and this sort especially, constitutes a stressor. These viewpoints may be correct. But what level of stress was it appropriate for Tess to experience? To be rattled even by tough negotiations was unlike her.

And I found Tess vulnerable on another front. Toward the end of one of our fifteen-minute reviews of Tess's sleep, appetite, and energy level, I asked about Jim, and she burst into uncontrollable sobs. Thereafter, our meetings took on a predictable form. Tess would report that she was substantially better. Then I would ask her about Jim, and her eyes would brim over with tears, her shoulders shake. People do cry about failed romances, but sobbing seemed out of character for Tess.

These are weak reeds on which to support a therapy. Here was a highly competent, fully functional woman who no longer considered herself depressed and who had none of the standard overt indicators of depression. Had I found her less remarkable, considered her less capable as a businesswoman, been less surprised by her fragility in the face of romantic disappointment, I might have declared Tess cured. My conclusion that we should try for a better medication response may seem to be based on highly subjective data—and I think this perception is correct. Pharmacotherapy, when looked at closely, will appear to be as arbitrary—as much an art, not least in the derogatory sense of being impressionistic where ideally it should be objective—as psychotherapy. Like any other serious assessment of human emotional life, pharmacotherapy properly rests on fallible attempts at intimate understanding of another person.

༺❀༻

When I laid out my reasoning, Tess agreed to press ahead. I tried raising the dose of imipramine; but Tess began to experience side effects—dry mouth, daytime tiredness, further weight gain—so we switched to similar medications in hopes of finding one that would allow her to tolerate a higher dose. Tess changed little.

And then Prozac was released by the Food and Drug Administration. I prescribed it for Tess, for entirely conventional reasons—to terminate her depression more thoroughly, to return her to her "premorbid self." My goal was not to transform Tess but to restore her.

⋅◦⟩⋅

But medications do not always behave as we expect them to.

Two weeks after starting Prozac, Tess appeared at the office to say she was no longer feeling weary. In retrospect, she said, she had been depleted of energy for as long as she could remember, had almost not known what it was to feel rested and hopeful. She had been depressed, it now seemed to her, her whole life. She was astonished at the sensation of being free of depression.

She looked different, at once more relaxed and energetic—more available —than I had seen her, as if the person hinted at in her eyes had taken over. She laughed more frequently, and the quality of her laughter was different, no longer measured but lively, even teasing.

With this new demeanor came a new social life, one that did not unfold slowly, as a result of a struggle to integrate disparate parts of the self, but seemed, rather, to appear instantly and full-blown.

"Three dates a weekend," Tess told me. "I must be wearing a sign on my forehead!"

Within weeks of starting Prozac, Tess settled into a satisfying dating routine with men. She had missed out on dating in her teens and twenties. Now she reveled in the attention she received. She seemed even to enjoy the trial-and-error process of learning contemporary courtship rituals, gauging norms for sexual involvement, weighing the import of men's professed infatuation with her.

I had never seen a patient's social life reshaped so rapidly and dramatically. Low self-worth, competitiveness, jealousy, poor interpersonal skills, shyness, fear of intimacy—the usual causes of social awkwardness—are so deeply ingrained and so difficult to influence that ordinarily change comes gradually if at all. But Tess blossomed all at once.

"People on the sidewalk ask me for directions!" she said. They never had before.

The circle of Tess's women friends changed. Some friends left, she said, because they had been able to relate to her only through her depression. Besides, she now had less tolerance for them. "Have you ever been to a party where other people are drunk or high and you are stone-sober? Their behavior annoys you, you can't understand it. It seems juvenile and self-centered. That's how I feel around some of my old friends. It is as if they are under the influence of a harmful chemical and I am all right—as if I had been in a drugged state all those years and now I am clearheaded."

The change went further: "I can no longer understand how they tolerate the men they are with." She could scarcely acknowledge that she had once thrown herself into the same sorts of self-destructive relationships. "I never think about Jim," she said. And in the consulting room his name no longer had the power to elicit tears.

This last change struck me as most remarkable of all. When a patient displays any sign of masochism, and I think it is fair to call Tess's relationship with Jim masochistic, psychiatrists anticipate a protracted psychotherapy. It is rarely easy to help a socially self-destructive patient abandon humiliating relationships and take on new ones that accord with a healthy sense of self-worth. But once Tess felt better, once the weariness lifted and optimism became possible, the masochism just withered away, and she seemed to have every social skill she needed. . . .

* * *

There is no unhappy ending to this story. It is like one of those Elizabethan dramas—Marlowe's *Tamburlaine*—so foreign to modern audiences because the Wheel of Fortune takes only half a turn: the patient recovers and pays no price for the recovery. Tess did go off medication, after about nine months, and she continued to do well. She was, she reported, not quite so sharp of thought, so energetic, so free of care as she had been on the medication, but neither was she driven by guilt and obligation. She was altogether cooler, better controlled, less sensible of the weight of the world than she had been.

After about eight months off medication, Tess told me she was slipping. "I'm not myself," she said. New union negotiations were under way, and she felt she could use the sense of stability, the invulnerability to attack, that Prozac gave her. Here was a dilemma for me. Ought I to provide medication to someone who was not depressed? I could give myself reason enough—construe it that Tess was sliding into relapse, which perhaps she was. In truth, I assumed I would be medicating Tess's chronic condition, call it what you will: heightened awareness of the needs of others, sensitivity to conflict, residual damage to self-esteem— all odd indications for medication. I discussed the dilemma with her, but then I did not hesitate to write the prescription. Who was I to withhold from her the bounties of science? Tess responded again as she had hoped she would, with renewed confidence, self-assurance, and social comfort.

* * *

I believe Tess's story contains an unchronicled reason for Prozac's enormous popularity: its ability to alter personality. Here was a patient whose usual method of functioning changed dramatically. She became socially capable, no longer a wallflower but a social butterfly. Where once she had focused on obligations to others, now she was vivacious and fun-loving. Before, she had pined after men; now she dated them, enjoyed them, weighed their faults and virtues. Newly confident, Tess had no need to romanticize or indulge men's shortcomings.

Not all patients on Prozac respond this way. Some are unaffected by the medicine; some merely recover from depression, as they might on any antidepressant. But a few, a substantial minority, are transformed. Like Garrison Keillor's marvelous Powdermilk biscuits, Prozac gives these patients the courage to do what needs to be done.

What I saw in Tess—a quick alteration in ordinarily intractable problems of personality and social functioning—other psychiatrists saw in their patients as well. Moreover, Prozac had few immediate side effects. Patients on Prozac do not feel drugged up or medicated. Here is one place where the favorable side-effect profile of Prozac makes a difference: if a doctor thinks there is even a modest chance of quickly liberating a chronically stymied patient, and if the risk to the patient is slight, then the doctor will take the gamble repeatedly.

And of course Prozac had phenomenal word of mouth, as "good responders" like Tess told their friends about it. I saw this effect in the second patient I put on Prozac. She was a habitually withdrawn, reticent woman whose cautious behavior had handicapped her at work and in courtship. After a long interval between sessions, I ran into her at a local bookstore. I tend to hang back when I see a patient in a public place, out of uncertainty as to how the patient may want to be greeted, and I believe that, while her chronic depression persisted, this woman would have chosen to avoid me. Now she strode forward and gave me a bold "Hello." I responded, and she said, "I've changed my name, you know."

I did not know. Had she switched from depression to mania and then married impulsively? I wondered whether I should have met with her more frequently. She had, I saw, the bright and open manner that had brought Tess so much social success.

"Yes," she continued, "I call myself Ms. Prozac."

There is no Ms. Asendin, no Ms. Pamelor. Those medicines are quite wonderful—they free patients from the bondage of depression. But they have not inspired the sort of enthusiasm and loyalty patients have shown for Prozac.

✦

No doubt doctors should be unreservedly pleased when their patients get better quickly. But I confess I was unsettled by Ms. Prozac's enthusiasm, and by Tess's as well. I was suspicious of Prozac, as if I had just taken on a cotherapist whose charismatic style left me wondering whether her magic was wholly trustworthy.

The more rational component to my discomfort had to do with Tess. It makes a psychiatrist uneasy to watch a medicated patient change her circle of friends, her demeanor at work, her relationship to her family. All psychiatrists have seen depressed patients turn manic and make decisions they later regret. But Tess never showed signs of mania. She did not manifest rapid speech or thought, her judgment remained sound, and, though she enjoyed life more than she had before, she was never euphoric or Pollyannaish. In mood and level of energy, she was "normal," but her place on the normal spectrum had changed, and that change, from "serious," as she put it, to vivacious, had profound consequences for her relationships to those around her.

As the stability of Tess's improvement became clear, my concern diminished, but it did not disappear. Just what did not sit right was hard to say. Might a severe critic find the new Tess a bit blander than the old? Perhaps her tortured intensity implied a complexity of personality that was now harder to locate. I wondered whether the medication had not ironed out too many character-giving wrinkles, like overly aggressive plastic surgery. I even asked myself whether Tess would now give up her work in the projects, as if I had administered her a pill to cure warmheartedness and progressive social beliefs. But in entertaining this thought I wondered whether I was clinging to an arbitrary valuation of temperament, as if the melancholy or saturnine humor were in some way morally superior to the sanguine. In the event, Tess did not forsake the projects, though she did make more time for herself.

Tess, too, found her transformation, marvelous though it was, somewhat unsettling. What was she to make of herself? Her past devotion to Jim, for instance—had it been a matter of biology, an addiction to which she was prone as her father had been to alcoholism? Was she, who defined herself in contrast to her father's fecklessness, in some uncomfortable way like him? What responsibility had she for those years of thralldom to degrading love? After a prolonged struggle to understand the self, to find the Gordian knot dissolved by medication is a mixed pleasure: we want some internal responsibility for our lives, want to find meaning in our errors. Tess was happy, but she talked of a mild, persistent sense of wonder and dislocation. . . .

⋅◉⋅

I wondered what I would have made of Tess had she been referred to me just before Jim broke up with her, before she had experienced acute depression. I might have recognized her as a woman with skills in many areas, one who had managed to make friends and sustain a career, and who had never suffered a mental illness; I might have seen her as a person who had examined her life with some thoroughness and made progress on many fronts but who remained frustrated socially. She and I might suspect the trouble stemmed from "who she is"—temperamentally serious or timid or cautious or pessimistic or emotionally unexpressive. If only she were a little livelier, a bit more carefree, we might conclude, everything else would fall into place.

Tess's family history—the depressed mother and alcoholic father—constitutes what psychiatrists call "affective loading." (Alcoholism in men seems genetically related to depression in women; or, put more cautiously, a family history of alcoholism is moderately predictive of depression in near relatives.) I might suspect that, in a socially stymied woman with a familial predisposition to depression, Prozac could prove peculiarly liberating. There I would sit, knowing I had in hand a drug that might give Tess just the disposition she needed to break out of her social paralysis.

Confronted with a patient who had never met criteria for any illness, what would I be free to do? If I did prescribe medication, how would we characterize this act?

For years, psychoanalysts were criticized for treating the "worried well," or for "enhancing growth" rather than curing illness. Who is not neurotic? Who is not a fit candidate for psychotherapy? This issue has been answered through an uneasy social consensus. We tolerate breadth in the scope of psychoanalysis, and of psychotherapy in general; few people today would remark on a patient's consulting a therapist over persistent problems with personality or social interactions, though some might object to seeing such treatments covered by insurance under the rubric of illness.

But I wondered whether we were ready for "cosmetic psycho-pharmacology." It was my musings about whether it would be kosher to medicate a patient like Tess in the absence of depression that led me to coin the phrase. Some people might prefer pharmacologic to psychologic self-actualization. Psychic steroids for mental gymnastics, medicinal attacks on the humors, anti-wallflower compound—these might be hard to resist. Since you only live once, why not do it as a blonde? Why not as a peppy blonde? Now that questions of personality and social stance have entered the arena of medication, we as a society will have to decide how comfortable we are with using chemicals to modify personality in useful, attractive ways. We may mask the issue by defining less and less severe mood states as pathology, in effect saying, "If it responds to an antidepressant, it's depression." Already, it seems to me, psychiatric diagnosis had been subject to a sort of "diagnostic bracket creep"—the expansion of categories to match the scope of relevant medications.

How large a sphere of human problems we choose to define as medical is an important social decision. But words like "choose" and "decision" perhaps misstate the process. It is easy to imagine that our role will be passive, that as a society we will in effect permit the material technology, medications, to define what is health and what is illness....

❧

An indication of the power of medication to reshape a person's identity is contained in the sentence Tess used when, eight months after first stopping Prozac, she telephoned me to ask whether she might resume the medication. She said, "I am not myself."

I found this statement remarkable. After all, Tess had existed in one mental state for twenty or thirty years; she then briefly felt different on medication. Now that the old mental state was threatening to re-emerge—the one she had experienced almost all her adult life—her response was "I am not myself." But who had she been all those years if not herself? Had medication somehow removed a false self and replaced it with a true one? Might Tess, absent the invention of the modern antidepressant, have lived her whole life—a successful life, perhaps, by external standards—and never been herself?

When I asked her to expand on what she meant, Tess said she no longer felt like herself when certain aspects of her ailment—lack of confidence, feelings of vulnerability—returned, even to a small degree. Ordinarily, if we ask a person why she holds back socially, she may say, "That's just who I am," meaning shy or hesitant or melancholy or overly cautious. These characteristics often persist throughout life, and they have a strong influence on career, friendships, marriage, self-image.

Suddenly those intimate and consistent traits are not-me, they are alien, they are defect, they are illness—so that a certain habit of mind and body that links a person to his relatives and ancestors from generation to generation is now "other." Tess had come to understand herself—the person she had been for so many years—to be mildly ill. She understood this newfound illness, as it were, in her marrow. She did not feel herself when the medicine wore off and she was rechallenged by an external stress.

On imipramine, no longer depressed but still inhibited and subdued, Tess felt "myself again." But while on Prozac, she underwent a redefinition of self. Off Prozac, when she again became inhibited and subdued—perhaps the identical sensations she had experienced while on imipramine—she now felt "not myself." Prozac redefined Tess's understanding of what was essential to her and what was intrusive and pathological.

This recasting of self left Tess in an unusual relationship to medication. Off medication, she was aware that, if she returned to the old inhibited state, she might need Prozac in order to "feel herself." In this sense, she might have a lifelong relationship to medication, whether or not she was currently taking it. Patients who undergo the sort of deep change Tess experienced generally say they never want to feel the old way again and would take quite substantial risks —in terms, for instance, of medication side effects—in order not to regress. This is not a question of addiction or hedonism, at least not in the ordinary sense of those words, but of having located a self that feels true, normal, and whole, and of understanding medication to be an occasionally necessary adjunct to the maintenance of that self.

Beyond the effect on individual patients, Tess's redefinition of self led me to fantasize about a culture in which this biologically driven sort of self-understanding becomes widespread. Certain dispositions now considered awkward or endearing, depending on taste, might be seen as ailments to be pitied and, where possible, corrected. Tastes and judgments regarding personality styles do change. The romantic, decadent stance of Goethe's young Werther and Chateaubriand's René we now see as merely immature, overly depressive, perhaps in need of treatment. Might we not, in a culture where overseriousness is a medically correctable flaw, lose our taste for the melancholic or brooding artists—Schubert, or even Mozart in many of his moods?

These were my concerns on witnessing Tess's recovery. I was torn simultaneously by a sense that the medication was too far-reaching in its effects and a sense that my discomfort was arbitrary and aesthetic rather than doctorly. I wondered how the drug might influence my profession's definition of illness and its understanding of ordinary suffering. I wondered how Prozac's success would interact with certain unfortunate tendencies of the broader culture. And I asked just how far we—doctors, patients, the society at large—were likely to go in the direction of permitting drug responses to shape our understanding of the authentic self.

My concerns were imprecisely formulated. But it was not only the concerns that were vague: I had as yet only a sketchy impression of the drug whose effects were so troubling. To whom were my patients and I listening? On that question depended the answers to the list of social and ethical concerns; and the exploration of that question would entail attending to accounts of other patients who responded to Prozac.

My first meeting with Prozac had been heightened for me by the uncommon qualities of the patient who responded to the drug. I found it astonishing that a pill could do in a matter of days what psychiatrists hope, and often fail, to accomplish by other means over a course of years: to restore to a person robbed of it in childhood the capacity to play. Yes, there remained a disquieting element to this restoration. Were I scripting the story, I might have made Tess's metamorphosis more gradual, more humanly comprehensible, more in sync with the ordinary rhythm of growth. I might even have preferred if her play as an adult had been, for continuity's sake, more suffused with the memory of melancholy. But medicines do not work just as we wish. The way neurochemicals tell stories is not the way psychotherapy tells them. If Tess's fairy tale does not have the plot we expect, its ending is nonetheless happy.

By the time Tess's story had played itself out, I had seen perhaps a dozen people respond with comparable success to Prozac. Hers was not an isolated case, and the issues it raised would not go away. Charisma, courage, character, social competency—Prozac seemed to say that these and other concepts would need to be re-examined, that our sense of what is constant in the self and what is mutable, what is necessary and what contingent, would need, like our sense of the fable of transformation, to be revised.

**Seymour Fisher and
Roger P. Greenberg**

Prescriptions for Happiness?

The air is filled with declarations and advertisements of the power of biological psychiatry to relieve people of their psychological distress. Some biological psychiatrists are so convinced of the superiority of their position that they are recommending young psychiatrists no longer be taught the essentials of doing psychotherapy. Feature stories in such magazines as *Newsweek* and *Time* have portrayed drugs like Prozac as possessing almost a mystical potency. The best-selling book *Listening to Prozac* by psychiatrist Peter Kramer, M.D., projects the idyllic possibility that psychotropic drugs may eventually be capable of correcting a spectrum of personality quirks and lacks.

As longtime faculty members of a number of psychiatry departments, we have personally witnessed the gradual but steadily accelerated dedication to the idea that "mental illness" can be mastered with biologically based substances. Yet a careful sifting of the pertinent literature indicates that modesty and skepticism would be more appropriate responses to the research accumulated thus far. In 1989, we first raised radical questions about such biological claims in a book, *The Limits of Biological Treatments for Psychological Distress: Comparisons with Psychotherapy and Placebo* (Lawrence Erlbaum). Our approach has been to filter the studies that presumably anchor them through a series of logical and quantitative (meta-analytic) appraisals.

How Effective Are Antidepressant Drugs?

Antidepressants, one of the major weapons in the biological therapeutic arsenal, illustrate well the largely unacknowledged uncertainty that exists in the biological approach to psychopathology. We suggest that, at present, no one actually knows how effective antidepressants are. Confident declarations about their potency go well beyond the existing evidence.

To get an understanding of the scientific status of antidepressants, we analyzed how much more effective the antidepressants are than inert pills called "placebos." That is, if antidepressants are given to one depressed group and a placebo to another group, how much greater is the recovery of those taking the active drug as compared to those taking the inactive placebo? Generous claims that antidepressants usually produce improvement in about 60 to 70 percent of patients are not infrequent, whereas placebos are said to benefit 25 to 30 percent. If antidepressants were, indeed, so superior to placebos, this would be a persuasive advertisement for the biological approach.

We found 15 major reviews of the antidepressant literature. Surprisingly, even the most positive reviews indicate that 30 to 40 percent of studies show no significant difference in response to drug versus placebo! The reviews indicate overall that one-third of patients do not improve with antidepressant treatment, one-third improve with placebos, and an additional third show a response to medication they would not have attained with placebos. In the most optimistic view of such findings, two-thirds of the cases (placebo responders and those who do not respond to anything) do as well with placebo as with active medication.

We also found two large-scale quantitative evaluations (meta-analyses) integrating the outcomes of multiple studies of antidepressants. They clearly indicated, on the average, quite modest therapeutic power.

We were particularly impressed by the large variation in outcomes of studies conducted at multiple clinical sites or centers. Consider a study that compared the effectiveness of an antidepressant among patients at five different research centers. Although the pooled results demonstrate that the drug was generally more effective than placebo, the results from individual centers reveal much variation. After six weeks of treatment, every one of the six measures of effectiveness showed the antidepressant (imipramine) to be merely equivalent to placebo in two or more of the centers. In two of the settings, a difference favoring the medication was detected on only one of 12 outcome comparisons.

In other words, the pooled, apparently favorable, outcome data conceal that dramatically different results could be obtained as a function of who conducted the study and the specific conditions at each locale. We can only conclude that a good deal of fragility characterized the apparent superiority of drug over placebo. The scientific literature is replete with analogous examples.

Incidentally, we also looked at whether modern studies, which are presumably better protected against bias, use higher doses, and often involve longer treatment periods, show a greater superiority of the antidepressant than did earlier studies. The literature frequently asserts that failures to demonstrate antidepressant superiority are due to such methodological failures as not using high enough doses, and so forth.

We examined this issue in a pool of 16 studies assembled by psychiatrists John Kane and Jeffrey Lieberman in 1984. These studies all compare a standard drug, such as imipramine or amitriptyline, to a newer drug and a placebo. They use clearer diagnostic definitions of depression than did the older studies and also adopt currently accepted standards for dosage levels and treatment duration. When we examined the data, we discovered that the advantage of drug over placebo was modest. Twenty-one percent more of the patients receiving a drug improved as compared to those on placebo. Actually, most of the studies showed no difference in the percentage of patients significantly improved by drugs. There was no indication that these studies, using more careful methodology, achieved better outcomes than older studies.

Finally, it is crucial to recognize that several studies have established that there is a high rate of relapse among those who have responded positively to an antidepressant but then are taken off treatment. The relapse rate may be 60 percent or more during the first year after treatment cessation. Many studies also show that any benefits of antidepressants wane in a few months, even while the drugs are still being taken. This highlights the complexity of evaluating antidepressants. They may be effective initially, but lose all value over a longer period.

Are Drug Trials Biased?

As we burrowed deeper into the antidepressant literature, we learned that there are also crucial problems in the methodology used to evaluate psychotropic drugs. Most central is the question of whether this methodology properly shields drug trials from bias. Studies have shown that the more open to bias a drug trial is, the greater the apparent superiority of the drug over placebo. So questions about the trustworthiness of a given drug-testing procedure invite skepticism about the results.

The question of potential bias first came to our attention in studies comparing inactive placebos to active drugs. In the classic double-blind design, neither patient nor researcher knows who is receiving drug or placebo. We were struck by the fact that the presumed protection provided by the double-blind design was undermined by the use of placebos that simply do not arouse as many body sensations as do active drugs. Research shows that patients learn to discriminate between drug and placebo largely from body sensations and symptoms.

A substance like imipramine, one of the most frequently studied antidepressants, usually causes clearly defined sensations, such as dry mouth, tremor, sweating, constipation. Inactive placebos used in studies of antidepressants also apparently initiate some body sensations, but they are fewer, more inconsistent, and less intense as indicated by the fact that they are less often cited by patients as a source of discomfort causing them to drop out of treatment.

Vivid differences between the body sensations of drug and placebo groups could signal to patients as to whether they are receiving an active or inactive agent. Further, they could supply discriminating cues to those responsible for the patients' day-to-day treatment. Nurses, for example, might adopt different attitudes toward patients they identify as being "on" versus "off" active treatment—and consequently communicate contrasting expectations.

The Body of Evidence

This is more than theoretical. Researchers have reported that in a double-blind study of imipramine, it was possible by means of side effects to identify a significant number of the patients taking the active drug. Those patients receiving a placebo have fewer signals (from self and others) indicating they are being actively treated and should be improving. By the same token, patients taking an active drug receive multiple signals that may well amplify potential placebo effects linked to the therapeutic context. Indeed, a doctor's strong belief in the power of the active drug enhances the apparent therapeutic power of the drug or placebo.

Is it possible that a large proportion of the difference in effectiveness often reported between antidepressants and placebos can be explained as a function of body sensation discrepancies? It is conceivable, and fortunately there are research findings that shed light on the matter.

Consider an analysis by New Zealand psychologist Richard Thomson. He reviewed double-blind, placebo-controlled studies of antidepressants completed between 1958 and 1972. Sixty-eight had employed an inert placebo and seven an active one (atropine) that produced a variety of body sensations. The antidepressant had a superior therapeutic effect in 59 percent of the studies using inert placebo—but in only one study (14 percent) using the active placebo. The active placebo eliminated any therapeutic advantage for the antidepressants, apparently because it convinced patients they were getting real medication.

How Blind Is Double-Blind?

Our concerns about the effects of inactive placebos on the double-blind design led us to ask just how blind the double-blind really is. By the 1950s reports were already surfacing that for psychoactive drugs, the double-blind design is not as scientifically objective as originally assumed. In 1993 we searched the world literature and found 31 reports in which patients and researchers involved in studies were asked to guess who was receiving the active psychotropic drug and who the placebo. In 28 instances the guesses were significantly better than chance—and at times they were surprisingly accurate. In one double-blind study that called for administering either imipramine, phenelzine, or placebo to depressed patients, 78 percent of patients and 87 percent of psychiatrists correctly distinguished drug from placebo.

One particularly systematic report in the literature involved the administration of alprazolam, imipramine, and placebo over an eight-week period to groups of patients who experience panic attacks. Halfway through the treatment and also at the end, the physicians and the patients were asked to judge independently whether each patient was receiving an active drug or a placebo. If they thought an active drug was being administered, they had to decide whether it was alprazolam or imipramine. Both physicians (with an 88 percent success rate) and patients (83 percent) substantially exceeded chance in the correctness of their judgments. Furthermore, the physicians could distinguish alprazolam from imipramine significantly better than chance. The researchers concluded that "double-blind studies of these pharmacological treatments for panic disorder was not really 'blind.'"

Yet the vast majority of psychiatric drug efficacy studies have simply *assumed* that the double-blind design is effective; they did not test the blindness by determining whether patients and researchers were able to differentiate drug from placebo.

We take the somewhat radical view that this means most past studies of the efficacy of psychotropic drugs are, to unknown degrees, scientifically untrustworthy. At the least, we can no longer speak with confidence about the true differences in therapeutic power between active psychotropic drugs and place-bos. We must suspend judgment until future studies are completed with more adequate controls for the defects of the double-blind paradigm.

Other bothersome questions arose as we scanned the cascade of studies focused on antidepressants. Of particular concern is how unrepresentative the patients are who end up in the clinical trials. There are the usual sampling problems having to do with which persons seek treatment for their discomfort, and, in addition, volunteer as subjects for a study. But there are others. Most prominent is the relatively high proportion of patients who "drop out" before the completion of their treatment programs.

Numerous dropouts occur in response to unpleasant side effects. In many published studies, 35 percent or more of patients fail to complete the research protocol. Various procedures have been developed to deal fairly with the question of how to classify the therapeutic outcomes of dropouts, but none can vitiate the simple fact that the final sample of fully treated patients has often been drastically reduced.

There are still other filters that increase sample selectivity. For example, studies often lose sizable segments of their samples by not including patients who are too depressed to speak, much less participate in a research protocol, or who are too disorganized to participate in formal psychological testing. We also found decisions not to permit particular racial or age groups to be represented in samples or to avoid using persons below a certain educational level. Additionally, researchers typically recruit patients whose depression is not accompanied by any other type of physical or mental disorder, a situation that does not hold for the depressed in the general population.

So we end up wondering about the final survivors in the average drug trial. To what degree do they typify the average individual in real life who seeks treatment? How much can be generalized from a sample made up of the "leftovers" from multiple depleting processes? Are we left with a relatively narrow band of those most willing to conform to the rather rigid demands of the research establishment? Are the survivors those most accepting of a dependent role?

The truth is that there are probably multiple kinds of survivors, depending upon the specific local conditions prevailing where the study was carried out. We would guess that some of the striking differences in results that appear in multicenter drug studies could be traced to specific forms of sampling bias. We do not know how psychologically unique the persons are who get recruited into, and stick with, drug research enterprises. We are not the first to raise this question, but we are relatively more alarmed about the potential implications.

Researcher Motivation and Outcome

We recently conducted an analysis that further demonstrates how drug effectiveness diminishes as the opportunity for bias in research design wanes. This analysis seized on studies in which a new antidepressant is compared (under double-blind conditions) with an older, standard antidepressant and a placebo. In such a context the efficacy of the newer drug (which the drug company hopes to introduce) is of central interest to the researcher, and the effectiveness of the older drug of peripheral import. Therefore, if the double-blind is breached (as is likely), there would presumably be less bias to enhance the efficacy of the older drug than occurred in the original trials of that drug.

We predicted that the old drug would appear significantly less powerful in the newer studies than it had in earlier designs, where it was of central interest of the researcher. To test this hypothesis, we located 22 double-blind studies in which newer antidepressants were compared with an older antidepressant drug (usually imipramine) and a placebo. Our meta-analysis revealed, as predicted, that the efficacy rates, based on clinicians's judgments of outcome, were quite modest for the older antidepressants. In fact, they were approximately one-half to one-quarter the average size of the effects reported in earlier studies when the older drug was the only agent appraised.

Let us be very clear as to what this signifies: When researchers were evaluating the antidepressant in a context where they were no longer interested in proving its therapeutic power, there was a dramatic decrease in that apparent power, as compared to an earlier context when they were enthusiastically interested in demonstrating the drug's potency. A change in researcher motivation was enough to change outcome. Obviously this means too that the present double-blind design for testing drug efficacy is exquisitely vulnerable to bias.

Another matter of pertinence to the presumed biological rationale for the efficacy of antidepressants is that no consistent links have been demonstrated between the concentration of drug in blood and its efficacy. Studies have found significant correlations for some drugs, but of low magnitude. Efforts to link plasma levels to therapeutic outcome have been disappointing.

Similarly, few data show a relationship between antidepressant dosage levels and their therapeutic efficacy. That is, large doses of the drug do not necessarily have greater effects than low doses. These inconsistencies are a bit jarring against the context of biological explanatory framework.

We have led you through a detailed critique of the difficulties and problems that prevail in the body of research testing the power of the antidepressants. We conclude that it would be wise to be relatively modest in claims about their efficacy. Uncertainty and doubt are inescapable.

While we have chosen the research on the antidepressants to illustrate the uncertainties attached to biological treatments of psychological distress, reviews of other classes of psychotropic drugs yield similar findings. After a survey of anti-anxiety drugs, psychologist Ronald Lipman concluded there is little consistent evidence that they help patients with anxiety disorders: "Although it seems natural to assume that the anxiolytic medications would be the most effective psychotropic medications for the treatment of anxiety disorders, the evidence does not support this assumption."

Biological Versus Psychological?

The faith in the biological approach has been fueled by a great burst of research. Thousands of papers have appeared probing the efficacy of psychotropic drugs. A good deal of basic research has attacked fundamental issues related to the nature of brain functioning in those who display psychopathology. Researchers in these areas are dedicated and often do excellent work. However, in their zeal, in their commitment to the so-called biological, they are at times overcome by their expectations. Their hopes become rigidifying boundaries. Their vocabulary too easily becomes a jargon that camouflages over-simplified assumptions.

A good example of such oversimplification is the way in which the term "biological" is conceptualized. It is too often viewed as a realm distinctly different from the psychological. Those invested in the biological approach all too often practice the ancient Cartesian distinction between somatic-stuff and soul-stuff. In so doing they depreciate the scientific significance of the phenomena they exile to the soul-stuff category.

But paradoxically, they put a lot of interesting phenomena out of bounds to their prime methodology and restrict themselves to a narrowed domain. For example, if talk therapy is labeled as a "psychological" thing—not biological—this implies that biological research can only hover at the periphery of what psychotherapists do. A sizable block of behavior becomes off limits to the biologically dedicated.

In fact, if we adopt the view that the biological and psychological are equivalent (biological monism), there is no convincing real-versus-unreal differentiation between the so-called psychological and biological. It *all* occurs in tissue and one is not more "real" than the other. A patient's attitude toward the therapist is just as biological in nature as a patient's response to an antidepressant. A response to a placebo is just as biological as a response to an antipsychotic drug. This may be an obvious point, but it has not yet been incorporated into the world views of either the biologically or psychologically oriented.

Take a look at a few examples in the research literature that highlight the overlap or identity of what is so often split apart. In 1992, psychiatrist Lewis Baxter and colleagues showed that successful psychotherapy of obsessive-compulsive patients results in brain imagery changes equivalent to those produced by successful drug treatment. The brain apparently responds in equivalent ways to both the talk and drug approaches. Even more dramatic is a finding that instilling in the elderly the illusion of being in control of one's surroundings (by putting them in charge of some plants) significantly increased their life span compared to a control group. What could be a clearer demonstration of the biological nature of what is labeled as a psychological expectation than the postponement of death?

Why are we focusing on this historic Cartesian confusion? Because so many who pursue the so-called biological approach are by virtue of their tunnel vision motivated to overlook the psychosocial variable that mediate the administration of such agents as psychotropic drugs and electroconvulsive therapy. They do not permit themselves to seriously grasp that psychosocial variables are just as biological as a capsule containing an antidepressant. It is the failure to understand this that results in treating placebo effects as if they were extraneous or less of a biological reality than a chemical agent.

Placebo Effects

Indeed, placebos have been shown to initiate certain effects usually thought to be reserved for active drugs. For example, placebos clearly show dose-level effects. A larger dose of a placebo will have a greater impact than a lower dose. Placebos can also create addictions. Patients will poignantly declare that they cannot stop taking a particular placebo substance (which they assume is an active drug) because to do so causes them too much distress and discomfort.

Placebos can produce toxic effects such as rashes, apparent memory loss, fever, headaches, and more. These "toxic" effects may be painful and even overwhelming in their intensity. The placebo literature is clear: Placebos are powerful body-altering substances, especially considering the wide range of body systems they can influence.

Actually, the power of the placebo complicates all efforts to test the therapeutic efficacy of psychotropic drugs. When placebos alone can produce positive curative effects in the 40 to 50 percent range (occasionally even up to 70–80 percent), the active drug being tested is hard-pressed to demonstrate its superiority. Even if the active drug exceeds the placebo in potency, the question remains whether the advantage is at least partially due to the superior potential of the active drug itself to mobilize placebo effects because it is an active substance that stirs vivid body sensations. Because it is almost always an inactive substance (sugar pill) that arouses fewer genuine body sensations, the placebo is less convincingly perceived as having therapeutic prowess.

Drug researchers have tried, in vain, to rid themselves of placebo effects, but these effects are forever present and frustrate efforts to demonstrate that psychoactive drugs have an independent "pure" biological impact. This state of affairs dramatically testifies that the labels "psychological" and "biological" refer largely to different perspectives on events that all occur in tissue. At present, it is somewhat illusory to separate the so-called biological and psychological effects of drugs used to treat emotional distress.

The literature is surprisingly full of instances of how social and attitudinal factors modify the effects of active drugs. Antipsychotic medications are more effective if the patient likes rather than dislikes the physician administering them. An antipsychotic drug is less effective if patients are led to believe they are only taking an inactive placebo. Perhaps even more impressive, if a stimulant drug is administered with the deceptive instruction that it is a sedative, it can initiate a pattern of physiological response, such as decreased heart rate, that it is sedative rather than arousing in nature. Such findings reaffirm how fine the line is between social and somatic domains.

What are the practical implications for distressed individuals and their physicians? Administering a drug is not simply a medical (biological) act. It is, in addition, a complex social act whose effectiveness will be mediated by such factors as the patient's expectations of the drug and reactions to the body sensations created by that drug, and the physician's friendliness and degree of personal confidence in the drug's power. Practitioners who dispense psychotropic medications should become thoroughly acquainted with the psychological variables modifying the therapeutic impact of such drugs and tailor their own behavior accordingly. By the same token, distressed people seeking drug treatment should keep in mind that their probability of benefiting may depend in part on whether they choose a practitioner they truly like and respect. And remember this: You are the ultimate arbiter of a drug's efficacy.

How to go about mastering unhappiness, which ranges from "feeling blue" to despairing depression, puzzles everyone. Such popular quick fixes as alcohol, conversion to a new faith, and other splendid distractions have proven only partially helpful. When antidepressant drugs hit the shelves with their seeming scientific aura, they were easily seized upon. Apparently serious unhappiness (depression) could now be chemically neutralized in the way one banishes a toothache.

But the more we learn about the various states of unhappiness, the more we recognize that they are not simply "symptoms" awaiting removal. Depressed feelings have complex origins and functions. In numerous contexts—for example, chronic conflict with a spouse—depression may indicate a realistic appraisal of a troubling problem and motivate a serious effort to devise a solution.

While it is true that deep despair may interfere with sensible problem-solving, the fact is that, more and more, individuals are being instructed to take antidepressants at the earliest signs of depressive distress and this could interfere with the potentially constructive signaling value of such distress. Emotions are feelings full of information. Unhappiness is an emotion, and despite its negativity, should not be classified single-mindedly as a thing to tune out. This in no way implies that one should submit passively to the discomfort of feeling unhappy. Actually, we all learn to experiment with a variety of strategies for making ourselves feel better, but the ultimate aim is long-term effective action rather than a depersonalized "I feel fine."

CHALLENGE QUESTIONS

Have Antidepressant Drugs Proven to Be Effective?

1. Assume that "mood brighteners" such as Prozac are as effective as Kramer says they are for Tess and that they are also perfectly safe. What would be some of the problems and prospects of this "brightened" world?
2. Fisher and Greenberg say that "depressed feelings have complex origins and functions." What function could such feelings have? How would their removal by antidepressants be problematic?
3. How would you account for what Fisher and Greenberg term "the power of the placebo"? How could this be used in psychotherapy?
4. Draw up a list of recommendations for improving drug evaluation research.
5. How do you account for the seemingly phenomenal success of Prozac as seen by psychiatrists such as Kramer?

On the Internet...

The C. G. Jung Page

The C. G. Jung Page was founded in 1995 to encourage new psychological ideas and conversations about what it means to be human in our time and place. It offers an introduction to Carl Jung, Jungian resources, Jungian articles, and much more.

http://www.cgjung.com

Knowledge Exchange Network (KEN)

The Center for Mental Health Services (CMHS) Knowledge Exchange Network (KEN) provides information about mental health via toll-free telephone services, an electronic bulletin board, and publications. It is a one-stop source for information and resources on prevention, treatment, and rehabilitation services for mental illness, and it also has many links to related sources.

http://www.mentalhealth.org

Sigmund Freud and the Freud Archives

Internet resources related to Sigmund Freud can be accessed through this site. A collection of libraries, museums, and biographical materials, as well as the Brill Library archives, can be found here.

http://plaza.interport.net/nypsan/freudarc.html

PART 6

Psychological Treatment

*C*oncerns over insurance coverage have highlighted discussions of the effectiveness of psychotherapy. Some argue, for example, that psychologists should limit therapy sessions to save money and to allow more people to be treated. However, is brief therapy as effective as long-term therapy? Also, the increase of pharmalogical treatment leads some to contend that psychologists should be allowed to prescribe drugs. Could this lead to an abuse of prescriptions? Finally, are diagnostic labels even useful for treatment? Could individuals benefit from more flexible therapies? All these concerns could drastically change traditional modes of psychological treatment.

- Is Brief Therapy as Effective as Long-Term Therapy?

- Should Psychologists Be Allowed to Prescribe Drugs?

- Classic Dialogue: Do Diagnostic Labels Hinder Treatment?

ISSUE 13

Is Brief Therapy as Effective as Long-Term Therapy?

YES: Brett N. Steenbarger, from "Toward Science-Practice Integration in Brief Counseling and Therapy," *The Counseling Psychologist* (July 1992)

NO: Charles J. Gelso, from "Realities and Emerging Myths About Brief Therapy," *The Counseling Psychologist* (July 1992)

ISSUE SUMMARY

YES: Researcher Brett N. Steenbarger argues that although psychologists may underestimate the long-lasting effects of brief therapy, studies show that the most dramatic changes in patient behavior take place after only eight therapy sessions.

NO: Therapist and researcher Charles J. Gelso contends that although initial behavior change may be rapid, long-term therapy is needed in order for a client to maintain lasting and deep personality changes.

To keep their therapy practices profitable, many psychologists are finding that they must participate in a health management organization (HMO). This participation allows them to be reimbursed for their services through their clients' health insurance providers. The problem is that many HMOs are concerned with rising health care costs, so they push therapists and counselors to cut costs and increase efficiency. This often means that therapists are "encouraged" to use medication and brief therapy to treat psychological disorders that would ordinarily be treated with long-term therapy or counseling. The question is, Is this really best for the client?

Some people argue that the most efficient methods are the best for the client. After all, if one can be cured by a psychologist in four weeks (or eight sessions), why waste one's time and money on six months or a year of therapy? Also, psychologists could treat and help many more people by limiting therapy sessions. From this viewpoint, it seems that a brief therapy approach would be good for everyone. But what if patients' symptoms come back? What if eight therapy sessions only addressed a patient's superficial needs, and six months later that patient had to start all over again? Wouldn't he or she feel cheated? Wouldn't that person give up on psychotherapy?

In the following selection, Brett N. Steenbarger contends that brief therapy is more efficient and just as effective as long-term therapy. He cites studies indicating that client improvement is most rapid in the first eight sessions of therapy. After that, change slows down significantly, and further therapy is really unnecessary. Steenbarger argues that therapists underestimate the effectiveness of brief therapy because they want to follow their clients through all their changes. Unfortunately, this desire is more for the emotional benefit of the therapist than for the psychological benefit of the clients. Putting therapists' desires aside, Steenbarger says, the evidence shows that clients who undergo brief therapy are just as psychologically healthy in the long run as those who undergo long-term therapy. Also, brief therapy allows clinicians and therapists to be more efficient without being less effective.

In the second selection, Charles J. Gelso disagrees. He contends that many clients who have undergone brief therapy have had to return to counseling within a year. He asserts that the empirical evidence comparing brief and long-term therapy is unclear. From his experience, he has found that long-term therapy results in more pervasive and more profound changes in client behavior. Just because the largest measurable changes are seen in the first eight sessions of therapy, he maintains, does not mean that eight sessions are all that are needed. The first eight sessions may contain the most obvious changes, but later sessions allow for subtler and deeper changes that are crucial to the client. Ultimately, Gelso concludes, if brief therapy cannot produce these deeper changes, then it is less effective and therefore less efficient.

POINT	COUNTERPOINT
• Brief therapy is just as effective as long-term therapy.	• Clients who receive brief therapy have higher relapse rates.
• The greatest changes in client behavior occur in the first eight sessions of therapy.	• The fact that the greatest changes in client behavior occur in the first eight sessions does not reduce the importance of the changes that occur in later sessions.
• Therapists and counselors resist brief therapy because they assume that change must take a long time to be meaningful.	• Since therapists know more about their clients than researchers do, therapists may be resisting brief therapy for good reasons.
• Brief therapy saves agencies time and money, cuts down on waiting lists, and decreases client dropout rates.	• Policies about therapy session duration should not be made simply to save time.

Brett N. Steenbarger

 **YES**

Toward Science-Practice Integration in Brief Counseling and Therapy

The past decade has witnessed an explosion of interest in short-term approaches to counseling and psychotherapy (Budman & Gurman, 1988; Garfield, 1989; Peake, Borduin, & Archer, 1988; Wells & Giannetti, 1990; Zeig & Gilligan, 1990). Surveys suggest that a substantial portion of mental health practice is brief in nature (Koss, 1979; Langsley, 1978), with the average client being seen for under 10 sessions (Garfield, 1989). Moreover, restrictions in third-party reimbursements (Kovacs, 1982), budget constraints affecting staffing patterns in college counseling centers (Stone & Archer, 1990) and community clinics (Kovacs, 1982), and trends in managed health care (Cummings, 1987) suggest that brevity in intervention will continue to affect psychologists in the years ahead.

Accompanying this practice trend has been a significant expansion of research into brief therapy. Counseling psychologists have contributed meaningfully to this effort, offering studies of outcome (Gelso & Johnson, 1983; Johnson & Gelso, 1980) and process (Hill, 1989; Tracey & Ray, 1984), as well as integrative syntheses of the practice literature (Burlingame & Fuhriman, 1987; Fuhriman, Paul, & Burlingame, 1986). The conclusions of the research literature, documenting the effectiveness of brief counseling (Butcher & Koss, 1978; Koss & Butcher, 1986), have no doubt helped to fuel the upsurge in practitioner interest.

Nevertheless, there are numerous signs of a science-practice schism in brief therapy. Equating longer therapy with deeper and more substantive change, therapists frequently resist the use of brief treatments, even when these have been demonstrated to be effective (Gelso & Johnson, 1983), and underestimate the effects of those brief interventions they do undertake (Gelso & Johnson, 1983; Johnson & Gelso, 1980). Among the practice approaches, there is a surprising lack of consensus on basic issues (Burlingame & Fuhriman, 1987), many of which (effective therapeutic elements, criteria for client inclusion and exclusion) have been meaningfully addressed in research studies....

Part 1: The Practice of Brief Counseling

As Wells (1982) notes, the concept of brief therapy is familiar to most practitioners, yet there is little consensus as to its defining features. Clearly, not all therapy of limited duration is "brief therapy." Burlingame and Fuhriman (1987), for example, distinguish between "conceptually planned" brevity and those limits on duration resulting from early client termination or administrative imposition. Conceptually planned brief counseling is typified by the intentional consideration of time limits throughout the change process, from treatment planning to management of the relationship and selection of interventions. Such use of time as a counseling variable may take the form of explicit limits on the number of sessions (time-limited therapy) or may remain open-ended within flexible, although still brief, parameters (short-term therapy). In the literature, as well as in this [selection], the terms *brief therapy* and *brief counseling* are used interchangeably to refer to both time-limited and short-term interventions....

Part 2: Integrative Themes in Brief Counseling Research

Accompanying the explosion of practitioner interest in brief counseling is an expanding research agenda, investigating both outcome and process. Indeed, an interesting problem facing a reviewer of the literature is determining which investigations do *not* pertain to brief work. Budman and Gurman (1988), noting that meta-analytic reviews of the effectiveness of therapy have studied treatments of 7 to 17 sessions in duration, wryly conclude that "virtually every major review of the efficacy of various individual therapies . . . has been an unacknowledged review of time-unlimited brief therapy" (p. 7). From this perspective, we probably know far more about the outcome, structure, and process of brief interventions than we know about long-term work. Unfortunately, much of this literature has been fragmented, with little integration of findings reported by dynamic, behavioral, cognitive, and strategic investigators. The sections that follow attempt to identify unifying themes in this sprawling literature, beginning with studies of outcomes and concluding with explorations of the client, therapist, and process factors that mediate outcome....

Outcome in Brief Counseling and Therapy

In their extensive reviews of the brief therapy literature, Butcher and Koss (1978; Koss & Butcher, 1986) conclude that the majority of studies show little difference between the outcomes of brief treatments and those of time-unlimited therapies. Clients in brief counseling routinely evidence change beyond that observed in no-treatment conditions, although there are few indications that any single approach consistently outperforms the other (Koss & Butcher, 1986). Those studies incorporating follow-up periods to determine whether change persists over time find that brief therapies are comparable to their longer-term counterparts (Johnson & Gelso, 1980; Koss & Butcher, 1986).

Interestingly, measures of the effectiveness of brief therapy are greatly influenced by who is doing the rating. Johnson and Gelso (1980), reviewing the outcome literature, report an impressive array of evidence that counselor ratings, unlike those of clients, tend to be biased toward longer-term therapies. Subsequent research (Gelso & Johnson, 1983) found that clients, observers, and standardized measures rate time-limited therapy as being as effective as time-unlimited treatment, whereas therapists tend to rate the unlimited modes more highly. Clients, unlike counselors, are likely to assume that change can occur over brief time frames (Garfield, 1989).

Studies that have looked at the relationship between time and counseling change identify a distinctive trajectory. Change occurs as a linear function of the logarithm of the number of sessions, with the greatest gains produced early in treatment and diminishing returns thereafter (Howard, Kopta, Krause, & Orlinsky, 1986). Indeed, most change appears to occur within the first eight sessions (Garfield, 1989). This may help to account for the failure of long-term therapies to produce more substantial gains than brief counseling when directly compared (Piper, Debbane, Bienvenu, & Garant, 1984).

Many provocative findings regarding brief outcomes are embedded in the literatures specific to the professions (social work, psychology, psychiatry) and schools (cognitive, dynamic, behavioral) from which the therapies emerged. Below appear several conclusions drawn from these studies.

Enduring change can occur through brief therapy. Studies and literature reviews evaluating the outcomes of individual approaches to brief therapy, including cognitive (Dobson, 1989; Miller & Berman, 1983), behavioral (Emmelkamp, 1986), dynamic (Barth et al., 1988; Husby et al., 1985), task-centered (Reid, 1978), interpersonal (Klerman et al., 1984), and paradoxical/strategic (DeBord, 1989; Dowd & Milne, 1986), find these to be effective change modalities. Moreover, the effectiveness of brief therapy has been demonstrated in a variety of practice settings, including college counseling centers (Gelso & Johnson, 1983; Muench, 1965), community clinics (Parad & Parad, 1968; Sledge, Moras, Hartly, & Levine, 1990), and private practice (Avnet, 1965).

Studies incorporating long-term follow-up periods in their design report that the changes produced in brief counseling hold up remarkably well over time. Investigations of the behavioral treatment of phobias (Burns, Thorpe, & Cavallaro, 1986; Emmelkamp & Kuipers, 1979; Lelliott, Marks, Monteiro, Tsakiris, & Noshirvani, 1987), cognitive counseling for depression (Kovacs, Rush, Beck, & Hollon, 1981; Simons, Murphy, Levine, & Wetzel, 1986), and brief psychodynamic treatment of neurosis (Barth et al., 1988; Husby, 1985) show changes maintained for periods of 1 year or longer. The long-term gains were observed across a variety of ratings systems, including structured interviews, standardized tests, behavioral measures, and the ratings of clients, counselors, and observers. Echoing Johnson and Gelso (1980), studies have found outcome differences based on the types of change being assessed. Barth et al. (1988), for example, note that brief counseling is most effective in producing and maintaining symptom relief and least effective in generating lasting changes in "specific internal predispositions." Indeed, there appear to be differential rates of change for the various outcome measures, with symptom relief occurring within relatively few sessions and changes in personality dimensions not becoming fully evident until well after the close of counseling (Barth et al., 1988; Husby, 1985). Evidence concerning relapse during the follow-up periods is mixed. Studies comparing brief behavioral and insight therapies (Cross, Shehan, & Khan, 1982; Sloane, Staples, Cristol, Yorkston, & Whipple, 1975) have found gains maintained at long-term follow-up with minimal relapse. Studies of cognitive therapy with depressed clients find a relapse rate in excess of 20% (Hollon, Shelton, & Loosen, 1991). Reports of outcome in the brief treatment of agoraphobia note that most clients experience improvement but that most also experience a continued degree of symptomatology (Burns et al., 1986; Jacobson, Wilson, & Tupper, 1988; Lelliott, Marks, Monteiro, Tsakiris, & Noshirvani, 1987). Indeed, a common observation in this literature is that a sizable proportion of clients followed up over periods of 1 year or more have sought therapy after their period of brief counseling. McLean and Hakstian (1990) found that behavior therapy clients maintained their gains over a 2.25-year period significantly better than those receiving nondirective treatment, suggesting that therapies preparing clients for relapse may be especially effective in sustaining change.

An expanding literature documents the efficacy of brief therapy relative to pharmacotherapies, especially among depressed adults. Although some studies report that drug therapies and brief therapies do not differ in their ability to yield overall symptom relief (Elkin et al., 1989), reviews find that effect sizes for behavioral, social learning/interpersonal, and cognitive therapies significantly exceed those for drug therapies (Fisher & Greenberg, 1989; Steinbrueck, Maxwell, & Howard, 1983). Moreover, there is growing evidence that cognitive therapy clients are more likely to maintain their gains over follow-up periods than are pharmacotherapy clients (Simons, Murphy, Levine, & Wetzel, 1986). Hollen et al. (1991), in their review, indicate that relapse rates among clients treated with tricyclic antidepressants are more than twice as high as those among cognitive therapy clients. Similarly, behavioral and cognitive therapies are more effective in generating and sustaining change among clients with panic disorder than drug therapies (Clum, 1989; Michelson & Marchione, 1991), with higher rates of attrition (due to side effects) plaguing the pharmacological treatments.

Brief counseling outcomes are demonstrated across a wide range of client types and are not linked to high-functioning clients alone. Traditionally, brief therapy has been seen as the intervention of choice for high-functioning clients only, with the presumption that "deeper" or more extensive problems could not change over a brief span. This assumption, however, finds almost no support in the literature. As noted earlier, brief counseling has been documented to produce lasting change among clients with depression (Dobson, 1989), phobias (Emmelkamp, 1986), compulsions (Foa, Steketee, & Milby, 1980), and panic disorder (Clum, 1989; Michelson & Marchione, 1991). Furthermore, brief therapies have been shown to facilitate change at a variety of levels, from targeted symptoms such as test anxiety (Goldfried, Linehan, & Smith, 1978; Wise & Haynes,

1983) and social skills deficits (Kazdin & Mascitelli, 1982; Linehan, Goldfried, & Goldfried, 1979) to global constructs of self-esteem and life satisfaction (Piper, Azim, McCallum, & Joyce, 1990). These findings suggest an applicability of brief counseling that exceeds traditional expectations.

A growing set of findings additionally suggests that brief approaches may even be effective with populations deemed highly disturbed. In a provocative study, a group of 300 clients appropriate for psychiatric hospitalization was randomly assigned to inpatient treatment or outpatient crisis counseling (Langsley, Machotka, & Flomenhaft, 1971). The outpatient group, followed up over an 18-month period, evidenced higher levels of adjustment and less frequent subsequent hospitalization than did the inpatient group. Similarly impressive brief treatment results have been reported among client groups suffering from posttraumatic stress (Brom, Kleber, & Defares, 1989), personality disorders (Pollack, Winston, McCullough, & Flegenheimer, 1990), bulimia (Agras, Schneider, Arnow, Raeburn, & Telch, 1989), and major depression (Gallagher-Thompson, Hanley-Peterson, & Thompson, 1990; Thompson, Gallagher, & Breckenridge, 1987). Within these groups, gains were achieved not only in symptom reduction but on personality dimensions such as self-esteem (Brom et al., 1989) and social maturity (Agras et al., 1989)....

Brief counseling is efficient as well as effective. Service providers are drawn to brief interventions in part because they promise a more efficient use of clinic and counseling center resources. A growing body of literature supports these expectations. Studies performed in a variety of practice settings find that the use of a brief intervention model yields favorable outcomes, even as it results in a savings in agency time (Avnet, 1965; Chubb & Evans, 1990; Gelso & Johnson, 1983; Langley et al., 1971; Muench, 1965; Parad & Parad, 1968). The adoption of a brief model reduces waiting lists at mental health sites (Muench, 1965; Parad & Parad, 1968), decreases levels of client dropout (Sledge et al., 1990), and results in lower levels of psychiatric hospitalization (Chubb & Evans, 1990; Langsley et al., 1971).

There are further indications that participation in brief therapy by medical patients decreases future medical expenditures (VandenBos & DeLeon, 1988). The amount of savings appears to be directly proportional to the number of therapy sessions undertaken, with diminishing rates of savings beyond 21 sessions (Schlesinger, Mumford, Glass, Patrick, & Sharfstein, 1983). Such savings are also manifested elsewhere, including vocational and social service systems (VandenBos & DeLeon, 1988)....

Summary

The present account finds that brief counseling is a promising family of applications, capable of producing sustained change among a variety of clients. Moreover, specific factors are identifiable that may enhance future brief therapeutic efforts. Change, it has been emphasized, possesses an underlying structure that blends the formation of an alliance with the provision of new perspectives and experiences at strategic points of client readiness. The role of brief counseling is to accelerate this process through the creation of time limits and favorable therapeutic contexts. Once initiated, this process can be consolidated and sustained, continuing well beyond the close of weekly meetings. As science and practice continue their reciprocal influence, sophisticated blendings of client, counselor, and intervention characteristics will become commonplace, extending the prescriptive dimensions of the present model.

Charles J. Gelso

 **NO**

Realities and Emerging Myths About Brief Therapy

I t has been a pleasure to read and reflect on [Brett N.] Steenbarger's (1992) treatise on brief therapy (BT). The goal of his article is to integrate the research and practice literatures on BT, and to develop a model of BT based on that integration. I believe that he has succeeded to a high degree. Steenbarger's integration of the practice and research literatures is a masterful piece of work; and, although the critical reader will naturally find one or another of the elements of his model insufficient or off the mark, the model is an eminently sensible one, infused with both clinical wisdom and scientific care.....

Needed Refinements and Elaborations

The concerns I do have with Steenbarger's otherwise enlightening treatise revolve around some apparent contradictions and points calling for elaboration....

Regarding the high-risk group, Steenbarger wisely addresses the issue of preventing relapse and maintaining gains. This is a hard group to work with, however, from the outset of therapy. We need considerably more research and theory on treatment methods with this group to enhance the likelihood that change occurs in the first place. It is fine and appropriate to worry about relapse, but as a therapist working with the kinds of clients included in Steenbarger's high-risk group, I would like more help on therapeutic procedures, that facilitate effective therapy from the beginning....

Some apparent contradictions are also in evidence. At one point, we hear that the "changes produced in brief counseling hold up remarkably well over time," whereas a short time later Steenbarger tells us that "a sizable proportion of clients followed up over periods of 1 year or more have sought therapy after their period of brief counseling" (p. 415). This seeming contradiction is badly in need of clarification. As I will amplify later, the data, including data gathered in the University of Maryland time-limited therapy (TLT) research program (Adelstein, Gelso, Haws, Reed, & Spiegel, 1983; Gelso, Speigel, & Mills, 1983), suggest that changes effected during BT hold up well because clients who do not get what they need seek additional help (at the same agency or elsewhere) after BT is terminated. . . .

Some Myths that the Brief Therapy Movement Has Lived By

I believe it is safe to say that interest in and advocacy of brief and time-limited therapies have coalesced into a movement, with all of the force and pitfalls of movements. One characteristic of movements is that they become enmeshed in their own versions of truth and reality, and in promoting those versions. Connected to this enmeshment, all movements, especially in their early stages, distort truth and reality to advance their aims. In this sense, movements carry and promote myths, that is, distortions of reality that fit the aims of the movement. In my view, the BT movement has carried and promoted several such myths. Below I note some of the major myths in BT and provide alternative views that better fit the empirical and clinical data. . . .

Myth 1: BT is as effective as, or more effective than, long-term therapy.   We simply do not have a sufficient number of well-controlled comparisons between brief and long-term therapy to justify any empirically based conclusions. The comparisons that do exist in the literature are often between brief time-limited therapy and longer, but still relatively brief, time-unlimited therapy. For example, the major outcome study of our TLT research program at the University of Maryland (Gelso et al., 1983) compared the outcomes of clients who participated in an average of 6 sessions (where there was an 8-session limit) with those who participated in approximately 20 sessions (where there was no time limit).

As part of the myth building of the BT movement, results that do not put BT in a favorable light are at times neglected. For example, whereas positive findings about TLT deriving from the Maryland research program are often cited in the BT literature, I have never seen mention of the fact that in our major outcome study, clients' and therapists' evaluations tended to favor the time-unlimited over time-limited treatments with 16 session and (especially) 8-session limits, particularly when clients and therapists were queried 18 months after termination. Also, for each of these groups separately, and for all combined, duration of counseling was positively related to outcome.

My reading of the empirical data, as well as my experience in the practice of BT and long-term therapy, leads me to believe that generally the impact of longer-term work is more pervasive and profound than that of BT. And I suspect that this will be ultimately documented empirically. At the same time, there is a large body of evidence documenting that BT does indeed have positive effects for a range of problems. Clients, therapists, and agencies need to be about the business of deciding how much of an effect is sufficient, given the resources of all involved.

Myth 2: Changes in BT are highly durable, as durable as those in long-term therapy. Although the data are also insufficient on the question of relapse, it appears that a substantially greater percentage of clients treated by BT return for more therapy than those receiving longer-term interventions. For example, when we combine two different studies of the TLT research program at Maryland (see Gelso & Johnson, 1983, chaps. 2,3), we find these return or "relapse" rates after 1 year to 18 months following termination: For clients in treatment with an 8-session time limit, return rate = 48%; 12-session TLT, return rate = 33%; 16-session TLT, return rate = 25%; and time-unlimited therapy, return rate = 23%. Thus it appears that the return rate following TLT may be inversely proportional to the duration limit. However, as the duration limit approaches the mean number of sessions for time-unlimited treatment in an agency, this inverse relationship will disappear.

What appears to happen is that if clients who end their BT feel they need more counseling, they seek it, either at the agency at which the initial therapy was received or elsewhere. This continued therapy may well at least partially account for the continued growth of clients who initially receive BT. Thus attributing the durable change to BT is not very compelling. At the same time, some preliminary data suggest that, even when considering return rate (to the same agency and somewhere else), brief time-limited counseling results in fewer total sessions (the brief intervention plus later ones) than the number of sessions for clients receiving time-unlimited counseling. This is so because when clients seek continued therapy following BT, that further help is also likely to be brief. It is as if, for better or worse, clients in BT come to think of problem solution in brief terms. The consequence of this from a service delivery standpoint is that brief TLT results in saving service delivery time, despite the greater return rate.

Myth 3: Because most measurable change occurs during the first few sessions, a few sessions of therapy are all that is needed. As Steenbarger notes, it does appear that the bulk of measured change occurs very early in counseling, for example, the first eight sessions. The key word here is *measured.* Any therapist worth his or her salt cannot help but notice this early "growth spurt" in counseling. In fact, it is so observable that it may be detected even with the crude measurement devices available to us currently. It is inappropriate and ultimately damaging to some clients, however, to conclude from this that only a few sessions are what is needed. To begin with, everything I have experienced and observed (in myself and other therapists) suggests to me that very profound and far-reaching changes may occur beyond the early sessions, but such changes unfold in a much more gradual fashion and are elusive from a measurement standpoint. Changes beyond early sessions are also a highly individualized matter, which makes it difficult to detect using the same measures for all clients. Yet especially for clients with chronic and more severe problems, these gradual changes may be tremendously important.

We do not need to minimize the value of long-term therapy and the gradual, elusive-to-measure changes that unfold after the initial stages, in order to "sell" BT. We simply need to demonstrate that BT possesses "sufficient" effectiveness for a range of clients and client problems.

Myth 4: Therapists-perceived lack of efficacy of BT is a perceptual error, whereas other rating sources (e.g., clients, outside observers) accurately see the true value of BT. This is part myth and part really. Regarding the reality, my research and observation have led me to believe that therapists who enjoy and are good at long-term therapy do tend to underestimate the positive effects of BT for three interrelated reasons: (a) they accurately see how slow certain changes are with their long-term clients; (b) they are geared toward deeper personality changes and have a hard time being satisfied with less pervasive changes; and (c) in long-term therapy a therapist gets to directly observe many of the client's changes, whereas in BT the changes are only beginning when therapy is terminated. (Because of the last reason, long-term follow-ups help the therapist as well as the client—that is, to see the change that has continued [see Gelso & Johnson, 1983, pp. 205–206].)

Although therapists who conduct long-term therapy appear to somewhat underemphasize the effects of BT, the myth I am referring to involves essentially dismissing therapists' reservations about BT—for example, as stemming from their own intrapsychic, interpersonal, and/or economic needs. It has become fashionable among researchers and participants in the BT movement to be dismissive of therapists' perceptions and to place much greater credence in both clients' and outside observers' reports. It is as if, because proponents of BT must advance this form of treatment and because therapists' ratings of BT are lower than those of their clients and outside judges, the therapists must be wrong. There is little recognition of the expertise of the therapist in making judgments about his or her client's progress and about the many subtle forces within the client that play into the extent to which progress is being made. This tendency to minimize the therapist's perceptions of BT has always struck me as a big mistake. Researchers and participants in the BT movement need to listen to therapists' reservations about BT, take them seriously, and incorporate them into their formulations about this form of treatment.

Myth 5: Abbreviating interventions through, for example, the establishment of duration limits inevitably saves agency time. There seems to be an assumption among BT aficionados that the establishment of a duration limit automatically saves agency time and thus reduces waiting lists. In fact, whether or not a limit saves time depends on precisely what that limit is in relation to the typical number of sessions (without a limit) at a given agency. For example, if the mean number of sessions at a counseling center is 6.5, setting a limit of 12 will save little if any time. Of course, the limit that is established ought to be based on more than saving agency time to shorten the waiting list. We need to be striving for an optimum blend of efficiency (with an eye toward saving time) and efficacy (with an eye toward attaining the level of outcome deemed satisfactory at a given agency). The limit can be too high to save time, but it also can be so low that efficacy is impeded. For example, in our early work at Maryland we found that 8 sessions TLT saved time but seemed too brief to attain outcomes that we viewed as satisfactory (Gelso & Johnson, 1983, pp. 58–60). . . .

Conclusions

. . . When considering any position paper such as this on BT, a treatment that has become part of a movement, I believe the scientist-practitioner needs to be mindful of certain myths that are part of that movement. Except for the early part of a movement (when movement-enhancing myths may be needed to marshal support), these myths tend to impede scientific and clinical progress. Thus such myths must be scrutinized, with an eye toward separating fact from movement-inspired fancy. Toward that end, I have delineated what I have come to believe are some of the major myths in the BT movement and have offered formulations that better fit the scientific and clinical data. The field of brief therapy will maintain, in fact ultimately increase, its strength and appeal without these myths, because sound clinical and empirical data do exist to support the efficacy of abbreviated interventions, although not for all clients and problems, not for all types of change, and not to a degree that is superior to that of longer-term interventions.

CHALLENGE QUESTIONS

Is Brief Therapy as Effective as Long-Term Therapy?

1. Would you feel comfortable going to a therapist who is required to practice brief therapy? Why, or why not?
2. Would you feel comfortable going to a therapist who practices only brief therapy because he or she believes it is in a client's best interests? Do you think this situation is different from that of therapists who are required by an HMO to practice brief therapy? Explain.
3. How might therapists cut costs and also be open to the needs of their clients? How might you balance the needs of insurance companies and the needs of clients if you were a therapist?
4. Steenbarger and Gelso seem to disagree on the type of change that is important to therapy. What should be the goal of therapy—behavior change or personality change? Why?

ISSUE 14

Should Psychologists Be Allowed to Prescribe Drugs?

YES: Patrick H. DeLeon and Jack G. Wiggins, Jr., from "Prescription Privileges for Psychologists," *American Psychologist* (March 1996)

NO: Steven C. Hayes and Elaine Heiby, from "Psychology's Drug Problem: Do We Need a Fix or Should We Just Say No?" *American Psychologist* (March 1996)

ISSUE SUMMARY

YES: Psychologist and lawyer Patrick H. DeLeon and Jack G. Wiggins, Jr., former president of the American Psychological Association, argue that giving prescription privileges to psychologists will allow them to address society's pressing needs.

NO: Psychologists Steven C. Hayes and Elaine Heiby maintain that prescription privileges will cost the discipline of psychology its unique professional identity and compromise public safety.

P sychology, like most disciplines, is continually modifying and expanding its caregiving role. A recent and highly controversial expansion of this role entails prescription privileges. That is, many psychologists are now seeking the legal privilege to prescribe drugs. Drugs have been increasingly recognized as contributing to the effective treatment of mental disorders. Because such treatment has traditionally been the province of psychology, many psychologists have advocated that they should be allowed to use all the effective treatments available, including prescription medications.

The most controversial aspect of this proposal, however, is that only psychiatrists (and a few other allied professionals) are currently permitted to prescribe drugs in the mental health field. Thus, if given prescription privileges, the psychologist would be moving into the professional and economic territory of the psychiatrist. Psychiatrists are medical doctors whose primary training is in the anatomy and physiology of the human body. Psychologists, on the other hand, are experts in human relations. Although some psychologists receive considerable education in pharmacology (the study of medications), few currently have the training necessary to competently prescribe drugs. The question then arises, What if an appropriate level of training were obtained? Couldn't psychologists then prescribe drugs to their patients?

Patrick H. DeLeon and Jack G. Wiggins, Jr., in the first selection, answer this question affirmatively. They assert that current technology would allow psychologists to safely prescribe psychoactive drugs without the medical knowledge required of a physician. The authors also describe several psychologists who have been functionally prescribing drugs with little or no training and who have experienced no problems. DeLeon and Wiggins see prescription privileges as a natural outgrowth of psychology's development as a discipline.

By contrast, in the second selection, Steven C. Hayes and Elaine Heiby see prescription privileges as radically changing psychology—ultimately into a field of medicine. This change would undermine the mental health professional's appreciation for psychology as a unique science. The granting of prescription privileges, Hayes and Heiby argue, undervalues the psychological side of people in favor of an exclusively biological emphasis. Rather than a fulfillment of psychology's disciplinary development, Hayes and Heiby see prescription privileges as a compromise of psychology's main objective—to better understand the nature of psychological phenomena.

POINT

- Current technology would allow psychologists to prescribe drugs with little medical training.

- Psychologists with prescription privileges could help prevent abuse of psychoactive drugs because they would have a fuller understanding of patients' psychological needs.

- The desire to treat patients more effectively with medications is widespread throughout the field.

- Obtaining access to a particular type of treatment will not cause psychology to forget its roots.

COUNTERPOINT

- To prescribe any drug, it is essential to have medical training to understand how the drug affects all of the body's systems.

- Psychologists would not understand patients' biological changes enough to ensure responsible use of medication.

- Most psychologists believe that the more important treatment is helping patients to understand the psychological aspects of their problems.

- Prescription privileges will change psychology into a medical field and cause psychological assessment to become undervalued.

Patrick H. DeLeon and
Jack G. Wiggins, Jr.

 **YES**

Prescription Privileges for Psychologists

From our vantage point, the issue of psychologists obtaining prescription privileges is a rather straight-forward one and one that is an outgrowth of the gradual maturation of the profession. In 1950, there were only 7,273 members of the American Psychological Association (APA); today, there are in excess of 110,000. In 1945, the Connecticut legislature provided psychology with its first state "scope of practice" (licensing–certification) act; by the year 1977, psychology had obtained statutory recognition in all 50 states as a fully autonomous profession (i.e., licensed–certified to independently "diagnose and treat"). Furthermore, we have no doubt that, for psychologists, obtaining the particular clinical responsibility of prescription authority ultimately represents both good public policy and good clinical policy....

Training Modules

In many ways, one can readily conceptualize the prescription privilege agenda as being primarily an educational one; that is, to what extent have our nation's health-professional training programs developed credible (and objectively measurable) training modules that ensure that their practitioners possess both a conceptual basis for making medication decisions (i.e., didactic training) and sufficient clinical experience to evaluate the consequences of those decisions (i.e., "hands-on" supervision)?...

In our judgment, the decision of whether or not to use specific psychotropic medications and at what dosage—once the correct diagnosis has been made by a licensed–certified mental health professional—represents little more than a probability algorithm, where various observable behavioral factors are computed such as symptomatology, patient age and body size, and drug-dosage response. These relatively few algorithms could easily be learned by psychologists. Furthermore, in today's practices, one should expect to use up-to-date desktop computer technology in making this determination. An analogy would be that one only needs to know how to use the most up-to-date computer software, not how to design one's own software or computer. This latter skill should be learned perhaps by true psychopharmacological specialists, but it absolutely should not be viewed as a requirement for doctoral-level psychologists to competently and safely serve their clients, notwithstanding organized psychiatry's alleged concerns.

Demonstration Projects

Historically, state governments have a long and impressive track record of exploring alternative health care delivery systems, including the development of innovative health professional training programs. For example, in 1965 the state of Colorado pioneered the establishment of pediatric nurse practitioners—a specialty that today, by federal mandate, must be reimbursed under every state's Medicaid plan, "whether or not (the practitioner) is under the supervision of, or associated with, a physician or other health care provider."

In 1982, the state of California released its landmark prescription report titled "Prescribing and Dispensing Pilot Projects." ... Under the California program, over one million patients were seen by nonphysician prescribing and dispensing trainees during a three-year period. The results clearly indicated that both the patients and supervising physicians were comfortable with the clinical performance of the trainees. Most important, there were no reported "quality of care" problems. Given the substantial potential cost savings involved, the state authorities ultimately recommended that clear statutory authority be enacted so that these nonphysicians would be able to prescribe and dispense drugs. Of particular interest to psychologists should be that 56% of these graduates possessed a bachelors degree or higher; that is, 44% did not! Furthermore, the principal teaching methods used were lectures and seminars, which varied from 16 hours to 95 hours in length—hardly comparable to a medical school curriculum.

The authors have admittedly become the focal point of much of the prescription debate in psychology, and, as a direct consequence, we have learned (among other things) that a very significant number of our professional colleagues have been "functionally prescribing" for years, often without any documented training, having learned, for example, of the psychoactive effects of medications their patients have received for cardiac, diabetic, thyroid, or other health conditions. And we have come to appreciate that, not surprisingly, they have not had any "quality of care" problems. This is particularly true in rural America and in the federal system (e.g., in the Veterans Administration and the military [Barclay, 1989]). There are many forms that this functional prescriptive practice takes, ranging from possessing pre-signed scrips (which would be legal in state and federal systems), to having developed close and long-standing relationships with physician colleagues where medication consultations are readily available. We have learned that a number of our colleagues are on the faculty of nursing, dental, and medical schools where they train the students in these professions to prescribe, particularly in narrowly defined specialties such as pediatrics....

Although some have suggested that only a vocal minority of psychologists are seriously interested in the prescription agenda, it has been our experience that the interest in obtaining relevant and targeted psychopharmacological training expressed by our child-oriented colleagues is becoming increasingly widespread throughout the field, thus enhancing the probability that in the foreseeable future, our (or perhaps nursing's) professional schools will make this experience readily available. Questions on prescription authority are becoming increasingly common in university doctoral comprehensive examinations and dissertation committees. At least two doctoral research projects (Evans, 1995; Smith, 1992) recently explored either attitudes of graduate students toward prescribing or the interest of directors of clinical programs in offering training in psychopharmacology. A survey of 40 APA-approved graduate schools across the nation found that second- and third-year students responded with strong support for these privileges, with 61% endorsing privileges for the field and 47% reporting they desired privileges for themselves (Smith, 1992). There were no significant differences in responses on the basis of program type, theoretical orientation, gender, age, undergraduate major, or the student's choice of future client population. It was felt that the two strongest supportive arguments for obtaining this privilege were (a) the ability to provide services to underserved groups and (b) the collection of third party reimbursement. The two strongest arguments opposing obtaining this authority were (a) damage to credibility and distinctiveness of psychology and (b) the possible impediment of collaboration with psychiatrists (Smith, 1992).

Another 1990 survey of the general APA membership similarly reported that, "There is very strong support for prescription privileges for psychologists (and that) the proposition that psychologists could do a better job of prescribing than the general practitioners who now prescribe most psychoactive drugs in the most effective argument in support of prescription privileges... There is overwhelming support for a demonstration project on prescription privileges (Frederick/Schneiders, 1990). Even among opponents of the general proposal, a majority support the demonstration project" (pp. 3-4).

Currently, we are aware of at least 25 state or country psychological associations that have formally established task forces on the issue and a number of educational institutions that are exploring how to best provide the type of didactic and hands-on training experiences that the field desires. Interestingly, within the educational leadership of professional nursing, a concerted effort is currently underway to identify commonalities and differences in their prescription training programs, not to mention developing appropriate programs targeted toward addressing the needs of their experienced clinicians (e.g., the establishment of special executive tracks or intensive summer workshops). With these developments in mind, the ongoing Department of Defense two- to three-year full-time training program clearly seems excessive.

Quality of Care Issues

It is of considerable interest to us that the prime argument those who are external to psychology consistently use to oppose our profession's obtaining prescription authority is the public health hazard allegation. Yet, none of the available objective evidence supports their emotional rhetoric. The nursing literature, for example, demonstrates that the medication decisions of nurse practitioners are very similar to those of their medical colleagues, and some researchers have found that they actually use medication less frequently than their physician counterparts. At the public policy level, we find it simply fascinating, to put it mildly, that no one seems to find it objectionable that in the mental health arena, of the 135.8 million psychotherapeutic scripts written in 1991, only 17.3% were by psychiatrists per se. That year, both internists and family practitioners prescribed more mental health medications than their mental health specialist colleagues. Stated slightly differently, of the psychotherapeutic medications prescribed that year by physicians, more than 82% were by practitioners who simply did not possess significant training in the mental health field. Given these data, for psychiatry to proclaim that doctoral-trained licensed psychologists cannot learn to safely use this particular clinical modality seems an incredible, if not downright arrogant, indictment of our educational system.

If one looks closely at the manner in which psychotropic medications are currently used, there are a number of troubling statistics. Study after study used indicated that even today certain populations are dramatically over medicated or inappropriately medicated—this is particularly true with minority, aging, and female clients—and there is even growing evidence that psychotherapy per se (and not medication) is crucial to resolving depression. More than 40% of nursing home patients receive psychotropic medications, despite the fact that most of them do not have mental health diagnoses. Why, we would rhetorically ask, did the Health Care Financing Administration (HCFA) recently feel it was necessary to promulgate federal regulations addressing the conditions under which certain medications could be used in nursing homes? Were not all issued medications being ordered by licensed physicians? Of course they were. In our judgment, one of the major clinical advances that will come with psychology obtaining prescription privileges will be the authority of behavioral scientists to determine with proper legal standing when and whether certain medications are necessary and appropriate; that is, the essence of the power to prescribe is the power not to prescribe. And this, we suggest, will ultimately revolutionize the delivery of mental health care in our nation.

Conclusion

In our judgment, there is no question that doctoral-trained psychologists can readily be trained to use psychotropic medications in a safe, cost-effective, and competent manner. This is psychology's next frontier, and we are confident that society will be well served by this evolution. We are not at all concerned that, by obtaining this particular clinical modality, psychology will lose its therapeutic expertise or forget its roots—our becoming intimately involved in the judicial system increased society's access to psychological care and did not negatively harm the field. In all candor, we have very little respect for the validity of the public health hazard allegations that have been made by those external to psychology and would merely suggest that those opposed should carefully review the available literature.

Psychology's Drug Problem

Prescription privileges for psychologists have only been considered seriously by most psychologists for the past few years. Just eight years have passed since American Psychological Association (APA) governance recommended "moving to the highest APA priority" the creation of "psychologically managed psychopharmacological intervention" (DeLeon et al., 1991, p. 391). Much has happened in those eight years. Slowly at first, but then with increased speed, continuing education curricula have been written, pilot projects have been launched, and legislatures have been lobbied. The prescription train gives many indications it is about to leave the station, whether or not all—or even most—of psychology is on board. . . .

Prescription Privilege Alternative

Driven by . . . professional pressures, intellectual changes, and market forces, the leadership of the practice community has for several years been working systematically to prepare the way for psychologists' use of chemical interventions. Prescription privileges, they purport, solve many of the problems facing the professional practice of psychology today. It solves the over-reliance on psychotherapy. Practitioners will be paid as much or more for medication visits, and only psychiatrists, other physicians, and psychologists will be eligible. It solves the problem of oversupply. For a time, master's-level providers will be held at bay. It solves the problem of managed care, or at least gives psychologists some way of differentiating their services from other mental health professionals in such a way that managed care organizations might be more interested in hiring doctoral-level psychologists. . . .

What This Issue Is Not About

It is sometimes difficult to remain focused on the real issues in this debate. Like combatants in a political campaign, both sides speak around each other

Excerpted from Steven C. Hayes and Elaine Heiby, "Psychology's Drug Problem: Do We Need a Fix or Should We Just Say No?" *American Psychologist,* vol. 51, no. 3 (1996), pp. 198, 201–203, 205. Copyright © 1996 by The American Psychological Association. Reprinted by permission. Notes and references omitted. This article has been reduced from its original appearance in *American Psychologist.*

for tactical reasons. We want to put aside two issues so as to avoid fruitless interactions.

False Issue 1: Psychologists Cannot Be Trained to Prescribe

Psychologists are generally quite bright people. With the right kind of curriculum they can surely be trained to prescribe. It also seems unlikely that it would take seven or eight years to do so, which is the time it takes to complete medical school and a psychiatric residency.

This does not mean that training psychologists to prescribe psychotropic medication will be easy. Many psychologists do not have the right kind of science background to make physiologically-oriented training readily accessible....

False Issue 2: Medications Do Not Work and Biology Is Not Involved in Behavior

Pro-prescription psychologists often equate opposition to prescription authority for psychologists with opposition to psychoactive medication per se or a failure to acknowledge that clients are also biological organisms (Brentar & McNamara, 1991; Fox, 1988). Some proponents accuse those who resist prescription authority of ascribing to a discredited mind–body dualism (Brentar & McNamara, 1991; Fox, 1988).

When the debate consists of exchanges about false issues, little productive discussion is likely. Some psychologists are indeed opposed to psychoactive medication, but most are not. Despite the substantial methodological difficulties in the pharmacotherapy literature (e.g., Fisher & Greenberg, 1993) most scientifically-oriented psychologists agree that at least under some circumstances, pharmacotherapy is helpful in the treatment of traditional psychological disorders. Thus, when the utility of medication is cast as a simple or absolute issue, pro-prescription advocates are on fairly firm ground. For example, Patrick DeLeon, a leading advocate of prescription authority for psychologists, recently responded to our own opposition against prescription authority as follows: "Dr. Hayes is talking about something he really does not understand... The data is clear that some individuals will benefit from appropriate medications" (Saeman, 1995, p. 10). Although DeLeon apparently meant it as a point of departure, we actually agree with the second sentence. But this issue is not about whether medications ever work. It is about whether psychologists should be the ones prescribing them....

Negative Impact of Drug Prescription Authority: Do We Really Want to Redefine Psychology?

There are three dominant areas in which prescription authority seems likely to lead to major negative impacts for psychology. Although these arguments are rapidly becoming well-worn, they deserve repeating. First, this authority seems likely to undermine an appreciation for the psychological level of analysis. Second, it could have a negative impact on clients. Third, if this negative impact on clients is avoided, prescriptive authority seems likely to have a major and negative impact on psychological training.

Level of Analysis: Psychology Is a Science in Its Own Right

... Some advocates have argued that prescription privileges would render no change in the definition of the discipline [of psychology] and would simply add biological assessment and treatment devices [of] the profession (Burns, DeLeon, Chemtob, Welch, & Samuels, 1988). This *additive effect* is not the only possible outcome, however (e.g., Butz, 1994). It assumes that the effects of prescription authority on the behavior of psychologists are linear and that the training involved to prescribe would be supplemental. It seems equally if not more likely that the medication of psychology would have a nonlinear dynamical effect— an irreversible qualitative shift in the discipline (Butz, 1994).

Psychologists who have also trained as psychiatrists generally take the latter view. For example, Kingsbury's (1992) experiences as a psychologist and a psychiatrist have convinced him that "the definition of psychology would have to be transformed if prescription privileges were granted" (p. 5). The limited experience with supplemental training for psychologists... tends toward the same conclusion. Indeed, some advocates of prescription privileges seem to agree with the dynamic view that psychology would be redefined (DeLeon, Fox, & Graham, 1991; Lorion, 1996). To prescription opponents, this redefinition "represents the ultimate denial or betrayal of our own, scientifically grounded knowledge-base and professional competency in favor of an alien, biomedical model, for no logical or conceptually defensible purpose" (McColskey, 1993, p. 57)....

Implications of science-based practice for this issue   Most APA-approved applied training programs in psychology claim that their training is based on the scientific discipline of psychology. If that is a central value, the issue of prescription privileges can be recast as follows: If the knowledge needed to prescribe drugs safely is part of psychology's technical, scientific knowledge base—if it is indeed part of the discipline of psychology—then drug prescriptions should be part of the practice of psychology. In order to make this argument, pro-prescription advocates need to be clear about what their view is of psychology as a discipline.

Pro-prescription advocates have generally argued vaguely that because medications can influence behavior, prescribing medications should be part of the discipline of psychology (e.g., Burns et al., 1988). This view (behavior = psychology) fails to draw reasonable distinctions among different parts of the discipline. By the same logic, brain surgery and electroconvulsive therapy are also part of psychology. Similarly, nonpsychiatric medicine, sociology, biochemistry, anthropology, political science, economics, law, and many other disciplines are part of psychology. Psychology overlaps with all of these fields and more, and some psychologists will fruitfully conduct research within each area of overlap. But that does not mean that psychology is the same as these other fields. The establishment of professional "boundaries is in no way an endorsement of an artificial mind-body dualism. The time has long passed when there was only one variety of health care provider who did everything for everybody" (DeNelsky, 1991, p. 191).

Drug–behavior relations are not enough There are clear reasons to distinguish between the disciplines of medicine and psychology. Responsibly prescribing the consumption of powerful chemicals requires the study of organ systems and their mutual interdependence, not just the study of the behavioral impact of these chemicals. For example, prescribing psychologists should know such things as how drugs affect the kidneys, now aging alters the functioning of the digestive system so that drugs are absorbed differently over time, how a diseased liver can make a specific drug combination more risky, or how exercise changes the excretion of particular drugs compared to others. These are inherently biological/medical topics because they deal with the physical relationship among organ systems per se. This kind of knowledge has never been the focus of psychology as a discipline....

To fail to make meaningful distinctions between disciplines—even when they overlap and interact—runs the risk of treating psychology as a branch of medicine and not as a science in its own right. If the role of prescribing psychologists is indeed the same as psychiatrists ... it is not because psychiatry has become more like psychology....

Risks to patients and prescribers Older adults often face many chronic ailments—each of which may be treated by a different provider, often through the use of drugs. They may have decreased abilities to tolerate chemical interventions. They may be unable to report to each provider how many medications are being taken and of what kind. Psychoactive medications are among the most harmful to this population. Some geropsychologists have estimated that the majority of behavioral disorders in older people are due to medical overprescribing or to drug interactions (Hayden & Safford, 1992). The third largest category of drugs used by older persons are the psychopharmacological agents such as antidepressants and antipsychotics (Wolfe, Fugate, Hulstrand, & Kamimoto, 1988). Adverse effects being very common, one recent review concluded that the excessive use of psychoactive medication with older people amounts to "a major public health problem" (Hayden & Safford, 1992, p. 42). Pro-prescription advocates argue that these problems support prescription privileges for psychologists (DeLeon, 1993; DeLeon, Fox, & Graham, 1991) because they believe that somehow psychologists would do a better job. Psychologists may better understand some of the developmental psychological processes involved with older adults, but it seems incredible that they would better understand development physiology—and ignoring that very knowledge base is at the core of prescription problems for older persons....

The same thing occurs at the other end of the age spectrum. Despite the fact that "there is a relative lack of empirical support for pediatric psychotropic safety and efficacy" (Kubiszyn, 1994), psychoactive medications are very widely prescribed to children. Highly variable responses due to children's developing physiological system can occur (American Medical Association, 1991).

Those who prescribe psychoactive medication are responsible for the general health status of the individual, as well as for adverse organic and behavioral side effects. The toxic nature of commonly prescribed psychoactive medications has been well established (Bezchlibnyk-Butler, 1990).

Historically, psychologists have studied how individual organisms interact over time with their social and nonsocial world. The structure of the organism is part of that interaction; as is the structure of the environment; as is the history of previous psychological interactions. Psychologists study these things to help elucidate the nature of the psychological interaction between an organism and its world. Psychologists, for example, study how the brain is part of a psychological interaction or how culture alters such interactions. But psychologists are not thereby biologists nor physicians, and they are neither anthropologists nor sociologists....

Does the public need more prescribers?   Psychology is a science in its own right, with a science-based practice that has a unique identity and that serves legitimate societal needs. There is no convincing evidence that mental health consumers are clamoring for medications to solve life's problems or that said consumers are dissatisfied with psychological knowledge. A survey recently prepared for the American Psychological Association's Practice Directorate (American Psychological Association, 1992) reported that 63% of psychologists who responded indicated that "helping a person understand" was the most important treatment for alleviating a mental health problem, whereas 15% indicated medication was most important. Generally, consumer surveys have indicated that psychological services are preferred over psychiatric services (Sanua, 1993).

Why then do pro-prescription psychologists so often emphasize the need for medications? Could it be that the loss of a clear focus on the psychological level of analysis is already occurring....

Conclusion

If a psychologist wants to prescribe medications, there are means to do so now in the form of MD/PhD, or physician's assistant programs. If psychiatry or pharmacotherapy require new models (e.g., more limited or more focused forms of medical training), these could be pursued more generally rather than by linking such changes to any specific nonmedical field. Prescription authority may permit psychologists to compete financially, but only by grafting some other profession onto the discipline.

A better and more honorable alternative is to build on psychology's traditional core through scientifically based standards of care, program development, and treatment manualization linked to these standards, training, supervision, and program evaluation (Hayes, Follette, Dawes, & Grady, 1995). Managed care companies need these services, and psychological scientist–practitioners are best positioned to deliver them. Direct delivery of services by doctoral psychologists paid by third parties may ultimately be focused on more complex cases not touched by manualized and validated therapy, and on areas in which doctoral providers have been shown to be more effective.

The title of this article asks if psychology needs a fix. The word *fix* means both to repair something that is broken and to hold something in place. Proprescription psychologists, who find it difficult to hold the independent practice of psychology in place, essentially argue that the practice of psychology is broken. It has a missing psychopharmacological piece. To the contrary, we argue that the independent practice of psychology needs to change rather than be held in place, and it needs to change in a way that fits with the best historical and scientific traditions of the discipline.

CHALLENGE QUESTIONS

Should Psychologists Be Allowed to Prescribe Drugs?

1. If psychologists were to obtain the privilege to prescribe medications, how would they be different from psychiatrists? How might your answer affect psychology's future?
2. Underlying this issue is what some theorists call reductionism. Reductionism is the notion that all psychological entities (e.g., mind, feelings, unconscious) can ultimately be reduced to biological entities. How might this theoretical notion be affecting the current controversy? How might one's stance on reductionism affect one's stance on this issue?
3. How does a profession like psychology balance the sometimes competing interests of its "marketability" with the good of the public?
4. Hayes and Heiby assert that most psychologists see their job as helping clients to understand their problems. How would psychologists who prescribe medications help their clients to understand their problems? Would you want a psychologist to prescribe medication for you if you were struggling with life issues? Support your answer.
5. DeLeon and Wiggins disagree with Hayes and Heiby about the medical knowledge required for psychologists to prescribe drugs safely. How much medical training would you require a mental health professional to have before you would feel comfortable accepting a prescription? Support your answer.

ISSUE 15

Classic Dialogue: Do Diagnostic Labels Hinder Treatment?

YES: D. L. Rosenhan, from "On Being Sane in Insane Places," *Science* (January 19, 1973)

NO: Robert L. Spitzer, from "On Pseudoscience in Science, Logic in Remission and Psychiatric Diagnosis: A Critique of 'On Being Sane in Insane Places,'" *Journal of Abnormal Psychology* (vol. 84, 1975)

ISSUE SUMMARY

YES: Psychologist D. L. Rosenhan describes an experiment that he contends demonstrates that once a patient is labeled "schizophrenic," his behavior is seen as such by mental health workers regardless of the true state of the patient's mental health.

NO: Psychiatrist Robert L. Spitzer argues that diagnostic labels are necessary and valuable and that Rosenhan's experiment has many flaws.

Traditionally, the first step in treating a disorder is to diagnose it. When a disorder is diagnosed, presumably the most effective treatment can then be applied. But diagnosis often involves classifying the person and attaching a label. Could such a label do more harm than good?

How would you think and behave if you were introduced to someone described as a high school dropout? A heroin addict? A schizophrenic? What would you think and how would you behave if, having recently taken a series of personality tests, you were told by an expert that you were schizophrenic?

Some people believe that diagnostic labels may actually serve as self-fulfilling prophecies. Labels seem to have a way of putting blinders on the way a problem is seen. Those who are labeled may behave differently toward others or develop self-concepts consistent with the diagnosis—and thereby exaggerate, or even create anew, behavior considered to be "abnormal."

In the following selection, D. L. Rosenhan asks the question, "If sanity and insanity exist, how shall we know them?" He then describes an experiment that he conducted to help answer this question. Rosenhan interprets the results of his investigation as demonstrating that "the normal are not detectably sane" by a mental hospital staff because "having once been labeled schizophrenic, there is nothing the [patient] can do to overcome this tag." He believes that mental institutions impose a specific environment in which the meaning of even normal behaviors can be construed as abnormal. If this is so, Rosenhan wonders, "How many people are sane... but not recognized as such in our psychiatric institutions?"

In the second selection, Robert L. Spitzer criticizes Rosenhan's experiment on many grounds and, in fact, contends that "a correct interpretation of his own [Rosenhan's] data contradicts his conclusions." Rosenhan's data, Spitzer contends, show that in "a psychiatric hospital, psychiatrists are remarkably able to distinguish the 'sane' from the 'insane.'" Although Spitzer recognizes some of the dangers of diagnostic classification, he argues that Rosenhan has not presented fairly the purpose and necessity of diagnoses. The misuse of diagnoses, he maintains, "is not a sufficient reason to abandon their use because they have been shown to be of value when properly used." They "enable mental health professionals to communicate with each other..., comprehend the pathological processes involved..., and control psychiatric disorders," says Spitzer.

POINT	COUNTERPOINT
• Psychiatric diagnoses are in the minds of the observers and do not reflect the behavior of the patients.	• A diagnosis based on real or false symptoms *is* based on a patient's behavior.
• A diagnosis can become a self-fulfilling prophecy for the doctor or the patient.	• Competent diagnoses derive from a necessary classification of the symptoms of a disorder.
• In the setting of a mental institution, almost any behavior could be considered abnormal.	• Mental patients *do* eventually get discharged when they continue to show no symptoms of behavioral pathology.
• Diagnostic labels serve no useful purpose, especially in view of the harm they do.	• Diagnoses enable psychiatrists to communicate, comprehend, and control disorders.

D. L. Rosenhan

 **YES**

On Being Sane in Insane Places

If sanity and insanity exist, how shall we know them?

The question is neither capricious nor itself insane. However much we may be personally convinced that we can tell the normal from the abnormal, the evidence is simply not compelling. It is commonplace, for example, to read about murder trials wherein eminent psychiatrists for the defense are contradicted by equally eminent psychiatrists for the prosecution on the matter of the defendant's sanity. More generally, there are a great deal of conflicting data on the reliability, utility, and meaning of such terms as "sanity," "insanity," "mental illness," and "schizophrenia." Finally, as early as 1934, Benedict suggested that normality and abnormality are not universal. What is viewed as normal in one culture may be seen as quite aberrant in another. Thus, notions of normality and abnormality may not be quite as accurate as people believe they are.

To raise questions regarding normality and abnormality is in no way to question the fact that some behaviors are deviant or odd. Murder is deviant. So, too, are hallucinations. Nor does raising such questions deny the existence of the personal anguish that is often associated with "mental illness." Anxiety and depression exist. Psychological suffering exists. But normality and abnormality, sanity and insanity, and the diagnoses that flow from them may be less substantive than many believe them to be.

At its heart, the question of whether the sane can be distinguished from the insane (and whether degrees of insanity can be distinguished from each other) is a simple matter: do the salient characteristics that lead to diagnoses reside in the patients themselves or in the environments and contexts in which observers find them? From Bleuler, through Kretchmer, through the formulators of the recently revised *Diagnostic and Statistical Manual* of the American Psychiatric Association, the belief has been strong that patients present symptoms, that those symptoms can be categorized, and, implicitly, that the sane are distinguishable from the insane. More recently, however, this belief has been questioned. Based in part on theoretical and anthropological considerations, but also on philosophical, legal, and therapeutic ones, the view has grown that psychological categorization of mental illness is useless at best and downright harmful, misleading, and pejorative at worst. Psychiatric diagnoses, in this view, are in the minds of the observers and are not valid summaries of characteristics displayed by the observed.

Gains can be made in deciding which of these is more nearly accurate by getting normal people (that is, people who do not have, and have never suffered, symptoms of serious psychiatric disorders) admitted to psychiatric hospitals and then determining whether they were discovered to be sane and, if so, how. If the sanity of such pseudopatients were always detected, there would be prima facie evidence that a sane individual can be distinguished from the insane context in which he is found. Normality (and presumably abnormality) is distinct enough that it can be recognized wherever it occurs, for it is carried within the person. If, on the other hand, the sanity of the pseudopatients were never discovered, serious difficulties would arise for those who support traditional modes of psychiatric diagnosis. Given that the hospital staff was not incompetent, that the pseudopatient had been behaving as sanely as he had been outside of the hospital, and that it had never been previously suggested that he belonged in a psychiatric hospital, such an unlikely outcome would support the view that psychiatric diagnosis betrays little about the patient but much about the environment in which an observer finds him.

This article describes such an experiment. Eight sane people gained secret admission to 12 different hospitals. Their diagnostic experiences constitute the data of the first part of this article; the remainder is devoted to a description of their experiences in psychiatric institutions. Too few psychiatrists and psychologists, even those who have worked in such hospitals, know what the experience is like. They rarely talk about it with former patients, perhaps because they distrust information coming from the previously insane. Those who have worked in psychiatric hospitals are likely to have adapted so thoroughly to the settings that they are insensitive to the impact of the experience. And while there have been occasional reports of researchers who submitted themselves to psychiatric hospitalization, these researchers have commonly remained in the hospitals for short periods of time, often with the knowledge of the hospital staff. It is difficult to know the extent to which they were treated like patients or like research colleagues. Nevertheless, their reports about the inside of the psychiatric hospital have been valuable. This article extends those efforts.

Pseudopatients and Their Settings

The eight pseudopatients were a varied group. One was a psychology graduate student in his 20s. The remaining seven were older and "established." Among them were three psychologists, a pediatrician, a psychiatrist, a painter, and a housewife. Three pseudopatients were women, five were men. All of them employed pseudonyms, lest their alleged diagnoses embarrass them later. Those who were in mental health professions alleged another occupation in order to avoid the special attentions that might be accorded by staff, as a matter of courtesy or caution, to ailing colleagues. With the exception of myself (I was the first pseudopatient and my presence was known to the hospital administrator and chief psychologist and, so far as I can tell, to them alone), the presence of pseudopatients and the nature of the research program was not known to the hospital staffs.

The settings were similarly varied. In order to generalize the findings, admission into a variety of hospitals was sought. The 12 hospitals in the sample are located in five different states on the East and West coasts. Some were old and shabby, some were quite new. Some were research-oriented, others not. Some had good staff-patient ratios, others were quite understaffed. Only one was a strictly private hospital. All the others were supported by state or federal funds or, in one instance, by university funds.

After calling the hospital for an appointment, the pseudopatient arrived at the admissions office complaining that he had been hearing voices. Asked what the voices said, he replied that they were often unclear, but as far as he could tell they said "empty," "hollow," and "thud." The voices were unfamiliar and were of the same sex as the pseudopatient. The choice of these symptoms was occasioned by their apparent similarity to existential symptoms. Such symptoms were alleged to arise from painful concerns about the perceived meaninglessness of one's life. It is as if the hallucinating person were saying, "My life is empty and hollow." The choice of these symptoms was also determined by the *absence* of a single report of existential psychoses in the literature.

Beyond alleging the symptoms and falsifying name, vocation, and employment, no further alterations of person, history, or circumstances were made. The significant events of the pseudopatient's life history were presented as they had actually occurred. Relationships with parents and siblings, with spouse and children, with people at work and in school, consistent with the aforementioned exceptions, were described as they were or had been. Frustrations and upsets were described along with joys and satisfactions. These facts are important to remember. If anything, they strongly biased the subsequent results in favor of detecting sanity, since none of their histories or current behaviors were seriously pathological in any way.

Immediately upon admission to the psychiatric ward, the pseudopatient ceased simulating *any* symptoms of abnormality. In some cases, there was a brief period of mild nervousness and anxiety, since none of the pseudopatients really believed that they would be admitted so easily. Indeed their shared fear was that they would be immediately exposed as frauds and greatly embarrassed. Moreover, many of them had never visited a psychiatric ward; even those who had, nevertheless had some genuine fears about what might happen to them. Their nervousness, then, was quite appropriate to the novelty of the hospital setting, and it abated rapidly.

Apart from that short-lived nervousness, the pseudopatient behaved on the ward as he "normally" behaved. The pseudopatient spoke to patients and staff as he might ordinarily. Because there is uncommonly little to do on a psychiatric ward, he attempted to engage others in conversation. When asked by staff how he was feeling, he indicated that he was fine, that he no longer experienced symptoms. He responded to instructions from attendants, to calls for medication (which was not swallowed), and to dining-hall instructions. Beyond such activities as were available to him on the admissions ward, he spent his time writing down his observations about the ward, its patients, and the staff.

Initially these notes were written "secretly," but as it soon became clear that no one much cared, they were subsequently written on standard tablets of paper in such public places as the dayroom. No secret was made of these activities.

The pseudopatient, very much as a true psychiatric patient, entered a hospital with no foreknowledge of when he would be discharged. Each was told that he would have to get out by his own devices, essentially by convincing the staff that he was sane. The psychological stresses associated with hospitalization were considerable, and all but one of the pseudopatients desired to be discharged almost immediately after being admitted. They were, therefore, motivated not only to behave sanely, but to be paragons of cooperation. That their behavior was in no way disruptive is confirmed by nursing reports, which have been obtained on most of the patients. These reports uniformly indicate that the patients were "friendly," "cooperative," and "exhibited no abnormal indications."

The Normal Are Not Detectably Sane

Despite their public "show" of sanity, the pseudopatients were never detected. Admitted, except in one case, with a diagnosis of schizophrenia each was discharged with a diagnosis of schizophrenia "in remission." The label "in remission" should in no way be dismissed as a formality, for at no time during any hospitalization had any question been raised about any pseudopatient's simulation. Nor are there any indications in the hospital records that the pseudopatient's status was suspect. Rather, the evidence is strong that, once labeled schizophrenic, the pseudopatient was stuck with that label. If the pseudopatient was to be discharged, he must naturally be "in remission"; but he was not sane, nor, in the institution's view, had he ever been sane.

The uniform failure to recognize sanity cannot be attributed to the quality of the hospitals, for, although there were considerable variations among them, several are considered excellent. Nor can it be alleged that there was simply not enough time to observe the pseudopatients. Length of hospitalization ranged from 7 to 52 days, with an average of 19 days. The pseudopatients were not, in fact, carefully observed, but this failure clearly speaks more to traditions within psychiatric hospitals than to lack of opportunity.

Finally, it cannot be said that the failure to recognize the pseudopatients' sanity was due to the fact that they were not behaving sanely. While there was clearly some tension present in all of them, their daily visitors could detect no serious behavioral consequences—nor, indeed, could other patients. It was quite common for the patients to "detect" the pseudopatients' sanity. During the first three hospitalizations, when accurate counts were kept, 35 of a total of 118 patients on the admissions ward voiced their suspicions, some vigorously. "You're not crazy. You're a journalist, or a professor [referring to the continual note-taking]. You're checking up on the hospital." While most of the patients were reassured by the pseudopatient's insistence that he had been sick before he came in but was fine now, some continued to believe that the pseudopatient was sane throughout his hospitalization. The fact that the patients often recognized normality when staff did not raises important questions.

Failure to detect sanity during the course of hospitalization may be due to the fact that physicians operate with a strong bias toward what statisticians call the type 2 error. This is to say that physicians are more inclined to call a healthy person sick (a false positive, type 2) than a sick person healthy (a false negative, type 1). The reasons for this are not hard to find: it is clearly more dangerous to mis-diagnose illness than health. Better to err on the side of caution, to suspect illness even among the healthy.

But what holds for medicine does not hold equally well for psychiatry. Medical illnesses, while unfortunate, are not commonly pejorative. Psychiatric diagnoses, on the contrary, carry with them personal, legal, and social stigmas. It was therefore important to see whether the tendency toward diagnosing the sane insane could be reversed. The following experiment was arranged at a research and teaching hospital whose staff had heard these findings but doubted that such an error could occur in their hospital. The staff was informed that at some time during the following 3 months, one or more pseudopatients would attempt to be admitted into the psychiatric hospital. Each staff member was asked to rate each patient who presented himself at admissions or on the ward according to the likelihood that the patient was a pseudopatient. A 10-point scale was used, with a 1 and 2 reflecting high confidence that the patient was a pseudopatient.

Judgments were obtained on 193 patients who were admitted for psychiatric treatment. All staff who had had sustained contact with or primary responsibility for the patient—attendants, nurses, psychiatrists, physicians, and psychologists—were asked to make judgments. Forty-one patients were alleged, with high confidence, to be pseudopatients by at least one member of the staff. Twenty-three were considered suspect by at least one psychiatrist. Nineteen were suspected by one psychiatrist *and* one other staff member. Actually, no genuine pseudopatient (at least from my group) presented himself during this period.

The experiment is instructive. It indicates that the tendency to designate sane people as insane can be reversed when the stakes (in this case, prestige and diagnostic acumen) are high. But what can be said of the 19 people who were suspected of being "sane" by one psychiatrist and another staff member? Were these people truly "sane," or was it rather the case that in the course of avoiding the type 2 error the staff tended to make more errors of the first sort—calling the crazy "sane"? There is no way of knowing. But one thing is certain: any diagnostic process that lends itself so readily to massive errors of this sort cannot be a very reliable one.

The Stickiness of Psychodiagnostic Labels

Beyond the tendency to call the healthy sick—a tendency that accounts better for diagnostic behavior on admission than it does for such behavior after a lengthy period of exposure—the data speak to the massive role of labeling in psychiatric assessment. Having once been labeled schizophrenic, there is nothing the pseudopatient can do to overcome this tag. The tag profoundly colors others' perceptions of him and his behavior.

From one viewpoint, these data are hardly surprising, for it has long been known that elements are given meaning by the context in which they occur. Gestalt psychology made this point vigorously, and Asch demonstrated that there are "central" personality traits (such as "warm" versus "cold") which are so powerful that they markedly color the meaning of other information in forming an impression of a given personality.

"Insane," "schizophrenic," "manic-depressive," and "crazy" are probably among the most powerful of such central traits. Once a person is designated abnormal, all of his other behaviors and characteristics are colored by that label. Indeed, that label is so powerful that may of the pseudopatients' normal behaviors were overlooked entirely or profoundly misinterpreted. Some examples may clarify this issue.

Earlier I indicated that there were no changes in the pseudopatient's personal history and current status beyond those of name, employment, and, where necessary, vocation. Otherwise, a veridical description of personal history and circumstances was offered. Those circumstances were not psychotic. How were they made consonant with the diagnosis of psychosis? Or were those diagnoses modified in such a way as to bring them into accord with the circumstances of the pseudopatient's life, as described by him?

As far as I can determine, diagnoses were in no way affected by the relative health of the circumstances of a pseudopatient's life. Rather, the reverse occurred: the perception of his circumstances was shaped entirely by the diagnosis. A clear example of such translation is found in the case of a pseudopatient who had had a close relationship with his mother but was rather remote from his father during his early childhood. During adolescence and beyond, however, his father became a close friend, while his relationship with his mother cooled. His present relationship with his wife was characteristically close and warm. Apart from occasional angry exchanges, friction was minimal. The children had rarely been spanked. Surely there is nothing especially pathological about such a history. Indeed, many readers may see a similar pattern in their own experiences, with no markedly deleterious consequences. Observe, however, how such a history was translated in the psycho-pathological context, this from the case summary prepared after the patient was discharged:

> This white 39-year-old male . . . manifests a long history of considerable ambivalence in close relationships, which begins in early childhood. A warm relationship with his mother cools during his adolescence. A distant relationship to his father is described as becoming very intense. Affective stability is absent. His attempts to control emotionality with his wife and children are punctuated by angry outbursts and, in the case of the children, spankings. And while he says that he has several friends, one senses considerable ambivalence embedded in these relationships also. . . .

The facts of the case were unintentionally distorted by the staff to achieve consistency with a popular theory of the dynamics of a schizophrenic reaction. Nothing of an ambivalent nature had been described in relations with parents, spouse, or friends. To the extent that ambivalence could be inferred, it was probably not greater than is found in all human relationships. It is true the pseudopatient's relationships with his parents changed over time, but in the ordinary context that would hardly be remarkable—indeed, it might very well be expected. Clearly, the meaning ascribed to his verbalizations (that is, ambivalence, affective instability) was determined by the diagnosis: schizophrenia. An entirely different meaning would have been ascribed if it were known that the man was normal.

All pseudopatients took extensive notes publicly. Under ordinary circumstances, such behavior would have raised questions in the minds of observers, as, in fact, it did among patients. Indeed, it seemed so certain that the notes would elicit suspicion that elaborate precautions were taken to remove them from the ward each day. But the precautions proved needless. The closest any staff member came to questioning these notes occurred when one pseudopatient asked his physician what kind of medication he was receiving and began to write down the response. "You needn't write it," he was told gently. "If you have trouble remembering, just ask me again."

If no questions were asked of the pseudopatients, how was their writing interpreted? Nursing records for three patients indicate that the writing was seen as an aspect of their pathological behavior. "Patient engages in writing behavior" was the daily nursing comment on one of the pseudopatients who was never questioned about his writing. Given that the patient is in the hospital, he must be psychologically disturbed. And given that he is disturbed, continuous writing must be a behavioral manifestation of that disturbance, perhaps a subset of the compulsive behaviors that are sometimes correlated with schizophrenia.

One tacit characteristic of psychiatric diagnosis is that it locates the sources of aberration within the individual and only rarely within the complex of stimuli that surrounds him. Consequently, behaviors that are stimulated by the environment are commonly misattributed to the patient's disorder. For example, one kindly nurse found a pseudopatient pacing the long hospital corridors. "Nervous, Mr. X?" she asked. "No, bored," he said.

The notes kept by pseudopatients are full of patient behaviors that were misinterpreted by well-intentioned staff. Often enough, a patient would go "berserk" because he had, wittingly or unwittingly, been mistreated by, say, an attendant. A nurse coming upon the scene would rarely inquire even cursorily into the environmental stimuli of the patient's behavior. Rather, she assumed that his upset derived from his pathology, not from his present interactions with other staff members. Occasionally, the staff might assume that the patient's family (especially when they had recently visited) or other patients had stimulated the outburst. But never were the staff found to assume that one of themselves or the structure of the hospital had anything to do with a patient's behavior. One psychiatrist pointed to a group of patients who were sitting outside the cafeteria entrance half an hour before lunchtime. To a group of young residents he indicated that such behavior was characteristic of the oral-acquisitive nature of the syndrome. It seemed not to occur to him that there were very few things to anticipate in a psychiatric hospital besides eating.

A psychiatric label has a life and an influence of its own. Once the impression has been formed that the patient is schizophrenic, the expectation is that he will continue to be schizophrenic. When a sufficient amount of time has passed, during which the patient has done nothing bizarre, he is considered to be in remission and available for discharge. But the label endures beyond discharge, with the unconfirmed expectation that he will behave as a schizophrenic again. Such labels, conferred by mental health professionals, are as influential on the patient as they are on his relatives and friends, and it should not surprise anyone that the diagnosis acts on all of them as a self-fulfilling prophecy. Eventually, the patient himself accepts the diagnosis, with all of its surplus meanings and expectations, and behaves accordingly.

The inferences to be made from these matters are quite simple. Much as Zigler and Phillips have demonstrated that there is enormous overlap in the symptoms presented by patients who have been variously diagnosed, so there is enormous overlap in the behaviors of the sane and the insane. The sane are not "sane" all of the time. We lose our tempers "for no good reason." We are occasionally depressed or anxious, again for no good reason. And we may find it difficult to get along with one or another person—again for no reason that we can specify. Similarly, the insane are not always insane. Indeed, it was the impression of the pseudopatients while living with them that they were sane for long periods of time—that the bizarre behaviors upon which their diagnoses were allegedly predicated constituted only a small fraction of their total behavior. If it makes no sense to label ourselves permanently depressed on the basis of an occasional depression, then it takes better evidence than is presently available to label all patients insane or schizophrenic on the basis of bizarre behaviors or cognitions. It seems more useful, as Mischel has pointed out, to limit our discussions to *behaviors*, the stimuli that provoke them, and their correlates.

It is not known why powerful impressions of personality traits, such as "crazy" or "insane," arise. Conceivably, when the origins of and stimuli that give rise to a behavior are remote or unknown, or when the behavior strikes us as immutable, trait labels regarding the *behaver* arise. When, on the other hand, the origins and stimuli are known and available, discourse is limited to the behavior itself. Thus, I may hallucinate because I am sleeping, or I may hallucinate because I have ingested a peculiar drug. These are termed sleep-induced hallucinations, or dreams, and drug-induced hallucinations, respectively. But when the stimuli to my hallucinations are unknown, that is called craziness, or schizophrenia—as if that inference were somehow as illuminating as the others.

The Experience of Psychiatric Hospitalization

The term "mental illness" is of recent origin. It was coined by people who were humane in their inclinations and who wanted very much to raise the station of (and the public's sympathies toward) the psychologically disturbed from that of witches and "crazies" to one that was akin to the physically ill. And they were at least partially successful, for the treatment of the mental ill *has* improved considerably over the years. But while treatment has improved, it is doubtful that people really regard the mentally ill in the same way that they view the physically ill. A broken leg is something one recovers from, but mental illness allegedly endures forever. A broken leg does not threaten the observer, but a crazy schizophrenic? There is by now a host of evidence that attitudes toward the mentally ill are characterized by fear, hostility, aloofness, suspicion, and dread. The mentally ill are society's lepers.

That such attitudes infect the general population is perhaps not surprising, only upsetting. But that they affect the professionals—attendants, nurses, physicians, psychologists, and social workers—who treat and deal with the mentally ill is more disconcerting, both because such attitudes are self-evidently pernicious and because they are unwitting. Most mental health professionals would insist that they are sympathetic toward the mentally ill, that they are neither avoidant nor hostile. But it is more likely that an exquisite ambivalence characterizes their relations with psychiatric patients, such that their avowed impulses are only part of their entire attitude. Negative attitudes are there too and can easily be detected. Such attitudes should not surprise us. They are the natural offspring of the labels patients wear and the places in which they are found.

Consider the structure of the typical psychiatric hospital. Staff and patients are strictly segregated. Staff have their own living space, including their dining facilities, bathrooms and assembly places. The glassed quarters that contain the professional staff, which the pseudopatients came to call "the cage," sit out on every dayroom. The staff emerge primarily for caretaking purposes—to give medication, to conduct a therapy or group meeting, to instruct or reprimand a patient. Otherwise, staff keep to themselves, almost as if the disorder that afflicts their charges is somehow catching.

So much is patient-staff segregation the rule that, for four public hospitals in which an attempt was made to measure the degree to which staff and patients mingle, it was necessary to use "time out of the staff cage" as the operational measure. While it was not the case that all time spent out of the cage was spent mingling with patients (attendants, for example, would occasionally emerge to watch television in the dayroom), it was the only way in which one could gather reliable data on time for measuring.

The average amount of time spent by attendants outside of the cage was 11.3 percent (range, 3 to 52 percent). This figure does not represent only time spent mingling with patients, but also includes time spent on such chores as folding laundry, supervising patients while they shave, directing ward clean-up, and sending patients to off-ward activities. It was the relatively rare attendant who spent time talking with patients or playing games with them. It proved impossible to obtain a "percent mingling time" for nurses, since the amount of time they spent out of the cage was too brief. Rather, we counted instances of emergence from the cage. On the average, daytime nurses emerged from the cage 11.5 times per shift, including instances when they left the ward entirely (range, 4 to 39 times). Late afternoon and night nurses were even less available, emerging on the average 9.4 times per shift (range, 4 to 41 times). Data on early morning nurses, who arrived usually after midnight and departed at 8 a.m., are not available because patients were asleep during most of this period.

Physicians, especially psychiatrists, were even less available. They were rarely seen on the wards. Quite commonly, they would be seen only when they arrived and departed, with the remaining time being spent in their offices or in the cage. On the average, physicians emerged on the ward 6.7 times per day (range 1 to 17 times). It proved difficult to make an accurate estimate in this regard, since physicians often maintained hours that allowed them to come and go at different times.

The hierarchical organization of the psychiatric hospital has been commented on before, but the latent meaning of that kind of organization is worth noting again. Those with the most power have least to do with patients, and those with the least power are most involved with them. Recall, however, that the acquisition of role-appropriate behaviors occurs mainly through the observation of others, with the most powerful having the most influence. Consequently, it is understandable that attendants not only spend more time with patients than do any other members of the staff—that is required by their station in the hierarchy—but also, insofar as they learn from their superiors' behavior, spend as little time with patients as they can. Attendants are seen mainly in the cage, which is where the models, the action, and the power are.

I turn now to a different set of studies, these dealing with staff response to patient-initiated contact. It has long been known that the amount of time a person spends with you can be an index of your significance to him. If he initiates and maintains eye contact, there is reason to believe that he is considering your requests and needs. If he pauses to chat or actually stops and talks, there is added reason to infer that he is individuating you. In four hospitals, the pseudopatient approached the staff member with a request which took the following form: "Pardon me, Mr. [or Dr. or Mrs.] X, could you tell me when I will be eligible for grounds privileges?" (or " . . . when I will be presented at the staff meeting?" or " . . . when I am likely to be discharged?"). While the content of the question varied according to the appropriateness of the target and the pseudopatient's (apparent) current needs, the form was always a courteous and relevant request for information. Care was taken never to approach a particular member of the staff more than once a day, lest the staff member become suspicious or irritated. In examining these data, remember that the behavior of the pseudopatients was neither bizarre nor disruptive. One could indeed engage in good conversation with them.

The data for these experiments are shown in Table 1, separately for physicians (column 1) and for nurses and attendants (column 2). Minor differences between these four institutions were overwhelmed by the degree to which staff avoided continuing contacts that patients had initiated. By far, their most common response consisted of either a brief response to the question offered while they were "on the move" and with head averted, or no response at all.

The encounter frequently took the following bizarre form: (pseudopatient) "Pardon me, Dr. X. Could you tell me when I am eligible for grounds privileges?" (physician) "Good morning Dave. How are you today?" (moves off without waiting for a response).

It is instructive to compare these data with data recently obtained at Stanford University. It has been alleged that large and eminent universities are characterized by faculty who are so busy that they have no time for students. For this comparison, a young lady approached individual faculty members who

Table 1

Self-Initiated Contact by Pseudopatients With Psychiatrists and Nurses and Attendants, Compared With Other Groups

Contact	Psychiatric hospitals		University campus (nonmedical)	University medical center Physicians		
	(1) Psychiatrists	(2) Nurses and attendants	(3) Faculty	(4) "Looking for a psychiatrist"	(5) "Looking for an internist"	(6) No additional comment
Responses						
Moves on, head averted (%)	71	88	0	0	0	0
Makes eye contact (%)	23	10	0	11	0	0
Pauses and chats (%)	2	2	0	11	0	0
Stops and talks (%)	4	0.5	100	78	100	90
Mean number of questions answered (out of 6)	*	*	6	3.8	4.8	4.5
Respondents (No.)	13	47	14	18	15	10
Attempts (No.)	185	1283	14	18	15	10

*Not applicable

seemed to be walking purposefully to some meeting or teaching engagement and asked them the following questions.

1. "Pardon me, could you direct me to Encina Hall?" (at the medical school: "... to the Clinical Research Center?").
2. "Do you know where Fish Annex is?" (there is no Fish Annex at Stanford).
3. "Do you teach here?"
4. "How does one apply for admission to the college?" (at the medical school: "... to the medical school?").
5. "Is it difficult to get in?"
6. "Is there financial aid?"

Without exception, as can be seen in Table 1 (column 3), all of the questions were answered. No matter how rushed they were, all respondents not only maintained eye contact, but stopped to talk. Indeed, many of the respondents went out of their way to direct or take the questioner to the office she was seeking, to try to locate "Fish Annex," or to discuss with her the possibilities of being admitted to the university.

Similar data, also shown in Table 1 (columns 4, 5, and 6), were obtained in the hospital. Here too, the young lady came prepared with six questions. After the first question, however, she remarked to 18 of her respondents (column 4), "I'm looking for a psychiatrist," and to 15 others (column 5), "I'm looking for an internist." Ten other respondents received no inserted comment (column 6). The general degree of cooperative responses is considerably higher for these university groups than it was for pseudopatients in psychiatric hospitals. Even so, differences are apparent with the medical school setting. Once having indicated that she was looking for a psychiatrist, the degree of cooperation elicited was less than when she sought an internist.

Powerlessness and Depersonalization

Eye contact and verbal contact reflect concern and individuation: their absence, avoidance and depersonalization. The data I have presented do not do justice to the rich daily encounters that grew up around matters of depersonalization and avoidance. I have records of patients who were beaten by staff for the sin of initiating verbal contact. During my own experience, for example, one patient was beaten in the presence of other patients for having approached an attendant and told him, "I like you." Occasionally, punishment meted out to patients for misdemeanors seemed so excessive that it could not be justified by the most radical interpretations of psychiatric canon. Nevertheless, they appeared to go unquestioned. Tempers were often short. A patient who had not heard a call for medication would be roundly excoriated, and the morning attendants would often wake patients with, "Come on, you m—— f——s, out of bed!"

Neither anecdotal nor "hard" data can convey the overwhelming sense of powerlessness which invades the individual as he is continually exposed to the depersonalization of the psychiatric hospital. It hardly matters *which* psychiatric hospital—the excellent public ones and the very plush private hospital were better than the rural and shabby ones in this regard, but again, the features that psychiatric hospitals had in common overwhelmed by far their apparent differences.

Powerlessness was evident everywhere. The patient is deprived of many of his legal rights by dint of his psychiatric commitment. He is shorn of credibility by virtue of his psychiatric label. His freedom of movement is restricted. He cannot initiate contact with the staff, but may only respond to such overtures as they make. Personal privacy is minimal. Patient quarters and possessions can be entered and examined by any staff member, for whatever reason. His personal history and anguish are available to any staff member (often including the "grey lady" and "candy striper" volunteer) who chooses to read his folder, regardless of their therapeutic relationship to him. His personal hygiene and waste evacuation are often monitored. The water closets may have no doors.

At times, the depersonalization reached such proportions that pseudopatients had the sense that they were invisible, or at least unworthy of account. Upon being admitted, I and other pseudopatients took the initial physical examination in a semipublic room, where staff members went about their own business as if we were not there.

On the ward, attendants delivered verbal and occasionally serious physical abuse to patients in the presence of other observing patients, some of whom (the pseudopatients) were writing it all down. Abusive behavior, on the other hand, terminated quite abruptly when other staff members were known to be coming. Staff are credible witnesses. Patients are not.

A nurse unbuttoned her uniform to adjust her brassiere in the presence of an entire ward of viewing men. One did not have the sense that she was being seductive. Rather, she didn't notice us. A group of staff persons might point to a patient in the dayroom and discuss him animatedly, as if he were not there.

One illuminating instance of depersonalization and invisibility occurred with regard to medications. All told, the pseudopatients were administered nearly 2100 pills, including Elavil, Stelazine, Compazine, and Thorazine, to name but a few. (That such a variety of medications should have been administered to patients presenting identical symptoms is itself worthy of note.) Only two were swallowed. The rest were either pocketed or deposited in the toilet. The pseudopatients were not alone in this. Although I have no precise records on how many patients rejected their medications, the pseudopatients frequently found the medications of other patients in the toilet before they deposited their own. As long as they were cooperative, their behavior and the pseudopatients' own in this matter, as in other important matters, went unnoticed throughout.

Reactions to such depersonalization among pseudopatients were intense. Although they had come to the hospital as participant observers and were fully aware that they did not "belong," they nevertheless found themselves caught up in and fighting the process of depersonalization. Some examples: a graduate student in psychology asked his wife to bring his textbooks to the hospital so he could "catch up on his homework"—this despite the elaborate precautions taken to conceal his professional association. The same student, who had trained for quite some time to get into the hospital, and who had looked forward to the experience, "remembered" some drag races that he had wanted to see on the weekend and insisted that he be discharged by that time. Another pseudopatient attempted a romance with a nurse. Subsequently, he informed the staff that he was applying for admission to graduate school in psychology and was very likely to be admitted, since a graduate professor was one of his regular hospital visitors. The same person began to engage in psychotherapy with other patients —all of this as a way of becoming a person in an impersonal environment.

The Sources of Depersonalization

What are the origins of depersonalization? I have already mentioned two. First, are attitudes held by all of us toward the mentally ill—including those who treat them—attitudes characterized by fear, distrust, and horrible expectations on the other. Our ambivalence leads us, in this instance as in others, to avoidance.

Second, and not entirely separate, the hierarchical structure of the psychiatric hospital facilitates depersonalization. Those who are at the top have least to do with patients, and their behavior inspires the rest of the staff. Average daily contact with psychiatrists, psychologists, residents, and physicians combined ranged from 3.9 to 25.1 minutes, with an overall mean of 6.8 (six pseudopatients over a total of 129 days of hospitalization). Included in this average are time spent in the admissions interview, ward meetings in the presence of a senior staff member, group and individual psychotherapy contacts, case presentation conferences, and discharge meetings. Clearly, patients do not spend much time in interpersonal contact with doctoral staff. And doctoral staff serve as models for nurses and attendants.

There are probably other sources. Psychiatric installations are presently in serious financial straits. Staff shortages are pervasive, staff time at a premium. Something has to give, and that something is patient contact. Yet, while financial stresses are realities, too much can be made of them. I have the impression that the psychological forces that result in depersonalization are much stronger than the fiscal ones and that the addition of more staff would not correspondingly improve patient care in this regard. The incidence of staff meetings and the enormous amount of record-keeping on patients, for example, have not been as substantially reduced as has patient contact. Priorities exist, even during hard times. Patient contact is not a significant priority in the traditional psychiatric hospital, and fiscal pressures do not account for this. Avoidance and depersonalization may.

Heavy reliance upon psychotropic medication tacitly contributes to depersonalization by convincing staff that treatment is indeed being conducted and that further patient contact may not be necessary. Even here, however, caution needs to be exercised in understanding the role of psychotropic drugs. If patients were powerful rather than powerless, if they were viewed as interesting individuals rather than diagnostic entities, if they were socially significant rather than social lepers, if their anguish truly and wholly compelled our sympathies and concerns, would we not *seek* contact with them, despite the availability of medications? Perhaps for the pleasure of it all?

The Consequences of Labeling and Depersonalization

Whenever the ratio of what is known to what needs to be known approaches zero, we tend to invent "knowledge" and assume that we understand more than we actually do. We seem unable to acknowledge that we simply don't know. The needs for diagnosis and remediation of behavioral and emotional problems are enormous. But rather than acknowledge that we are just embarking on understanding, we continue to label patients "schizophrenic," "manic-depressive," and "insane," as if in those words we had captured the essence of understanding. The facts of the matter are that we have known for a long time that diagnoses are often not useful or reliable, but we have nevertheless continued to use them. We now know that we cannot distinguish insanity from sanity. It is depressing to consider how that information will be used.

Not merely depressing, but frightening. How many people, one wonders, are sane but not recognized as such in our psychiatric institutions? How many have been needlessly stripped of their privileges of citizenship, from the right to vote and drive to that of handling their own accounts? How many have feigned insanity in order to avoid the criminal consequences of their behavior, and, conversely, how many would rather stand trial than live interminably in a psychiatric hospital—but are wrongly thought to be mentally ill? How many have been stigmatized by well-intentioned, but nevertheless erroneous, diagnoses? On the last point, recall again that a "type 2 error" in psychiatric diagnosis does not have the same consequences it does in medical diagnosis. A diagnosis of cancer that has been found to be in error is cause for celebration. But psychiatric diagnoses are rarely found to be in error. The label sticks, a mark of inadequacy forever.

Finally, how many patients might be "sane" outside the psychiatric hospital but seem insane in it—not because craziness resides in them, as it were, but because they are responding to a bizarre setting, one that may be unique to institutions which harbor nether people? Goffman calls the process of socialization to such institutions "mortification"—an apt metaphor that includes the processes of depersonalization that have been described here. And while it is impossible to know whether the pseudopatients' responses to these processes are characteristic of all inmates—they were after all, not real patients—it is difficult to believe that these processes of socialization to a psychiatric hospital provide useful attitudes or habits of response for living in the "real world."

Summary and Conclusions

It is clear that we cannot distinguish the sane from the insane in psychiatric hospitals. The hospital itself imposes a special environment in which the meanings of behavior can easily be misunderstood. The consequences to patients hospitalized in such an environment—the powerlessness, depersonalization, segregation, mortification, and self-labeling—seem undoubtedly countertherapeutic.

I do not, even now, understand this problem well enough to perceive solutions. But two matters seem to have some promise. The first concerns the proliferation of community mental health facilities, of crisis intervention centers, of the human potential movement, and of behavior therapies that, for all of their own problems, tend to avoid psychiatric labels, to focus on specific problems and behaviors, and to retain the individual in a relatively nonpejorative environment. Clearly, to the extent that we refrain from sending the distressed to insane places, our impressions of them are less likely to be distorted. (The risk of distorted perceptions, it seems to me, is always present, since we are much more sensitive to an individual's behaviors and verbalizations than we are to the subtle contextual stimuli that often promote them. At issue here is a matter of magnitude. And, as I have shown, the magnitude of distortion is exceedingly high in the extreme context that is a psychiatric hospital).

The second matter that might prove promising speaks to the need to increase the sensitivity of mental health workers and researchers to the *Catch-22* position of psychiatric patients. Simply reading materials in this area will be of help to some such workers and researchers. For others, directly experiencing the impact of psychiatric hospitalization will be of enormous use. Clearly, further research into the social psychology of such total institutions will both facilitate treatment and deepen understanding.

I and the other pseudopatients in the psychiatric setting had distinctly negative reactions. We do not pretend to describe the subjective experiences of true patients. Theirs may be different from ours, particularly with the passage of time and the necessary process of adaptation to one's environment. But we can and do speak to the relatively more objective indices of treatment within the hospital. It could be a mistake, and a very unfortunate one, to consider that what happened to us derived from malice or stupidity on the part of the staff. Quite the contrary, our overwhelming impression of them was of people who really cared, who were committed and who were uncommonly intelligent. Where they failed, as they sometimes did painfully, it would be more accurate to attribute those failures to the environment in which they too, found themselves than to personal callousness. Their perceptions and behavior were controlled by the situation, rather than being motivated by a malicious disposition. In a more benign environment, one that was less attached to global diagnosis, their behaviors and judgments might have been more benign and effective.

Robert L. Spitzer

 **NO**

On Pseudoscience in Science, Logic in Remission and Psychiatric Diagnosis

Some foods taste delicious but leave a bad aftertaste. So it is with Rosenhan's study, "On Being Sane in Insane Places" (Rosenhan, 1973a), which, by virtue of the prestige and wide distribution of *Science,* the journal in which it appeared, provoked a furor in the scientific community. That the *Journal of Abnormal Psychology,* at this late date, chooses to explore the study's strengths and weaknesses is a testament not only to the importance of the issues that the study purports to deal with but to the impact that the study has had in the mental health community.

Rosenhan apparently believes that psychiatric diagnosis is of no value. There is nothing wrong with his designing a study the results of which might dramatically support this view. However, "On Being Sane in Insane Places" is pseudoscience presented as science. Just as his pseudopatients were diagnosed at discharge as "schizophrenia, in remission," so a careful examination of this study's methods, results, and conclusions leads me to a diagnosis of "logic, in remission."

Let us summarize the study's central question, the methods used, the results reported, and Rosenhan's conclusions. Rosenhan (1973a) states the basic issue simply: "Do the salient characteristics that lead to diagnoses reside in the patients themselves or in the environments and contexts in which observers find them?" Rosenhan proposed that by getting normal people who had never had symptoms of serious psychiatric disorders admitted to psychiatric hospitals "and then determining whether they were discovered to be sane" was an adequate method of studying this question. Therefore, eight "sane" people, pseudopatients, gained secret admission to 12 different hospitals with a single complaint of hearing voices. Upon admission to the psychiatric ward, the pseudopatients ceased simulating any symptoms of abnormality.

The diagnostic results were that 11 of the 12 diagnoses on admission were schizophrenia and 1 was manic-depressive psychosis. At discharge, all of the patients were given the same diagnosis, but were qualified as "in remission."[1]

Despite their "show of sanity" the pseudopatients were never detected by any of the professional staff, nor were any questions raised about their authenticity during the entire hospitalization.

Rosenhan (1973a) concluded: "It is clear that we cannot distinguish the sane from the insane in psychiatric hospitals" (p. 257). According to him, what is needed is the avoidance of "global diagnosis," as exemplified by such diagnoses as schizophrenia or manic-depressive psychosis, and attention should be directed instead to "behaviors, the stimuli that provoke them, and their correlates."

The Central Question

One hardly knows where to begin. Let us first acknowledge the potential importance of the study's central research question. Surely, if psychiatric diagnoses are, to quote Rosenhan, "only in the minds of the observers," and do not reflect any characteristics inherent in the patient, then they obviously can be of no use in helping patients. However, the study immediately becomes confused when Rosenhan suggests that this research question can be answered by studying whether or not the "sanity" of pseudopatients in a mental hospital can be discovered. Rosenhan, a professor of law and psychology, knows that the terms "sane" and "insane" are legal, not psychiatric, concepts. He knows that no psychiatrist makes a diagnosis of "sanity" or "insanity" and that the true meaning of these terms, which varies from state to state, involves the inability to appreciate right from wrong—an issue that is totally irrelevant to this study.

Detecting the Sanity of a Pseudopatient

However, if we are forced to use the terms "insane" (to mean roughly showing signs of serious mental disturbance) and "sane" (the absence of such signs), then clearly there are three possible meanings to the concept of "detecting the sanity" of a pseudopatient who feigns mental illness on entry to a hospital, but then acts "normal" throughout his hospital stay. The first is the recognition, when he is first seen, that the pseudopatient is feigning insanity as he attempts to gain admission to the hospital. This would be detecting sanity in a sane person simulating insanity. The second would be the recognition, after having observed him acting normally during his hospitalization, that the pseudopatient was initially feigning insanity. This would be detecting that the currently sane never was insane. Finally, the third possible meaning would be the recognition, during hospitalization, that the pseudopatient, though initially appearing to be "insane," was no longer showing signs of psychiatric disturbance.

These elementary distinctions of "detecting sanity in the insane" are crucial to properly interpreting the results of the study. The reader is misled by Rosenhan's implication that the first two meanings of detecting the sanity of the pseudopatient to be a fraud, are at all relevant to the central research question. Furthermore, he obscures the true results of his study—because they fail to support his conclusion—when the third meaning of detecting sanity is considered, that is, a recognition that after their admission as "insane," the pseudopatients were not psychiatrically disturbed while in the hospital.

Let us examine these three possible meanings of detecting the sanity of the pseudopatient, their logical relation to the central question of the study, and the actual results obtained and the validity of Rosenhan's conclusions.

The Patient Is No Longer "Insane"

We begin with the third meaning of detecting sanity. It is obvious that if the psychiatrists judged the pseudopatients as seriously disturbed while they acted "normal" in the hospital, this would be strong evidence that their assessments were being influenced by the context in which they were making their examination rather than the actual behavior of the patient, which is the central research question. (I suspect that many readers will agree with Hunter who, in a letter to *Science* (Hunter, 1973), pointed out that, "The pseudopatients did *not* behave normally in the hospital. Had their behavior been normal, they would have walked to the nurses' station and said, 'Look, I am a normal person who tried to see if I could get into the hospital by behaving in a crazy way or saying crazy things. It worked and I was admitted to the hospital, but now I would like to be discharged from the hospital'" [p. 361].)

What were the results? According to Rosenhan, all the patients were diagnosed at discharge as "in remission."[2] The meaning of "in remission" is clear: It means without signs of illness. Thus, all of the psychiatrists apparently recognized that all of the pseudopatients were, to use Rosenhan's term, "sane." However, lest the reader appreciate the significance of these findings, Rosenhan (1973a) quickly gives a completely incorrect interpretation: "If the pseudopatient was to be discharged, he must naturally be 'in remission'; but he was not sane, nor, in the institution's view, had he ever been sane" (p. 252). Rosenhan's implication is clear: The patient was diagnosed "in remission" not because the psychiatrist correctly assessed the patient's hospital behavior but only because the patient had to be discharged. Is this interpretation warranted?

I am sure that most readers who are not familiar with the details of psychiatric diagnostic practice assume, from Rosenhan's account, that it is common for schizophrenic patients to be diagnosed "in remission" when discharged from a hospital. As a matter of fact, it is extremely unusual. The reason is that a schizophrenic is rarely completely asymptomatic at discharge. Rosenhan does not report any data concerning the discharge diagnoses of the real schizophrenic patients in the 12 hospitals used in his study. However, I can report on the frequency of a discharge diagnosis of schizophrenia "in remission" at my hospital, the New York State Psychiatric Institute, a research, teaching, and community hospital where diagnoses are made in a routine fashion, undoubtedly no different from the 12 hospitals of Rosenhan's study. I examined the official book that the record room uses to record the discharge diagnoses and their statistical codes for all patients. Of the over 300 patients discharged in the last year with a diagnosis of schizophrenia, not one was diagnosed "in remission." It is only possible to code a diagnosis of "in remission" by adding a fifth digit (5) to the 4-digit code number for the subtype of schizophrenia (e.g., paranoid schizophrenia is coded as 295.3, but paranoid schizophrenia "in remission" is coded as 295.35). I therefore realized that a psychiatrist might intend to make a discharge diagnosis of "in remission" but fail to use the fifth digit, so that the official recording of the diagnosis would not reflect his full assessment. I therefore had research assistants read the discharge summaries of the last 100 patients whose discharge diagnosis was schizophrenia to see how often the term "in remission," "recovered," "no longer ill," or "asymptomatic" was used, even if not recorded by use of the fifth digit in the code number. The result was that only one patient, who was diagnosed paranoid schizophrenia, was described in the summary as being "in remission" at discharge. The fifth digit code was not used.

To substantiate my view that the practice at my hospital of rarely giving a discharge diagnosis of schizophrenia "in remission" is not unique, I had a research assistant call the record room librarians of 12 psychiatric hospitals, chosen catch as catch can.[3] They were told that we were interested in knowing their estimate of how often, at their hospital, schizophrenics were discharged "in remission" (or "no longer ill" or "asymptomatic"). The calls revealed that 11 of the 12 hospitals indicated that the term was either never used or, at most, used for only a handful of patients in a year. The remaining hospital, a private hospital, estimated that the terms were used in roughly 7 percent of the discharge diagnoses.

This leaves us with the conclusion that, because 11 of the 12 pseudopatients were discharged as "schizophrenia in remission," a discharge diagnosis that is rarely given to real schizophrenics, the diagnoses given to the pseudopatients were a function of the patients' behaviors and not of the setting (psychiatric hospital) in which the diagnoses were made. In fact, we must marvel that 11 psychiatrists all acted so rationally as to use at discharge the category of "in remission" or its equivalent, a category that is rarely used with real schizophrenic patients.

It is not only in his discharge diagnosis that the psychiatrist had an opportunity to assess the patient's true condition incorrectly. In the admission mental status examination, during a progress note or in his discharge note the psychiatrist could have described any of the pseudopatients as "still psychotic," "probably still hallucinating but denies it now," "loose associations," or "inappropriate affect." Because Rosenhan had access to all of this material, his failure to report such judgments of continuing serious psychopathology strongly suggests that they were never made.

All pseudopatients took extensive notes publicly to obtain data on staff and patient behavior. Rosenhan claims that the nursing records indicate that "the writing was seen as an aspect of their pathological behavior." The only datum presented to support this claim is that the daily nursing comment on one of the pseudopatients was, "Patient engaged in writing behavior." Because nursing notes frequently and intentionally comment on nonpathological activities that patients engage in so that other staff members have some knowledge of how the patient spends his time, this particular nursing note in no way supports Rosenhan's thesis. Once again, the failure of Rosenhan to provide data regarding instances where normal hospital behavior was categorized as pathological is remarkable. The closest that Rosenhan comes to providing such data is his report of an instance where a kindly nurse asked if a pseudopatient, who was pacing the long hospital corridors because of boredom, was "nervous." It was, after all, a question and not a final judgment.

Let us now examine the relation between the other two meanings of detecting sanity in the pseudopatients: the recognition that the pseudopatient was a fraud, either when he sought admission to the hospital or during this hospital stay, and the central research question.

Detecting "Sanity" Before Admission

Whether or not psychiatrists are able to detect individuals who feign psychiatric symptoms is an interesting question but clearly of no relevance to the issue of whether or not the salient characteristics that lead to diagnoses reside in the patient's behavior or in the minds of the observers. After all, a psychiatrist who believes in a pseudopatient who feigns a symptom *is* responding to the pseudopatient's behavior. And Rosenhan does not blame the psychiatrist for believing the pseudopatient's fake symptom of hallucinations. He blames him for the diagnosis of schizophrenia. Rosenhan (1973b) states:

> The issue is not that the psychiatrist believed him. Neither is it whether the pseudopatient should have been admitted to the psychiatric hospital in the first place.... The issue is the diagnostic leap that was made between the single presenting symptom, hallucinations, and the diagnosis schizophrenia (or in one case, manic-depressive psychosis). Had the pseudopatients been diagnosed "hallucinating," there would have been no further need to examine the diagnosis issue. The diagnosis of hallucinations implies only that: no more. The presence of hallucinations does not itself define the presence of "schizophrenia." And schizophrenia may or may not include hallucinations. (p. 366)

Unfortunately, as judged by many of the letters to *Science* commenting on the study (Letters to the editor, 1973), many readers, including psychiatrists, accepted Rosenhan's thesis that it was irrational for the psychiatrists to have made an initial diagnosis of schizophrenia as *the most likely condition* on the basis of a single symptom. In my judgment, these readers were wrong. Their acceptance of Rosenhan's thesis was aided by the content of the pseudopatients' auditory hallucinations, which were voices that said "empty," "hollow," and "thud." According to Rosenhan (1973a), these symptoms were chosen because of "their apparent similarity to existential symptoms [and] the *absence* of a single report of existential psychoses in the literature" (p. 251). The implication is that if the content of specific symptoms has never been reported in the literature, then a psychiatrist should somehow know that the symptom is fake. Why then, according to Rosenhan, should the psychiatrist have made a diagnosis of hallucinating? This is absurd. Recently I saw a patient who kept hearing a voice that said, "It's O.K. It's O.K." I know of no such report in the literature. So what? I agree with Rosenhan that there has never been a report of an "existential psychosis." However, the diagnoses made were schizophrenia and manic-depressive psychosis, not existential psychosis.

Differential Diagnosis of Auditory Hallucinations

Rosenhan is entitled to believe that psychiatric diagnoses are of no use and therefore should not have been given to the pseudopatients. However, it makes no sense for him to claim that within a diagnostic framework it was irrational to consider schizophrenia seriously as the most likely condition without his presenting a consideration of the differential diagnosis. Let me briefly give what I think is a reasonable differential diagnosis, based on the presenting picture of the pseudopatient when he applied for admission to the hospital.

Rosenhan says that "beyond alleging the symptoms and falsifying name, vocation, and employment, no further alterations of person, history, or circumstances were made" (p. 251). However, clearly the clinical picture includes not only the symptom (auditory hallucinations) but also the desire to enter a psychiatric hospital, from which it is reasonable to conclude that the symptom is a source of significant distress. (How often did the admitting psychiatrist suggest what would seem to be reasonable care: outpatient treatment? Did the pseudopatient have to add other complaints to justify inpatient treatment?) This, plus the knowledge that the auditory hallucinations are of 3 weeks duration,[4] establishes the hallucinations as significant symptoms of psychopathology as distinguished from so-called "pseudohallucinations" (hallucinations while falling asleep or awakening from sleep, or intense imagination with the voice heard from inside of the head).

Auditory hallucinations can occur in several kinds of mental disorders. The absence of a history of alcohol, drug abuse, or some other toxin, the absence of any signs of physical illness (such as high fever), and the absence of evidence of distractibility, impairment in concentration, memory or orientation, and a negative neurological examination all make an organic psychosis extremely unlikely. The absence of a recent precipitating stress rules out a transient situational disturbance of psychotic intensity or (to use a nonofficial category) hysterical psychosis. The absence of a profound disturbance in mood rules out an effective psychosis (we are not given the mental status findings for the patient who was diagnosed manic-depressive psychosis).

What about simulating mental illness? Psychiatrists know that occasionally an individual who has something to gain from being admitted to a psychiatric hospital will exaggerate or even feign psychiatric symptoms. This is a genuine diagnostic problem that psychiatrists and other physicians occasionally confront and is called "malingering." However, with the pseudopatients there was no reason to believe that any of them had anything to gain from being admitted into a psychiatric hospital except relief from their alleged complaint, and therefore no reason to suspect that the illness was feigned. Dear Reader: There is only one remaining diagnosis for the presenting symptom of hallucinations under these conditions in the classification of mental disorders used in this country, and that is schizophrenia.

Admittedly, there is a hitch to a definitive diagnosis of schizophrenia: Almost invariably there are other signs of the disorder present, such as poor premorbid adjustment, affective blunting, delusions, or signs of thought disorder. I would hope that if I had been one of the 12 psychiatrists presented with such a patient, I would have been struck by the lack of other signs of the disorder, but I am rather sure that having no reason to doubt the authenticity of the patients' claim of auditory hallucinations, I also would have been fooled into noting schizophrenia as the most likely diagnosis.

What does Rosenhan really mean when he objects to the diagnosis of schizophrenia because it was based on a "single symptom"? Does he believe that there are real patients with the single symptom of auditory hallucinations who are misdiagnosed as schizophrenic when they actually have some other condition? If so, what is the nature of that condition? Is Rosenhan's point that the psychiatrist should have used "diagnosis deferred," a category that is available but rarely used? I would have no argument with this conclusion. Furthermore, if he had presented data from real patients indicating how often patients are erroneously diagnosed on the basis of inadequate information and what the consequences were, it would have been a real contribution.

Until now, I have assumed that the pseudopatients presented only one symptom of psychiatric disorder. Actually, we know very little about how the pseudopatients presented themselves. What did the pseudopatients say in the study reported in *Science,* when asked as they must have been, what effect the hallucinations were having on their lives and why they were seeking admission into a hospital? The reader would be much more confident that a single presenting symptom was involved if Rosenhan had made available for each pseudopatient the actual admission work-up from the hospital record.

Detecting Sanity After Admission

Let us now examine the last meaning of detecting sanity in the pseudopatients, namely, the psychiatrist's recognition, *after* observing him act normally during his hospitalization, that the pseudopatient was initially feigning insanity and its relation to the central research question. If a diagnostic condition, by definition, is always chronic and never remits, it would be irrational not to question the original diagnosis if a patient were later found to be asymptomatic. As applied to this study, if the concept of schizophrenia did not admit the possibility of recovery, then failure to question the original diagnosis when the pseudopatients were no longer overtly ill would be relevant to the central research question. It would be an example of the psychiatrist allowing the context of the hospital environment to influence his diagnostic behavior. But neither any psychiatric textbook nor the American Psychiatric Association's *Diagnostic and Statistical Manual of Mental Disorders* (American Psychiatric Association, 1968) suggests that mental illnesses endure forever. Oddly enough, it is Rosenhan (1973a) who, without any reference to the psychiatric literature, says: "A broken leg is something one recovers from, but mental illness allegedly endures forever" (p. 254). Who, other than Rosenhan, alleges it?

As Rosenhan should know, although some American psychiatrists restrict the label of schizophrenia to mean chronic or process schizophrenia, most

American psychiatrists include an acute subtype. Thus, the *Diagnostic and Statistical Manual*, in describing the subtype, acute schizophrenic episode, states that "in many cases the patient recovers within weeks."

A similar straw man is created when Rosenhan (1973a) says,

> The insane are not always insane ... the bizarre behaviors upon which their (the pseudopatients) behaviors were allegedly predicated constituted only a small fraction of their total behavior. If it makes no sense to label ourselves permanently depressed on the basis of an occasional depression, then it takes better evidence than is presently available to label all patients insane or schizophrenic on the basis of behaviors or cognitions. (p. 254)

Who ever said that the behaviors that indicate schizophrenia or any other diagnostic category comprise the total of a patient's behavior? A diagnosis of schizophrenia does not mean that all of the patient's behavior is schizophrenic anymore than a diagnosis of carcinoma of the liver means that all of the patient's body is diseased.

Does Rosenhan at least score a point by demonstrating that, although the professional staff never considered the possibility that the pseudopatient was a fraud, this possibility was often considered by other patients? Perhaps, but I am not so sure. Let us not forget that all of the pseudopatients "took extensive notes publicly." Obviously this was highly unusual patient behavior and Rosenhan's quote from a suspicious patient suggests the importance it had in focusing the other patients' attention on the pseudopatients: "You're not crazy. You're a journalist or a professor (referring to the continual note-taking). You're checking up on the hospital." (Rosenhan, 1973a, p. 252)

Rosenhan presents ample evidence, which I find no reason to dispute, that the professional staff spent little time actually with the pseudopatients. The note-taking may easily have been overlooked, and therefore they developed no suspicion that the pseudopatients had simulated illness to gain entry into the hospital. Because there were no pseudopatients who did not engage in such unusual behaviors, the reader cannot assess the significance of the patients' suspicions of fraud when the professional staff did not. I would predict, however, that a pseudopatient in a ward of patients with mixed diagnostic conditions would have no difficulty in masquerading convincingly as a true patient to both staff and patients if he did nothing unusual to draw attention to himself.

Rosenhan presents one way in which the diagnosis affected the psychiatrist's perception of the patient's circumstances: Historical facts of the case were often distorted by the staff to achieve consistency with psychodynamic theories. Here, for the first time, I believe Rosenhan has hit the mark. What he described happens all the time and often makes attendance at clinical case conferences extremely painful, especially for those with a logical mind and a research orientation. Although his observation is correct, it would seem to be more a consequence of individuals attempting to rearrange facts to comply with an unproven etiological theory than a consequence of diagnostic labeling. One could as easily imagine a similar process occurring when a weak-minded, behaviorally-oriented clinician attempts to rewrite the patient's history to account for "hallucinations reinforced by attention paid to patient by family members when patient complains of hearing voices." Such is the human condition.

One final finding requires comment. In order to determine whether "the tendency toward diagnosing the sane insane could be reversed," the staff of a research and teaching hospital was informed that at some time during the following three months, one or more pseudopatients would attempt to be admitted. No such attempt was actually made. Yet approximately 10 percent of the 193 real patients were suspected by two or more staff members (we are not told how many made judgments) to be pseudopatients. Rosenhan (1973a) concluded: "Any diagnostic process that lends itself so readily to massive errors of this sort cannot be a very reliable one" (p. 179). My conclusion is that this experimental design practically assures only one outcome.

Elementary Principles of Reliability of Classification

Some very important principles that are relevant to the design of Rosenhan's study are taught in elementary psychology courses and should not be forgotten. One of them is that a measurement or classification procedure is not reliable or unreliable in itself but only in its application to a specific population. There are serious problems in the reliability of psychiatric diagnosis as it is applied to the population to which psychiatric diagnoses are ordinarily given. However, I fail to see, and Rosenhan does not even attempt to show, how the reliability of psychiatric diagnoses applied to a population of pseudopatients (or one including the threat of pseudopatients). The two populations are just not the same. Kety (1974) has expressed it dramatically:

> If I were to drink a quart of blood and, concealing what I had done, come to the emergency room of any hospital vomiting blood, the behavior of the staff would be quite predictable. If they labeled and treated me as having a bleeding peptic ulcer, I doubt that I could argue convincingly that medical science does not know how to diagnose that condition. (p. 959)

(I have no doubt that if the condition known as pseudopatient ever assumed epidemic proportions among admittants to psychiatric hospitals, psychiatrists would in time become adept at identifying them, though at what risk to real patients, I do not know.)

Attitudes Toward the Insane

I shall not dwell on the latter part of Rosenhan's study, which deals with the experience of psychiatric hospitalization. Because some of the hospitals participated in residency training programs and were research oriented, I find it hard to believe that conditions were quite as bad as depicted, but they may well be. I have always believed that psychiatrists should spend more time on psychiatric wards to appreciate how mind dulling the experience must be for patients. However, Rosenhan does not stop at documenting the horrors of life on a psychiatric ward. He asserts, without a shred of evidence from his study, that "negative attitudes [toward psychiatric patients] are the natural offspring of the labels patients wear and the places in which they are found." This is nonsense. In recent years large numbers of chronic psychiatric patients, many of them chronic schizophrenics and geriatric patients with organic brain syndromes, have been discharged from state hospitals and placed in communities that have no facilities to deal with them. The affected communities are up in arms not primarily because they are mental patients labeled with psychiatric diagnoses (because the majority are not recognized as ex-patients) but because the behavior of some of them is sometimes incomprehensible, deviant, strange, and annoying.

There are at least two psychiatric diagnoses that are defined by the presence of single behaviors, much as Rosenhan would prefer a diagnosis of hallucinations to a diagnosis of schizophrenia. They are alcoholism and drug abuse. Does society have negative attitudes toward these individuals because of the diagnostic label attached to them by psychiatrists or because of their behavior?

The Uses of Diagnosis

Rosenhan believes that the pseudopatients should have been diagnosed as having hallucinations of unknown origin. It is not clear what he thinks the diagnosis should have been if the pseudopatients had been sufficiently trained to talk, at times, incoherently, and had complained of difficulty in thinking clearly, lack of emotion, and that their thoughts were being broadcast so that strangers knew what they were thinking. Is Rosenhan perhaps suggesting multiple diagnoses of (a) hallucinations, (b) difficulty thinking clearly, (c) lack of emotion, and (d) incoherent speech... all of unknown origin?

It is no secret that we lack a full understanding of such conditions as schizophrenia and manic-depressive illness, but are we quite as ignorant as Rosenhan would have us believe? Do we not know, for example, that hallucinations of voices accusing the patient of sin are associated with depressed affect, diurnal mood variation, loss of appetite, and insomnia? What about hallucinations of God's voice issuing commandments, associated with euphoric affect, psychomotor excitement, and accelerated and disconnected speech? Is this not also an entirely different condition?

There is a purpose to psychiatric diagnosis (Spitzer & Wilson, 1975). It is to enable mental health professionals to (a) communicate with each other about the subject matter of their concern, (b) comprehend the pathological processes involved in psychiatric illness, and (c) control psychiatric disorders. Control consists of the ability to predict outcome, prevent the disorder from developing, and treat it once it has developed. Any serious discussion of the validity of psychiatric diagnosis, or suggestions for alternative systems of classifying psychological disturbance, must address itself to these purposes of psychiatric diagnosis.

In terms of its ability to accomplish these purposes, I would say that psychiatric diagnosis is moderately effective as a shorthand way of communicating the presence of constellations of signs and symptoms that tend to cluster together, is woefully inadequate in helping us understand the pathological processes of psychiatric disorders, but does offer considerable help in the control of many mental disorders. Control is possible because psychiatric diagnosis often yields information of value in predicting the likely course of illness (e.g., an early recovery, chronicity, or recurrent episodes) and because for many mental disorders it is useful in suggesting the best available treatment.

Let us return to the three different clinical conditions that I described, each of which had auditory hallucinations as one of its manifestations. The reader will have no difficulty in identifying the three hypothetical conditions as schizophrenia, psychotic depression, and mania. Anyone familiar with the literature on psychiatric treatment will know that there are numerous well-controlled studies (Klein & Davis, 1969) indicating the superiority of the major tranquilizers for the treatment of schizophrenia, of electroconvulsive therapy for the treatment of psychotic depression and, more recently, of lithium carbonate for the treatment of mania. Furthermore, there is convincing evidence that these three conditions, each of which is often accompanied by hallucinations, are influenced by separate genetic factors. As Kety (1974) said, "If schizophrenia is a myth, it is a myth with a strong genetic component."

Should psychiatric diagnosis be abandoned for a purely descriptive system that focuses on simple phenotypic behaviors before it has been demonstrated that such an approach is more useful as a guide to successful treatment or for understanding the role of genetic factors? I think not. (I have a vision. Traditional psychiatric diagnosis has long been forgotten. At a conference on behavioral classification, a keen research investigator proposes that the category "hallucinations of unknown etiology" be subdivided into three different groups based on associated symptomatology. The first group is characterized by depressed affect, diurnal mood variation, and so on, the second group by euphoric mood, psychomotor excitement. . . .)

If psychiatric diagnosis is not quite as bad as Rosenhan would have us believe, that does not mean that it is all that good. What is the reliability of psychiatric diagnosis prior to 1972? Spitzer & Fleiss (1974) revealed that "reliability is only satisfactory for three categories: mental deficiencies, organic brain syndrome, and alcoholism. The level of reliability is no better than fair for psychosis and schizophrenia, and is poor for the remaining categories." So be it. But where did Rosenhan get the idea that psychiatry is the only medical specialty that is plagued by inaccurate diagnosis? Studies have shown serious unreliability in the diagnosis of pulmonary disorders (Fletcher, 1952), in the interpretation of electrocardiograms (Davis, 1958), in the interpretation of X-rays (Cochrane & Garland, 1952; Yerushalmy, 1947), and in the certification of causes of death (Markush, Schaaf, & Siegel, 1967). A review of diagnostic unreliability in other branches of physical medicine is given by Garland (1960) and the problem of the vagueness of medical criteria for diagnosis is thoroughly discussed by Feinstein (1967). The poor reliability of medical diagnosis, even when assisted by objective laboratory tests, does not mean that medical diagnosis is of no value. So it is with psychiatric diagnosis.

Recognition of the serious problems of the reliability of psychiatric diagnosis has resulted in a new approach to psychiatric diagnosis—the use of specific inclusion and exclusion criteria, as contrasted with the usually vague and ill-defined general descriptions found in the psychiatric literature and in the standard psychiatric glossary of the American Psychiatric Association. This approach was started by the St. Louis group associated with the Department of Psychiatry of Washington University (Feighner, Robins, Guze, Woodruff, Winokur, & Munoz, 1972) and has been further developed by Spitzer, Endicott, and Robins (1974) as a set of criteria for a selected group of functional psychiatric disorders, called the Research Diagnostic Criteria (RDC). The Display shows the specific criteria for a diagnosis of schizophrenia from the latest version of the RDC.[5]

Diagnostic Criteria for Schizophrenia from the Research Diagnostic Criteria

1. At least two of the following are required for definite diagnosis and one for probable diagnosis:

   a. Thought broadcasting, insertion, or withdrawal (as defined in the RDC).
   b. Delusions of control, other bizarre delusions, or multiple delusions (as defined in the RDC), of any duration as long as definitely present.
   c. Delusions other than persecutory or jealousy, lasting at least 1 week.
   d. Delusions of any type if accompanied by hallucinations of any type for at least 1 week.
   e. Auditory hallucinations in which either a voice keeps up a running commentary on the patient's behaviors or thoughts as they occur, or two or more voices converse with each other (of any duration as long as definitely present).
   f. Nonaffective verbal hallucinations spoken to the subject (as defined in this manual).
   g. Hallucinations of any type throughout the day for several days or intermittently for at least 1 month.
   h. Definite instances of formal thought disorder (as defined in the RDC).
   i. Obvious catatonic motor behavior (as defined in the RDC).

2. A period of illness lasting at least 2 weeks.
3. At no time during the active period of illness being considered did the patient meet the criteria for either probable or definite manic or depressive syndrome (Criteria 1 and 2 under Major Depressive or Manic Disorders) to such a degree that it was a prominent part of the illness.

Reliability studies using the RDC with case record material (from which all cues as to diagnosis and treatment were removed), as well as with live patients, indicate high reliability for all of the major categories and relia-bility coefficients generally higher than have ever been reported (Spitzer, Endicott, Robins, Kuriansky, & Garland, in press). It is therefore clear that the reliability of psychiatric diagnosis can be greatly increased by the use of specific criteria. (The interjudge reliability [chance corrected agreement, K] for the diagnosis of schizophrenia using an earlier version of RDC cri-teria with 68 newly admitted psychiatric inpatients at the New York State Psychiatric Institute was .88, which is a thoroughly respectable level of re-liability). It is very likely that the next edition of the American Psychiatric Association's *Diagnostic and Statistical Manual* will contain similar specific criteria.

There are other problems with current psychiatric diagnosis. The recent controversy over whether or not homosexuality per se should be considered a mental disorder highlighted the lack of agreement within the psychiatric pro-fession as to the definition of a mental disorder. A definition has been proposed by Spitzer (Spitzer & Wilson, 1975), but it is not at all clear whether a consensus will develop supporting it.

There are serious problems of validity. Many of the traditional diagnostic categories, such as some of the subtypes of schizophrenia and of major affective illness, and several of the personality disorders, have not been demonstrated to be distinct entities or to be useful for prognosis or treatment assignment. In addition, despite considerable evidence supporting the distinctness of such conditions as schizophrenia and manic-depressive illness, the boundaries sepa-rating these conditions from other conditions are certainly not clear. Finally, the categories of the traditional psychiatric nomenclature are of least value when applied to the large numbers of outpatients who are not seriously ill. It is for these patients that a more behaviorally or problem-oriented approach might be particularly useful.

I have not dealt at all with the myriad ways in which psychiatric diagnos-tic labels can be, and are, misused to hurt patients rather than to help them. This is a problem requiring serious research which, unfortunately, Rosenhan's study does not help illuminate. However, whatever the solutions to that prob-lem the misuse of psychiatric diagnostic labels is not a sufficient reason to abandon their use because they have been shown to be of value when prop-erly used.

In conclusion, there are serious problems with psychiatric diagnosis, as there are with other medical diagnoses. Recent developments indicate that the reliability of psychiatric diagnosis can be considerably improved. However, *even with the poor reliability of current psychiatric diagnosis, it is not so poor that it cannot be an aid in the treatment of the seriously disturbed psychiatric patient.* Rosenhan's study, "On Being Sane in Insane Places," proves that pseudopatients are not detected by psychiatrists as having simulated signs of mental illness. This rather remarkable finding is not relevant to the real problems of the relia-bility and validity of psychiatric diagnosis and only serves to obscure them. A correct interpretation of his own data contradicts his conclusions. In the set-ting of a psychiatric hospital, psychiatrists are remarkably able to distinguish the "sane" from the "insane."

Notes

1. The original article only mentions that the 11 schizophrenics were diagnosed "in remission." Personal communication from D. L. Rosenhan indicates that this also applied to the single pseudopatient diagnosed as manic-depressive psychosis.

2. In personal communication D. L. Rosenhan said that "in remission" referred to a use of that term or one of its equivalents, such as recovered or no longer ill.

3. Rosenhan has not identified the hospitals used in this study because of his concern with issues of confidentiality and the potential for ad hominem attack. However, this does make it impossible for anyone at those hospitals to corroborate or challenge his account of how the pseudopatients acted and how they were perceived. The 12 hospitals used in my mini-study were: Long Island Jewish-Hillside Medical Center, New York; Massachusetts General Hospital, Massachusetts; St. Elizabeth's Hospital, Washington, D.C.; McLean Hospital, Massachusetts; UCLA, Neuropsychiatric Institute, California; Meyer-Manhattan Hospital (Manhattan State), New York; Vermont State Hospital, Vermont; Medical College of Virginia, Virginia; Emory University Hospital, Georgia; High Point Hospital, New York; Hudson River State Hospital, New York, and New York Hospital-Cornell Medical Center, Westchester Division, New York.

4. This was not in the article but was mentioned to me in personal communication by D. L. Rosenhan.

5. For what it is worth, the pseudopatient would have been diagnosed as "probable" schizophrenia using these criteria because of 1(f). In personal communication, Rosenhan said that when the pseudopatients were asked how frequently the hallucinations occurred, they said "I don't know." Therefore, Criterion 1(g) is not met.

References

American Psychiatric Association. *Diagnostic and statistical manual of mental disorders* (2nd ed.). Washington, D.C.: American Psychiatric Association, 1968.

Cochrane, A. L., & Garland, L. H. Observer error in interpretation of chest films: International Investigation. *Lancet,* 1952, 2, 505–509.

Davies, L. G. Observer variation in reports on electrocardiograms. *British Heart Journal,* 1958, 20, 153–161.

Feighner, J. P., and Robins, E., Guze, S. B., Woodruff, R. A., Winokur, G., & Munoz, R. Diagnostic criteria for use in psychiatric research. *Archives of General Psychiatry,* 1972, *26,* 57–63.

Feinstein, A. *Clinical judgment.* Baltimore, Md.: Williams & Wilkins, 1967.

Fletcher, C. M. Clinical diagnosis of pulmonary emphysema—an experimental study. *Proceedings of the Royal Society of Medicine,* 1952, *45,* 577–584.

Garland, L. H. The problem of observer error. *Bulletin of the New York Academy of Medicine,* 1960, *36,* 570–584.

Hunter, F. M. Letters to the editor. *Science,* 1973, *180,* 361.

Kety, S. S. From rationalization to reason. *American Journal of Psychiatry,* 1974, *131,* 957–963.

Klein, D., & Davis, J. *Diagnosis and drug treatment of psychiatric disorders.* Baltimore, Md.: Williams & Wilkins, 1969.

Letters to the editor. *Science,* 1973, *180,* 356–365.

Markush, R. E., Schaaf, W. E., & Siegel, D. G. The influence of the death certifier on the results of epidemiologic studies. *Journal of the National Medical Association,* 1967, *59,* 105–113.

Rosenhan, D. L. On being sane in insane places. *Science,* 1973, *179,* 250–258. (a)

Rosenhan, D. L. Reply to letters to the editor. *Science,* 1973, *180,* 365–369. (b)

Spitzer, R. L., Endicott, J., & Robins, E. *Research diagnostic criteria.* New York: Biometrics Research, New York State Department of Mental Hygiene, 1974.

Spitzer, R. L., Endicott, J., Robins, E., Kuriansky, J., & Garland, B. Preliminary report of the reliability of research diagnostic criteria applied to psychiatric case records. In A. Sudilofsky, B. Beer, & S. Gershon (Eds.), *Prediction in psychopharmacology,* New York: Raven Press, in press.

Spitzer, R. L. & Fleiss, J. L. A reanalysis of the reliability of psychiatric diagnosis. *British Journal of Psychiatry,* 1974. *125,* 341–347.

Spitzer, R. L., & Wilson, P. T. Nosology and the official psychiatric nomenclature. In A. Freedman & H. Kaplan (Eds.), *Comprehensive textbook of psychiatry.* New York: Williams & Wilkins, 1975.

Yerushalmy, J. Statistical problems in assessing methods of medical diagnosis with special reference to X-ray techniques. *Public Health Reports,* 1947, *62,* 1432–1449.

CHALLENGE QUESTIONS

Classic Dialogue: Do Diagnostic Labels Hinder Treatment?

1. Would society be better off if there were no names (such as "normal" or "abnormal") for broad categories of behavior? Why, or why not?
2. Who would you consider best qualified to judge a person's mental health: a parent, a judge, or a doctor? Why?
3. If a person at any time displays symptoms of a mental disorder, even fraudulently, is it helpful to consider that the same symptoms of disorder may appear again? Why, or why not?
4. Is there any danger in teaching the diagnostic categories of mental behavior to beginning students of psychology? Explain.

On the Internet ...

Journal of Personality and Social Psychology

This site contains a description of the *Journal of Personality and Social Psychology*, the current issue's table of contents (with abstracts), and past tables of contents. Looking over the tables of contents should provide you with an overview of current topics of interest to social psychologists.

http://www.apa.org/journals/psp.html

Psychology of Religion Pages

This site serves as a resource for the psychological aspects of belief and behavior. It starts with a general introduction to the psychology of religion and connects to other links related to religion's influence on people's lives.

http://www.psychwww.com/psychology/index.htm

Society for the Psychological Study of Social Issues (SPSSI)

This home page for the Society for the Psychological Study of Social Issues (SPSSI) provides information about current research in social psychology as well as abstracts of issues of the *Journal of Social Issues*.

http://www.spssi.org

PART 7

Social Psychology

*S*ocial psychology is the study of humans in their social environment. A central concern of social psychologists is how society affects the individual. For example, does religiosity improve mental health and well-being? Another particularly controversial example is the question of whether or not pornography negatively influences men's treatment of women. Of more recent concern is the effect that the Internet has on psychological health. These concerns are addressed in this section.

- Does the Internet Have Psychological Benefits?

- Does Religious Commitment Improve Mental Health?

- Does Pornography Cause Men to Be Violent Toward Women?

ISSUE 16

Does the Internet Have Psychological Benefits?

YES: James E. Katz and Philip Aspden, from "A Nation of Strangers?" *Communications of the ACM* (December 1997)

NO: Robert Kraut et al., from "Internet Paradox: A Social Technology That Reduces Social Involvement and Psychological Well-Being?" *American Psychologist* (September 1998)

ISSUE SUMMARY

YES: Research scientist James E. Katz and Philip Aspden, executive director of the Center for Research on the Information Society, contend that the Internet has positive effects on the lives of its users. They also maintain that the Internet creates more opportunities for people to foster relationships with people, regardless of their location.

NO: Robert Kraut, a professor of social psychology and human computer interaction, and his colleagues at Carnegie Mellon University question how beneficial Internet use really is. They argue that Internet use reduces the number and quality of interpersonal relationships that one has.

A few years ago, phrases like "surfing the Web" were understood by only the most technologically advanced. Now the Internet is accessible by almost anyone from almost anywhere, including classrooms, homes, and businesses. People can even check their e-mail in some malls. People spend increasing amounts of time on the Internet and use it for an increasing number of things. With the touch of a button, people can gain access to oceans of information and all sorts of new activities. What effects does the explosion of Internet access have on the psychological well-being of Internet users? Is it beneficial or harmful?

Many people feel that the Internet gives them greater opportunities to meet new friends in chat rooms and through other forms of Internet communication. The Internet offers the potential for thousands of new relationships and the protection of relative anonymity. No one knows if a user is attractive, has a particular ethnicity, or has a good job. All that an individual's chat room companions know is what she or he tells them. The problem is that Internet relationships require people to spend time in relative isolation—time in front of a machine. This has spurred some to predict that the Internet will decrease community and family involvement. They feel that the time spent in front of a computer monitor, communicating with people who cannot be seen, greatly detracts from more healthy relationships. Instead of talking to immediate family members or friends, the Internet user spends hours talking to people who require little from the user. Critics maintain that Internet relationships are largely superficial and that some are even deceptive.

James E. Katz and Philip Aspden contend that the Internet is anything but harmful. They indicate that the Internet is, in fact, beneficial to the psychological health of its users. Internet use merely adds to traditional forms of social ties, they argue, and users of the Internet are just as active in social organizations as nonusers. Rather than shrinking a person's social contacts, the Internet expands social opportunities. Katz and Aspden also argue that Internet use does not negatively influence the quantity or quality of time spent with family and friends.

Robert Kraut et al., on the other hand, hold that Internet use not only decreases family communication but also increases depression and loneliness. Although they acknowledge that the Internet does allow for a greater number of friendships, they argue that the kinds of friendships gained on the Internet are of a poorer quality than more traditional friendships. They suggest that "people are substituting poorer quality social relationships for better relationships, that is, substituting weak ties for strong ones." Kraut et al. maintain that Internet use should be carefully balanced with real-life social involvement in order to curtail negative psychological effects of reliance on Web friends.

POINT

- Internet use leads to more relationships, regardless of geography or convenience.

- Internet use does not have a significant effect on time spent with friends and family.

- The number one use of the Internet is interpersonal communication.

- Sixty percent of the people who have met friends on the Internet also went on to meet them face-to-face.

COUNTERPOINT

- Relationships gained on the Internet block people from "real," more satisfying relationships and reduces social involvement.

- Greater use of the Internet causes declines in family communication, as well as increased rates of depression and loneliness.

- Internet use is associated with physical inactivity and less face-to-face contact.

- Only 22 percent of people who have used the Internet for at least two years have ever made a new friend on the Internet.

James E. Katz and Philip Aspden **YES**

A Nation of Strangers?

Readers of New York tabloid newspapers may have been shocked [in 1997] by a front-page photograph showing a local computer expert being led away in handcuffs, having been arrested on charges of raping a woman he had met via the Internet. But troubles with Internet acquaintances are by no means unique. Stories appear in the news media with disturbing frequency about young boys or girls running away from their homes with adults they met through computer bulletin boards or chat groups.... As similar stories arise about Internet friendships going awry, or even of these "friendships" being malicious cons in the first place, concerns over the Internet's social impact will increase. Of course the concern is by no means limited to the one-on-one level of interpersonal friendships. National and international bodies are grappling with questions about what to do about various extremist political or religious groups who are aiming to suborn or recruit large groups of people. The mass suicide of the Heaven's Gate cult, which had a presence on the Internet, was a ready target for those who fear the way the Internet is changing society.

But the Internet situation is not unique. Every new technology finds dour critics (as well as ebullient proponents). Communication technologies in particular can be seen as opening the doors to all varieties of social ills. When the telegraph, telephone and the automobile were in their infancy, each of these three earlier "communication" technologies found vitriolic critics who said these "instruments of the devil" would drastically alter society (which they did) with disastrous consequences for the quality of life and the moral order (readers may judge for themselves about this point). The Internet is no exception to this rule. Indeed, it has stimulated so many commentators that not even the most indefatigable reader can stay abreast of the flood of speculation and opinion. Yet, as might be expected in light of the conflicts, difficulties, and tragedies associated with the Internet mentioned previously, one area in particular has been singled out for comment: the way the Internet affects social relationships generally and participation in community life in particular. Among those who have criticized the Internet are MIT's Sherry Turkle, who claims that it leads to the destruction of meaningful community and social integration, and Berkeley's Cliff Stoll, who says it reduces people's commitment to and enjoyment of real friendships....

By contrast, optimists argue that genuinely meaningful communities can be established in cyberspace, and indeed even fostered via online communications. Rheingold holds that since virtual interfacing obscures social categories we ordinarily use to sift our relationships (race, sex, age, location), the possibility of new relationships and hence new communities is multiplied. An even more utopian argument is that new, powerful communities will arise in cyberspace, supplanting physical ones of the past, and becoming to an unprecedented extent cohesive, democratic, and meaningful for its members. Indeed, Internet pioneer and Lotus Corporation cofounder Mitch Kapor sees virtual communities ringing in at last the Jeffersonian ideal of community. "Life in cyberspace seems to be shaping up exactly like Thomas Jefferson would have wanted: founded on the primacy of individual liberty and a commitment to pluralism, diversity, and community."

But all these theories have been based on personal impressions, anecdotal evidence or case studies rather than systematic investigation. We wanted to get a broader, more objective picture of what is going on in terms of friendship formation and community involvement for the denizens of the Internet. (We use the term Internet to encompass such aspects of cyberspace as networked computers, computer bulletin boards, and email). Hence in late 1995 we carried out a national random telephone survey which had among its objectives to: compare "real-world" participation for Internet users and non-users, and to examine friendship creation via the Internet.

Our approach was to consider the perspectives of five different Internet awareness/usage groups:

- Those not aware of the Internet,
- Non-users who were aware of the Internet,
- Former users,
- Recent users—those who started using the Internet in 1995,
- Longtime users—those who started using the Internet prior to 1995.

By comparing those who were on the Internet versus those who were not, and controlling statistically for demonstrable demographic differences among user categories, we would be in a position to see if, on average, Internet users were less likely to belong to various voluntary organizations, thus strengthening the hand of those who see the Internet as socially pernicious. Of course if they belonged to more organizations than their non-Internet-using counterparts, the celebrationists would be supported. Likewise, by getting a representative sample of Internet users to speak about their experiences with friendship formation, we would also have some more reliable views of what the typical or majority experiences have been in this regard, without having our understanding biased by a few extraordinary reports.

Our October 1995 survey yielded 2,500 respondents—8% reported being Internet users, 8% reported being former Internet users, 68% reported being aware of the Internet but not being users, and 16% reported not being aware of the Internet. The sample of Internet users was augmented by a national random telephone sample of 400 Internet users. Of the total of 600 Internet users, 49%

reported being longtime Internet users. As a whole, our survey of 2,500 respondents closely matches socioeconomic patterns of the U.S. population on key variables: compared to 1990/91 U.S. Census data, our sample reflects national averages in gender, ethnic mix, and age, and is slightly wealthier and better educated.

No Evidence of Internet Users Dropping Out of Real Life

We explored respondents' community involvement in the real world by asking them how many religious, leisure, and community organizations they belonged to.

Religious organizations. Our survey showed no statistically significant differences across the five awareness/usage categories in membership rates of religious organizations. Fifty-six percent of respondents reported belonging to one religious organization, while a further 8% reported belonging to two or more religious organizations....

Leisure organizations. Here we found that non-users reported belonging to fewer organizations than users, both former and current. Non-users who were not aware of the Internet reported being members of fewest leisure organizations—11% reported belonging to one leisure organization and a further 13% belonged to two or more leisure organizations. Non-users who were aware of the Internet reported belonging to significantly more leisure organizations—21% reported belonging to one leisure organization and a further 19% belonged to two or more leisure organizations.

Reported membership rates for former and current users were much higher—21% of former users reported belonging to one leisure organization and 28% to two or more; 24% of recent users reported belonging to one leisure organization and 25% to two or more; and 24% of longtime users reported belonging to one leisure organization and 29% to two or more. However when we statistically controlled for demographic variables, these differences disappeared.

Community organizations. The aggregate responses to the question about membership of community organizations did not appear to display a pattern relating to the awareness/usage categories. Those who were not aware of the Internet and recent users appeared to belong to the fewest community organizations....

Non-users who were aware of the Internet and former users belonged to more community organizations....

Longtime Internet users reported belonging to most community organizations—27% reported belonging to one organization and a further 22% to two or more. Overall, the survey results provide no evidence that Internet users belong to fewer community organizations....

The Internet Is Augmenting Involvement in Existing Communities

... Contact with family members.   An area where the Internet appeared to have a significant impact on social involvement was communications with family members where just under half the users reported contacting family members at least once or twice. Longtime users reported contacting family members more often than recent members. Thirty-five percent of longtime users reported contacting family members at least several times a month, twice the proportion of recent users.

Participation in Internet communities.   We also asked users the extent they participated in Internet communities. Again we found a significant degree of participation—31% of longtime users and 17% of recent users reported doing so. The distribution of the number of communities belonged to for both longtime and recent users was not statistically different (Chi square $= 3.6$, sig. $= 0.6$, with 5 degrees of freedom). Of those who reported participating in various Internet communities, 58% participated in one or two communities, 28% participated in three or four communities, and 14% participated in five or more communities.

Change in face-to-face/phone communications.   For the vast majority of both longtime and recent users, use of the Internet did not appear to have much impact on the time spent with friends and family. The two groups' views were not statistically different. Eighty-eight percent of users reported that the time spent with friends and family face-to-face or by phone since they started using Internet had not changed. The same proportions (6%) of users reported they spent more time with friends and family face-to-face or by phone, as those who spent less time.

The Internet Is Emerging as a Medium for Friendship Creation

Friendship formation.   As part of our survey, we asked Internet users whether they knew people only through the Internet whom they considered their friends. Of our 601 Internet users, a significant minority (82 respondents, 14% of our sample of Internet users) reported knowing people in this way.

Propensity to form friendships through the Internet appeared to relate more strongly to general measures of Internet usage and experience, rather than demographic variables. For example, those with self-identified higher Internet skill levels appeared more likely to make Internet friends. Nine percent of novices, 13% of those with average skill levels, 22% of those with above average skill levels, and 27% of those with excellent skill levels reported making Internet friendships.

Somewhat surprisingly, we found no statistical relationships between propensity to make friends and a wide range of measures of traditional forms of social connectedness and measures of personality attributes.... This perhaps points to the Internet deemphasizing the importance of sociability and personality differences.

Number of friendships formed. For the 81 users who reported establishing friendships via the Internet, a substantial proportion said they had made numerous friendships. Thirty percent of the group (24 respondents) reported having established friendships with 1 to 3 people, 40% (32 respondents) with 4 to 10 people, 22% (18 respondents) with 11 to 30 people, and 9% (7 respondents) with 31 or more people. The best predictor of the number of friends made was again a general measure of Internet usage. Longtime users reported making more friends....

Internet friendships leading to meetings. A majority of people who reported making friends through the Internet met one or more of them. Of the 81 respondents who reported making friends via the Internet, 60% reported meeting one or more of these friends. Those reporting higher numbers of Internet friends were more likely to have met at least one of them....

Number of friends met. For the 49 users who reported meeting Internet friends, a substantial number of meetings were reported. Thirty-seven percent of the group (18 respondents) reported meeting with 1 to 3 Internet friends, 29% (14 respondents) with 4 to 10 Internet friends, 22% (11 respondents) with 11 to 30 Internet friends, and 12% (6 respondents) met with 31 or more Internet friends....

Although it is always dangerous to extrapolate, we will do so nonetheless. Based on the data, it would be our guess that perhaps two million new face-to-face meetings have taken place due to participation on the Internet. We do not know, since we did not ask, what the purpose of these meetings might have been (dating services, support groups, hobbyists, political activism?). We hope to explore questions along these lines in our future work.

Pessimism for Pessimistic Theories

Based on our national snapshot, we found no support for the pessimistic theories of the effects of cyberspace on community involvement. When controlling for demographic differences between users and non-users, we found no statistical differences in participation rates in religious, leisure, and community organizations.

Moreover, the Internet appeared to augment existing traditional social connectivity. Just under half of Internet users reported contacting family members at least once or twice via the Internet. A significant minority of users also reported participating in Internet communities. In addition, the vast majority of both longtime and recent users reported that time spent with friends and family in face-to-face contact or by phone had not changed since they started using the Internet.

Further, our survey suggests that the Internet is emerging as a medium for cultivating friendships which, in a majority of cases, lead to meetings in the real world. The Internet is currently a medium where Internet skills appear to be the most important determinant of friendship formation, eclipsing personality characteristics such as sociability, extroversion, and willingness to take risks.

... We also found—due to people's Internet activities, the formation of many new friendships, the creation of senses of community, and reports of voluminous contact with family members. In sum, although the "Jeffersonian ideal" may not be realized, a high proportion of Internet users are engaging in lots of social contact and communication with friends and family. Many family members are keeping in touch and new friendships are being formed. Far from creating a nation of strangers, the Internet is creating a nation richer in friendships and social relationships.

Robert Kraut et al.

 **NO**

Internet Paradox

Fifteen years ago, computers were mainly the province of science, engineering, and business. By 1998, approximately 40% of all U.S. households owned a personal computer; roughly one third of these homes had access to the Internet. Many scholars, technologists, and social critics believe that these changes and the Internet, in particular, are transforming economic and social life (e.g., Anderson, Bikson, Law, & Mitchell, 1995; Attewell & Rule, 1984; King & Kraemer, 1995). However, analysts disagree as to the nature of these changes and whether the changes are for the better or worse. Some scholars argue that the Internet is causing people to become socially isolated and cut off from genuine social relationships, as they hunker alone over their terminals or communicate with anonymous strangers through a socially impoverished medium (e.g., Stoll, 1995; Turkle, 1996). Others argue that the Internet leads to more and better social relationships by freeing people from the constraints of geography or isolation brought on by stigma, illness, or schedule. According to them, the Internet allows people to join groups on the basis of common interests rather than convenience (e.g., Katz & Aspden, 1997; Rheingold, 1993)....

Whether the Internet is increasing or decreasing social involvement could have enormous consequences for society and for people's personal well-being. In an influential article, Putnam (1995) documented a broad decline in civic engagement and social participation in the United States over the past 35 years. Citizens vote less, go to church less, discuss government with their neighbors less, are members of fewer voluntary organizations, have fewer dinner parties, and generally get together less for civic and social purposes. Putnam argued that this social disengagement is having major consequences for the social fabric and for individual lives. At the societal level, social disengagement is associated with more corrupt, less efficient government and more crime. When citizens are involved in civic life, their schools run better, their politicians are more responsive, and their streets are safer. At the individual level, social disengagement is associated with poor quality of life and diminished physical and psychological health. When people have more social contact, they are happier and healthier, both physically and mentally (e.g., S. Cohen & Wills, 1985; Gove & Geerken, 1977).

Although changes in the labor force participation of women and marital breakup may account for some of the declines in social participation and increase in depression since the 1960s, technological change may also play a role. Television, an earlier technology similar to the Internet in some respects, may have reduced social participation as it kept people home watching the set. By contrast, other household technologies, in particular, the telephone, are used to enhance social participation, not discourage it (Fischer, 1992). The home computer and the Internet are too new and, until recently, were too thinly diffused into American households to explain social trends that originated over 35 years, but, now, they could either exacerbate or ameliorate these trends, depending on how they are used. . . .

Internet for Entertainment, Information, and Commerce

If people use the Internet primarily for entertainment and information, the Internet's social effects might resemble those of television. Most research on the social impact of television has focused on its content; this research has investigated the effects of TV violence, educational content, gender stereotypes, racial stereotypes, advertising, and portrayals of family life, among other topics (Huston et al., 1992). Some social critics have argued that television reinforces sociability and social bonds (Beniger, 1987, pp. 356–362; McLuhan, 1964, p. 304). One study comparing Australian towns before and after television became available suggests that the arrival of television led to increases in social activity (Murray & Kippax, 1978). However most empirical work has indicated that television watching reduces social involvement (Brody, 1990; Jackson-Beeck & Robinson, 1981; Neuman, 1991; Maccoby, 1951). Recent epidemiological research has linked television watching with reduced physical activity and diminished physical and mental health (Anderson, Crespo, Bartlett, Cheskin, & Pratt, 1998; Sidney et al., 1998). . . .

Like watching television, using a home computer and the Internet generally imply physical inactivity and limited face-to-face social interaction. Some studies, including our own, have indicated that using a home computer and the Internet can lead to increased skills and confidence with computers (Lundmark, Kiesler, Kraut, Scherlis, & Mukopadhyay, 1998). However, when people use these technologies intensively for learning new software, playing computer games, or retrieving electronic information, they consume time and may spend more time alone (Vitalari, Venkatesh, & Gronhaug, 1985). Some cross-sectional research suggests that home computing may be displacing television watching itself (Danko & McLachlan, 1983; Kohut, 1994) as well as reducing leisure time with the family (Vitalari et al., 1985).

Internet for Interpersonal Communication

The Internet, like its network predecessors (Sproull & Kiesler, 1991), has turned out to be far more social than television, and in this respect, the impact of the Internet may be more like that of the telephone than of TV. Our research has shown that interpersonal communication is the dominant use of the Internet at home (Kraut, Mukhopadhyay, Szczypula, Kiesler, & Scherlis, 1998). That people use the Internet mainly for interpersonal communication, however, does not imply that their social interactions and relationships on the Internet are the same as their traditional social interactions and relationships (Sproull & Kiesler, 1991), or that their social uses of the Internet will have effects comparable to traditional social activity.

... Strong ties are relationships associated with frequent contact, deep feelings of affection and obligation, and application to a broad content domain, whereas weak ties are relationships with superficial and easily broken bonds, infrequent contact, and narrow focus. Strong and weak ties alike provide people with social support. Weak ties (Granovetter, 1973), including weak on-line ties (Constant, Sproull, & Kiesler, 1996), are especially useful for linking people to information and social resources unavailable in people's closest, local groups. Nonetheless, strong social ties are the relationships that generally buffer people from life's stresses and that lead to better social and psychological outcomes (S. Cohen & Wills, 1985; Krackhardt, 1994). People receive most of their social support from people with whom they are in most frequent contact, and bigger favors come from those with stronger ties (Wellman & Wortley, 1990).

Generally, strong personal ties are supported by physical proximity. The Internet potentially reduces the importance of physical proximity in creating and maintaining networks of strong social ties. Unlike face-to-face interaction or even the telephone, the Internet offers opportunities for social interaction that do not depend on the distance between parties. People often use the Internet to keep up with those whom they have preexisting relationships (Kraut et al., 1998). But they also develop new relationships on-line. Most of these new relationships are weak....

Whether a typical relationship developed on-line becomes as strong as a typical traditional relationship and whether having on-line relationships changes the number or quality of a person's total social involvements are open questions....

Current Data

Katz and Aspden's national survey (1997) is one of the few empirical studies that has compared the social participation of Internet users with nonusers. Controlling statistically for education, race, and other demographic variables, these researchers found no differences between Internet users' and nonusers' memberships in religious, leisure, and community organizations or in the amount of time users and nonusers reported spending communicating with family and friends. From these data, Katz and Aspden concluded that "[f]ar from creating a nation of strangers, the Internet is creating a nation richer in friendships and social relationships" (p. 86).

Katz and Aspden's (1997) conclusions may be premature because they used potentially inaccurate, self-report measures of Internet usage and social participation that are probably too insensitive to detect gradual changes over time. Furthermore, their observation that people have friendships on-line does not necessarily lead to the inference that using the Internet increases the people's social participation or psychological well-being; to draw such a conclusion, one needs to know more about the quality of their on-line relationships and the impact on their off-line relationships. Many studies show unequivocally that people can and do form on-line social relationships (e.g., Parks & Floyd, 1995). However, these data do not speak to the frequency, depth, and impact of on-line relationships compared with traditional ones or whether the existence of on-line relationships changes traditional relationships or the balance of people's strong and weak ties.

Even if a cross-sectional survey were to convincingly demonstrate that Internet use is associated with greater social involvement, it would not establish the causal direction of this relationship. In many cases, it is as plausible to assume that social involvement causes Internet use as the reverse. For example, many people buy a home computer to keep in touch with children in college or with retired parents. People who use the Internet differ substantially from those who do not in their demographics, skills, values, and attitudes. Statistical tests often under-control for the influence of these factors, which in turn can be associated with social involvement (Anderson et al., 1995; Kraut, Scherlis, Mukhopadhyay, Manning, & Kiesler, 1996; Kohut, 1994).

A Logitudinal Study of Internet Use

The research described here uses longitudinal data to examine the causal relationship between people's use of the Internet, their social involvement, and certain likely psychological consequences of social involvement. The data come from a field trial of Internet use, in which we tracked the behavior of 169 participants over their first one or two years of Internet use. It improves on earlier research by using accurate measures of Internet use and a panel research design. Measures of Internet use were recorded automatically, and measures of social involvement and psychological well-being were collected twice, using reliable self-report scales. Because we tracked people over time, we can observe change and control statistically for social involvement, psychological states, and demographic attributes of the trial participants that existed prior to their use of the Internet. With these statistical controls and measures of change, we can draw stronger causal conclusions than is possible in research in which the data are collected once.

Method

Sample

The HomeNet study consists of a sample of 93 families from eight diverse neighborhoods in Pittsburgh, Pennsylvania.... Children younger than 10 and uninterested members of the households are not included in the sample....

Families received a computer and software, a free telephone line, and free access to the Internet in exchange for permitting the researchers to automatically track their Internet usage and services, for answering periodic questionnaires, and for agreeing to an in-home interview....

Data Collection

We measured demographic characteristics, social involvement, and psychological well-being of participants in the HomeNet trial on a pretest questionnaire, before the participants were given access to the Internet. After 12 to 24 months, participants completed a follow-up questionnaire containing the measures of social involvement and psychological well-being. During this interval, we automatically recorded their Internet usage using custom-designed logging programs. The data reported here encompass the first 104 weeks of use after a HomeNet family's Internet account was first operational for the 1995 subsample and 52 weeks of use for the 1996 subsample....

Internet usage.   Software recorded the total hours in a week in which a participant connected to the Internet. Electronic mail and the World Wide Web were the major applications that participants used on the Internet and account for most of their time on-line. Internet hours also included time that participants read distribution lists such as listservs or Usenet newsgroups and participated in real-time communication using the Web chat lines, MUDs, and Internet Relay Chat. For the analyses we report here, we averaged weekly Internet hours over the period in which each participant had access to the Internet, from the pretest up to the time he or she completed the follow-up questionnaire. Our analyses use the log of the variable to normalize the distribution.

Personal electronic mail use.   We recorded the number of e-mail messages participants sent and received. To better distinguish the use of the Internet for interpersonal communication rather than for information and entertainment, we excluded e-mail messages in which the participant was not explicitly named as a recipient in our count of received mail. These messages typically had been broadcast to a distribution list to which the participant had subscribed. We believe these messages reflect a mix of interpersonal communication and information distribution....

Social Involvement

Family communication.   ... The analysis of family communication showed that teenagers used the Internet more hours than did adults, but Whites did not differ from minorities, and female participants did not differ from male participants in their average hours of use. Different families varied in their use of the Internet... but the amount of communication that an individual family member had with other members of the family did not predict subsequent Internet use.... For our purposes, the most important finding is that greater use of the Internet was associated with subsequent declines in family communication.

Size of participants' social networks. ... Greater social extroversion and having a larger local social circle predicted less use of the Internet during the next 12 to 24 months. Whites reported increasing their distant social circles more than minorities did, and teens reported increasing their distant circles more than adults did; these groups did not differ in changes to their local circles. Holding constant these control variables and the initial sizes of participants' social circles, greater use of the Internet was associated with subsequent declines in the size of both the local social circles ($p < .05$) and, marginally, the size of the distant social circle ($p < .07$)....

Psychological Well-Being

Loneliness. ... Note that initial loneliness did not predict subsequent Internet use. Loneliness was stable over time. People from richer households increased loneliness more than did those from poorer households, men increased loneliness more than did women, and minorities increased loneliness more than did Whites. Controlling for these personal characteristics and initial loneliness, people who used the Internet more subsequently reported larger increases in loneliness. The association of Internet use with subsequent loneliness was comparable to the associations of income, gender, and race with subsequent loneliness....

Depression. ... Initial depression did not predict subsequent Internet use. Minorities reported more increases in depression than did Whites, and those with higher initial stress also reported greater increases in depression. For the purposes of this analysis, the important finding is that greater use of the Internet was associated with increased depression at a subsequent period, even holding constant initial depression and demographic, stress, and support variables that are often associated with depression. This negative association between Internet use and depression is consistent with the interpretation that use of the Internet caused an increase in depression. Again, it is noteworthy that depression... did not predict using the Internet subsequently.

Discussion

Evaluating the Causal Claim

The findings of this research provide a surprisingly consistent picture of the consequences of using the Internet. Greater use of the Internet was associated with small, but statistically significant declines in social involvement as measured by communication within the family and the size of people's local social networks, and with increases in loneliness, a psychological state associated with social involvement. Greater use of the Internet was also associated with increases in depression. Other effects on the size of the distant social circle, social support, and stress did not reach standard significance levels but were consistently negative.

Our analyses are consistent with the hypothesis that using the Internet adversely affects social involvement and psychological well-being. The panel research design gives us substantial leverage in inferring causation, leading us to believe that in this case, correlation does indeed imply causation. Initial Internet use and initial social involvement and psychological well-being were included in all of the models assessing the effects of Internet use on subsequent social and psychological outcomes. Therefore, our analysis is equivalent to an analysis of change scores, controlling for regression toward the mean, unreliability, contemporaneous covariation between the outcome and the predictor variables, and other statistical artifacts (J. Cohen & Cohen, 1983). Because initial social involvement and psychological well-being were generally not associated with subsequent use of the Internet, these findings imply that the direction of causation is more likely to run from use of the Internet to declines in social involvement and psychological well-being, rather than the reverse. The only exception to this generalization was a marginal finding that people who initially had larger local social circles were lighter users of the Internet.

The major threat to the causal claim would arise if some unmeasured factor varying over time within individuals were to simultaneously cause increases in their use of the Internet and declines in their normal levels of social involvement and psychological well-being. One such factor might be developmental changes in adolescence, which could cause teenagers to withdraw from social contact (at least from members of their families) and to use the Internet as an escape. Our data are mixed regarding this interpretation. In analyses not reported . . . , statistical interactions of Internet use with age showed that increases in Internet use were associated with larger increases in loneliness ($\beta = -.16$, $p < .02$) and larger declines in social support ($\beta = -.13$, $p < .05$) for teenagers than for adults. On the other hand, increases in Internet use were associated with smaller increases in daily stress for teenagers than adults ($\beta = -.16$, $p < .02$). There were no statistical interactions between Internet use and age for family communication, depression, or size of social circle. . . .

Finally, we can generalize our results only to outcomes related to social behavior. In particular, we are not reporting effects of the Internet on educational outcomes or on self-esteem related to computer skill learning. Participants gained computer skills with more Internet usage. Several parents of teenagers who had spent many hours on-line judged that their children's positive educational outcomes from using the Internet outweighed possible declines in their children's social interaction. Future research will be needed to evaluate whether such trade-offs exist. . . .

Displacing social activity.   The time that people devote to using the Internet might substitute for time that they had previously spent engaged in social activities. According to this explanation, the Internet is similar to other passive, nonsocial entertainment activities, such as watching TV, reading, or listening to music. Use of the Internet, like watching TV, may represent a privatization of entertainment, which could lead to social withdrawal and to declines in psychological well-being. Putnam (1995) made a similar claim about television viewing.

The problem with this explanation is that a major use of the Internet is explicitly social. People use the Internet to keep up with family and friends through electronic mail and on-line chats and to make new acquaintances through MUDs, chats, Usenet newsgroups, and listservs. Our previous analyses showed that interpersonal communication was the dominant use of the Internet among the sample studied in this research (Kraut et al., 1998). They used the Internet more frequently for exchanging electronic mail than for surfing the World Wide Web and, within a session, typically checked their mail before looking at the Web; their use of electronic mail was more stable over time than their use of the World Wide Web; and greater use of e-mail relative to the Web led them to use the Internet more intensively and over a longer period (Kraut et al., 1998). Other analyses, not reported here, show that even social uses of the Internet were associated with negative outcomes. For example, greater use of electronic mail was associated with increases in depression.

Displacing strong ties.   The paradox we observe, then, is that the Internet is a social technology used for communication with individuals and groups, but it is associated with declines in social involvement and the psychological well-being that goes with social involvement. Perhaps, by using the Internet, people are substituting poorer quality social relationships for better relationships, that is, substituting weak ties for strong ones (e.g., Granovetter, 1973; Krackhardt, 1994). People can support strong ties electronically. Indeed, interviews with this sample revealed numerous instances in which participants kept up with physically distant parents or siblings, corresponded with children when they went off to college, rediscovered roommates from the past, consoled distant friends who had suffered tragedy, or exchanged messages with high school classmates after school.

However, many of the on-line relationships in our sample, and especially the new ones, represented weak ties rather than strong ones. Examples include a woman who exchanged mittens with a stranger she met on a knitting listserv, a man who exchanged jokes and Scottish trivia with a colleague he met through an on-line tourist website, and an adolescent who exchanged (fictional) stories about his underwater exploits to other members of a scuba diving chat service. A few participants met new people on-line and had friendships with them. For instance, one teenager met his prom date on-line, and another woman met a couple in Canada whom she subsequently visited during her summer vacation. However, interviews with participants in this trial suggest that making new friends on-line was rare. Even though it was welcomed when it occurred, it did not counteract overall declines in real-world communication with family and friends. Our conclusions resonate with Katz and Aspden's (1997) national survey data showing that only 22% of the respondents who had been using the Internet for two or more years had ever made a new friend on the Internet. Although neither we nor Katz and Aspden provide comparison data, we wonder whether, in the real world, only a fifth of the population make a friend over a two-year period.

On-line friendships are likely to be more limited than friendships supported by physical proximity. On-line friends are less likely than friends developed at school, work, church, or in the neighborhood to be available for help with tangible favors, such as offering small loans, rides, or baby-sitting.

Because on-line friends are not embedded in the same day-to-day environment, they will be less likely to understand the context for conversation, making discussion more difficult (Clark, 1996) and rendering support less applicable. Even strong ties maintained at a distance through electronic communication are likely to be different in kind and perhaps diminished in strength compared with strong ties supported by physical proximity (Wellman & Wortley, 1990). Both frequently of contact and the nature of the medium may contribute to this difference. For example, one of our participants who said that she appreciated the e-mail correspondence she had with her college-aged daughter also noted that when her daughter was homesick or depressed, she reverted to telephone calls to provide support. Although a clergyman in the sample used e-mail to exchange sermon ideas with other clergy, he phoned them when he needed advice about negotiating his contract. Like that mother and clergyman, many participants in our sample loved the convenience of the Internet. However, this convenience may induce people to substitute less involving electronic interactions for more involving real-world ones. The clergyman in the sample reported that his involvement with his listserv came at the expense of time with his wife. . . .

Both as a nation and as individual consumers, we must balance the value of the Internet for information, communication, and commerce with its costs. Use of the Internet can be both highly entertaining and useful, but if it causes too much disengagement from real life, it can also be harmful. Until the technology evolves to be more beneficial, people should moderate how much they use the Internet and monitor the uses to which they put it.

CHALLENGE QUESTIONS

Does the Internet Have Psychological Benefits?

1. Do you use the Internet? Discuss how it has increased or decreased your ability to create and sustain relationships. Integrate your experiences with current research.
2. One of the issues embedded in this controversy is the importance of face-to-face contact. How significant are a body, nonverbal communication, and the environment of communication in such contact?
3. Are there benefits of the Internet other than social? Review the research on this, and discuss it in light of the social relationship issue.
4. Take a survey of at least 20 people who use the Internet. Ask them questions about how and why they use the Internet. Use your results to support or disprove a hypothesis that you might have regarding social relationships.

ISSUE 17

Does Religious Commitment Improve Mental Health?

YES: David B. Larson, from "Have Faith: Religion Can Heal Mental Ills," *Insight* (March 6, 1995)

NO: Albert Ellis, from "Dogmatic Devotion Doesn't Help, It Hurts," *Insight* (March 6, 1995)

ISSUE SUMMARY

YES: David B. Larson, president of the National Institute for Healthcare, maintains that religious commitment improves mental health and that spirituality can be a medical treatment.

NO: Albert Ellis, president of the Institute for Rational-Emotive Therapy, challenges Larson's studies and questions particularly whether a religious commitment of "fanatic" proportions is truly mentally healthy.

Before the modern forms of medicine and psychotherapy were ever formulated, many religious people were considered healers. The Judeo-Christian tradition and its literature are filled with claims about healing powers and reports of healing even psychological disorders. Part of the reason that these healing claims have been discounted is that some periods of history equated religious sin with psychological disorder. The people of these periods assumed that what we would now call "schizophrenia" and "depression" were really the results of sin or the indwelling of an evil spirit.

Recently, however, the healing claims of some religious people have gained a new hearing. Few of these people would contend that all psychological and emotional problems are simply sin or an evil spirit. But they caution us that although medical and living problems play an important role in psychological disorders, religious factors may also be influential. And although biological and psychological treatments have enjoyed some success, religious variables, such as spirituality, can also be important factors in alleviating mental or emotional problems. At the very least, they argue, this is an empirical rather than a religious question. Do religious factors, such as spirituality and religious commitment, improve one's mental health?

David B. Larson believes that this type of improvement has been demonstrated in numerous empirical studies. In the following selection, he presents research findings showing that spirituality is an effective treatment for drug and alcohol abuse and depression as well as an effective reducer of teen suicide and divorce. Larson explains how spirituality and religious commitment accomplish these results. Unfortunately, Larson says, psychologists' bias against religion has resulted in a continuing neglect of research on religious factors. Such bias has prevented therapists and policymakers from fully understanding the role of religion in health care. This, in turn, has deprived patients of a vital tool in coping with psychological disorders.

In the second selection, Albert Ellis questions how vital this "tool" really is. Ellis distrusts the objectivity of the studies that Larson cites. Nearly all the studies, he contends, were conducted by religious believers and published in religious journals. These people, according to Ellis, can hardly be considered to be dispassionate observers of "reality." Ellis also asserts that the more seriously people take their religious beliefs, the more fanatical they can become. Fanaticism, he suggests, is mentally and emotionally unhealthy. Therefore, the seriously religious—those who are committed and convinced—cannot be the psychologically healthy.

POINT

- The religiously committed report a higher rate of marital satisfaction than the nonreligious.
- Many mental health professionals resist positive findings on religious people because of antireligious views.
- Religious people have a greater sense of overall life satisfaction than nonreligious people.
- Mental health status improves for those who attend religious services on a regular basis.
- Studies show that religious commitment is the best predictor of a lack of substance abuse.

COUNTERPOINT

- Religious people are more likely than nonreligious people to respond in a socially desirable fashion.
- Many studies of religious people do not present a true picture of the mental health benefits of being religious.
- Many religious people have a tendency to claim happier and less stressful lives than they actually have.
- There is a high degree of correlation between dogmatic religiosity and mental disorder.
- Most of these studies are conducted by religious believers who are motivated to prove that religionists are healthier than nonreligionists.

David B. Larson

 **YES**

Have Faith: Religion Can Heal Mental Ills

If a new health treatment were discovered that helped to reduce the rate of teenage suicide, prevent drug and alcohol abuse, improve treatment for depression, reduce recovery time from surgery, lower divorce rates and enhance a sense of well-being, one would think that every physician in the country would be scrambling to try it. Yet, what if critics denounced this treatment as harmful, despite research findings that showed it to be effective more than 80 percent of the time? Which would you be more ready to believe—the assertions of the critics based on their opinions or the results of the clinical trials based upon research?

As a research epidemiologist and board-certified psychiatrist, I have encountered this situation time and again during the last 15 years of my practice. The hypothetical medical treatment really does exist, but it is not a new drug: It is spirituality. While medical professionals have been privately assuming and publicly stating for years that religion is detrimental to mental health, when I actually looked at the available empirical research on the relationship between religion and health, the findings were overwhelmingly positive.

Just what are the correlations that exist between religion and mental health? First, religion has been found to be associated with a decrease in destructive behavior such as suicide. A 1991 review of the published research on the relationship between religious commitment and suicide rates conducted by my colleagues and I found that religious commitment produced lower rates of suicide in nearly every published study located. In fact, Stephen Stack, now of Wayne State University, showed that non-church attenders were four times more likely to kill themselves than were frequent attenders and that church attendance predicted suicide rates more effectively than any other factor including unemployment.

What scientific findings could explain these lower rates of suicide? First, several researchers have noted that the religiously committed report experiencing fewer suicidal impulses and have a more negative attitude toward suicidal behavior than do the nonreligious. In addition, suicide is a less-acceptable alternative for the religiously committed because of their belief in a moral accountability to God, thus making them less susceptible than the nonreligious to this life-ending alternative. Finally, the foundational religious beliefs in an

From David B. Larson, "Have Faith: Religion Can Heal Mental Ills," *Insight* (March 6, 1995). Copyright © 1995 by News World Communications, Inc. Reprinted by permission of *Insight*.

afterlife, divine justice and the possibility of eternal condemnation all help to reduce the appeal of potentially self-destructive behavior.

If religion can reduce the appeal of potentially self-destructive behavior such as suicide, could it also play a role in decreasing other self-destructive behavior such as drug abuse? When this question has been examined empirically, the overwhelming response is yes. When Richard Gorsuch conducted a review of the relationship between religious commitment and drug abuse nearly 20 years ago, he noted that religious commitment "predicts those who have not used an illicit drug regardless of whether the religious variable is defined in terms of membership, active participation, religious upbringing or the meaningfulness of religion as viewed by the person himself."

More recent reviews have substantiated the earlier findings of Gorsuch, demonstrating that even when employing varying measures of religion, religious commitment predicted curtailed drug abuse. Interestingly, a national survey of 14,000 adolescents found the lowest rates of adolescent drug abuse in the most "politically incorrect" religious group—theologically conservative teens. The drug-abuse rates of teens from more liberal religious groups rose a little higher but still sank below rates of drug abuse among nonreligious teens. The correlations between the six measures of religion employed in the survey and the eight measures of substance abuse all were consistently negative. These findings lead the authors of the study to conclude that the amount of importance individuals place on religion in their lives is the best predictor of a lack of substance abuse, implying that "the (internal) controls operating here are a result of deeply internalized norms and values rather than fear ... or peer pressure." For teens living in a society in which drug rates continue to spiral, religion may not be so bad after all.

Just as religious commitment seems to be negatively correlated with drug abuse, similar results are found when examining the relationship between religious commitment and alcohol abuse. When I investigated this area myself, I found that those who abuse alcohol rarely have a strong religious commitment. Indeed, when my colleagues and I surveyed a group of alcoholics, we found that almost 90 percent had lost interest in religion during their teenage years, whereas among the general population, nearly that same percentage reported no change or even a slight increase in their religious practices during adolescence. Furthermore, a relationship between religious commitment and the nonuse or moderate use of alcohol has been extensively documented in the research literature. Some of the most intriguing results have been obtained by Acheampong Amoateng and Stephen Bahr of Brigham Young University, who found that whether or not a religion specifically proscribed alcohol use, those who were active in a religious group consumed substantially less than those who were not active.

Not only does religion protect against clinical problems such as suicide and drug and alcohol abuse, but religious commitment also has been shown to enhance positive life experiences such as marital satisfaction and personal well-being. When I reviewed the published studies on divorce and religious commitment, I found a negative relationship between church attendance and divorce in nearly every study that I located.

To what can these lower rates of divorce be attributed? Some critics argue that the religiously committed stay in unsatisfactory marriages due to religious prohibitions against divorce. However research has found little if any support for this view. In my review I found that, as a group, the religiously committed report a higher rate of marital satisfaction than the nonreligious. In fact, people from long-lasting marriages rank religion as one of the most important components of a happy marriage, with church attendance being strongly associated with the hypothetical willingness to remarry a spouse—a very strong indicator of marital satisfaction. Could these findings be skewed because, as is believed by some in the mental-health field, religious people falsify their response to such questions to make themselves look better? When the studies were controlled for such a factor the researchers found that the religiously committed were not falsifying their responses or answering in a socially acceptable manner and truly were more satisfied in their marriages.

Although the religiously committed are satisfied with their marriages, is this level of satisfaction also found in the sexual fulfillment of married couples? Though the prevailing public opinion is that religious individuals are prudish or even sexually repressed, empirical evidence has shown otherwise. Using data from *Redbook* magazine's survey of 100,000 women in 1975, Carole Tavris and Susan Sadd contradicted the longstanding assumption that religious commitment fosters sexual dysfunction. Tavris and Sadd found that it is the most religious women who report the greatest happiness and satisfaction with marital sex—more so than either moderately religious or nonreligious women. Religious women also report reaching orgasm more frequently than nonreligious women and are more satisfied with the frequency of their sexual activity than the less pious. Thus, while surprising to many, research suggests that religious commitment may play a role in improving rather than hindering sexual expression and satisfaction in marriage.

Not only has religious commitment been found to enhance sexual satisfaction, but overall life satisfaction as well. For example, David Myers of Hope College reviewed well-being literature and found that the religiously committed have a greater sense of overall life satisfaction than the nonreligious. Religion not only seems to foster a sense of well-being and life satisfaction but also may play a role in protecting against stress, with religiously committed respondents reporting much lower stress levels than the less committed. Even when the religiously committed have stress levels that are similar to the nonreligious, the more committed report experiencing fewer mental-illness problems than do the less committed.

Mental-health status has been found to improve for those attending religious services on a regular basis. Indeed, several studies have found a significant reduction in diverse psychiatric symptomatology following increased religious involvement. Chung-Chou Chu and colleagues at the Nebraska Psychiatric Institute in Omaha found lower rates of rehospitalization among schizophrenics who attended church or were given supportive aftercare by religious homemakers and ministers. One of my own studies confirmed that religious commitment can improve recovery rates as well. When my colleagues and I examined elderly women recovering from hip fractures, we found that those women with stronger religious beliefs suffered less from depression and thus were more likely to walk sooner and farther than their nonreligious counterparts.

⋅✦⋅

Yet, despite the abundance of studies demonstrating the beneficial effects of religious commitment on physical and mental health, many members of the medical community seem immune to this evidence. This resistance to empirical findings on the mental-health benefits of religious commitment may stem from the anti-religious views espoused by significant mental-health theorists. For example, Sigmund Freud called religion a "universal obsessional neurosis" and regarded mystical experience as "infantile helplessness" and a "regression to primary narcissism." More recently, Albert Ellis, the originator of rational-emotive therapy, has argued that "unbelief, humanism, skepticism and even thoroughgoing atheism not only abet but are practically synonymous with mental health; and that devout belief, dogmatism and religiosity distinctly contribute to, and in some ways are equal to, mental or emotional disturbance." Other clinicians have continued to perpetuate the misconception that religion is associated with psychopathology by labeling spiritual experiences as, among other things, borderline psychosis, a psychotic episode or the result of temporal-lobe dysfunction. Even the consensus report, "Mysticism: Spiritual Quest or Psychological Disturbance," by the Group for the Advancement of Psychiatry supported the long-standing view of religion as psychopathology; calling religious and mystical experiences "a regression, an escape, a projection upon the world of a primitive infantile state."

What is perhaps most surprising about these negative opinions of religion's effect on mental health is the startling absence of empirical evidence to support these views. Indeed, the same scientists who were trained to accept or reject a hypothesis based on hard data seem to rely solely on their own opinions and biases when assessing the effect of religion on health. When I conducted a systematic review of all articles published in the two leading journals of psychiatry, the *American Journal of Psychiatry* and the *Archives of General Psychiatry,* which assessed the association between religious commitment and mental health, I found that more than 80 percent of the religious-mental health associations located were clinically beneficial while only 15 percent of the associations were harmful—findings that run counter to the heavily publicized opinion of mental-health professionals. Thus, even though the vast majority of published research studies show religion as having a positive influence on mental health, religious commitment remains at best ignored or at worst, maligned by the professional community.

The question then begs to be asked: Why do medical professionals seem to ignore such positive evidence about religion's beneficial effect on mental health? One possible source of this tension could lie in clinicians' unfamiliarity with or rejection of traditional religious expression. For example, not only do mental-health professionals generally hold levels of religious commitment that diverge significantly from the general population, but they have much higher rates of atheism and agnosticism as well. The most recent survey of the belief systems of mental-health professionals found that less than 45 percent of the members of the American Psychiatric Association and the American Psychological Association believed in God—a percentage less than half that of the general population. When asked whether they agreed with the statement, "My whole approach to life is based on my religion," only one-third of clinical psychologists and two-fifths of psychiatrists agreed with that statement—again, a percentage that is nearly half that of the U.S. population. Indeed, more than 25 percent of psychiatrists and clinical psychologists and more than 40 percent of psychoanalysts claimed that they had abandoned a theistic belief system, compared with just less than 5 percent of the general population reporting the same feelings.

Science is assumed to be a domain that progresses through the gradual accumulation of new data or study findings, yet the mental-health community seems to be stalled in its understanding of the interface between religion and mental health. If a field is to progress in its knowledge and understanding of a controversial issue such as religion, empirical data and research must be relied upon more than personal opinions and biases. At a time when the rising cost of health care is causing so much discussion in our country, no factor that may be so beneficial to health can be ignored. The continuing neglect of published research on religion prevents clinicians and policymakers from fully understanding the important role of religion in health care and deprives patients as well as themselves of improved skills and methods in clinical prevention, coping with illness and quality of care. The mental health establishment needs to begin to recognize that it is treating a whole person—mind, body and, yes, even spirit.

NO

Albert Ellis

Dogmatic Devotion Doesn't Help, It Hurts

According to the psychological studies cited by David Larson, religious believers have more satisfying marriages, more enjoyable sex lives, less psychological stress, less depression and less drug and alcohol abuse than nonreligious people. Do these studies present a "true" picture of the mental health benefits of being religious? Probably not, for several reasons. First, the scientific method itself has been shown by many postmodernists to be far from "objective" and unassailable because it is created and used by highly subjective, often biased individuals. Scientists are never purely dispassionate observers of "reality" but frequently bring their own biases to their experiments and conclusions.

Second, practically all the studies that Larson cites were conducted by religious believers; some were published in religious journals. Many of the researchers were motivated to structure studies to "prove" that religionists are "healthier" than nonreligionists and only to publish studies that "proved" this.

None of the studies cited—as I noted when I read many of them myself—eliminated the almost inevitable bias of the subjects they used. I showed, in two comprehensive reviews of personality questionnaires that were published in the *Psychological Bulletin* in 1946 and 1948 and in several other psychological papers, that people often can figure out the "right" and "wrong" answers to these questionnaires and consequently "show" that they are "healthy" when they actually are not. I also showed, in an article in the *American Sociological Review* in 1948, that conservative and religious subjects probably more often were claiming falsely to have "happier" marriages on the Burgess-Locke Marriage Prediction Test than were liberal and nonreligious subjects.

This tendency of conservative, religious, job-seeking and otherwise motivated individuals to overemphasize their "good" and deemphasize their "poor" behavior on questionnaires has been pointed out by a number of other reviewers of psychological studies. Because all these studies included a number of strongly religious subjects, I would guess that many of these religionists had a distinct tendency to claim to be happier, less stressful and less addictive personalities than a good clinician would find them to be. I believe that this is a common finding of psychologists and was confirmed by my reviews mentioned previously.

Although Larson has spent a number of years locating studies that demonstrated that religious believers are healthier than nonreligious subjects, a large number of researchers have demonstrated the opposite. Several other studies have found that people who rigidly and dogmatically maintain religious views are more disturbed than less-rigid religious followers. But all these studies, once again, are suspect because none of them seem to have eliminated the problem of the biased answers of some of their subjects who consciously or unconsciously want to show how healthy they are.

Larson points out that many psychologists are sure that religionists are more disturbed than nonreligionists in spite of their having no real scientific evidence to substantiate their opinions. He is largely right about this, in view of what I have already said. Nonetheless, some reasonably good data back up the views of these psychologists that devout religionists often are disturbed.

Antiabortion killers such as Paul Hill have demonstrated that fanatical beliefs can have deadly consequences. But lesser-known fanatical religious believers have used ruthless tactics to oppose such "enlightened" views as birth control, women's liberation and even separation of church and state. Some religious zealots have jailed, maimed or even killed liberal proponents of their own religions. Nobel laureate Naguib Mahfouz is still recovering from stab wounds inflicted by Muslim extremists last October near his home in Cairo. (Mahfouz, considered by many to be a devout Muslim, frequently has ridiculed religious hypocrisy in his work.) Indian-born author Salman Rushdie has lived for seven years under a death sentence pronounced by the late Ayatollah Khomeini. Rushdie explained to the *New York Times* that dissidents within the Muslim world become "persons whose blood is unclean and therefore deserves to be spilled."

Religious persecution and wars against members of other religions have involved millions of casualties throughout human history Islamic fundamentalists from North Africa to Pakistan have established, or done their best to establish, state religions that force all the citizens of a country or other political group to strictly obey the rules of a specific religious group.

People diagnosed as being psychotic and of having severe personality disorders frequently have been obsessed with religious ideas and practices and compulsively and scrupulously follow religious teachings.

The tragic, multiple suicides of members of the Switzerland-based Order of the Solar Temple last October is only the most recent illustration of an extremist religious cult which manipulated its adherents and induced some of them to harm and kill themselves.

Do these manifestations of religious-oriented fanaticism, despotism, cultism and psychosis prove that religious-minded people generally are more disturbed than nonreligious individuals? Of course not. Many—probably most—religionists oppose the extreme views and practices I have just listed, and some actually make efforts to counteract them. One should not conclude, then, that pious religiosity in and of itself equals emotional disturbance.

However, as a psychotherapist and the founder of a school of psychotherapy called rational emotive behavior therapy, I have for many years distinguished between people who hold moderate religious views and those who espouse devout, dogmatic, rigid religious attitudes. In my judgment, most intelligent and educated people are in the former group and temperately believe God (such as Jehovah) exists, that He or She created the universe and the creatures in it, and that we preferably should follow religious, ethical laws but that a Supreme Being forgives us fallible humans when we do not follow His or Her rules. These "moderate" religionists prefer to be "religious" but do not insist that the rest of us absolutely and completely always must obey God's and the church's precepts. Therefore, they still mainly run their own lives and rarely damn themselves (and others) for religious nonobservance. In regard to God and His or Her Commandments, they live and let live.

The second kind of religious adherents—those who are devout, absolutistic and dogmatic—are decidedly different. They differ among themselves but most of them tend to believe that there absolutely has to be a Supreme Being, that He or She specifically runs the universe, must be completely obeyed and will eternally damn all believers and nonbelievers who deviate from His or Her sacred commands.

Another devout and absolutistic group of people do not believe in anything supernatural, but do rigidly subscribe to a dogmatic, secular belief system —such as Nazism, Fascism or Communism—which vests complete authority in the state or in some other organization and which insists that nonallegiance or opposition to this Great Power must be ruthlessly fought, overthrown, punished and annihilated.

As an advocate of mental and emotional health, I have always seen "moderate" religious believers as reasonably sound individuals who usually are no more neurotic (or otherwise disturbed) than are skeptical, nonreligious people. Like nonbelievers, they are relatively open-minded, democratic and unbigoted. They allow themselves to follow and experience "religious" and "secular" values, enjoyment and commitments. Therefore, they infrequently get into serious emotional trouble with themselves or with others because of their religious beliefs and actions.

This is not the case with fanatical, pietistic religionists. Whether they are righteously devoted to God and the church or to secular organizations and cults (some of which may be atheistic) these extreme religionists are not open-minded, tolerant and undamning. Like nonreligious neurotics and individuals with severe personality disorders, they do not merely wish that other religionists and nonbelievers agree with them and worship their own Supreme Being and their churchly values. They insist, demand and command that their God's and their church's will be done.

Since the age of 12, I have been skeptical of anything supernatural or god-like. But I always have believed that undogmatic religionists can get along well in the world and be helpful to others, and I relate nicely to them. Many, if not most, of the mental-health professionals with whom I have worked in the field of rational emotive behavior therapy are religious. A surprisingly large number of them have been ordained as Protestant ministers, Catholic priests or nuns or Jewish rabbis. A few have even been fundamentalists! So some forms of psychotherapy and moderate religious belief hardly are incompatible.

The important question remains: Is there a high degree of correlation between devout, one-sided, dogmatic religiosity and neurosis (and other personality disorders)? My experience as a clinical psychologist leads me to conclude that there well may be. Some of the disturbed traits and behaviors that pietistic religionists tend to have (but, of course, not always have) include these:

A dearth of enlightened self-interest and self-direction. Pietistic religionists tend to be overdevoted, instead, to unduly sacrificing themselves for God, the church (or the state) and to ritualistic self-deprivation that they feel "bound" to follow for "sacred" reasons. They often give masochistic and self-abasing allegiance to ecclesiastical (and/or secular) lords and leaders. Instead of largely planning and directing their own lives, they often are mindlessly overdependent on religious-directed (or state-directed) creeds, rules and commandments.

Reduced social and human interest. Dogmatic religionists are overly focused on godly, spiritual and monastic interests. They often give greater service to God than to humanity and frequently start holy wars against dissidents to their deity and their church. Witness the recent murders by allegedly devout antiabortionists!

Refusal to accept ambiguity and uncertainty. In an obsessive-compulsive fashion, they hold to absolute necessity and complete certainty, even though our universe only seems to include probability and chance. They deny pliancy, alternative-seeking and pluralism in their own and other people's lives. They negate the scientific view that no hypothesis is proved indisputably "true" under all conditions at all times.

Allergy to unconditional self-acceptance. Emotionally healthy people accept themselves (and other humans) unconditionally—that is, whether they achieve success and whether all significant others approve of them. Dogmatic religionists unhealthily and conditionally accept themselves (and others) only when their God, their church (or state) and similar religionists approve of their thoughts, feelings and behaviors. Therefore, they steadily remain prone to, and often are in the throes of, severe anxiety, guilt and self-condemnation.

In rational-emotive therapy we show people that they "get" emotionally disturbed not only by early or later traumas in their lives but mainly by choosing goals and values that they strongly prefer and by unrealistically, illogically and defeatingly making them into one, two or three grandiose demands: (1) "I absolutely must succeed at important projects or I am an utterly worthless person"; (2) "Other people must treat me nicely or they are totally damnable"; (3) "Life conditions are utterly obligated to give me everything that I think I need or my existence is valueless."

When people clearly see that they are largely upsetting themselves with these godlike commandments, and when they convert them to reasonable—but often still compulsive—desires, they are able to reconstruct their disturbed thoughts, feelings and actions and make themselves much less anxious, depressed, enraged and self-hating and much more self-actualizing and happy.

Being a philosophical system of psychotherapy, rational emotive behavior therapy has much to learn from theological and secular religions. But individuals who choose to be religious also may learn something important from it, namely: Believe whatever you wish about God, the church, people and the universe. But see if you can choose a moderate instead of a fanatical form of religion. Try to avoid a doctrinal system through which you are dogmatically convinced that you absolutely must devote yourself to the one, only, right and unerring deity and to the one, true and infallible church. And try to avoid the certitude that you are God. Otherwise, in my view as a psychotherapist, you most probably are headed for emotional trouble.

CHALLENGE QUESTIONS

Does Religious Commitment Improve Mental Health?

1. Explain why Ellis feels that the data concerning the benefits of religion are not objective. Could his explanation be applied to other types of psychological research?
2. Ellis is the founder of a major school of psychotherapy—rational-emotive therapy. Find a description of this therapy, and discuss how Ellis's own nonreligious values might influence his formulation of this therapy.
3. If it were generally agreed that religious factors were beneficial for mental health, how might psychotherapists use these factors? What problems might a person encounter in employing these factors?
4. How does Ellis distinguish between those who adopt moderate forms of religion and those who adopt fanatical forms of religion? How is this distinction different from the distinction between those who consider their religion relatively superficially and those who take their religious beliefs seriously?
5. For the last few centuries, religion and science have been considered completely separate endeavors. How might this historical separation play into the controversy between Larson and Ellis?

ISSUE 18

Does Pornography Cause Men to Be Violent Toward Women?

YES: Elizabeth Cramer et al., from "Violent Pornography and Abuse of Women: Theory to Practice," *Violence and Victims* (vol. 13, no. 4, 1998)

NO: Kimberly A. Davies, from "Voluntary Exposure to Pornography and Men's Attitudes Toward Feminism and Rape," *The Journal of Sex Research* (vol. 34, no. 2, 1997)

ISSUE SUMMARY

YES: Author Elizabeth Cramer and her colleagues maintain that pornography often depicts women in violent and degrading ways, thus desensitizing the viewer of such pornography and making violence acceptable.

NO: Professor of sociology Kimberly A. Davies argues that pornography is a scapegoat for many societal problems, including violence and abuse toward women.

It is a sad fact that the United States has some of the highest rates of violence of all of today's advanced societies. Of special concern are the high rates of violence against women. What causes such violence, especially at such high rates? Finding the answer to this question has led numerous psychological researchers to conclude that pornography, especially violent pornography, is the culprit. Pornography is believed to reduce appreciation and consideration for women, thus increasing male violence against their female partners.

Psychologists have extensively debated beliefs and hypotheses about the relationship between pornography and violence against women for many years. Those who view pornography as a prime cause of violence against women contend that pornography depicts women as objects to be degraded and abused. How could continual exposure to such degradation and abuse not eventually lead viewers to the same kind of behavior? Researchers who hold this opinion look to *social learning theory,* a prominent psychological explanation of behavior, as a rationale for their arguments: what people see is eventually what people do. Other psychologists contend that pornography does not negatively affect viewers' attitudes and actions toward women. They consider pornography to be a scapegoat for society's ills, and they maintain that the research does not indicate the effect that feminists against violence believe exists.

In the following selection, Elizabeth Cramer and her colleagues mince no words in indicting pornography: "Pornography is the theory and rape is the practice." That is, using pornographic material leads to the belief that women are mere objects to be used by men. Violent pornography also encourages men to assume that women enjoy having their male partners be violent toward them. Cramer et al. cite evidence to support these assertions, including the finding that a high proportion of men who abuse their female partners have used pornographic materials. Cramer et al. conclude that the link between pornography and violence is too strong to ignore any longer.

In the second selection, Kimberly A. Davies disagrees with Cramer et al.'s interpretation of the relevant research as well as their conclusions. In studying the findings relevant to pornography, Davies found no substantial evidence to support the contention that pornography causes violence toward women. She also found no reason to believe that pornography causes men to be desensitized toward women as people or toward women's issues. Davies argues that antipornography feminists are prejudiced in designing and interpreting pornography research. Even if pornography has had some negative effect, Davies asserts, it is too minuscule to be of importance; it is, in effect, a product of the feminist agenda, and attention should be focused elsewhere.

POINT

- Of the women who reported abuse by their partners, a high percentage of their partners used pornographic material.
- Pornography demeans and degrades women in the eyes of its viewers.
- The evidence clearly shows that pornography leads to violence against women.
- Prolonged exposure to pornography leads to greater acceptance of rape and abuse of women.

COUNTERPOINT

- Male dominance and the power structure in our society, not pornography, cause violence against women.
- Watching pornography does not affect men's attitudes toward equal rights for women or toward feminism.
- An unbiased look at the research does not support any such negative effect of pornography.
- Greater exposure to pornography does not lead to a greater acceptance of rape.

Elizabeth Cramer et al.  **YES**

Violent Pornography and Abuse of Women: Theory to Practice

The charge has been made that pornography is the theory and rape is the practice (Kramarae & Treechler, 1985). The final report of the Attorney General's Commission on Pornography (1986), also known as the Meese Commission, stated that there was indeed a connection between persons' use of violent pornography and their use of violence in intimate relationships. The Meese Commission defined pornography as "material predominantly sexually specific and intended for the purpose of sexual arousal" (p. 228–29). They further divided pornography into two subcategories: (1) erotica, which features nudity and explicit consensual sex, and (2) pornography, which contains both nonviolent materials depicting domination and humiliation, and sexually explicit material containing violence. Only the latter category was used to define pornography in the present study. Degrading and violent sexual materials have been identified as potentially the most damaging of all types of erotica to the formation of egalitarian, mutually satisfying relationships (Linz, Donerstein, & Penrod, 1988).

Theory to Practice

Does the theory of pornography (that using pornographic materials actually teaches the user that women are there for the gratification of men, and that women enjoy the sexual "liberation" that violence brings) become the practice of pornography? Social learning theory states that we learn about how to act in social situations by observing society around us (Bandura, 1977). Cowan, Lee, Levy, and Smyer (1988) did a content analysis of 45 adult only, x-rated films randomly selected from a list of 121 adult movie titles readily available from a family videocassette store. They found that 60% of the video time was devoted to explicit portrayals of sexual acts. Of these depictions, 78% were coded as dominant and 82% as exploitive, with men doing almost 80% of the dominating/exploiting. Where women were shown as dominating/exploiting, their targets were most frequently other women. A woman's rape was shown in over half of the films, and 90% of the rapists were men. Physically aggressive acts

From Elizabeth Cramer, Judith McFarlane, Barbara Parker, Karen Soeken, Concepcion Silva, and Sally Reel, "Violent Pornography and Abuse of Women: Theory to Practice," *Violence and Victims*, vol. 13, no. 4 (1998). Copyright © 1998 by Springer Publishing Company, Inc. Reprinted by permission. References omitted.

appeared in 73% of the movies. Status inequities were shown with the men portrayed as professionals, and the women as secretaries, homemakers, students.... The authors state that "the message that men receive from these videos ... is a distorted characterization of both male and female sexuality that is particularly degrading to women" (p. 309)....

There is also a racist component in portrayals of pornographic sex. In an examination of the covers of 60 pornographic magazines and a content analysis of 7 pornographic books, Mayall and Russell (1993) found that African American women were "portrayed in a variety of derogatory and stereotypic ways —as animalistic, incapable of self-control, sexually depraved, impulsive, unclean...." Jewish women were also identified as a separate class, with these women being spoken of as "Jewish whores," "Yiddish swine," etc., and portrayed as submitting to, and enjoying, sexual degradation by Aryan "masters" (p. 176)....

Since more than 25% of all women will suffer from a sexual attack during their lifetime (Remer & Witten, 1988) and women's enjoyment of rape is a common theme in pornography (Cowan et al., 1988; Russell et al., 1993), the question of whether viewers of pornography have callous views of rape and/or are more likely to deny men's responsibility in cases of rape has been raised. Malamuth (1981) in a study of 271 male and female students found that exposure to sexually violent films increased men's acceptance of both rape myths ("women say no when they mean yes," "most women who have been raped were asking for it," "many women secretly want to be raped") and interpersonal violence against women. (Interestingly, women in the study were less accepting of rape myths and interpersonal violence after viewing sexually violent films.) Findings similar to these have been supported by Demare, Briere and Lips (1988), Garcia (1986), Linz, Donnerstein, and Penrod (1988), Malamuth and Check (1985). Linz, Donnerstein and Penrod (1984) found that exposure to one film juxtaposing sexual situations and violence per day for 5 days lowered the subjects' anxiety and depressive reactions to the violence in these films over the course of viewing. Subjects who rated the material as progressively less offensive or violent over the course of the series were also more likely to view the victim as responsible for her assault, judged her as offering less resistance to her abuser, and found her less sympathetic, less attractive and less worthy as an individual at the end of the series.

All of the studies mentioned above have taken place in a laboratory setting, and the criticism can be leveled at them that a laboratory is very different from real life. Does pornography relate to the abuse of women outside of the laboratory setting? The authors' previous study found a correlation between battering of women and pornography use by the abuser in a more naturalistic setting (Cramer & McFarlane, 1994). In this study, 87 women pressing charges of physical abuse against an intimate partner were asked if this partner used violent pornography. Forty percent of the women reported pornography use by the abuser. Of these, 35 women (53%) stated that they had been asked or forced to enact scenes they had been shown. Thirty-six (40%) of the subjects had been raped and of these, 74% stated that their partner had used pornography. Twenty-six percent of the women had been reminded of pornography during the abuse incidents. Sommers and Check (1987) also found that battered women experienced significantly more sexual aggression from their partners than the nonbattered control group and that 39% of these women (vs. 3% of the controls) answered yes to the question of whether their partner had ever tried to get them to act out pornographic scenes they had viewed. Russell and colleagues (1985) stated that 14% of a random selection of 930 women from the San Francisco area reported that they had been asked to pose for pornographic pictures, and 10% had been upset by a partner trying to enact scenes from the pornography that had been seen. In a study with current and former prostitutes in the San Francisco Bay area Silbert and Pines (1993) found that 24% of 193 women who had been raped mentioned allusions to pornographic material on the part of the rapist during the assault. This figure is even more significant when it is understood that these comments were spontaneously offered by correspondents during the course of interviews soliciting information about their sexual assault experiences, with no reference to the issues of pornography being made by the interviewer....

Procedures

A prospective cohort design was followed. Approximately equal numbers of African American, non-Hispanic Anglo-American, and Hispanic women, who reported abuse in the year prior to or during pregnancy, were assessed for severity of abuse and their partners use of pornography, and then assigned to an intervention or control group and followed until the baby was 12 months of age....

Sample.   This report is from 198 abused women of whom 35.4% ($n = 70$) are African American, 32.8% ($n = 65$) Hispanic (primarily Mexican and Mexican-American), and 31.8% ($n = 63$) are White American women. (Hispanic was defined as non-Anglo and non-African American and of Spanish speaking decent.)

The women were between the ages of 14 and 42, with a mean age of 23.2 years (standard deviation = 5.6); 29.6% were teenagers (i.e., 19 years or less). All women had incomes below the poverty level as defined using each state's criteria for Women, Infants, and Children (WIC) program eligibility.

Instruments

Abuse Screen

The Abuse Screen consists of five questions to determine abuse status and perpetrator within a defined period of time. (See Box)....

Index of Spouse Abuse (ISA)

The ISA is a 30-item, self-report scale designed to measure the severity or magnitude of physical (ISA-P) and nonphysical (ISA-NP) abuse inflicted on a woman by her male partner (Hudson & McIntosh, 1981)....

Danger Assessment Scale (DAS)

The DAS, consisting of 14 items with yes/no response format, is designed to assist abused women in determining their potential danger of homicide (Campbell, 1986). All items refer to risk factors that have been associated with homicides in situations involving battering....

(CIRCLE <u>YES</u> OR <u>NO</u> FOR EACH QUESTION)

1. Have you **EVER** been emotionally or physically abused by your **partner or someone** important to you?   YES   NO

2. **IN THE YEAR BEFORE YOU WERE PREGNANT**, were you pushed, shoved, slapped, hit, kicked or otherwise physically hurt by someone?   YES   NO
   If YES, by whom?_____

3. **WHILE YOU WERE PREGNANT** were you pushed, shoved, slapped, hit, kicked or otherwise physically hurt by someone?   YES   NO
   If YES, by whom?_____

4. **IN THE YEAR BEFORE YOU WERE PREGNANT**, did anyone force you to have sexual activities?   YES   NO
   If YES, who?_____

5. **WHILE YOU WERE PREGNANT** did anyone force you to have sexual activities?   YES   NO
   If YES, who?_____

6. Are you afraid of your partner or anyone you listed above?   YES   NO

Severity of Violence Against Women Scales (SVAWS)

The SVAWS is a 46-item questionnaire designed to measure two major dimensions: behaviors which threaten physical violence and actual physical violence (Marshall, 1992). Included are nine factors or subscales that have been demonstrated valid through factor analytic techniques: Symbolic Violence and Mild, Moderate, and Serious Threats (Threats of Violence Dimension), and Mild, Minor, Moderate, Serious, and Sexual Violence (Actual Violence Dimension)....

Relationship Inventory

The authors designed the Relationship Inventory to assess the status of the relationship including information about the abusers' use of pornography. The following introductory comment was read by the investigators to each woman. "The next questions are about pornography and abuse. We define pornography as sexually violent scenes where a woman is being hurt. For example, the woman is held or tied down." Four questions with a yes/no response option were asked: Does the man who abuses you EVER use pornographic magazines films, or videos? Does the man who abuses you EVER show you or make you look at pornographic scenes in magazines, films or videos? Does the man who abuses you EVER ask you or force you to act out the pornographic scenes he has looked at? Does the man who abuses you EVER ask you or force you to pose for pornographic pictures? . . .

Discussion and Conclusions

The findings of this ethnically stratified cohort study of 198 abused women indicate that 40.9% of the women report use of pornographic material by the abuser with the proportion of pornographic use significantly higher for Whites compared to Blacks and Hispanics. Ethnic differences exist for all four pornographic questions, with a greater proportion of White women responding "yes" to all the pornographic questions. If one accepts social learning theory, this would tend to confirm findings of the 1970 Commission on Pornography and Obscenity which stated that White males use more pornography than other ethnic or racial groups, since most of the relationships in this study did not cross racial lines. These ethnic differences also agree with the authors' earlier study of abuse during pregnancy that found both frequency and severity of physical abuse significantly higher for White women compared to African American and Hispanic women (McFarlane, Parker, Soeken, & Bullock, 1992).

In this study, when three groups were formed according to the abuser's use of pornography and associated involvement of the woman in pornographic activities, violence scores were highest for women reporting the abuser asked or forced them to look at, act out or pose for pornographic scenes, pictures. Severity of violence was not related simply to whether the abuser used pornography.

. . . Stated differently, one out of four abusive men forced their partner to participate with them in their use of pornography. Using other measures of violence, this subsample of abusers was consistently the most violent.

Although some would argue that since forcing a woman to participate in a sexual act is violence, the relationship between these variables is tautological. However, the entire sample was of women currently in a relationship with a violent man and only one fourth of the women reported being forced to participate in pornographic activities. Additional research is needed to further describe the differences between these groups of abusive men.

In considering these findings, several points need to be emphasized. First, in collecting the data, we were careful to define pornography by saying "We are talking about when women are held down or hurt," thus making sure that the women were not reporting on simple nudity. Second, the entire sample was women who had been physically or sexually assaulted by their male partner in the previous 12 months. To summarize, in this sample of 198 women, 2 out of 5 reported that their husband or male partner had used pornographic materials that depicted women in sexually violent scenes. The rate was highest for White women, followed by Hispanic women, with Black women reporting the lowest rate. Of those who did report any use of pornography, approximately 55% of the men forced the women to participate. . . .

Implications exist for both women and men. Requested or forced involvement of women in pornographic activities may indicate the likelihood for increased violence and associated trauma for women. This information can be offered to abused women as part of comprehensive counseling, advocacy, and education. Women provided with information on behaviors associated with increased violence can make informed decisions that protect not only their own safety, but that of their children. Equally important is to provide men with information regarding the degree to which pornography may influence their behavior toward women. Of particular concern is the degree to which pornography is used by men for sexual information. Certainly, to present sexual information to both males and females with an egalitarian relationship of mutual respect will contribute to decreasing violence toward women.

Kimberly A. Davies

 **NO**

Voluntary Exposure to Pornography and Men's Attitudes Toward Feminism and Rape

The effects that pornography have on men's attitudes toward women remains an issue of contention. Most previous researchers who have examined the relationship between pornography and attitudes toward women have used experimental studies or aggregate studies. Instead, I examined a sample of men who voluntarily viewed sexually explicit videos of their choosing in a non-experimental setting. I examined the relationship between these men's renting of pornographic videos and their attitudes toward feminism and rape. More specifically, the purpose of this research was to determine whether men who rented more X-rated videos displayed more negative attitudes toward feminism and if they were more likely to condone violence toward women than were men who rented fewer X-rated videos. In this article, I used cross tabulation to compare 194 men who rented X-rated videos of their choosing from a single pornography establishment in a large metropolitan county during 1988. The men were compared on their attitudes concerning the Equal Rights Amendment, a law against marital rape, and punishment for date rape and marital rape. No correlations were found between the number of videos a man had rented and his attitudes toward feminism and rape. These findings suggest that calloused attitudes toward women may not be generated by sexually explicit videos but are more deeply ingrained in our society.

The availability of pornography and the effects it may have on the public, men in particular, continues to be controversial. Anti-pornography feminists argue that pornography teaches men to despise women. Through pornography, these feminists believe, men learn that women are to be abhorred, seen as less human than themselves, and used. Robin Morgan (1980, p. 128) asserted that "pornography is the theory; rape is the practice." Andrea Dworkin and others believe that pornography trivializes rape (Everywoman, 1988) and makes men "increasingly callous to cruelty, to infliction of pain, to violence against persons, to abuse of women" (Dworkin, 1988, p. 205). Pornography and men's attitudes about violence and women are clearly linked, according to anti-pornography feminists. Yet, empirical research on the possible effects of pornography remains contradictory.

The purpose of my research was to explore the relationship between men's viewing of sexually explicit videos and their attitudes toward feminism and rape. This work is different from much previous experimental and aggregate research in that I examined a sample of men who rented sexually explicit videos of their choosing.

For the most part, two methodological approaches have been used in social science research to explore the links between exposure to pornography and aggressive attitudes and actions toward women (Baron, 1990; Childress, 1991; also see Davis & Bauserman, 1993, for a more inclusive literature review). First, researchers have used aggregate studies to examine the relationship between the availability of pornography and officially reported rape rates within particular geographic areas. Second, in experiments, men have been exposed to pornography in a laboratory setting and then either given the opportunity to aggress against a female confederate or given questionnaires intended to measure attitudes toward women and rape. The findings of these aggregate and experimental studies are mixed, and the limitations of these types of research are many.

During the 1960s, pornography was decriminalized in Denmark, and its production and sales increased. This situation allowed researchers to compare reported rates of sex crimes before and after decriminalization. Both Kutchinsky (1973) and Ben-Veniste (1971) reported a significant decrease in reported sex crimes, including rape, during the years in which widespread dissemination of pornography increased in Copenhagen, Denmark. This finding leads to the belief that pornography may actually lead to a decrease in the number of sex crimes rather than to an increase in calloused behavior toward women (Ben-Veniste, 1971; Kutchinsky, 1973). On the other hand, Court (1984) argued that, although the number of sex crimes overall may have decreased in Denmark after the decriminalization of pornography, rape actually increased. Yet, Danish crime experts argued that this increase in rape reports was not a result of a greater tolerance of rape but a "greater willingness to report rape because of increased public awareness" (Donnerstein, Linz, & Penrod, 1987). Overall, the Denmark experience is inconclusive and may not be generalizable to the U.S. because of differences in cultural norms.

Others have compared the consumption of pornography with rape rates in different geographic areas. Both Baron and Straus (1984) and Scott and Schwalm (1988b) compared the circulation rates of sex-oriented magazines and rape rates for each state in the U.S. Findings in both studies supported anti-pornography feminists' claims about the connection between pornography and rape. Both Baron and Straus (1984) and Scott and Schwalm (1988b) found that circulation rates of sexually explicit magazines and rape rates were positively correlated. On the other hand, Scott and Schwalm (1988a) compared the numbers of adult theaters with rape rates in 41 areas of the U.S. (either individual states or 2 states together) and found that the relationship between rape rates and adult theater rates was nonsignificant. Similarly, Gentry (1991) essentially replicated the research of Scott and Schwalm (1988b) and Baron and Straus

(1984) but used standard metropolitan statistical areas (cities and the surrounding metropolitan areas) as her units of analyses, resulting in the finding of no relationship between the circulation of sexually-oriented magazines and rape rates. Furthermore, Baron (1990) compared gender equality (measured with an index reflecting the status of women relative to men in politics, economics, and legal rights) and pornography circulation rates in states and found that gender equality and pornography were positively correlated.

The findings of Baron and Straus (1984) and Scott and Schwalm (1988a) suggest that pornography may be harmful to women. However the research by Baron (1990), Scott and Schwalm (1988a), and Gentry (1991) indicates that, on a macro level, claims about pornography's harm to women are not certain. In fact, Baron's findings suggest that gender equality is greater where pornography is more prevalent, suggesting perhaps that liberal attitudes about portrayals of sex extend to liberal ideas about gender equality. Furthermore, although some aggregate studies suggest a relationship between pornography and rape, it is not clear that those men who view pornography are the same men who are committing rapes.

In most studies of pornography since 1970, researchers have used an experimental approach (Childress, 1991). Researchers have not directly studied the link between pornography and sexual offenses. Rather, researchers have attempted to look at the relationship between pornography and aggression or the relationship between pornography and attitudes toward women.

Zillmann and Bryant's research (1982, 1984) is supportive of the argument that pornography is detrimental to women. These researchers exposed both women and men undergraduate students to sexually explicit (what Zillmann and Bryant called "erotic," 1984) films for six weeks to assess the effects of "massive" exposure to pornography on perceptions and attitudes about women and rape. These experimenters found that the men (and women) exposed to massive doses of pornography (parts of 36 erotic films viewed for 4 hours, 48 minutes in 6 weeks) became less supportive of statements about sexual equality and became more lenient in assigning punishment to a rapist whose crime was described in a newspaper account than did men and women in control groups with less (parts of 18 erotic films viewed for 2 hours, 20 minutes in 6 weeks) or no exposure to pornography (Zillmann & Bryant, 1982).

Linz, Donnerstein, and Penrod (1988) exposed male college students to nonerotic violent films and nonviolent erotic films and failed to support Zillmann and Bryant's (1982, 1984) findings that sexually explicit films negatively affect beliefs and attitudes about women. Instead, Linz et al. (1988) found that participants exposed to R-rated film violence against women showed a tendency to be less sympathetic to a rape victim when compared with control groups, including those exposed to nonviolent erotic films. In other words, Linz et al. (1988) found that violent nonsexual depictions were more likely to lead to calloused attitudes toward rape victims than sexual or pornographic depictions.

Although experimental researchers attempt to avoid the difficulties involved with aggregate studies, the problems of experiments focusing on pornography's possible connection to violence against women are well known (Childress, 1991; Fisher & Grenier, 1994). [For a critique of Zillmann and

Bryant's experimental work, see Branigan (1987), Christensen (1986), and Zill-mann and Bryant's replies (Zillmann & Bryant, 1986, 1987).] Childress (1991) included the following possible limiting factors of experiments:

1. the unreal nature of lab violence
2. lack of real punishment or social control
3. respondents' inhibitions while being observed or interviewed
4. the use of willing college students as the norm
5. an experimenter demand effect
6. publication of studies, mainly if they have positive results
7. lack of precise definitions of violence and aggression
8. the ethical inability to produce real violence

[See Childress (1991) for a detailed discussion of these problems and Berkowitz and Donnerstein (1982) for a discussion of the artificiality of laboratory experiments.]

A handful of researchers (Boeringer, 1994; Garcia, 1986; Padgett, Brislin-Slutz, & Neal, 1989) have avoided some concerns expressed about experimental research, such as the artificiality of exposing participants to sexual material in a lab. (Also see Malamuth & Check, 1981, and Weisz & Earls, 1995, for an examination of the effects of exposure to non-X-rated films in a non-experimental setting.)

Garcia (1986) employed questionnaires to determine male undergraduates' previous experience with sexually explicit material and their attitudes toward women and rape. In agreement with Zillmann and Bryant's findings (1982, 1984), Garcia found that those most exposed to coercive sexual material held more traditional attitudes toward women and believed rapists should not be severely punished. However, those exposed to mostly nonviolent pornography believed that rape is an act of power, not sex, which is a contention of feminists, findings that are more in agreement with the work of Linz et al. (1988).

Boeringer (1994) also asked college men about their exposure to pornography using questions about his respondents' involvement in sexually coercive behavior and propensity to commit rape as dependent variables. Boeringer's findings were in line with Linz et al. (1988) in that he found that the strongest correlates of sexual coercion were exposure to violent pornography and pornography depicting rape. However, Boeringer's (1994) findings may at the same time support Zillmann and Bryant's (1982, 1984) findings. Boeringer (1994, p. 299) found that reported exposure to milder materials found in "soft-core pornography" was positively related to "coercive verbal behavior and the hypothetical likelihood of using sexual force."

Unlike Garcia (1986), Boeringer (1994), and other experimental researchers, Padgett et al. (1989) did not limit their investigation to college students. Rather, they compared college students who they exposed to erotic materials with 21 male patrons of an "adult" movie theater who completed questionnaires about experience with pornography and attitudes toward women. Although the "adult patron" group had more experience with sexually explicit material, they held more favorable attitudes toward women than did the college students. Again, these findings are counter to Zillmann's and Bryant's (1982, 1984) laboratory findings. However, they must be viewed with caution, as there were only 21 adult patrons, and they voluntarily completed a questionnaire displayed at the "adult" movie theater, which they may have answered in ways that would appear favorable for pornography.

The research findings thus far are conflicting. Moreover, little is known about the relationship between voluntary X-rated video viewing and attitudes about rape and feminism. Researchers such as Garcia (1986) and Boeringer (1994), who studied the relationship of pornography and attitudes toward women among those who view sexually explicit materials on their own, have been limited by the use of college students as the sample. Padgett et al.'s (1989) study was limited by their small non-college sample who volunteered to complete a survey inside an "adult" theater. In this study, I move beyond some of these limitations by examining a random sample of men who voluntarily viewed sexually explicit material. Thus, this work adds to the literature to investigate the relationship between sexually explicit material and attitudes about women.

Methods

I used data collected by a research firm to explore the relationship between viewing of sexually explicit material and attitudes about rape and feminism. Using questions similar to those used by Zillmann and Bryant (1982), I tested hypotheses about rape attitudes and attitudes about feminism and the equality of women as related to the number of sexually explicit videos rented by men.

The data were collected in a large Southern metropolitan county that had a population of 450,800 in 1986 (U.S. Bureau of Census, 1988). Originally, the data were collected as part of a court case about obscenity. Although the data were collected at the request of attorneys representing an establishment that rented and sold sexually explicit materials, the collection of data was overseen by a market research firm.

Participants

Two hundred two persons who had rented X-rated videos during 1988 were surveyed between January 26 and February 17, 1989. Although both men and women completed surveys, only eight women in the sample of renters had rented X-rated videos in the past year. As a result of the low number of women renters in the survey, and because feminists often argue that exposure to pornography affects men's attitudes about women, the data were reduced to a sample of 194 men for the renter population (see Table 1). Although it cannot be determined if those surveyed are a representative sample of the establishment's renter population in 1988, it is at least representative of the county in terms of race. In 1986, this metropolitan county's population was 72.19% White and 26.52% Black (U.S. Bureau of Census, 1988). Similarly, 70.1% (136)

Table 1

Frequency Distribution of the Number of Videos Rented by Men in 12 Months

X-rated Videos Rented	Frequency	Percent
1	29	14.9%
2	58	29.9%
3 or more	107	55.2%
Total	194	100%

of the male respondents were White, 25.3% (49) were Black, and 2% (4) were other (2.6% or 5 did not give answers for the race question).

Measures

The primary independent variable for this analysis was the number of X-rated videos an individual had rented in 1988 from one of two "adult" establishments that rented and sold X-rated videos in a large metropolitan county in the southern United States. The number of X-rated videos rented was recorded for each respondent at the time the data set was created. Table 1 presents a frequency distribution of the number of X-rated videos that the men rented in 1988. The numbers of videos rented ranged from 1 to 59 (mean = 5.72, standard deviation, 7.58; median number or videos rented = 3, and the modal number = 2). I divided the renters into those who had rented one video, those who had rented two videos, and those who had rented three or more videos in 1988. Users were broken into these categories because they are somewhat equal groupings. Further, someone who rented three or more videos was defined as a regular user and thus was expected to be more affected or influenced by the videos than someone who had only rented one or two in a single year. Additionally, Eysenck (1984) argued that people make their way to more hard-core pornography as they rent more. Thus, although I did not know which videos each respondent rented, those who rented larger numbers of videos may have rented more violent videos than those who rented fewer videos. Last, the same results were found if the men were split into 1, 2, 3, 4–60, and other combinations.

Dependent variables for this analysis were obtained through four questions. First, I used the following question as to whether the Constitution should be amended to include the Equal Rights Amendment: "There has been considerable discussion about amending the U.S. Constitution with an Equal Rights Amendment. What about you? Do you *favor* or *oppose* an Equal Rights Amendment?" This question reflects participants' support or lack of support for feminism.

The second question I used asked whether a law against marital rape should be passed: "Do you *favor* or *oppose* having a law in *(State)* that would permit a wife to accuse her husband of rape?" This question reflects respondents' attitudes about the individuality of women as well as exposing general attitudes toward rape. Last, I used two similar questions about the punishment, if any, a man who has committed date rape or marital rape should receive:

> There has been a considerable amount of discussion in the mass media about *"marital rape,"* which is when a man, with the use of physical force or threat of force, has sexual relations with his *wife*. Some people feel this is a serious crime while others feel this should not be considered a crime. What about you? Which of the following statements comes closest to your opinion about what, if anything, should happen to a man who with the use of such force has sexual relations with his wife?
>
> 1. He should serve a long term, 10 years or more, in prison.
> 2. He should serve a short term, at least 1 or 2 years in prison.
> 3. He should serve a few months in a local jail.
> 4. He should be required to have counseling and do community service work.
> 5. This should not be treated as a crime, but should be grounds for divorce.
> 6. Do nothing—this is a private issue between a husband and a wife.
> 7. Don't know/no answer.

> There has been a considerable amount of discussion in the mass media about *"date rape,"* which is when a man, with the use of physical force or threat of force, has sexual relations with his *date*. Some people feel this is a serious crime while others feel this should not be considered a crime. What about you? Which of the following statements comes closest to your opinion about what, if anything, should happen to a man who with the use of such force has sexual relations with his *date*?
>
> 1–4. Same as first four responses above.
> 5. This should not be treated as a crime, but the woman should be able to sue him.
> 6. Do nothing—this is a private issue between a man and his date.
> 7. Don't know/no answer.

As with Zillmann and Bryant's (1984) study, a longer period of incarceration represents disapproval for these types of rape. Sexual callousness toward women is expected to be expressed in no punishment or less severe punishment for the rapists.

The questionnaire used for this research was designed to help secure completion. It contained 30 questions. Except for the final three questions about date and marital rape, the questionnaire was originally designed and previously used to measure community obscenity standards. Questions about the media and the community's acceptance of nudity and sexual activities in movies and magazines were included in addition to the four questions used in my analysis. The first questions were general media questions such as whether a person subscribed to a newspaper and if his or her television was connected to cable.

Then, the Equal Rights Amendment question was included along with questions about a person's religious and political conservatism/liberalism. Next, questions about community standards of obscenity were included, followed by common demographic questions such as the respondent's age and educational level. Finally, the last three questions asked were the marital and date rape questions that I used in my analysis.

Procedure

One of two establishments in the county that rented sexually explicit materials in 1988 granted access to the store's 1988 video rental records. These records contained names of 1,064 renters, their phone numbers, and the number of X-rated videos that they had rented from this establishment in 1988. From these records a list of all 1,064 persons and their phone numbers was constructed. Numbers of X-rated videos rented was not recorded on the phone list. Instead, each person was assigned an anonymous code so that the number of videos that each respondent had rented during 1988 could be recorded when creating the data file for completed surveys.

The phone list was given to a market research firm that was hired to complete 200 surveys with respondents residing in the county in which the court case was taking place. The research firm employed 10 interviewers (mean age 33.1 years), with an average of 5.1 years of experience to phone the respondents and complete the surveys over the telephone.

In training interviewers, great care was taken to avoid bias so that the data would be accepted in court. Interviewers were not told details about the court case or that the data were being collected at the request of defense attorneys. Further, the interviewers were instructed not to speculate about the reasons for the data being collected. They were simply to read the survey questions to the respondents and direct any questions about the purpose of the survey to the social scientist who oversaw data collection.

The research firm personnel told the interviewers that the sample was randomly generated; they were not told that the names were obtained from a video-rental establishment. Interviewers, however, were instructed to record a respondent's code on surveys as they interviewed that person.

Upon completion of training, interviewers dialed the numbers listed on individual calling records and read the following statement:

> Hello, my name is (*interviewer's name*) with (*research firm*). Let me assure you that we are not selling anything but rather interviewing a sample of adults concerning a variety of current issues. To make this survey scientific, I need to speak with (*sampled video-renter's name from the phone list*). Is (*he or she*) home?

If the person they asked for was not at home, they noted that and attempted the call later. If the person was there but had not answered the phone, the interviewer repeated the opening statement when the requested person came to the phone.

After the intended respondent was on the phone, he or she was told that the survey would only take a few minutes and that the answers would remain confidential and anonymous. A question as to which state and county he or she lived in was used as a screening question. If a person did not live in the southern county where the court case was taking place, the interview was terminated at that time, and the respondent was excluded from the sample. One hundred forty-five (21% of 689) were excluded in this way.

Care was taken so that the respondents remained anonymous and their answers remained confidential, as promised. Respondents' names were not recorded on the surveys. Only the first three digits of the respondent's phone number and his or her assigned identification number were recorded on the completed surveys to ensure that the respondent and the numbers of videos rented were correctly matched. Respondent identification number lists were carefully locked away separately from the surveys to ensure confidentiality and anonymity.

Of the 1,064 numbers provided by the pornography outlet, 184 were non-working, 35 went to business or government offices, 53 were out of the area code, and 103 were never contacted. Of the 689 (65% of 1,064) remaining numbers, 145 (21%) respondents were not eligible to respond because they lived outside of the county of interest. One hundred fourteen (16.5%) refused to answer the survey, and six (.9%) terminated the interview before completing the survey. Two hundred two (29.3%) completed the telephone survey. Upon completion of the 202 interviews, no other attempts to complete additional surveys were made, because 200 completions was the number that the researchers wanted for the court case.

Twenty-six or 12.9% of the 202 respondents who completed the survey (22% of those who had originally refused to answer the survey) agreed to answer the survey on a subsequent call. This refusal-conversion population did not differ significantly by age, education, race, income, marital status, political party, or any dependent variables from those who completed the survey. This suggests that those who refused may not have differed in a significant way from those who completed surveys.

Results

Tabular analysis was used to examine the relationship between renting X-rated videotapes and attitudes about rape and the Equal Rights Amendment. Chi-square was calculated to determine whether there were statistically significant differences between those who rented one video or two videos and those who rented three or more videos.

Because the numbers of X-rated videos rented did not vary significantly for any demographic variables (age, education in years, income, marital status, and political party), one can be more certain that the results from a cross-tabulation measure effects of renting sexually explicit videos rather than these demographic variables. If a respondent refused to answer the question of interest, he was not included in that particular analysis.

First, I performed a cross-tabulation of men who rented different numbers of sexually explicit videos and their opinions on whether a law against marital rape should be passed. In contrast to Zillmann and Bryant (1984) and what is expected based on anti-pornography feminists' beliefs about pornography, these results suggested that there was no significant difference between those who rented one, two, and three or more X-rated videos during 1988. Of the 177 men who answered this question, only 53.8% of those who had rented one explicit video favored a marital rape law, whereas at least 70% of those who had seen two, three, or more X-rated videos did so.

There were also no significant differences between those who rented one, two, and three or more X-rated videos with regard to opinions on what punishment one deserves for marital rape. The responses were varied. About half of the men (79 of 184 who answered, or 47%) reported that they believed that a man who forces his wife to have sexual relations should spend one or more years in prison. Forty six percent (12) of the single renters, 43.6% (20) of those who rented 2 videos and 52.4% (47) of those who rented more than 2 videos favored a year of more punishment for a man convicted of raping his wife. Approximately 58% (15) of those who rented 1 video, 43.6% (24) of those who rented 2 videos, and 52.4% (53) of those who rented 3 or more videos believed that marital rape deserved some length of incarceration. Likewise, there were no significant differences found when punishment categories were divided by those who were in favor of serving some time incarcerated versus no time incarcerated or when the punishments were divided into the categories of incarceration, counseling or grounds for divorce, and nothing. Of those who rented 1 video, 23% felt that a man who rapes his wife should receive counseling, 3.8% (1) believed marital rape was grounds for divorce, and 15.3%, or 4, thought that nothing should be done to the husband. Thirteen (23.6%) of those who rented 2 videos believed that the man should be counseled, 13 believed that marital rape was grounds for divorce, and 5, or 9.1%, believed that nothing should be done. Finally, 25.2% (26) of those who rented 3 or more videos believed that a man who raped his wife should receive counseling, 14.6% (15) thought it was grounds for divorce, and 7.8% (8) believed that there should be no punishment.

Similarly, the number of videos rented did not result in significantly different opinions on assigning punishment for date rape. However, date rape appears to be seen as more serious than marital rape, with 84 of the 186 respondents (45%) calling for 10 years in prison and 140 of the 186 respondents (75%) saying that date rape should be punished with 1 year or more of incarceration. Of those who rented 1 video, 35.7% believed that the punishment for date rape should be 10 years, 32.1% felt it should be 1–2 years, 10.7% answered 1–2 months, 10.7% thought the punishment should be counseling, 3.7% thought the victim should be able to sue, and 7.1% thought that nothing should be done. Approximately 49% of those who rented 2 videos thought that the punishment for date rape should be 10 years, 23.6% felt it should be 1–2 years, 10.9% said 1–2 months, 12.7% selected counseling, 3.6% said [the victim should be able to sue], and 0 thought that the punishment for date rape should be nothing. Of those renting 3 or more videos, 45.6% responded that the punishment for date rape should be 10 years, 33% said 1–2 years, 2.9% felt 1–2 months was sufficient, 12.6% responded that the punishment for date rape should be counseling, and 5.8% said that the victim should be permitted to sue.

Last, men who have viewed one, two, or three or more X-rated videos are not significantly different from one another in their support or opposition for the ERA. Unlike Zillmann and Bryant (1982, 1984), who found less support for feminism among those exposed to sexually explicit videos, only 18.2% of those who had rented 3 or more videos were opposed to the Equal Rights Amendment, suggesting that viewing pornography in a non-laboratory setting is not related to negative attitudes toward women and/or feminism. The percentage opposed in other categories is similar, with 18.5% of those who had rented 1 X-rated video in 1988 opposed and 25% of those who had rented 2 opposed to the Equal Rights Amendment. At least 75% of all X-rated film renters favored the Equal Rights Amendment.

Discussion

The purpose of this research was to examine the effects of viewing sexually explicit materials on men's attitudes toward feminism and rape. Attitudes about rape and feminism of a sample of 194 men who were known to have rented sexually explicit videos during 1988 were compared by numbers of X-rated videos rented.

The number of X-rated self-chosen videos rented by these men during 1988 was not significantly related to their support for the Equal Rights Amendment, a law against marital rape, or opinions on punishment for marital and date rape. Those who rented more pornographic videos did not differ from those renting fewer videos. These findings suggest that greater exposure to pornography did not result in more negative opinions toward feminism or to a greater acceptance of marital or date rape. Men who voluntarily rent greater numbers of sexually explicit videos of their choosing in a non-experimental setting do not appear any more likely to have negative attitudes toward feminism or condone violence against women than those who rent fewer X-rated videos.

Of those men who rented X-rated videos in 1988, 79.7% favored the Equal Rights Amendment, 68.9% favored a marital rape law, 81.7% believed that a man who is found guilty of date rape should be incarcerated (defined as serving *any* jail or prison time), and 68.9% believed that a man found guilty of marital rape should be incarcerated. Men who view sexually explicit videos of their choosing are not necessarily likely to have negative attitudes toward feminism or condone violence toward women.

These findings are contrary to those in many previous studies, such as those by Zillmann and Bryant (1982, 1984), in which exposure to sexually explicit videos was found to be correlated with calloused attitudes toward women. My research suggests that pornographic videos may not have the effects on men that anti-pornography feminists have previously argued. Instead, it suggests that calloused attitudes toward women are not generated by sexually explicit videos but arise elsewhere in our society. Furthermore, the results of this research indicate that experimental studies may not, as has been suggested, be a valid representation of what occurs outside of an experimental laboratory when men view sexually explicit videos of their choosing (Eysenck, 1984).

Overall, this research introduces an alternative approach for exploring relationships between sexually explicit materials and men's attitudes toward women. However, this research has some limitations, including willingness of store owners to make records available, as they might not do. Also, in this research, I assumed that those who rented the videos and participated in this survey actually viewed the videos they rented. Similarly, it cannot be ascertained as to how representative these men are with regard to men who rent sexually explicit videos in other places. Additionally, in this study I reported only the number of videos rented at this video store. I do not know if these men rented videos from the other video store in the county that rented X-rated videos or if they purchased X-rated material from other outlets. Furthermore, I did not know which X-rated videos these men rented, and thus it is not known if these men rented violent or nonviolent X-rated videos. Although this study and surveys of college respondents are a beginning, more data collected from general populations of individuals who voluntarily view sexually explicit materials would be helpful in exploring the connection between sexually explicit material and men's attitudes toward women and rape. Further research should include methods such as those used here, with data from different areas of the country and studies that include types of videos rented.

Ultimately, however, if the goal is to explain negative attitudes and actions directed at women in our society, closer examination of male dominance and the power structure of our society may be needed instead of a narrow focus on how pornography affects men. More important questions need to be asked: How can it be that violent material showing women bruised, battered, and beaten are created with the intention of arousing men? Why are the obvious physical sufferings of certain individuals portrayed in some pornography arousing to other individuals in our society? It seems that violent depictions of women as portrayed in some pornography are not generating violent actions against women but are a symptom of a greater underlying problem.

CHALLENGE QUESTIONS

Does Pornography Cause Men to Be Violent Toward Women?

1. If pornography does cause men to be violent toward women, what might this imply about other types of media and other types of behavior?
2. To say that an aspect of our environment, such as pornographic material, causes violent behavior may imply determinism. That is, if pornography does cause men to be violent, does this mean that these men could not have chosen to act differently? Research the free will/determinism issue in philosophy, and apply your philosophical conclusion to the pornography debate.
3. Research *social learning theory.* How might Albert Bandura—perhaps the leading proponent of this theory—explain violence toward women?
4. How might the First Amendment to the U.S. Constitution be implicated in the pornography and violence debate?

Contributors to This Volume

EDITOR

BRENT SLIFE is a clinical psychologist and a professor of psychology at Brigham Young University in Provo, Utah. A fellow of the American Psychological Association, he has published over 80 articles and books, including *What's Behind the Research? Discovering Hidden Assumptions in the Behavioral Sciences,* coauthored with Richard N. Williams (Sage Publications, 1995), which attempts to make accessible to students the many conceptual issues of psychology. Recently voted Teacher of the Year at Brigham Young, he is also editor of the *Journal of Theoretical and Philosophical Psychology* and serves in editorial capacities on the *Journal of Mind and Behavior* and *Theory and Psychology.* He received his Ph.D. from Purdue University, where he and Joseph Rubinstein, coeditor of the first seven editions of *Taking Sides: Clashing Views on Controversial Psychological Issues,* began the dialogue approach to psychology that is the basis of this volume.

STAFF

Theodore Knight   List Manager
David Brackley   Senior Developmental Editor
Juliana Poggio   Developmental Editor
Rose Gleich   Administrative Assistant
Brenda S. Filley   Production Manager
Juliana Arbo   Typesetting Supervisor
Diane Barker   Proofreader
Lara Johnson   Design/Advertising Coordinator
Richard Tietjen   Publishing Systems Manager
Larry Killian   Copier Coordinator

AUTHORS

NANCY C. ANDREASEN is a doctor in the Mental Health Clinical Research Center of the University of Iowa Hospitals and Clinics and College of Medicine.

PHILIP ASPDEN is executive director of the Center for Research on the Information Society (CRIS) in Pennington, New Jersey. He has consulted in telecommunications and technology-based economic development for a wide range of high-tech firms, public bodies, and foundations in both the United States and Europe. He has also been a scientific civil servant in the British Civil Service and a research scholar at the International Institute for Applied Systems Analysis.

ELIZABETH BALDWIN is a research ethics officer for the American Psychological Association's Science Directorate. Her work involves a broad range of research ethics issues, including those relating to the use of animals in research. She has also worked at the Congressional Research Service in the Division of Science Policy. She holds a B.A. in biology, an M.S. in entomology, and an M.A. in science, technology, and public policy.

DIANA BAUMRIND is a research psychologist and the principal investigator for the Family Socialization and Developmental Competence Project of the University of California's Institute for Human Development in Berkeley, California. She has contributed numerous articles to professional journals and books, and she is on the editorial board of *Developmental Psychology*. She is also the author of *Child Maltreatment and Optimal Caregiving in Social Contexts* (Garland, 1995).

MAY BENATAR is a clinical social worker in private practice in Montclair, New Jersey. She currently teaches and lectures to professional groups on sexual abuse and the treatment of dissociative disorders.

MARISSA S. BEYERS is a freelance writer with an M.A. in theoretical psychology.

ALAN D. BOWD is a professor of educational psychology and director of the School of Education at Lakehead University in Thunder Bay, Ontario, Canada. He received an M.A. in psychology from the University of Sydney and a Ph.D. in educational psychology from the University of Calgary. His main interest is in the ethical treatment of animals, and his published research has focused on the development of beliefs and attitudes about animals during childhood.

BRANDON S. CENTERWALL is an assistant professor of epidemiology in the School of Public Health and Community Medicine at the University of Washington in Seattle, Washington.

ZACK Z. CERNOVSKY is an associate professor of psychiatry in the Department of Psychology at the University of Western Ontario in London, Ontario, Canada.

ANDREW CHRISTENSEN is a professor of psychology at the University of California, Los Angeles. He is coauthor, with Neil S. Jacobson, of *Integrative Couple Therapy: Promoting Acceptance and Change* (W. W. Norton, 1996).

ELIZABETH CRAMER is an author who writes about the abuse of women.

KIMBERLY A. DAVIES is an assistant professor of sociology and criminal justice. Her research and teaching interests include feminist criminology, deviance, and homicide. She received her Ph.D. in sociology from Ohio State University in 1996.

PATRICK H. DeLEON is a psychologist and a lawyer.

ALBERT ELLIS, founder of rational-emotive therapy, is president of the Institute for Rational-Emotive Therapy, located in New York City. He received his Ph.D. in clinical psychology from Columbia University, and he has authored or coauthored more than 600 articles and over 50 books on psychotherapy, marital and family therapy, and sex therapy, including *Why Some Therapies Don't Work: The Dangers of Transpersonal Psychology,* coauthored with Raymond Yaeger (Prometheus Books, 1989).

HELEN FISHER is a member of the Center for Human Evolutionary Studies and a research associate in the Department of Anthropology at Rutgers University. She received her Ph.D. from the University of Colorado in 1975, and she is a fellow of the American Anthropological Association and of the American Association of Physical Anthropologists. Her research interests include human evolution, primatology, human sexual behavior, reproductive strategies, and the neurological and biological basis of behavior. She is the author of *The First Sex: The Natural Talents of Women and How They Are Changing the World* (Random House, 1999).

SEYMOUR FISHER is a professor of psychology and coordinator of research training in the Department of Psychiatry and Behavioral Sciences at the University of New York Health Science Center at Syracuse. He has published 16 books and approximately 200 scientific papers. His scholarly work has focused on such areas as body image, sexual behavior, the validity of psychoanalytic theory, the psychodynamics of comedians, and the efficacy of psychotropic drugs.

HOWARD GARDNER is the John H. and Elisabeth A. Hobbs Professor in Cognition and Education at the Harvard Graduate School of Education. He also holds positions as adjunct professor of psychology at Harvard, adjunct professor of neurology at the Boston University School of Medicine, and codirector of Harvard Project Zero. He has received numerous honors, including a MacArthur Prize Fellowship in 1981. He is the author of several hundred articles and 18 books, including *Extraordinary Minds* (Basic Books, 1997) and *The Disciplined Mind: What All Students Should Understand* (Simon & Schuster, 1999).

CHARLES J. GELSO is a licensed psychologist and a professor in the Department of Psychology at the University of Maryland. He received his M.S. from Florida State University in 1964 and his Ph.D. from Ohio State University in 1970. His interests include the client-therapist relationship in therapy, the application of psychoanalytic concepts to short- and long-term counseling, and the research training environment in graduate education.

He is coauthor, with J. A. Hayes, of *The Psychotherapy Relationship: Theory, Research, and Practice* (John Wiley, 1998).

ROGER P. GREENBERG is a professor in and head of the Division of Clinical Psychology, as well as director of psychology internship training, at the State University of New York Health Science Center at Syracuse. His more than 150 publications and presentations include the award-winning books *The Scientific Credibility of Freud's Theories and Therapy* (Columbia University Press, 1985) and *A Critical Appraisal of Biological Treatments for Psychological Distress: Comparisons With Psychotherapy and Placebo* (Lawrence Erlbaum, 1989), both coauthored with Seymour Fisher.

STEVEN C. HAYES is a professor in the Department of Psychology at the University of Nevada in Reno, Nevada. He is the editor of *Rule-Governed Behavior: Cognition, Contingencies, and Instructional Control* (Plenum Press, 1989) and coeditor of *Acceptance and Change: Content and Context in Psychotherapy* (Context Press, 1994).

ELAINE HEIBY is a professor in the Department of Psychology at the University of Hawaii at Manoa.

NEIL S. JACOBSON is a professor of psychology at the University of Washington in Seattle, Washington. His research interests include behavior, marital therapy, depression, and family therapy. He is coauthor, with John M. Gottman, of *When Men Batter Women: New Insights into Ending Abusive Relationships* (Simon & Schuster, 1998).

JAMES E. KATZ is a professor of communication at Rutgers University and a senior scientist at Bellcore (Bell Communications Research) in New Jersey. He has examined a variety of issues concerning the Internet and its societal consequences, and he is an expert in privacy policy. He has also been involved in the World Wide Web Consortium and U.S. National Science Foundation planning exercises for research on knowledge networks.

PERRY D. KLEIN is an assistant professor in the Faculty of Education at the University of Western Ontario. His interests include metacognition and concept development in science and language learning. His current research focuses on students' construction of scientific explanations through informal writing.

PETER D. KRAMER is a psychiatrist and the author of *Moments of Engagement: Intimate Psychotherapy in a Technological Age* (W. W. Norton, 1989).

ROBERT KRAUT is a professor of social psychology and human computer interaction at Carnegie Mellon University, with joint appointments in the Department of Social and Decision Sciences, the Human Computer Interaction Institute, and the Graduate School of Industrial Administration. His current research focuses on the design and social impacts of information technologies in small groups, in the home, and between organizations. He is coauthor of *Research Recommendations to Facilitate Distributed Work* (National Academy Press, 1994).

DAVID B. LARSON is an assistant secretary of planning at the Department of Health and Human Services in Washington, D.C.

STANLEY MILGRAM (1933–1984) was an experimental social psychologist and a professor of psychology at the Graduate School and University Center of the City University of New York. He is especially well known for his series of controversial investigations regarding obedience to authority, which were performed at Yale University from 1960 to 1963. His publications include *Obedience to Authority: An Experimental View* (Harper & Row, 1975).

JEFFREY S. REBER is a freelance writer with an M.A. in social psychology.

KATHARINE A. RIMES is affiliated with the University of Oxford Department of Psychiatry, Warneford Hospital, in the United Kingdom.

SUSAN P. ROBBINS is an associate professor in the Graduate School of Social Work at the University of Houston in Texas. She is the author of *River and Jungle* (Random House, 1993).

JOHN K. ROSEMOND is head of the Center for Affirmative Parenting in Gastonia, North Carolina, as well as a family psychologist and syndicated columnist. He is the author of several books, including *Because I Said So!* (Andrews & McMeel, 1996).

D. L. ROSENHAN (b. 1929) is a professor of law and psychology at Stanford University and a social psychologist whose focal concern has been clinical and personality matters. He has also been a faculty member at Princeton University, the University of Pennsylvania, and Swarthmore College.

J. PHILIPPE RUSHTON is a John Simon Guggenheim Fellow and a professor of psychology at the University of Western Ontario in London, Ontario, Canada. He holds a Ph.D. and a D.Sc. from the University of London, and he is a fellow of the American Association for the Advancement of Science and of the American, British, and Canadian Psychological Associations. He is the author of *Race, Evolution, and Behavior* (Transaction Publishers, 1995).

PAUL M. SALKOVSKIS is a Wellcome Trust Senior Research Fellow in Basic Biomedical Science in the University of Oxford Department of Psychiatry, Warneford Hospital, in the United Kingdom.

VICTOR D. SANUA is an adjunct professor of psychology at St. John's University in New York City. He is the editor of *Fields of Offerings: Studies in Honor of Raphael Patai* (Fairleigh Dickinson University Press, 1983). He earned his B.A. at American University and his M.A. and Ph.D. at Michigan State University.

MARTIN E. P. SELIGMAN is a professor in the Department of Psychology at the University of Pennsylvania and is well known for his formulation of the learned helplessness model. A member of the APA's Public Education Campaign Advisory Task Force, Seligman has published over 15 books, including *What You Can Change and What You Can't: The Complete Guide to Successful Self-Improvement* (Alfred A. Knopf, 1994) and *Helplessness: On Depression, Development, and Death* (W. H. Freeman, 1992).

KENNETH J. SHAPIRO is executive director of Psychologists for the Ethical Treatment of Animals and editor of the academic biannual *Society and Animals*. His background is in clinical psychology, phenomenological psychology, and intellectual history. He has published scholarly work in phenomenological psychology, developing and applying methods for the study of both human and nonhuman animals.

BRIAN SIANO is a writer and researcher based in Philadelphia, Pennsylvania. His column "The Skeptical Eye" appears regularly in *The Humanist.*

ROBERT L. SPITZER is affiliated with the New York State Psychiatric Institute in New York City. He is a former chairman of the American Psychiatric Association and its Task Force on Nomenclature and Statistics.

BRETT N. STEENBARGER is on the faculty of the M.D. and Ph.D. graduate program at the State University of New York Health Science Center at Syracuse, where he also staffs the Student Counseling Service. He received his Ph.D. from the University of Kansas, and his research interests include mental health care delivery systems, managed care, and brief treatment models.

MURRAY A. STRAUS is a professor of sociology and codirector of the Family Research Laboratory at the University of New Hampshire in Durham, New Hampshire. He has held academic appointments at Cornell University, the University of Minnesota, the University of Wisconsin, and Washington State University, as well as at universities in England, India, and Sri Lanka. He has published over 150 articles and 15 books, including *Physical Violence in American Families,* coauthored with Richard J. Gelles (Transaction Publishers, 1995).

CAROL LYNN TRIPPITELLI is House Staff Fellow of the Department of Psychiatry in the School of Medicine at the Johns Hopkins University, where she is also a resident of the Johns Hopkins Hospital.

JACK G. WIGGINS, JR., is a member of the board of trustees for the American Psychological Foundation.

Index